SALES AND
LEASES OF GOODS

SALES AND LEASES OF GOODS

By

ALFRED W. MEYER
Seegars Chair-in-Law Professor
Valparaiso University School of Law

RICHARD E. SPEIDEL
Beatrice Kuhn Professor of Law
Northwestern University School of Law

BLACK LETTER SERIES®

WEST PUBLISHING CO.
ST. PAUL, MINN.
1993

Black Letter Series and Black Letter Series design appearing on the front cover are registered trademarks used herein under license.

COPYRIGHT © 1993 By WEST PUBLISHING CO.
        610 Opperman Drive
        P.O. Box 64526
        St. Paul, MN 55164–0526
        1–800–328–9352

ISBN 0–314–01068–8

 TEXT IS PRINTED ON 10% POST CONSUMER RECYCLED PAPER

4th Reprint — 2002

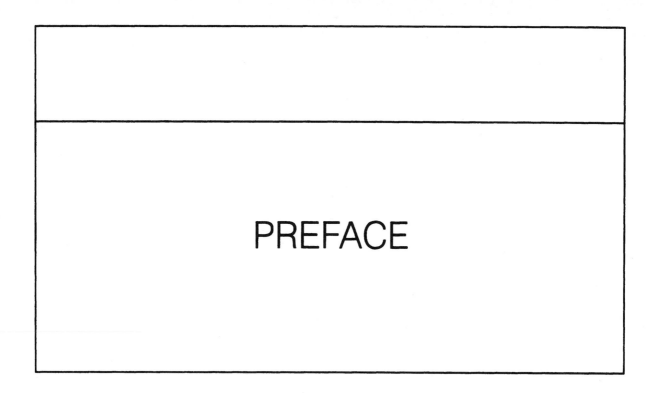

PREFACE

While preserving the general format of the Black Letter Series, this edition differs from its 1984 predecessor in two significant respects. Retitled "Sales and Leases of Goods" from the original "Sales and Sales Financing," the change reflects 1) an editorial judgment that the subject of sales financing is sufficiently independent to warrant its own treatment in a separate edition, and 2) the need to include coverage of the new Article 2A of the UCC, the Article which deals with lease of goods transactions. Promulgated by the National Conference of Commissioners on Uniform State Laws and the American Law Institute in 1987 and amended in 1990, Article 2A responds to the critical need for codifying the law of a type of commercial transaction which was closely related to but significantly different from sales transactions.

The Convention on the International Sale of Goods (CISG) became effective in the United States in January, 1988. Where applicable, CISG preempts Article 2 of the UCC. Even if there is no preemption, CISG exists as a competing body of sales law for the international transaction. Upon occasion, we will identify important differences between Article 2 and CISG. For a more complete comparison, see Winship, *Domesticating International Commercial Law: Revising U.C.C. Article 2 in Light of the United Nations Sales Convention*, 37 Loyola L.Rev. 43 (1991).

*

PUBLISHER'S PREFACE

This "Black Letter" is designed to help a law student recognize and understand the basic principles and issues of law covered in a law school course. It can be used both as a study aid when preparing for classes and as a review of the subject matter when studying for an examination.

Each "Black Letter" is written by experienced law school teachers who are recognized national authorities in the subject covered.

The law is succinctly stated by the author of this "Black Letter." In addition, the exceptions to the rules are stated in the text. The rules and exceptions have purposely been condensed to facilitate quick review and easy recollection. For an in-depth study of a point of law, citations to major student texts are given. In addition, a **Text Correlation Chart** provides a convenient means of relating material contained in the "Black Letter" to appropriate sections of the casebook the student is using in his or her law school course.

If the subject covered by this text is a code or code-related course, the code section or rule is set forth and discussed wherever applicable.

FORMAT

The format of this "Black Letter" is specially designed for review. (1) **Text.** First, it is recommended that the entire text be studied, and, if deemed necessary, supplemented by the student texts cited. (2) **Capsule Summary.** The Capsule Summary is an abbreviated review of the subject matter which can be used both before and after studying the main body of the text. The headings in the Capsule Summary follow the main text of the "Black Letter." (3) **Table of Contents.** The Table of Contents is in outline form to help you organize the details of the subject and the Summary of Contents gives you a final overview of the materials. (4) **Practice Examination.** The Practice Examination in Appendix B gives you the opportunity of testing yourself with the type of question asked on an exam, and comparing your answer with a model answer.

In addition, a number of other features are included to help you understand the subject matter and prepare for examinations:

Short Questions and Answers: This feature is designed to help you spot and recognize issues in the examination. We feel that issue recognition is a major ingredient in successfully writing an examination.

Perspective: In this feature, the authors discuss their approach to the topic, the approach used in preparing the materials, and any tips on studying for and writing examinations.

Analysis: This feature, at the beginning of each section, is designed to give a quick summary of a particular section to help you recall the subject matter and to help you determine which areas need the most extensive review.

Examples: This feature is designed to illustrate, through fact situations, the law just stated. This, we believe, should help you analytically approach a question on the examination.

Glossary: This feature is designed to refamiliarize you with the meaning of a particular legal term. We believe that the recognition of words of art used in an examination helps you to better analyze the question. In addition, when writing an examination you should know the precise definition of a word of art you intend to use.

We believe that the materials in this "Black Letter" will facilitate your study of a law school course and assure success in writing examinations not only for the course but for the bar examination. We wish you success.

THE PUBLISHER

SUMMARY OF CONTENTS

APPENDICES

*

TABLE OF CONTENTS

*

CAPSULE SUMMARY

PART ONE: GENERAL CONSIDERATIONS

I. COMMERCIAL LAW IN GENERAL

Commercial law defines the rights, duties and remedies of parties to and persons affected by exchange transactions. Under the Uniform Commercial Code (UCC), (1) these transactions take various forms, (2) the subject matter is personal property, and (3) the parties include merchants and consumers. The primary sources of commercial law are the agreement of the parties and the UCC. Other sources include state law not preempted by the UCC, federal and state law protecting consumer interests, the Bankruptcy Code and the Convention of the International Sale of Goods (CISG), effective in the United States since January, 1988. Of the many transactions generating a need for commercial law, this BLACK LETTER will deal primarily with contracts for the sale and lease of goods, UCC Articles 2 and 2A. Where relevant, it will discuss the provisions of UCC Article 9, Secured Transactions. Occasionally we will highlight some relevant provisions of CISG.

II. THE UNIFORM COMMERCIAL CODE
A. Legislative History

The UCC, first enacted in Pennsylvania in 1953, is now law in 49 States, the District of Columbia and Puerto Rico. The 1990 Official Text contains the latest substantive revisions, but these have not been enacted in every state. Each state's

1

version of the UCC must be consulted to determine the degree of conformance to the 1990 Official Text.

B. Nature of the UCC
The UCC has many features of a "true" code. To the extent applicable, it is preemptive, systematic and comprehensive. Yet it is a code in the common law rather than the civil law tradition, with the expressed recognition in 1–103 that it is supplemented by other principles of state law not displaced by particular provisions of the UCC.

C. Basic Policies: Article 1
UCC Article 1 provides structure by expressing the Code's underlying policies, 1–102(1), defining the extent to which the effect of Code provisions may be varied by agreement, 1–102(3), providing general definitions, 1–201, and dealing with matters of substance, such as imposing a duty of good faith upon the performance and enforcement of contracts, 1–203, and stating the content of and exclusions from remedial policy, 1–106(1). Article 1, therefore, plays an important role in resolving disputes arising under Articles 2 and 2A.

D. Substantive Content
The substantive articles of the UCC are: Article 2, Sales; Article 2A, Leases; Article 3, Commercial Paper; Article 4, Bank Deposits and Collections; Article 4A, Funds Transfers; Article 5, Letters of Credit; Article 6, Bulk Sales; Article 7, Documents of Title; Article 8, Investment Securities; and Article 9, Secured Transactions. Two or more of these articles may apply to disputes arising under the same transaction. This BLACK LETTER will deal primarily with Articles 1, 2, and 2A, with discussion of Article 9 where relevant.

E. Commercial Law Not in the UCC
There are limitations upon the scope of the UCC. For example, a transaction may be excluded from coverage, such as a contract to sell land, and certain principles of state law, such as the law of fraud, are not displaced by the Code. See 1–103. In addition, other state law or federal legislation or treaties may preempt or supplement the Code. Finally, under conflict of laws principles, the law or Code of a state other than the forum may govern.

F. Methodology
A methodology for approaching Code problems and reaching sound solutions involves the following steps: (1) Analyze the problem and develop the general issue(s); (2) Determine whether the Code applies and, if so, which Article(s) and what sections; (3) Develop precise statutory issues; (4) Consult the applicable statutory language, relevant definitions and cross-references to other sections to determine the principal purpose(s) and policies applicable to the issues at hand; (5) Enhance interpretation by consulting the comments, relevant legislative history and persuasive secondary sources, such as treatises and law reviews; and (6)

Analyze judicial decisions interpreting the same sections, with the caveat that the Code, not judicial interpretation, is the best evidence of its meaning.

PART TWO: SALE OF GOODS

III. GENERAL SCOPE AND POLICIES
A. Scope and Definitions
Although 2–102 uses the phrase "transactions in goods" to define the scope of Article 2, the vast majority of its sections apply literally only to contracts for the *sale* of goods. Nowhere is the term "transaction" defined and the various sections repetitively use the terms "buyer" and "seller" to state the rules of law. Thus, gifts, bailments, consignments, leases (now covered by Article 2A, see Part Three), and service and construction contracts are subject to other state law. Article 2 may, however, apply to particular segments of these other transactions and it may apply either directly or by analogy where the transaction is one of mixed sales and services.

B. Special Policies
Article 2 has a number of special policies.

    1. Standards rather than rules dominate. The standards must be particularized in each case from evidence in the relevant commercial context.

    2. Title is deemphasized as a problem solving device. Title is relevant only where made so by a particular section.

    3. Article 2, by permitting a broad range for agreement, encourages and rewards pre-transaction planning. If the parties intend to contract even though material terms are left open or incomplete, Article 2 supplies "reasonable" terms to fill the gaps in agreement.

    4. When a seller or buyer is a "merchant" different and higher standards of conduct are required.

    5. Abuses at the time of contracting are regulated by the "unconscionability" doctrine and abuses at the time of performance or enforcement of the contract are regulated by the requirement of good faith.

IV. CONTRACT FORMATION
A. The Importance of Agreement
A contract is formed when Article 2 gives legal effect to the parties' agreement in fact. An agreement is the bargain in fact of the parties as found in their language or by "implication" from other circumstances, such as course of dealing, course of performance or usage of trade. Whether that agreement creates a contract is determined by Article 2, Part 2.

B.   General Policies

Contract formation under Article 2 differs from the common law in the following respects: 1. The emphasis is upon agreement rather than "promise" or consideration; 2. Formalities are deemphasized and the best evidence of agreement may be what the parties do, i.e., their conduct, rather than what they say; 3. The "intention" of the parties to "make" a contract is afforded legal protection, even though the moment of contract formation cannot be determined or material terms have not been agreed; and 4. If the parties have intended to "make" a contract but a material term has not been agreed, the court will supply a reasonable term and enforce the bargain if there is a reasonably certain basis for giving a remedy. Thus, if the conduct of both parties manifests an intention to make some contract, the court will work to fill in the pages and provide a reasonably certain basis for enforcement.

C.   Offers and Acceptance

Offer is not defined in Article 2, Part 2. A "firm" offer, i.e., an option, however, may be created without consideration or reliance in a writing signed by a merchant. Unless unambiguously indicated in the offer, an acceptance may be in any method or manner reasonable in the circumstances. Thus, an offeree may be able to accept by promise, performance or by commencing performance. At common law, a response which contained additional or different terms was a counteroffer. This rule was thought to be unrealistic and to give an offeree an unfair advantage. Section 2–207 provides that a contract is formed if the offeree gives a definite acceptance accompanied by additional or different terms or if there is conduct by both parties recognizing a contract even though their writings do not agree. If some contract is formed, the additional or different terms may become part of the agreement if the offeror has expressly assented to them. Otherwise, they "drop out" and the court may supply reasonable terms to fill any gap.

D.   The Statute of Frauds

The statute of frauds conditions enforceability of an agreement on the presence of a writing indicating that a contract for sale has been made and signed by the party to be charged. The requirement is satisfied, however, even though the writing does not contain all of the material terms or where a merchant fails to object to a satisfactory confirmation in writing sent by another merchant. Even without a writing, there are other ways around the statute, i.e., specially manufactured goods, part performance, admission in court and, in some states, by reliance. In all cases, the agreement is not enforceable beyond the quantity of goods shown in the writing or evidenced by the part-performance or admission.

V.   PERFORMANCE OF THE CONTRACT FOR SALE

A.   Introduction

After formation, the order and content of performance will be determined by the agreement, as supplemented by Article 2. If the agreement is not sufficient, the performance obligations of the seller and buyer will be supplied by Article 2, Part

3, so long as the parties intended to contract and a remedy can be provided with reasonable certainty. In the absence of agreement, Article 2 also governs the risk of loss problem and determines when one party is excused by post-contract events which arguably make continued performance impracticable. Article 2 encourages agreed risk allocation and supports agreements during performance which modify the contract.

B. Scope and Meaning of Agreement

The parol evidence rule determines the scope of and principles of contract interpretation help to determine the meaning of the agreement. The parol evidence rule applies when the parties intend a writing to be a partial or total integration of the agreement. It does not bar evidence tending to show that no contract was formed or that a modification has been made. In a partial integration, prior terms that contradict those in the writing are excluded but consistent additional terms are not. In a total integration, all prior terms excluded, although evidence intended to explain the writing is not. The key question is whether the parties intended any integration and, if so, what is its exclusionary effect. Principles of contract interpretation assist in ascertaining the meaning of terms included in the agreement. The question is whose meaning is more reasonable in the commercial setting, and the answer is facilitated by resort to evidence of prior course of dealing, trade usage and course of performance. If a meaning cannot be determined yet the parties intended to contract, the court will supply reasonable terms from Article 2, Part 3.

C. General Obligations of the Parties

The obligation of the seller is to "transfer and deliver" and that of the buyer is to "accept and pay for" the goods in accordance with the contract. The agreement may cover whether either party extends credit to the other, the time and order of performance, and the duration and termination of the contract. In the absence of agreement, neither party extends credit to the other and Article 2, Part 3 supplies "reasonable" terms on order of performance, duration and termination. A non-excludable duty of good faith is imposed upon both parties in performing the contract.

D. Seller's Obligations

Performance obligations unique to the seller include delivery of the goods. In the absence of agreement, the seller's obligation is to transfer and deliver the goods in a single lot unless circumstances justify an apportionment. The place of delivery depends upon location of the goods and, in the absence of agreement, neither the seller nor a bailee has an obligation to ship them to the buyer. What the seller must do to tender delivery and where the tender must be made depends upon the location of the goods, whether the seller has an obligation to ship and, if so, the nature of the shipment obligation. The technicalities of tender of delivery are further enhanced when a documentary transaction is agreed upon. The quantity obligation of the seller must be agreed and is not enforceable beyond the quantity set forth in a signed writing. The seller may agree to supply his "output" or the buyer may promise to order his "requirements." The exercise of discretion by both parties is controlled by the duty of good faith and a concept of reasonableness expressed in Section 2–306.

E. Seller's Obligation of Quality: Herein of Warranty

The seller's quality obligation is measured by three frequently overlapping warranties, one express and two implied. There are different requirements for each and the ease with which they can be disclaimed depends upon the type of warranty involved. Express warranties come in more varieties and offer the buyer the greatest potential protection. The implied warranty of merchantability is made only by a merchant and assures that the goods, among other things, are fit for "ordinary" purposes. The implied warranty of fitness warrants the special suitability of goods and is made when the seller has reason to know of the buyer's special needs and that the buyer is relying on the seller's skill and judgment. A seller who first makes and then tries to disclaim one of these warranties must satisfy the conditions of Section 2–316. Code warranties may be extended to a person other than the seller's immediate purchaser, but this depends upon the version of Section 2–318 enacted by the state. Where dangerously defective goods cause damage to person or property, the plaintiff may sue the manufacturer or seller in tort without privity of contract and without regard to Code conditions of notice or disclaimers or agreed remedies. In most states, however, a buyer who has suffered economic loss from a defective or unmerchantable product cannot recover in tort and can recover for breach of warranty only where there is privity of contract or where Alternative C to Section 2–318 has been enacted.

F. Buyer's Obligations

The buyer's obligation is to "accept and pay in accordance with the contract." The price can be paid in money, goods or an interest in realty. The pricing mechanism takes various forms, each of which allocates risks in a different way. If the parties have intended to contract but fail to agree on price or the pricing mechanism fails, the court may supply a reasonable price. The buyer has no duty to accept and pay until it has a reasonable opportunity to inspect the goods or documents. An exception is where the buyer agrees to pay before inspection. The buyer may accept goods by affirmative action or by failing to reject them after having a reasonable inspection opportunity. If the goods are accepted, the buyer is liable for their price, loses the right to reject and has the burden of establishing breach, among other things. Unless otherwise agreed, the buyer must pay at the time and place where it is to receive goods, even though the seller has shipped them FOB point of shipment. The same rule applies where documents are involved. In most cases, payment by check—a conditional payment—is proper. Where agreed, the method of payment may be "against documents of title" or by letter of credit. Here, the buyer pays in advance of delivery and inspection and, in effect, extends credit to the seller.

G. Risk of Loss

Unless otherwise agreed, risk of loss rules determine which party bears the risk when goods are lost or damaged without the fault of either party before the buyer has taken delivery. The answer turns upon who is in the best position to prevent or insure against the loss rather than who has title. Where there is no breach by either party, the guidelines are as follows: (1) If the seller has agreed to ship the goods, risk of loss passes to the buyer upon tender of delivery to the carrier unless the seller has agreed to ship to a particular destination; (2) If the goods are in the possession of a bailee to be delivered without being moved, risk of loss passes when the buyer has a right to obtain possession from the bailee, such as where the buyer is in possession of a negotiable document duly negotiated to him or the bailee has acknowledged to the buyer it's right to possession; and (3) In other cases, where the seller is a merchant the risk passes when the buyer takes physical possession and, if he is not, the risk passes when the seller tenders delivery. In these cases, the buyer may have a special property interest or an insurable interest in goods before the risk passes. These rules change when one party is in breach and the other has a deficiency in effective insurance coverage. In these cases, a risk that should have passed is reallocated to the breacher to the extent of the deficiency. Once reallocated, insurance companies who pay cannot change the situation through subrogation. The effect of breach on the normal risk of loss rules is complicated and somewhat difficult to justify.

H. Excusable Nonperformance

Unless the risk is allocated by agreement, rules of excusable nonperformance determine when events occurring after formation justify relief from contract obligations. Cases where relief will be granted include: (1) Goods identified to the contract at the time of formation and required for performance are damaged or destroyed without the fault of either party and before the risk of loss passes; (2) Circumstances which both parties assumed would not occur make performance as agreed impracticable; and (3) An agreed method or manner of performance fails and there is no commercially reasonable substitute. If relief short of a complete discharge is appropriate, the seller may have a duty to allocate remaining goods among customers and the buyer may have an option to take and pay for the goods remaining, whether damaged or not. A hope is that the parties will adjust their obligations in light of changed conditions, but neither party has a duty to negotiate over an adjustment in good faith or to agree to a modification. The Code's excuse provisions do not explicitly apply to the buyer, but the principles do apply by implication.

I. Modification of the Contract

If the parties agree to a modification in light of changed circumstances, it will be enforced without consideration. The modification, however, must be in good faith. A bad faith modification includes extortion of the modification without a legitimate commercial reason. Most commentators argue that the purpose of the good faith requirement is to prevent duress, but some courts have found bad faith where there was no duress. A modification may also occur by waiver through election or by inducing reliance. In any case, a modification must satisfy the requirements of the statute of frauds.

VI. REMEDIES FOR BREACH OF CONTRACT FOR SALE
A. In General
Conduct by the seller or buyer may either impair the other's expectation of receiving due performance or constitute a breach. In the impairment case, remedies are provided by Section 2–609. In the breach case, Article 2 specifies what is a breach, provides a general remedial policy, and organizes the seller's and the buyer's cumulative remedies in separate parts. Thus, the seller's remedies are set out in Sections 2–702 through 2–710 and the buyer's remedies are set out in Sections 2–711 through 2–717. The effect of agreements liquidating or limiting damages or modifying or limiting remedies is governed by Sections 2–718 and 2–719. Within the classic requirements of proof, mitigation, cause and foreseeability, these remedies seek to protect the aggrieved party's expectation interest.

B. Breach of Contract
Where one party impairs the other's expectations but does not breach, the aggrieved party may suspend performance and demand adequate assurance from the other. In this process, the response or lack of it may lead to renewed performance, a modification or, in some cases may constitute a repudiation. Either the seller or the buyer may breach by repudiation. Upon repudiation, the other has several remedial choices, including cancellation of the contract and the pursuit of damages. Other types of breach flow from the conduct of the seller or buyer during the course of performance. Thus, the seller may fail to deliver on time or tender defective goods and the buyer may pursue the remedies listed in Section 2–711. Or, the buyer may fail to pay on time or make a wrongful rejection and the seller may pursue the remedies listed in Section 2–703. The aggrieved party's remedies respond to the type and the timing of the breach by the other.

C. Seller's Remedies
Upon breach by the buyer, the seller may exercise "self help" remedies, such as suspending performance, withholding delivery of goods in its possession and, in more limited circumstances, stopping the delivery of goods in transit. The seller may also cancel the contract for specified types of breaches and seek damages. The seller's damage remedies include an action for the price, the resale to a third party of goods completed before or after the breach, an action for damages measured by the difference between the contract price and the market price at the time and place for tender and an action for lost profit, including reasonable overhead, measured by subtracting total variable costs from the contract price. Each remedy has its own set of conditions, with the "contract price/market price" formula existing as a fall back position when all else fails. Thus, the seller may fail to satisfy the conditions of the resale remedy yet still prove damages under the formula. The damages may be augmented by "incidental" damages, incurred after the breach, and adjusted downward for savings realized by the breach. The

administration of these remedies is complicated by uncertainty over when, if ever, the seller "elects" one remedy over the other, the effect of "lost volume" and the applicability and application of the "components" approach in the infamous Section 2–708(2).

D. Buyer's Remedies

Upon breach by the seller, the buyer may exercise "self help" remedies, such as withholding payments otherwise due, and may, for specified breaches, cancel the contract and seek damages, including recovery of any price paid. If the seller repudiates or fails to deliver, the buyer has certain "goods oriented" remedies, namely specific performance if the goods are unique or special circumstances exist, replevin if the goods are identified and cover is not reasonably available and recovery of the goods in limited cases where the seller is insolvent. If specific performance or replevin are not available, the buyer may "cover" by purchasing substitute goods in the market or seek damages based upon the difference between the contract price and the market price at specified places when the buyer learned of the breach. For "cover," the buyer may recover the difference between the contract price and the cost to cover if specified conditions are met. The failure to effect cover does not preclude damages measured by the formula. An effective cover, however, may foreclose formula damages, even though that amount is higher. The damage remedies are augmented by provable incidental or consequential damages and are adjusted downward for expenses saved. The damage remedies are also available where the buyer has rightfully rejected the goods or justifiably revoked an acceptance.

If the seller makes a non-conforming tender which is discovered upon inspection, the buyer may reject the goods, cancel the contract and pursue damage remedies. Rejection must occur within a reasonable time and the buyer, to avoid prejudicing the seller's right to cure, should state the grounds. The limitations upon the power to reject include the general obligation of good faith, the requirement in installment contracts that the non-conformity be material and the limited right of the seller to cure the non-conformity. A buyer in possession of rightfully rejected goods has a security interest for amounts paid and expenses incurred and, in addition, has varying duties regarding their care and disposition. If the goods have been accepted, the buyer has a limited power to revoke that acceptance and then cancel the contract and pursue damage remedies. The revocation remedy must be exercised by notice within a reasonable time, and is influenced by the importance of the non-conformity, whether the buyer discovered or should have discovered it and the condition of the goods at the time of revocation. If the buyer is unable to revoke acceptance, it may still recover damages to accepted goods, provided that notice of the breach has been given to the seller within a reasonable time after the buyer discovered or should have discovered it.

Damages where the goods are accepted are measured in various ways. If a breach of warranty occurs, the buyer's direct damages are the difference in value between the goods as warranted and the goods as accepted measured at the time and place of acceptance, unless "special circumstances" show a different amount. This flexible standard is augmented, when proved, by incidental and consequential damages. Consequential damages result from the buyer's inability to put the promised goods to productive use. The damages must result from needs of the buyer of which the seller had reason to know at the time of contracting and the buyer must make reasonable efforts to avoid them by "cover or otherwise." In addition, they must be proved with reasonable certainty. If defective goods cause damage to the buyer's person or property, he may also recover them under the Code, unless preempted by strict products liability.

By agreement, the parties may attempt to liquidate damages upon breach. A forecast of damages reasonable at the time of contracting will be enforced unless, in light of actual damages, the amount was unreasonably large or was unconscionably low. The parties may also add or limit other remedies, provided that the agreement does not deprive the aggrieved party of a "fair quantum" of remedy. Other controls are that a clause excluding liability for consequential damages must be conscionable and that if an exclusive remedy fails its "essential purpose," normal Code remedies will prevail. These limitations are frequently tested in warranty litigation where the seller is unable, after a reasonable time, to repair or replace defective parts or workmanship as agreed.

VII. THIRD PARTY CLAIMS TO THE GOODS
A. In General
Claims to goods involved in a sale are frequently made by persons who are not parties to the contract. These claimants include creditors of or purchasers from either party to the sale. Thus, an alleged owner or the holder of a security interest may claim goods that have been sold and delivered by S to B. If these claimants are successful, B will lose the goods but may have a damage claim against S for breach of warranty of title. Claims to goods delivered asserted by the seller or a consignor may compete with claims of purchasers from or creditors of B. Similarly, a buyer's claims to possession of goods left with S may compete with claims of purchasers from or creditors of S. Some of these disputes can be resolved under Article 2. When a secured party is involved, however, Article 9 may apply.

B. Ownership Claims
When an owner seeks to replevin goods sold by S to B, the basic rule is that S can convey to B no greater title than he has. The exceptions are when O has delivered the goods to S in a transaction of purchase later claimed to be voidable and when O has entrusted the goods but not power to sell to a merchant and B buys in the ordinary course of business.

C. Security Interest Claims
Security interests in goods are created and perfected under Article 9. The general rule is that if a secured party creates a perfected security interest in S's goods and S sells them to B, B is subject to the security interest. The buyer takes free

of the security interest if the secured party has authorized the sale or if B is a buyer in the ordinary course of business and the security interest was created by his seller.

D. Seller's Warranty of Title
Unless disclaimed by language or circumstances, the seller makes a warranty to the buyer that the title conveyed is good, its transfer rightful and that the goods are free of any security interest. B's damages for breach are measured under Section 2–714(2) and include incidental and consequential damages.

E. Claims of Other Creditors and Purchasers
After delivery, a seller has a limited right to reclaim the goods from a buyer in a credit sale where the buyer was insolvent or a cash sale where a check issued in payment is dishonored. This Article 2 reclamation power is subject to purchasers, including a secured party, whose rights intervene before a demand is made. A consignor of goods is protected from the claims of the consignee's creditors and secured parties if appropriate notice is given. A buyer who leaves identified goods in the seller's possession may be entitled to them as against the seller through specific performance, replevin or reclamation. A purchaser of those goods from S may prevail if the retention of possession is an entrusting to a merchant and the sale was in the ordinary course of business. A creditor of S may prevail over B if the retention or identification was fraudulent. Some courts have held that a BIOCB prevails over a perfected security interest even though the goods have been left with the seller, thereby suggesting that an Article 2 special property interest has priority over an Article 9 security interest.

F. Security Interests Arising Under Article 2
If the seller creates a security interest by agreement or retention of title in goods sold and delivered to a buyer, the problems of perfection of the security interest, priority and enforcement are governed by Article 9. If the seller retains or lawfully regains possession of goods upon default by the buyer, he may have a possessory security interest arising by operation of law under Article 2. The security interest is created without the need of a security agreement and perfected without filing a financing statement. In this hybrid situation, priority disputes with creditors of and purchasers from the buyer are governed by Article 9 but enforcement of the security interest through resale of the goods is governed by Article 2.

PART THREE: LEASING OF GOODS: ARTICLE 2A

VIII. GENERAL SCOPE AND POLICIES
A. The Need for 2A
Article 2A is the first completely new article to be added to the Uniform Commercial Code. It responds to the need to codify the law governing what has become an increasingly important institution in the commercial world: the leasing

of goods. Prior law was fraught with litigation as courts struggled to apply to the leasing transaction the provisions of Articles 2 and 9 by analogy. The uncomfortable fit produced wide ranging disagreement and resultant uncertainty especially with reference to the foundational issue of whether a given transaction should be classified as a "true lease" with analogical application of Article 2 law or as a "security interest" disguised as a lease and therefore subject to Article 9. To resolve this issue, the definition of "security interest" in Article 9 was amended and the new Article 2A was drafted to govern the lease transaction thereby eliminating the need to resort to the uncertainties of analogical reasoning and common law precedents.

B. The Scope of 2A
The scope of 2A includes "any transaction, regardless of form, that creates a lease." Lease, in turn, is defined as a "transfer of the right to possession and use of goods for a term in return for consideration, but a sale . . . is not a lease."

C. The "True" Lease
The new definition of "security interest" focuses on economic factors to distinguish the lease from the security interest disguised as a lease. Two factors predominate: The transaction should be considered a security interest if 1) the economic life of the goods coincides with the term of the lease or 2) the lessee may acquire the goods at the termination of the lease for a nominal consideration.

IX. GENERAL PROVISIONS
A. Definitions Unique to 2A
The most significant definitions of 2A are those for "Consumer lease" and "Finance lease". The former means ". . . a lease that a lessor regularly engaged in the business of leasing or selling makes to a lessee who is an individual and who takes under the lease primarily for a personal, family, or household purpose. . . ." Although far from being a consumer protection statute, 2A does contain particular sections providing special protection for consumers. In this respect, the definition and its use do not differ substantially from the "buyer in ordinary course" concept in Article 9. By contrast, the concept of a "finance lease" is innovative and unique to Article 2A. The definition describes a three party transaction in which the lessor purchases goods from a supplier (goods which have been preselected by the lessee) and then leases the goods to the lessee. The definition lays the groundwork for later sections which recognize the reality of the transaction by insulating the lessor from the implied warranty liability and by extending the supplier's warranties and promises in the purchase contract to the lessee through third party beneficiary theory.

B. Choice of Law and Forum
To protect the consumer from inconvenient choice of law and forum clauses, 2A requires 1) that the law chosen by that of a jurisdiction in which the lessee either resides or will reside within 30 days or a jurisdiction in which the goods are to be used and 2) that the forum chosen not be one that would otherwise not have

jurisdiction over the lessee. Choice of law rules governing leases which are subject to Certificate of Title legislation are similar to those provided in Article 9.

C. Private Autonomy

The provisions of 2A may be varied by agreement except 1) obligations of good faith, diligence, reasonableness and care may not be disclaimed, 2) provisions which protect the rights of third parties, and 3) provisions protecting consumers from abusive clauses in consumer leases.

D. Unconscionability

The 2A counterpart to Article 2's provision on unconscionability differs in two respects: 1) conduct is expressly recognized as a potential source of unconscionability and 2) courts are authorized to award attorney's fees to the lessee where a lease is found to be unconscionable or to the lessor when the lessee claiming unconscionability knew the claim to be groundless.

X. FORMATION AND CONSTRUCTION
A. In General

With two significant exceptions, 2A mirrors the provisions of Article 2 on formation and construction. The two exceptions: 1) the Statute of Frauds section does not require a writing ". . . if the contract as modified is within its provisions", and 2) Article 2's "battle of the forms" section (2–207) does not have an Article 2A counterpart.

B. Statute of Frauds

For reasons designed to accommodate leasing practices, 2A's Statute of Frauds provisions depart from their Article 2 analogue by 1) omitting the provision dispensing with the requirement of a signature where a merchant does not respond to a written memorandum and 2) omitting the exception for cases in which payment for goods has been made.

C. Finance Lessee, a Third Party Beneficiary

2A–209 provides that the promises and warranties of the supplier under the purchase contract extend to the lessee under the lease contract.

D. Warranties

Except in the case of the finance lease (see C. above), 2A provides that unless properly disclaimed, lessors grant implied warranties of merchantability and fitness of purpose to lessees.

XI. EFFECT OF LEASE CONTRACT
A. In General

The initial section of Part 3 of 2A is modeled after a similar section on validity and enforceability in Article 9 (9–201). It states: "Except as otherwise provided in this Article, a lease contract is effective and enforceable between the parties, against purchasers of the goods and against creditors of the parties." The

(M.& S.) Sales & Leases of Goods BLS—2

"except" clause covers a host of provisions which are treated in the subsequent sections of 2A and which are treated in the following paragraphs of this capsule summary.

B. Transfer and Alienability

In general, rights of lessors and lessees are freely transferable. Exceptions involve contractual restrictions on transfer or transfers which materially increase the burden or risk on the other parties without having received adequate assurance of return performance.

C. Priority Disputes

Priority disputes involving non-creditor transferees resulting from transfers by lessors and lessees are governed by the twin sections of 2A–304 and 2A–305. In general, these sections provide that the transferees will take subject to the existing leases. The exceptions involve situations where the transactions involve transferees who qualify as buyers or lessees "in the ordinary course of business", i.e., parties who have bought or leased in good faith from a person in the business of selling or leasing "goods of that kind". 2A–302(2) and 2A–305(2).

Creditors of the lessee are subject to the rights of the lessor and therefore have rights to the leasehold interest of the lessee but not to the residual interest of the lessor. Creditors of the lessor also take subject to the lease contract with the exception which would give a secured creditor priority if that secured creditor would have had priority under Article 9 by having filed its interest before the time when the lease contract became enforceable.

D. Competing Claims in Fixtures

2A–309 is modeled after the fixture section of Article 9 with minor changes made to reflect leasing terminology and practices. One of the subsections subjects the fixture lessor's interest to the filing requirements of Article 9 even though the lease agreement does not create a security interest.

E. Sale and Leaseback

The "sale and leaseback" transaction is one where the seller sells goods to a buyer but possession is retained by the seller pursuant to a lease contract between the buyer as lessor and the seller as lessee. The transaction is a financing transaction qualifying as a "finance lease". 2A validates this transaction and therefore immunizes it from statutory or case law attack from those jurisdictions which had treated the retention of possession by sellers as fraudulent per se or prima facie fraudulent.

XII. PERFORMANCE

Part 4 of 2A largely duplicates the parallel sections of Article 2. The significant difference is the special treatment afforded to the "finance lease". Unless a consumer lease is involved, once goods have been accepted by the lessee, the lessee's promise to pay rent must be performed "come hell or high water". Its promise is "irrevocable and independent". 2A–407. The section recognizes the reality that the lessee is only a financer of the transaction and that the lessee's remedy for breaches of express and implied warranties is against the supplier of the goods, a remedy expressly recognized in 2A–209.

XIII. DEFAULT
A. In General
The remedial sections of Part 5 of 2A are similar to their Article 2 counterparts. They emphasize, however, that whether a party is in default is determined by 2A as well as the agreement thus giving rise to what commentators are referring to as "statutory" and "contractual" defaults. Remedies are stated to be cumulative and selective, limited only by the concept that the selection or cumulation should not place a party in a better position than if performance had been rendered.

B. Default by Lessor
The remedy of "cover" differs from its Article 2 analogue to address the issue that the difference between two sales contracts are likely to be less than the difference between two leases. 2A–518 therefore provides that the covering lease agreement be "substantially similar" to account for adjustments which may need to be made for what will frequently be the different time periods of the two leases. Also recognized is the need to convert the periodic future payments of the covering lease into their present value to make the proper comparison.

Cover is not mandatory and the aggrieved lessee may choose to use the "contract/market" differential measure of damages, once again recognizing the need to adjust the future contract and market rental payments to their present values.

C. Default by Lessee
Lessee remedies include 1) repossession and disposition (the counterpart to a seller's resale remedy), 2) contract/market differential, 3) profits where the contract/market differential is inadequate to fully compensated the lessor (the lost volume lessor), 4) action for the rent where the lessor is unable to dispose of the goods at a reasonable price or rental (the counterpart to a seller's action for the price), and 5) a residual action for damages recognizing that the lessor need not choose any of the foregoing remedies but may seek to recover the loss resulting in the ordinary course of events from the lessee's default as determined in any reasonable manner, together with incidental damages, less expenses saved in consequence of the lessee's default.

*

PERSPECTIVE

The transition from common law to statutory courses comes as a shock to most students. The tremor occurs when the grand principles of "general" contract law are replaced by the complex and often perplexing language of the Uniform Commercial Code (UCC). The purpose of this BLACK LETTER is to ease that transition in two areas, contracts for the sale of goods, governed by Article 2 of the UCC, and contracts for the lease of goods under Article 2A of the UCC. You may have learned a little Article 2 in the first year contracts course but the odds are against you having had much exposure to the principles of personal property leasing elaborated in Article 2A. So we will spend considerable time on these two Articles and Article 1 of the UCC with the following objectives in mind: (1) What is the nature of the UCC and what methodology must be employed to use it well; (2) What are the nature and purposes of the transactions governed by Articles 2 and 2A; (3) To what extent do these Articles give the parties power to plan their transaction by agreement and how should this planning proceed to insure maximum effectiveness; and (4) In what manner and with what policy objectives should a court apply relevant UCC provisions to decide disputes that the parties cannot resolve by agreement.

To achieve these objectives, you must read the text, puzzle over the many examples provided and answer the review questions in the BLACK LETTER. To do this, you must have a copy of the 1990 Official Text of the UCC and occasional access to relevant sections of the Bankruptcy Code, federal and state consumer protection legislation and CISG. The compilations of commercial and consumer statutes prepared

17

annually by the West Publishing Company or the Foundation Press will normally provide all that you need. Because you will have the UCC before you as you read, there is no need to provide a Glossary of Terms in the BLACK LETTER. They appear in the Code itself.

Because the Code and its comments provide the best evidence of its meaning, we have resisted the temptation to cite many cases in the text, examples and questions. There are literally hundreds of cases and, frequently, the trends or decisions have been summarized for you. We have cited a few leading cases to support basic points. If you wish to consult the cases, appropriate examples can be found in the Casebooks and Treatises which are cited and crossindexed in Appendix C. Finally, you must remember that this BLACK LETTER is just an introduction to a mystifying field of law that could take a lifetime to master. Our objective is to put the foundation in place. We hope that by working with the Code, this BLACK LETTER, your Casebook and other appropriate readings, you will survive the trip into the Code catacombs and emerge triumphant.

To test the extent of your triumph, we have, in addition to endless review questions (with answers), provided several examination questions on Sales and Leases of Goods (with answers). Examinations never write themselves. Please read the text, study the Examples and answer the review questions *before* peeking at the answers. Resist the temptation to rely on someone else's answers. Otherwise, your capacity to work with the UCC will not be fully developed.

*

PART ONE

GENERAL CONSIDERATIONS

Analysis

I

COMMERCIAL LAW IN GENERAL

Analysis

A. Definition and Scope
B. Parties and Persons Affected
   1. Parties
   2. Persons Affected
C. Types of Commercial Transactions
D. Sources and Nature of Commercial Law
   1. Agreement of the Parties
   2. State Law
   3. Federal Law
E. Review Questions

A. DEFINITION AND SCOPE

Commercial law is a body of rules and standards that defines the rights and duties of and the remedies available to the parties to and third persons affected by business contracts. The potential scope is enormous, for the subject could include disputes arising under all bargains. In this BLACK LETTER, however, the scope is limited generally to those agreements governed by the Uniform Commercial Code (UCC) and more particularly to contracts for the sale and lease of goods, governed by Articles 2 and 2A. In short, we will focus upon the creation, performance and enforcement of contracts by which goods are sold and leased. This focus insures that, *first,* in most transactions one of the parties will be a merchant, *second,* the subject matter will involve personal rather than real property, and *third,* the primary Articles of the UCC under study will be Articles 1, 2 and 2A. Nevertheless, certain aspects of the sales or security transaction *may* be affected by other Articles of the UCC, e.g., Article 9 when the seller or third parties attempt to create and perfect a security interest in goods sold, Article 7 when goods sold are shipped by carrier to the buyer, other statutes or common law principles in the state where the UCC was enacted, and federal law, e.g., the Bankruptcy Code, enacted in 1978 and substantially revised in 1984. Despite these potentially conflicting or overlapping sources of law, however, the unifying theme of this BLACK LETTER will be found in the function of the contracts under study: contracts for the sale or lease of goods.

B. PARTIES AND PERSONS AFFECTED

1. PARTIES

The parties to a contract for sale will be a seller, 2–103(1)(d), and a buyer, 2–103(1)(a). These parties sell or buy or contract to sell or buy goods. The parties to a lease of goods are a lessor, 2A–103(1)(p), and a lessee, 2A–103(1)(n). These parties transfer and acquire the right to possession and use of goods under the lease. In a finance lease, 2A–103(1)(g), an additional party is a supplier, i.e., the person from whom a lessor buys or leases goods for lease to the lessee. 2A–103(1)(x).

Many of these parties to the contracts will be engaged in a business conducted for profit and most will qualify as merchants, in that they deal regularly in the goods or transactions involved or have knowledge of and skill in the relevant usages and practices. See 2–104(1). Article 2 calls contracts where both parties are merchants a transaction "between merchants." 2–104(2). Commercial law developed over time as the needs of merchants and their transactions evolved and Article 2, at least, was drafted with these interests in mind. Article 2A, on the other hand, contains fewer "merchant" rules than Article 2, see 2A–103(1)(t), comment (t).

One of the parties to a sale or lease may be a consumer—an individual who buys or leases primarily for personal, family or household purposes. See 2A–103(1)(e). Compare 9–109(1). In recent years, the interests of consumers as a class have been given greater protection by state and federal legislation and administrative rules. The UCC in general and Article 2 in particular, however, was not drafted with the special needs of consumer sellers or buyers in mind. In a departure from this posture of neutrality, Article 2A does contain some special rules for consumer leases, see, e.g., 2A–106, and is explicitly made subject to other consumer protection statutes or "final consumer protection of a court." 2A–104(1)(c). Otherwise, consumers are governed by the general rules and standards of Articles 2 and 2A.

2. PERSONS AFFECTED

Not all persons affected by a particular commercial transaction will be parties to the contract. Consider three examples: (1) E, an employee, was injured in person by defects in goods sold by S to B, E's employer. The question is whether E has a claim for breach of warranty against S without "privity" of contract? (2) T, a thief, stole goods from O, the owner, and sold them to S, who paid value in good faith and without notice of the theft. S then sold the goods to B, who also was a bona fide purchaser. Can O replevin the goods from B, even though he was not a party to the sale? (3) Under a finance lease, Lessor purchased unmerchantable goods from Supplier and leased them to Lessee, disclaiming all warranties express or implied. Can Lessee sue Supplier for breach of warranty?

In each case, the UCC was drafted with the interests of these non-parties in mind. Thus, in the three situations above, (1) E would have a claim against S if any warranty S made to B was extended by Section 2–318 to E, (2) O would be able to replevin the goods from B, see 2–403(1), and (3) Lessee, under a finance lease, is made a beneficiary of warranties made by Supplier to Lessor. 2A–209.

> *Example I(1):* S sold and delivered goods to B on credit, with payment to be made in 30 days. Two days later S discovered that B was insolvent at the time of delivery and promptly demanded the return of the goods. B refused and shortly thereafter resold the goods for value to C who took them in good faith. S may reclaim the goods from B, since a timely demand was made, but is subject to the rights of C, a good faith purchaser. 2–702(2) and (3).

> *Example I(2):* Lessor leased goods to Lessee, a merchant who dealt in goods of that kind. The lease prohibited Lessee from disposing of the goods. Nevertheless, Lessee sold the goods to B, a buyer in the ordinary course of business. Since Lessor entrusted the goods to Lessee, a merchant, B takes free of the rights of Lessor and Lessee and the lease contract. 2A–305(2).

C. TYPES OF COMMERCIAL TRANSACTIONS

Most commercial transactions are contracts, i.e., there are "legal obligations" resulting from the parties' agreement. 1–201(11). These contracts are frequently specialized and have evolved over time in response to the needs and practices of merchants in the various markets. They are the grist of commercial law. The subject matter of these transactions is goods and other forms of tangible and intangible personal property. Land or interests in land are not involved. Some typical and recurring commercial transactions governed in whole or in part by the UCC include:

Sales or contracts to sell goods as they move in the distribution process from producer to manufacturer to retailer to the ultimate customer;

Leases of goods;

Consignments of goods to factors for sale or return;

Contracts, evidenced by documents of title, with carriers for the shipment of goods and with warehouses for the storage of goods;

Assignments of accounts receivable or other forms of intangible personal property for security;

Contracts extending credit, either by the loan of money or by a sale, where the price is to be paid after delivery of the goods;

Contracts securing an obligation to pay by the creation of a security interest in personal property;

Promissory notes issued as evidence of debt;

Transfers by negotiation or otherwise for value of negotiable instruments, documents of title, investment securities and the like;

Checks issued to pay obligations which are collected through the banking system;

Letters of credit issued to insure that goods shipped are paid for before delivery;

Payments by cash, credit card or electronic fund transfer;

And more.

D. SOURCES AND NATURE OF COMMERCIAL LAW

Whether involved in planning the commercial transaction or representing the client after a dispute arises, the attorney must have a firm grasp of the sources of commercial law. These sources are varied and frequently overlap. Some of the possibilities, interspersed with some informal history, are discussed below. Throughout it is assumed that claims and disputes arising from commercial transactions will, if they cannot be settled by agreement, be decided by courts, or if the parties have agreed, by mediation or arbitration. Thus, whatever the source and nature of commercial law, it will be authoritatively applied, when one party requests it, through the judicial or arbitral process.

1.   AGREEMENT OF THE PARTIES

In commercial law, it can be said that the transaction comes first and the law comes thereafter. This is because the Anglo–American legal system has rarely compelled people to contract and has seldom made the contract or its making a crime. Thus, from the time of the Law Merchant in 13th Century England, through its gradual absorption by the common law, through the codification movement, starting in the late 19th Century, to the more current legislative and administrative regulation of the market, the primary requisite for commercial law is the fact of some agreement between the parties. That agreement *may* have been shaped by preexisting law but its primary inducement is economic: the parties are seeking to conclude an agreed exchange involving personal property for value with the hope that both will be better off. *A major source of commercial law, therefore, is the agreement of the parties, whether that be an agreement to sell or to lease goods.* One must know what the parties intended before a decision to enforce the agreement can be made. And in commercial law, the intention of the parties, if clearly and completely expressed, frequently controls the legal outcome. Under the UCC, the definition and concept of agreement play an important role in determining the scope of obligation. See, e.g., 1–102(3) & 1–201(3).

2.   STATE LAW

Whether the agreement of the parties is enforceable as a contract and the scope and meaning of that agreement are, normally, questions of state law. Until the late 19th Century, the source of that law was judicial precedents developed in the common law process. In the interest of increased uniformity, certainty and conformity of law to business practice, the states began to enact legislation governing sales and bulk sales of goods, negotiable instruments, documents of title and certain aspects of personal property security. Unfortunately, this early "uniform" legislation was not adopted by every state and was not interpreted and applied uniformly by the courts. To some, this legislation also reflected an approach to commercial law that was rigid, mechanical and out of touch with business reality.

In the late 1940's, a project was commenced to draft a comprehensive, integrated and systematic code to cover various commercial transactions. The result was the Uniform Commercial Code (UCC), which has now been enacted, with some deviations, by 49 states, the District of Columbia and the territories. Louisiana has enacted some Articles of the UCC, but not Article 2. With this development, when a commercial dispute arises and it is clear that state law applies, the first question is whether the UCC or non-Code law applies. If the UCC *does not* apply, then the applicable non-Code state law must be found. For example, in disputes where consumers are involved, the state may have a Deceptive Practices Act or a "Lemon" law. If the UCC *does* apply, then the next questions are which article(s) and what section(s) are applicable to the dispute. We will have much more to say about UCC scope and methodology. See *infra* at II(F)(1).

3.   FEDERAL LAW

The Bankruptcy Code. Federal treaties, statutes and regulations that may preempt state law, including the Uniform Commercial Code, and thus govern the commercial transaction. Except for the Bankruptcy Code, the bulk of relevant federal law deals with the international sale of goods or various aspects of consumer credit transactions or consumer warranties. The Bankruptcy Code comes into play when a "case" in bankruptcy is commenced by or against a debtor and regulates the claims of secured and unsecured creditors against the estate. A frequent source of tension is a claim to specific property by a secured party under Article 9 of the Code or by a "reclaiming" seller or consignor under Article 2. In some cases, the trustee in bankruptcy may be able to avoid or subordinate these claims.

Consumer Protection Legislation. Federal consumer protection legislation takes various forms.

(1) The Consumer Credit Protection Act, 15 U.S.C.A. § 1601 *et seq.*, requires the disclosure of credit information and regulates various aspects of consumer credit reporting, equal credit opportunity, debt collection practices, and some aspects of electronic fund transfers where consumers are involved. The Act also regulates certain aspects of consumer leases. For example, lessors must make certain disclosures to consumer lessees and their advertising is regulated. In addition, the lessee's liability upon termination of the lease and the civil liability of the lessor for violations of the Act are spelled out. See 15 U.S.C.A. §§ 1667–1667(e).

(2) In 1988, Congress enacted the Expedited Funds Availability Act, 12 U.S.C.A. §§ 4001–4010, which specifies when funds represented by checks and other items deposited for collection are available for withdrawal and provides authority for a more expeditious collection and return of all items in the banking system. This legislation is implemented by Regulation CC, issued by the Board of Governors of the Federal Reserve System.

(3) The Federal Trade Commission has issued regulations regulating the "holder-in-due-course" doctrine and certain practices in door-to-door sales. Compliance with the former virtually abolishes the HDC doctrine while the latter grants the buyer power to cancel a home sale after a three day "cooling off" period.

(4) Finally, the Magnuson–Moss Warranty Act, 15 U.S.C.A. § 2301 *et seq.*, provides increased information about consumer warranties when a written warranty is given by a "supplier" and both limit the disclaimer of implied warranties and bolster the legal protection available when the warranty is not met. The term "supplier" is broad enough to include both a seller and a lessor of goods.

The Convention on the International Sale of Goods

On January 1, 1988, the Convention on the International Sale of Goods (CISG) became law in the United States. Unless otherwise agreed, CISG applies to contracts for the sale of goods where private parties reside in different countries both of which have adopted the Convention. CISG, which applies only to commercial transactions, contains many provisions that parallel and several provisions that deviate from Article 2. For example, CISG's risk of loss provisions are similar to those in Article 2, but unlike Article 2, CISG has no statute of frauds or provision dealing with the so-called "battle of the forms." In part, these differences reflect the somewhat distinct needs of domestic and international sales contracts.

E. REVIEW QUESTIONS

I-A. Who other than the parties to a sale or a lease of goods may be affected by the contract?

I-B. How are "consumers" and "merchants" to be distinguished from "ordinary" parties to commercial transactions? What difference does it make?

I-C. In light of applicable Federal legislation, evaluate the following statement: In commercial transactions, the law comes first and the transaction comes second.

I-D. *True or False:* When the Uniform Commercial Code applies, it is the exclusive source of law governing the transaction.

*

II

THE UNIFORM COMMERCIAL CODE

A. LEGISLATIVE HISTORY

After World War II, there was growing dissatisfaction with the condition of commercial law in the United States. The so-called "uniform" acts, such as the Uniform Sales Act, the Uniform Negotiable Instrument Act, and the Uniform Warehouse Receipts Act, did not meet the needs of national commerce. They were fragmentary in enactment and not uniformly applied by the courts. Frequently, they revealed an approach to commercial law that was doctrinal and rigid rather than flexible and responsive to the needs of merchants. From this dissatisfaction, the project to draft a uniform commercial code as state rather than federal law was born.

The Code was a joint project of the American Law Institute (ALI) and the National Conference of Commissioners on Uniform State Law (NCCUSL). The task of reviewing and commenting on its nine substantive and two transitional articles was delegated to the Permanent Editorial Board for the Uniform Commercial Code (PEB). The task of revising the UCC, however, remains with the ALI and NCCUSL.

Since Pennsylvania enacted an early version in 1953, the Code has undergone several major revisions. The 1958 Official Text became the model for state enactment through the 1960's and 1970's. The 1972 Official Text contained major revisions in Article 9, Secured Transactions. The 1978 Official Text contained major revisions in Article 8, Investment Securities. The 1988 Official Text contained a completely revamped Article 6, Bulk Sales, and two new Articles, Article 2A, Leases, and Article 4A, Funds Transfers. The 1990 Official Text contained further revisions in Article 2A, Leases, a complete reorganization and revision of Article 3, Negotiable Instruments, and a revised Article 4, Bank Deposits—Collections.

Some version of the 1961 Official Text was enacted in 49 states, the District of Columbia and Territories. At this writing, all but one state (Vermont) have enacted the 1972 revisions to Article 9 and 44 states have enacted the 1978 amendments to Article 8. Efforts are currently underway to persuade the states to enact the new articles and revisions contained in the 1988 and 1990 Official Texts. Tables showing both the deviations from state to state from the Official Text and the extent to which the states have adopted new and revised articles are found in many Code services. They *must* be consulted in every situation.

B. NATURE OF THE UCC

It has been suggested that the UCC is simply a collection of statutes in the common law rather than the civil law tradition. It goes as far as it goes and no further. This view is supported by Section 1–103 which provides that if the general principles of law and equity are not displaced by particular provisions of the Code, they "shall supplement its provisions." Similarly, courts sometimes interpret code sections as if they were common law precedents to be manipulated and stretched rather than legislative policy which, within the bounds of sound statutory construction, controls the outcome of the dispute. *Nevertheless, there are certain features which justify calling the UCC a code rather than a collection of statutes. First, it is preemptive in that it displaces all other law in its subject area save only that which the statute excepts, e.g., Section 1–103. Second, it is systematic in that all of its parts, arranged in an orderly fashion and stated with a consistent terminology, form an interlocking integrated body, revealing its own plan and containing its own methodology. Finally, it is comprehensive in that it is sufficiently inclusive and independent to enable it to be administered in accordance with its own basic policies.*

C. BASIC POLICIES: ARTICLE 1

Article 1 of the UCC, entitled General Provisions, sets forth some general policies, definitions and principles of interpretation that control in the interpretation and application of the following eight substantive articles. Since we will not discuss all of these general provisions here, you should read through Article 1 with these organizing thoughts in mind.

1. UNDERLYING PURPOSES AND POLICIES
Section 1–102(1) states that the UCC "shall be liberally construed and applied to promote" the following underlying purposes and policies:

> *(a) to simplify, clarify and modernize commercial law;*
>
> *(b) to permit the continued expansion of commercial practices through custom, usage and agreement of the parties;*
>
> *(c) to make uniform the law among the various jurisdictions. Section 1–102(2). See also 1–205, covering Course of Dealing and Usage of Trade.*

In construing the UCC in accordance with these purposes and policies, the "text of each section should be read in the light of the purpose and policy of the rule or principle in question, as also of the Act as a whole, and the application of the language should be construed narrowly or broadly, as the case may be, in conformity with the purposes and policies involved." Comment 1, 1–102.

Section 1–106(1) also provides a basic policy for remedies:

> *"The remedies provided by this Act shall be liberally administered to the end that the aggrieved party may be put in as good a position as if the other had fully performed but neither consequential or special nor penal damages may be had except as specifically provided in this Act or by other rule of law."*

Thus, UCC remedies are designed to compensate the aggrieved party rather than to punish the breacher and to measure that compensation against the yardstick of the aggrieved party's reasonable expectations.

2. VARIATION BY AGREEMENT

Section 1–102(3) provides that the "effect of provisions of this Act may be varied by agreement. . . ." See 1–201(3) for the definition of agreement. There are limitations, however.

First, Section 1–102(3) imposes a general limitation: "except as otherwise provided in this Act." Thus, the specific language or general purpose of a section may foreclose variation by agreement. For an example of specific language, see Sections 2–318 and 2A–106(1). For an example of a general purpose, see Section 2–201.

Second, Section 1–102(3) also provides:

> *except that the obligation of good faith, diligence, reasonableness and care prescribed by this Act may not be disclaimed by agreement but the parties may by agreement determine the standards by which the performance of such obligations is to be measured if such standards are not manifestly unreasonable*

For example, Section 2–607(3)(a) provides that a buyer who has accepted nonconforming goods "must within a reasonable time after he discovers or should have discovered any breach notify the seller of breach or be barred from any remedy." It is clear that the parties by agreement could not delete the requirement of *reasonable* time but that they could by agreement establish a specific time so long as it was not "manifestly unreasonable." See 1–204(1).

Third, many sections of the UCC explicitly state that "unless otherwise agreed" the following rules or principles apply. See, e.g., 2–319(1). Section 1–102(4) provides, however, that the presence of "unless otherwise agreed" or similar language in some sections "does not imply that the effect of other provisions may not be varied by agreement. . . ." In each case, the scope of the power to vary by agreement must be determined from Section 1–102(3) and the underlying purpose and policy of the particular section sought to be varied.

3. GENERAL OBLIGATIONS: GOOD FAITH

Section 1–203 provides: "Every contract or duty within this Act imposes an obligation of good faith in its performance or enforcement." This supervening principle, applicable throughout the UCC, cannot be disclaimed by agreement, 1–102(3), and thus, rescues the transaction the dishonest if not unreasonable practices sometimes condoned in the marketplace. As we shall see, there is considerable disagreement about the scope and content of the good faith duty.

4. GENERAL DEFINITIONS

Section 1–201 provides 46 "general definitions" which are applicable throughout the Code, unless the "context otherwise requires" or the general definition is supplemented or modified by additional definitions contained in specific articles. The definition of good faith provides one example. In Section 1–201(19), good faith means "honesty in fact in the conduct or transaction involved." In Section

|

THE UNIFORM COMMERCIAL CODE

2–103(1)(b), however, good faith "in the case of a merchant means honesty in fact and the observance of reasonable commercial standards of fair dealing in the trade." Thus, a higher standard of good faith is imposed upon merchants buying and selling goods and this standard is imposed by the definitions provided in Article 2. This same objective standard applies to merchants who lease goods under Article 2A. See 2A–103(3). In all other cases where the good faith duty is involved under Articles 2 and 2A, the "honesty in fact" definition applies unless the "context otherwise requires." Since the context should never require less than honesty in fact, the clear inference is that the context—perhaps one where trade practice is clear—may require more than simple honesty even though no definition so requiring is applicable.

The importance of Article 1 in the overall UCC scheme cannot be overestimated. It provides an undergirding of purpose, policy, principle and definition that structures and influences all that follows.

D. SUBSTANTIVE CONTENT

In addition to Article 1, General Provisions, and Articles 10 and 11, dealing with effective date, repealers and transition provisions, the 1990 Official Text of the UCC contains 10 articles dealing with substantive commercial law: Article 2, Sales; Article 2A, Leases; Article 3, Commercial Paper; Article 4, Bank Deposits and Collections; Article 4A, Funds Transfers; Article 5, Letters of Credit; Article 6, Bulk Transfers; Bulk Sales; Article 7, Documents of Title; Article 8, Investment Securities; and Article 9, Secured Transactions. In the following text, a basic transaction will be used to illustrate the general content of each article, some of the overlaps, and the support provided by the general provisions of Article 1.

1. ARTICLE 2, SALES

Article 2 deals with the formation, adjustment, construction, performance and enforcement of contracts for sale of goods. Although a specialized version of contract law, its principles and policies have had a strong influence upon the Restatement (Second) of Contracts. Article 2 rejects the concept of title as a general problem solving device, but does define when title passes in contracts for the sale of goods, see 2–401. This definition is important in disputes over when a seller can pass better title to a buyer than it has, see 2–403, and in disputes outside of Article 2, such as the scope of insurance protection and the incidence of state and local personal property taxation.

The last major revision of Article 2 occurred in 1958. At this writing, the National Conference of Commissioners on Uniform State Law (NCCUSL) has appointed a drafting committee to recommend appropriate revisions.

Example II(1): Smersh, a manufacturer, owns a stock of kerosene stoves to be sold in the ordinary course of business to wholesalers or retailers. The stoves are goods, 2–105(1). S contracts to sell 50 stoves to Bunson, a retailer, for $10,000. The stoves are delivered by S and accepted and paid for by B. Later, B claims that the stoves were defective when delivered, that S must take them back and that B is entitled to recover the price paid plus damages. Is B correct?

B is correct only if S made and breached a warranty and B's acceptance of the goods can be revoked. The steps to an answer are as follows: (1) This is a dispute to which Article 2 applies, since the parties have entered a contract for the sale of goods. See 2–102, 2–106(1); (2) The first question is whether S made and breached an express or implied warranty? See 2–313, 2–314 & 2–315. If not, B, who has accepted the goods, 2–606, and has the burden of proof, 2–607(4), has no claim. If so, the buyer may resort to available remedies; (3) What are they? If timely notice has been given to the seller, 2–607(3)(a), the next question is whether B can "revoke" acceptance of the goods. To do so, B must satisfy the conditions of 2–608. If revocation is proper, B may recover the price paid plus direct and consequential damages. See 2–608(3), 2–711(1) & 2–715(2). (4) If revocation is not proper, B must keep the goods but may deduct damages as determined under 2–714(2) & 2–715(2) from the price. See 2–717.

2. ARTICLE 2A, LEASES

Although covering all leases of goods, Article 2A is primarily concerned with the institution of equipment and finance leasing. Organized similarly to Article 2, its five parts cover General Provisions, Formation and Construction of Lease Contract, Effect of Lease Contract, Performance of Lease Contract, and Default. Since a sale and a lease each involve the transfer of an interest in property, one should expect to find similar principles in their governance. But the difference between a transfer for a *limited* period of time (the lease) and one which transfers ownership from a seller to a buyer (the sale) requires different treatment of a variety of issues.

Example II(2): Suppose, in *Example II(1)*, above, that B selected a large stove for its plant from S at a retail price of $2,500. B then asked L, a commercial lessor, for assistance in financing. L, in turn, purchased the stove from S for $2,250 and then leased the stove to B for 4 years for a total rent of $2,500. At the end of the lease, B had an option to purchase the stove from L for $500. At the time of the lease, L provided B with a copy of the supply contract by which L obtained the furnace from S. Soon after delivery, B, claiming that the stove was unmerchantable, refused to pay further rent.

The probable outcome is as follows: (1) The transaction between L and B is a lease rather than a secured transaction (or a "disguised" sale), since B had an option to purchase at the fair market value of the goods determined at the time the option is to be performed. 1–201(37)(x). This means that L did not have to file an Article 9 financing statement; (2) The lease is a "finance" lease because L met the requirements of 2A–103(1)(g); [Read that subsection, please.] (3) Under a finance lease, B is the beneficiary of any warranties, express or implied, made by S to L under their supply contract. Thus, if S made and breached a warranty to L, B can enforce that warranty under Article 2 directly against S. See 2A–209; (4) L, as a finance lessor, made no implied warranties to B. B, then, is in default under the lease and L can pursue the appropriate remedies against B. See 2A–523. In this circular situation, B has no defense against L, who does not assume the risk of product defects, but may recover its losses for breach of warranty directly from S.

3. ARTICLE 3, COMMERCIAL PAPER

Article 3 deals with the negotiability, negotiation, rights and liabilities of parties to, and the enforcement and discharge of commercial paper, including drafts, checks, certificates of deposits and notes. It does not apply to documents of title, Article 7, and investment securities, Article 8, even though they may be negotiable and negotiated for value. When issued by a maker or drawer, the underlying obligation to pay is suspended and the instrument becomes the tangible and legal embodiment of that obligation. As such, the instrument can be the subject of a gift and is frequently transferred for value to various purchasers. To maximize certainty and minimize costs that might impede the instrument's free transfer, Article 3 imposes rigid requirements on its form, transferability and enforcement.

Article 3 has been substantially revised and renumbered in the 1990 Official Text. Citations in the following example are to the 1990 text.

> **Example II(3):** S contracted to sell B 50 stoves on credit for $10,000. B signed and issued a promissory note to S, promising to pay $10,000 in 90 days. S promptly transferred the note to Bank for $9,500. Later, B claimed that the stoves were defective and refused to pay when Bank presented the note for payment 90 days later. Assuming that B has a breach of warranty claim against S, (an Article 2 question), can B assert that breach as a defense against Bank who seeks to enforce the note?
>
> Article 3 applies to the dispute between B and Bank. 3–102(a). Bank will prevail if *all* of the following requirements are met: (1) the promissory note is negotiable, thereby qualifying as an instrument, 3–104(a) & 3–102(a); (2) S negotiated the instrument to Bank so as to qualify Bank as a holder, 3–201(a); and (3) Bank, as a holder, took the instrument in due course, that is, for value, in good faith and without notice of the defense. 3–302(a). If so, Bank is a holder in due course (HDC) of the instrument and takes free of B's breach of warranty defense against S. 3–305(a)(2) & (b). If Bank is not a HDC, the defense may be asserted by B. Note, however, that if B were a consumer, either state consumer legislation or the FTC regulations might limit or foreclose Bank's status as a HDC.

4.   ARTICLE 4, BANK DEPOSITS—COLLECTIONS

Article 4 deals with checks, see 3–104(f), and other demand items which are drawn on a bank, called a Payor Bank, and collected through the banking system. The contractual relationship between Payor Bank and the drawer of the check, its customer, is regulated in Article 4, Part 4. The relationship between the drawee or payee of the check and the bank in which the check is deposited for collection, called the Depositary Bank, and other collecting banks is regulated in Article 4, Part 2. The responsibilities of the Payor Bank when a check is presented for payment are spelled out in Article 4, Part 3.

Article 4 is complicated and highly specialized law and governs Articles 3 and 8 to the extent there are conflicts. See 4–102(a). It begins to operate at the point where the check is deposited by the payee in the Depositary Bank for collection or presented by the payee holder to the Payor Bank for payment. In addition, when the check collection process involves the Federal Reserve System, the banks are subject to Federal Reserve Regulation J and other operating circulars. See, e.g., 4–103(b). More generally, all banks in the collection process are subject to the Expedited Funds Availability Act and Federal Reserve Regulation CC. This federal law states, inter alia, when a Customer is entitled to withdraw funds deposited in a bank and the obligations of the various banks when a check is dishonored.

Article 4 was revised and, to some extent, renumbered in the 1990 Official Text. Citations in the following example are to the 1990 text.

> *Example II(4):* S contracts to sell 50 stoves to B for $10,000. B issues to S a check for $10,000, drawn on Payor Bank, in payment. The check is negotiable and, up to this point at least, the transaction is subject to Article 3. S promptly deposited the check in Depositary Bank for collection. The check was presented through the Federal Reserve system to Payor Bank for payment on March 1. On March 2, B discovered that the stoves were defective and requested the bank to stop payment on the check. Payor Bank stopped payment and dishonored the check by promptly notifying Depositary Bank [Regulation CC 229.33(a) now requires a paying bank to give notice of dishonor directly to the depositary bank for checks of $2,500 or more] and returning the check through the banking system to S. S, the payee, however, claims that Payor Bank paid the check and is accountable for the amount of the item to S. Is S correct?
>
> This is a dispute to which Article 4 applies. Payor Bank is not accountable for the item if it returns the check or sends notice of dishonor before its "midnight deadline." 4–302(a)(1). See 4–215(a)(3). On these facts, the "midnight deadline" is midnight on March 2, the banking day after the banking day on which the check was received. 4–104(a)(10). Assuming that B's stop payment order was timely, 4–303(a), and in proper form, 4–403(a), the dishonor was timely and Payor Bank has no liability to S. S, however,

can now sue B either on the check or the underlying obligation, see 3–310(b) but, in either case, S would be subject to B's breach of warranty defense. Note, however, if B's stop order came too late and the check was not dishonored, Payor Bank's payment and debit of B's account were proper. See 4–401(a). B, then, has no claim against Payor Bank and is left to its Article 2 remedies against S.

5. ARTICLE 4A, FUNDS TRANSFERS

Article 4A, which was first promulated in the 1987 Official Text, governs the transfer of funds by wire between commercial parties. It does not govern electronic transfers where consumers are involved. These transfers are, in all probability, governed by the Electronic Fund Transfer Act, 15 U.S.C.A. §§ 1693–1693r. Article 4A does involve a credit (not a debit) transfer by a Sender to a Beneficiary over the Federal Reserve wire transfer network (Fedwire) or the New York Clearing House Interbank Payments Systems (CHIPS). The transfer is initiated by a payment order issued by the Sender to its Bank and concluded when the Beneficiary's bank accepts the payment order "for the benefit of the beneficiary of the originator's payment order." 4A–104(a). Article 4A details the procedures to be followed to effect the transfer and deals with the many problems that may arise after the payment order is issued. An excellent analysis and overview is contained in the Prefatory Note to the Official Text of Article 4A.

6. ARTICLE 5, LETTERS OF CREDIT

Article 5 regulates the process whereby obligations are paid by a letter of credit. In a typical case, S has contracted to sell goods and agreed to ship them by carrier to B. S wants payment shortly after the goods are shipped and B agrees to pay by letter of credit. B then goes to a local Bank and, for a fee, obtains a written, signed "engagement" that Bank, upon presentation of a draft drawn by S upon B and a bill of lading in proper form, will pay the amount of the draft to S. B then sends the letter of credit to S, called Beneficiary, and a Correspondent Bank at the point of shipment is advised of the arrangement. When S ships the goods and presents the draft, the letter of credit and a bill of lading in proper form to Correspondent Bank, payment of the price is made, thereby discharging the contract. If payment is improperly refused, B has a claim for damages against the issuing bank and S may require payment for the goods directly from B. The general rule is that the bank must pay according to the terms of credit in the letter. If the letter and documents are in order, the bank must pay even though the goods shipped are defective.

At this writing, a Drafting Committee has been appointed by NCCUSL to study Article 5 and make recommendations for revision.

7. ARTICLE 6, BULK TRANSFERS; BULK SALES

The 1958 Official Text of Article 6 was designed to protect a seller's unsecured creditors against the risk of a "bulk sale," i.e., the sale of a "major part" of the inventory not in the ordinary course of business for cash, and a subsequent dissipation by the seller of the proceeds. If a "bulk" sale is made, see 6–102(1), it is ineffective against unsecured creditors unless the buyer has met the requirements of 6–104(1) and given the notice to creditors required by Section 6–105. See 6–107. If the transfer is ineffective, the defrauded unsecured creditors may obtain a judgment against S and levy upon the inventory sold to and still in the hands of B.

The 1987 Official Text rejected the premises of Article 6 and, in Alternative A, recommended its repeal. In Alternative B, the 1987 Official Text recommends both the repeal of the "old" Article 6 and the enactment of a revised version of Article 6 that provides better protection to creditors of the seller and minimizes the impediments to good faith purchases.

8. ARTICLE 7, DOCUMENTS OF TITLE

Documents of title include bills of lading, 1–201(6), and warehouse receipts, 1–201(45). The former is the contract between a shipper and carrier when goods are shipped and the latter is the contract between an owner and warehouse when goods are stored. These documents may or may not be negotiable. Article 7 governs the form and issuance, negotiation and transfer and obligations of the parties to these documents.

> ***Example II(5):*** S contracts to sell 50 stoves, agreeing to ship them "FOB origin," and B agrees to pay the $10,000 "against documents of title." S made a proper contract with Carrier for shipment to B, see 2–319(1)(a), 2–504, and Carrier issued a bill of lading promising to deliver the goods to "S or order." S then drew a draft ordering B to pay "S or his order" the sum of $10,000 on "sight," see 3–104(a)(2), and delivered the bill of lading and the "sight" draft to an agent who presented them to B at its place of business. If B pays the draft, Agent will "duly negotiate," 7–501(4) the bill of lading to B and remit the payment to S. B, upon surrender of the document of title to Carrier, will be entitled to the goods when they arrive. If B fails to pay without justification, it will be a breach of contract and Agent will return the bill of lading to S. Note that this transaction involves Articles 2, 3 and 7. But Article 7 determines who is entitled to the goods under the document, 7–403(4), and the rights and duties of the Carrier. See Article 7, Part 3.

9. ARTICLE 8, INVESTMENT SECURITIES

Article 8 sets forth the rights and duties of the issuer of investment securities. The issuer is usually a corporation, the securities are typically stocks and bonds and the parties are shareholders, bondholders, brokers and purchasers. The primary emphasis is upon how investment securities, whether certificated or not, are transferred and how security interests in them are created and the rights and duties of various parties. The 1978 Official Text made important revisions to cover the "uncertificated" security, i.e., the security that is not represented by a writing or a negotiable document.

10. ARTICLE 9, SECURED TRANSACTIONS

Article 9 regulates agreements intended to create a security interest in personal property, 9–102(1), i.e., an "interest in personal property or fixtures which secures payment or performance of an obligation." 1–201(37). It governs the creation, perfection, priority and enforcement of security interests in personal property, including goods. Note, however, that Article 8 governs the creation and perfection of a security interest in investment securities and that the reversionary interest in a "true" lease, governed by Article 2A, does not create a security interest in leased goods.

> ***Example II(6):*** S contracted to sell 50 stoves to B for $10,000 on credit. B issued a promissory note payable in 60 days and S, in the contract for sale, reserved "title" in the goods until the price was paid. Thirty days after delivery, C, an unsecured creditor, obtained a judicial lien on the stoves in B's possession. S claims that as owner of the stoves he can reclaim them from B free from C's lien. Is S correct? The answer, which is found in Article 9, is no.
>
> By reserving title in goods delivered to B until the price is paid, S has, in effect, created a security interest in them. See 1–201(37) & 2–401(1). Its effect against B, C and other third parties, is governed by Article 9. Unless S has perfected the security interest by the proper filing of a financing statement, the unperfected security interest is "subordinate" to C, who became a lien creditor before it was perfected. 9–301(1)(c). If S had perfected the security interest, however, it would have had priority over C's interest as a lien creditor, 9–201, 9–301(1)(a), 9–312(5).

E. COMMERCIAL LAW NOT IN THE UCC

In Chapter 2(B) it was stated that the UCC is preemptive, systematic and comprehensive. That does not mean, however, that all commercial law matters are within its scope. The UCC in general and each Article in particular have definite scope limitations. These can be organized under five headings. Because this BLACK LETTER deals with Sales and Leases of Goods, we will illustrate the limitations with examples taken primarily from Articles 2 and 2A.

1. SPECIFIC EXCLUSIONS FROM SCOPE

Unless the "context otherwise requires," Article 2 "applies to transactions in goods," 2–102. In most cases, the transaction will be a contract for the sale of goods. 2–106(1). See 2–105(1) for a definition of goods. Thus, a safe starting point is that Article 2 will *not* apply to a "true" lease of goods or a contract to sell real estate. But see 2–107. Similarly, Article 2 will not apply to a contract for personal services or a gift of goods. See 2–403 & 2–326(3). Article 2 may apply to a "mixed" transaction of goods and services where the sale of goods predominates.

Article 2A "applies to any transaction, regardless of form, that creates a lease." 2A–102. "Lease" is defined to mean "a transfer of the right to possession and use of goods for a term in return for consideration . . ." and "unless the context clearly indicates otherwise . . . includes a sublease." 2A–103(1)(j). Thus, Article 2A will *not* apply to a purported lease that is in fact a sale of (Article 2 applies) or that creates a security interest in goods (Article 9 applies). Similarly, Article 2A will not directly apply to a lease without consideration or to a lease of personal property other than goods. See 2A–103(1)(h) for a definition of goods. The Official Comment to 2A–102, however, invites courts to apply Article 2A by analogy to leases of personal property other than goods or to other bailments of personal property, gratuitous or for hire.

Note that transactions excluded from the scope of Articles 2 and 2A may be governed either by law outside of the UCC or by other articles of the UCC. Thus, a contract where personal services predominates over the transfer of goods will be governed by general contract law and a purported lease which is in substance a security interest will be governed by Article 9. See 1–201(37), 9–102(1).

2. GENERAL PRINCIPLES NOT DISPLACED: SECTION 1–103

The link between the UCC and other state law is Section 1–103, which provides:

> *Unless displaced by the particular provisions of this Act, the principles of law and equity, including the law merchant and the law relative to capacity to contract, principal and agent, estoppel, fraud, misrepresentation, duress, coercion, mistake, bankruptcy, or other validating or invalidating cause shall supplement its provisions.*

Section 1–103 supports the view that the UCC, as a code, goes as far as it goes and no farther. Unless a pre-existing principle of state law is "displaced" by a "particular provision" of the UCC, that pre-existing principle shall "supplement its provisions." On the other hand, 1–103 creates some tension with the view that the UCC is comprehensive and capable of being administered in accordance with its own basic policies. Suppose, for example, that in negotiations leading toward a proposed contract for the sale of goods, a dispute arises over whether S made an offer to B. Although Article 2 uses the word "offer," see 2–205, 2–206(1) & 2–207(1), it does not define it. Does this mean that a court must use the general contract law of the state to provide that definition regardless of how it conforms to general policies of contract formation under Article 2? Or, may the court provide a definition of offer that is constructed from within the UCC? Undoubtedly, the courts have some discretion in these matters and, if there is an obvious policy conflict, the court should construct a definition that is consistent with overall UCC policy.

> ***Example II(7):*** S sold goods to B on credit. At the time of delivery, B was insolvent but did not tell S. Under pre-code law, assume that B's failure to inform S of his insolvency was fraud and S was entitled to reclaim the goods

and to recover damages. This principle of state law is, however, displaced by Subsections 2–702(2) & (3) which provide that under certain conditions S may reclaim the goods but that this "excludes all other remedies with respect to them." 2–702(3). Fraud claims in general, however, are displaced by Article 2 and, with the exception of some remedies, see 2–721, are governed by non-code law. See 1–103.

3. OTHER STATE LEGISLATION PREEMPTS OR SUPPLEMENTS

Other state legislation, not repealed by the enactment of UCC, may supplement or preempt it. Thus, both sellers to consumer buyers and institutions which finance consumer lessees might be subject to regulation contained in the Uniform Consumer Credit Code or similar legislation or a final judicial decision that is not found in either Article 2 or Article 2A. See 2–102 & 2A–104(1)(d). Similarly, a lease of goods may be covered by a certificate of title act that requires notation of the lessor's reversionary interest on the certificate. See 2A–104(1)(b). *The message is clear: the UCC does not exist in a legislative vacuum and the careful lawyer must be aware of other state legislation that supplements or preempts it.*

> *Example II(8):* State A enacted a Consumer Protection Act which provided *inter alia,* that upon default by a debtor under a security agreement or a lessee under a lease the secured party or the lessor must give notice and an opportunity for a hearing before repossessing the goods. Lessee, a consumer, defaulted and Lessor, in full compliance with 2A–525, peacefully repossessed and resold the goods. See 2A–527. Although Lessor did not violate Article 2A's requirements, it did violate the Consumer Protection Act to which Article 2A was subject. As such, Lessor is subject only to the sanctions imposed by that statute. 2A–104(3).

4. FEDERAL LAW PREEMPTS OR SUPPLEMENTS

Some potential sources of federal law which preempt or supplement the UCC were discussed in Chapter I(D)(3). These sources appear to be always increasing and changing in content. Here are some brief illustrations.

> *Example II(9):* On June 1, Lessor and Lessee entered into what they thought was a four year lease, at the end of which Lessee had an option to purchase the goods for $10. On August 1, Lessor's attorney advised that the transaction was not a "true" lease. Rather, it created a security interest subject to Article 9. See 1–201(37). On September 15, Lessor perfected that security interest by filing a financing statement in the proper place. On October 1, D defaulted and declared bankruptcy. Lessor's security interest, although enforceable and perfected under Article 9, is avoidable by the trustee in bankruptcy as a preference under Section 547 of the Bankruptcy Code. In most cases, a delayed perfection is a transfer for an antecedent debt. See § 547(e)(2).

Example II(10): SP, a retailer, sold goods to B, a consumer, on credit. SP created a security interest in the goods sold and, as additional security, a security interest in goods previously sold to B. This was an enforceable security interest under Article 9. In the disclosure required by the Federal Consumer Credit Protection Act, however, SP failed to provide a "clear identification of the property to which the security interest relates." 15 U.S.C.A. § 1639(a)(8). See Regulation Z 226.8(b)(5). This failure was a violation of federal law for which SP may be liable to B.

Example II(11): S, a New York corporation, sold goods to B, an Australian corporation. The contract provided that the "law of New York" shall govern the transaction. Since both the United States and Australia have ratified the Convention for the International Sale of Goods (CISG) (they are contracting parties) and S and B have places of business in the contracting states, that Convention governs the transaction, see CISG Art. 1(1), unless the parties have "excluded the application of this Convention." CISG Art. 6. They have not done so on the facts of this case. Federal treaties, as the Supreme law of the land, are part of the law of New York unless the parties have clearly excluded their application. Since they did not limit the choice to local and domestic New York law, CISG would apply.

Example II(12): S, a retailer, sold B, a consumer, a refrigerator and warranted in writing that the goods were free from defects in material and workmanship for a 90 day period. The writing also provided that the exclusive remedy for breach was repair or replacement of defective parts and, in small print, excluded any liability for consequential damages. Assuming that this agreement is enforceable under the UCC, S must still comply with the Magnuson–Moss Warranty Act, 15 U.S.C.A. § 2301 *et seq.* Since S has made a "written warranty," it must, at a minimum, designate the warranty as either "full" or "limited" and must "fully and conspicuously disclose in simple and readily understood language the terms and conditions of such warranty." The failure to meet these and other requirements is a violation of federal law for which S may be liable to B.

5. THE CODE OF ANOTHER STATE APPLIES

Choice of law principles are important in commercial litigation. For example, the forum state may have enacted the 1990 Official Text of Article 2A and another state with which the transaction has contacts may have enacted the 1987 Official Text or failed to enact 2A at all. Or, one state may have enacted a comprehensive consumer protection statute and the other may not. The outcome may depend upon which state's law applies.

Under Section 1–105, the conflict should be resolved as follows: *first,* if the transaction bears a "reasonable relation" to the forum and to some other state, the parties may agree that the law of the forum or that other state "shall govern their rights and duties," 1–105(1); *second,* if there is no agreement, the UCC enacted by the forum state applies if the transaction bears "an appropriate relation" to the forum state and, if not, the law of the state to which the transaction does bear an appropriate relation should apply; and *third,* special choice rules apply when one of the six sections listed in Section 1–105(2) are applicable. One of these sections is 2–402, which provides that the "law of the state where the goods are situated" controls whether a creditor of the seller can void a sale because the seller has retained possession. See 2–402(2). Another is 2A–105, which specifies which law governs the "effect of compliance or noncompliance" with a certificate of title statute covering leased motor vehicles.

> ***Example II(13):*** Lessee, a consumer, drove from Indiana to Wisconsin to lease a new stereo system for use in her Indiana home. The lease provided that the law of Wisconsin governed the transaction. Even though this agreement would be enforceable under 1–105(1), 2A–106(1), which is listed in 1–105(2), provides that the choice of law is not enforceable in a consumer lease: The jurisdiction chosen was "other than a jurisdiction in which the lessee resides at the time the lease agreement becomes enforceable. . . or in which the goods are to be used."

F. CODE METHODOLOGY

Methodology involves the approach that lawyers and judges should take to maximize the possibility that sound and uniform interpretations of the UCC, particularly Articles 2 and 2A, can be achieved. This approach contains three important ingredients. For a more detailed discussion, see Gedid, *U.C.C. Methodology: Taking A Realistic Look at the Code,* 29 Wm. & Mary L.Rev. 341 (1988).

1. STEPS IN SOUND CODE METHODOLOGY
First, remember that the UCC was enacted in a Code form. Its sections, subsections, definitions and comments are arranged in an orderly manner within a semi-complete system to achieve textual unity. The UCC is *authoritative,* in that it is enacted by the legislature, it is *selective,* in that it states only the leading principles, it is *comprehensive* in that it states all of the leading principles, and it is *unified,* in that it speaks completely on a given subject. But the UCC is not totally preemptive: It goes as far as it goes and no farther. See 1–103; Hawkland, Uniform Commercial Code Methodology, 1962 U.Ill.L.Rev. 29.

Second, the drafting techniques employed in the Code, particularly Article 2, suggest that courts should employ a purposeful interpretation of its provisions. Thus, 1–102(1) states that the Code "shall be liberally construed and applied to promote its underlying purposes and policies." Whether those "purposes or policies" are expressed in the general principles of Article 1 or the more specific provisions of Articles 2 and 2A, the court is directed to find and implement them. *Put differently, the governing principle should be ascertained from the statute itself and the court should then engage in a purposeful implementation of that principle.*

Third, there are several rather mechanical steps that should be taken in this process. They are:

(a) Analyze the problem and develop the general issue(s).

(b) Determine whether the UCC applies and, if so, which Article(s) and what Section(s).

(c) Using the applicable language, develop a precise statutory issue.

(d) Determine whether the question can be resolved satisfactorily from the applicable statutory language, as amplified by applicable statutory cross references and definitions.

(e) If not, can the question be resolved when the specific purposes and policies underlying the particular section and the general purposes and policies underlying the UCC are considered? These purposes and policies may be found in the Comments to the UCC, persuasive judicial opinions, the drafting history of the particular section(s) and the work of commentators.

(g) If, after these steps have been taken, the answer is still not clear, the choice is between a return to supplemental principles of law via Section 1–103 or the development of an answer that is consistent with perceived purposes and policies of the Code. See, generally, White & Summers, Uniform Commercial Code §§ 1–8 (3d ed. 1988).

2. ILLUSTRATION: FIRM OFFERS UNDER SECTION 2–205

Suppose that after informal negotiations, B mailed to seller a printed form prepared by B inviting S to make an offer to sell 50 kerosene stoves for $10,000. The form contained 5 paragraphs on a single sheet of paper, with blank spaces filled in ink. In the third paragraph above the signature line the following language appeared: THIS OFFER WILL BE HELD OPEN FOR 30 DAYS AFTER RECEIPT BY OFFEREE. S signed on the signature line and returned the form. Ten days later the market price of kerosene stoves rose sharply and S telephoned B to revoke the offer. B argued that the offer was not revocable and, shortly thereafter, telegraphed an acceptance. Assume that S had read the form before signing. Assume, further, that the form would constitute an offer and that S received no consideration for the assurance that the offer would be held open for 30 days. Is there a contract? Let's see where the methodological steps take us.

(a) The general issue is whether an assurance that an offer will be held open contained in a writing signed by the offeror where no consideration has been received or recited in the writing is enforceable as an option contract? The answer at common law was no. See Restatement (Second) Contracts § 87(1)(a).

(b) The precise question is governed by Section 2–205 of the UCC. To understand why, you must first have a general understanding of the scope of the various articles and the arrangement of the parts and sections within each article. This is a transaction in goods, with negotiations leading to the possible formation of a contract for the sale of goods. As such, it is within the general scope of Article 2, see 2–102 & 2–105(1), and, more particularly, Part 2 of Article 2. After examining part 2, it is clear that the dispositive section is 2–205, Firm Offers.

(c) The precise statutory issue is this: If S is a merchant and all other conditions imposed by Section 2–205 up to the semicolon are met (they appear to be), has the "term of assurance on a form supplied by the offeree" been "separately signed by the offeror" when the offeror has signed only on the signature line. If so, the offer is "firm" and cannot be revoked and B's timely acceptance creates a contract.

(d) Can the statutory issue be answered from the language of the statute as appropriately defined in other sections of the UCC? Look first at the definitional cross references to Section 2–205 and note that four key words, "goods," "merchant", "signed" and "writing", are defined, some in Article 1 and some in Article 2. (What a "reasonable time" depends on is spelled out in Section 1–204.) The words "offer" and "consideration" are not defined by the UCC. But see Restatement (Second) Contracts § 24 & § 71. But must S "separately sign" the form by a second signature at the place on the form where the "term of assurance" appears? The plain meaning of "separately" and the definition of "signed," 1–201(39), supports an affirmative answer. So does an apparent purpose of the requirement, which is to insure that one party is aware of important provisions in standard forms supplied by the other. Is there anything else to support this conclusion?

(e) Other sections of Article 2 reveal a general concern of the drafters that one party to a transaction in goods might be unfairly surprised by the fine print in a standard form contract prepared by the other. The Cross References to 2–205 refer to one such general provision, Section 2–302, but not to another where the language "separately signed" is used. 2–209(2). See also 2–207. This general policy against unfair surprise certainly reinforces the affirmative answer reached above. But suppose B, who wants to enforce the option argues that S was not unfairly surprised: the "term of assurance" was in conspicuous print and S read it before signing the signature line. See 1–201(10). Furthermore, B might argue that during the days before S attempted to revoke, B relied to his detriment on the assurance by foregoing other business opportunities.

(f) Legislative history and Comment 4 to Section 2–205 indicate that B's argument should be rejected. The purpose is to protect the offeror "against the inadvertent signing" of a firm offer on a form supplied by the offeree and the method of protection is the requirement of separate authentication: "If the offer clause is called to the offeror's attention and he separately authenticates it, he will be bound." Comment 4. See 1 N.Y. State Law Rev. Comm'n Report 615 (1955). Thus, the drafters of the UCC did not intend that the issue turn on whether the offeror was in fact surprised. Rather, a separate element of formality, perhaps to replace the seal, see 2–203, was required before the assurance was enforceable. To date, there have been no judicial decisions on this point and it has not been fully treated by the commentators. See, e.g., White & Summers, Uniform Commercial Code § 1–4 (3d ed. 1988).

G. REVIEW QUESTIONS

II–A.   S sold B a used car. During negotiations, S knowingly misrepresented the odometer reading to B. In fact, it had been set back 20,000 miles. Later, B discovered the truth and sought to rescind the contract for fraud and recover the price. In addition, B sought punitive damages. S argued that the false representation was an express warranty under Section 2–313 and that it was not part of the agreement because of the parol evidence rule. See 2–202. S also argued that B could not recover punitive damages under the UCC, citing Section 1–106(1). What is B's best argument in response?

II–B.   In what ways is the UCC designed to accommodate change?

II–C.   S sold B yarn which required processing before it could be used to manufacture sweaters. In the contract, B agreed to give S notice of "any defects within 10 days of receipt of the yarn" or be barred from any remedy. S delivered a batch of yarn and B took 15 days to process it. Defects, latent at the time of delivery, then appeared. B gave notice and S claimed that it was "too late." Assuming that 15 days was usual for processing, is S correct?

II–D.   *True or False:* The parties may alter by agreement the legal effect of the statute of frauds for the sale of goods. See 1–102(3) and 2–201.

II–E.   *Exercise:* Using the definitions in Sections 1–201 and Article 2, Part 1 (§ 2–101 through § 2–107), what words and phrases in Section 2–205 are separately defined? Make a list with the complete definition.

II–F.   *Exercise:* In the discussion of Substantive Content, See II(D), identify the *business purposes* served by the transactions involved and the *interests* asserted by the parties and persons affected. Start making a list. . . .

II–G.   *True or False:*

1. Article 9 does not apply to a "true" lease but Article 2 may be applied.

2. What an "offer" is must be determined from non-Code law.

3. In the case of consumer goods, a clause excluding the seller's liability for consequential damages is enforceable if it satisfies the requirements of Section 2–719(3).

4. Section 9–103 governs choice of law problems where leases of goods are involved.

5. The analysis in II(F), Code Methodology, is absolutely brilliant.

II–H. **A *final problem*.** Buyer accepted goods tendered by Seller under a contract for sale but later complained that they did not conform to the contract. S disagreed and insisted that B pay the contract price of $5,000. B claimed that the goods were worth only $2,500. After somewhat bitter discussions, B sent a messenger to S with $3,000 in cash and a letter stating that the cash was offered "in full settlement" of our dispute. S accepted the cash and wrote a letter in response, which was duly delivered by the clerk. The letter insisted that B owed S $5,000 and that S, although accepting the cash, reserved all rights against B. The letter also stated that the cash was accepted "without prejudice" to those rights. Later, S sued B for $2,000 and B defended on the ground that there had been an accord and satisfaction. S responded that it had reserve rights under 1–207 and that B's duty to pay the full price was not discharged. What result?

*

PART TWO

SALE OF GOODS: ARTICLE 2

Analysis

*

III

GENERAL SCOPE AND POLICIES

Analysis

51

A. SCOPE AND DEFINITIONS

Article 2 applies to "transactions in goods," unless the "context otherwise requires" and with other exceptions to be discussed below. 2–102. The prototype transaction is a contract between a "seller," 2–103(1)(d), and a "buyer," 2–103(1)(a), for the sale of goods. This includes both a present sale of goods, i.e., the passing of title from the seller to the buyer for a price, 2–106(1), and a "contract to sell them at a future time." 2–106(1).

Goods, with exceptions to be discussed, mean "all things (including specially manufactured goods) which are movable at the time of identification to the contract for sale. . . ." 2–105(1). Goods also include "minerals or the like (including oil and gas) . . . if they are to be severed by the seller." 2–107(1). *Thus, Article 2, with its particular approach to liability and remedy, applies directly to any contract for the present or future sale of goods. See 2–106(1), first sentence.*

1. WHAT ARE "TRANSACTIONS IN GOODS"?

Scope questions are very important, especially in warranty disputes. Assume S, a retailer, contracts to sell a color T.V. set to B, a consumer, for $300. Later, B claims that the T.V. is defective and that S breached an implied warranty of merchantability. This prototype transaction is clearly within the scope of Article 2. The "transaction in goods" is a contract for their sale. Thus, Article 2 rather than some other source of state law governs such questions as whether S made any warranties, and, if so, whether B has any remedies upon breach. See 2–314(1) & 2–714(2).

Some transactions in goods, however, do not involve a contract for their sale. This does not necessarily mean that Article 2 is inapplicable. Article 2 may still apply directly or a court may decide to apply it by analogy.

Here are some examples.

(a) Gifts

Suppose that S made a gift of the T.V. to B. Later, B claimed that the set was "unmerchantable" and sued S for breach of warranty. The quick answer here is that Article 2 does not apply. A gift is a "transaction" in goods, but S makes no implied warranty of merchantability unless he has contracted for their sale. 2–314(1). A gift is not a sale because title did not pass from S to B "for a price." 2–106(1). *In general, Article 2 does not apply directly or by analogy to transactions in goods where no bargain was involved. See 1–201(3), which defines agreement as the parties' "bargain in fact."*

(b) Bailments

In a bailment, S delivers the T.V. to another for a stated and limited purpose, e.g., shipment, storage or repair. Or B, the owner of components, may deliver them to S for finishing and assembly. Even though a bargain is involved, i.e., the bailor agrees to pay for the service, the transaction is not a sale. Thus, Article 2 does not govern such questions as contract formation, performance and remedies.

Article 2, however, might apply to some narrow issues in and around a bailment. For example, if S "entrusts" goods to a merchant for repairs, the merchant may have power to transfer good title to a buyer in the ordinary course of business. 2–403(2). Similarly, if B properly rejects goods sold to and in its possession, see 2–601, B, as a bailee of S's goods, has some duty to preserve and dispose of them. See 2–602(2), 2–603 & 2–604. *In a bailment, however, the assumption is that Article 2 does not apply unless explicitly stated otherwise.*

(c) Consignments

If S sells the T.V. to B "on approval," the usual understanding is that if B does not approve, the goods can be returned even though they conform to the contract. Similarly, S may sell the goods to B "primarily for resale" and agree to their return if B is unable to sell them. These are conditional sales within the general scope of Article 2 and are regulated in particular by Sections 2–326 and 2–327.

In a consignment, however, the goods are delivered by the Owner to a Factor (or Agent) who has power to sell. But they are not sold to Factor: O retains title until they are sold and, at that time, title passes directly to the buyer. If they are not sold by F, they are returned to O. The consignment is not within the general scope of Article 2, but, as with some bailments, particular aspects of the transaction may be regulated. *Thus, unless O has given public notice that F may be trading in the goods of others, the consignment goods may be subject to the claims of F's creditors.* See 2–326(3) and Chapter VII(E)(1)(c).

> *Example III(1):* F is a merchant, see 2–104(1), who deals in new and used T.V.s. C, a consumer, delivered a used T.V. to F for repair. S, a manufacturer, consigned 20 new T.V.s to F for sale in the ordinary course of business. Thereafter, L, a creditor of F, obtained a judicial lien on all of the T.V.s in F's possession: (1) Article 2 does not govern the dispute between C, the bailor, and L, F's lien creditor. Since there is no provision protecting F's creditors in a bailment, C should be able, under other state law, to replevy the goods free from the judicial lien; (2) Article 2 does govern the dispute between S, the consignor and L: Section 2–326(3) protects L unless S has complied with the notice requirements. See also, 9–114.

> *Example III(2):* In Example III(1), above, suppose that F had sold the goods delivered by both C and S to B, a buyer in the ordinary course of business. Article 2 does govern the dispute between the owners of the

goods, the bailor and consignor, and B, the buyer. In short, B wins. See 2–403(2).

(d) Leases

For tax or other business reasons, a manufacturer may prefer to lease rather than to sell goods to customers. Leases of goods are now governed by Article 2A, thereby partially resolving a number of complicated scope questions that had plagued the courts.

For example, suppose the party in possession under a transaction called a "lease" claimed that the goods were unmerchantable. Prior to Article 2A, the party in possession would have every incentive to argue that the transaction was really a sale rather than a lease. If a sale, Article 2's warranty provisions would apply. If a "true" lease, Article 2 would not directly apply and the lessee's protection was less certain. Many courts, however, extended Article 2's warranty provisions by analogy to disputes arising under leases. They reasoned that both the substance of the transaction and the expectations of the lessee were similar to a contract for sale and that it would be unsound to have different bodies of state law governing transactions where the economic effect was the same. For a good example, see *Cucchi v. Rollins Protective Services Co.*, 524 Pa. 514, 574 A.2d 565 (1990).

With the promulgation of Article 2A and its comprehensive warranty provisions, there is less tension at the border with Article 2.

(e) Mixed Transactions: The Predominant Purpose Test

At one extreme are contracts where only personal or professional services are involved. These are not "transactions in goods" and Article 2 does not apply. At the other extreme are contracts for sale where only goods are involved. Article 2 does apply. In most cases, however, the contract will involve both services and the sale of goods. For example, B may contract with S for the development and licensing of specialized software, the supply and installation of computer hardware within which the software is to operate and for maintenance and repair services after installation. This transaction involves a sale of goods (the hardware), but the software is licensed rather than sold. Furthermore, services are involved: S is to develop the software, install the hardware and maintain the system. Does Article 2 apply to this mixed transaction of goods and services? For an answer, see *Example III(7), infra.*

For most courts, the answer depends upon which part predominates, the furnishing of services or the sale of goods. See, e.g., Coakley & Williams, Inc. v. Shatterproof Glass Corp., 706 F.2d 456 (4th Cir.1983). If the former, Article 2 does not apply to any of the transaction. If the latter, Article 2 applies to the entire transaction. There is no middle ground. Moreover, this "either-or" outcome depends upon the somewhat uncertain application of several factors in each case:

(1) The nature and language of the contract. Is the nature of the contract (i.e., a franchise agreement) or the contractual language more consistent with the transfer of goods or the rendition of a service?

(2) The nature of the business of the supplier. Is the supplier's business essentially the rendition of services (such as the stripping and refinishing of wood flooring) or the sale of goods (such as supply and installation of carpeting)?

(3) The price or value allocation in the contract between goods and services. Is there an allocation of price to goods and services and, if so, to which part was most of the price allocated?

(4) The issues involved in the dispute. Is the primary dispute over the quality of the goods supplied, the services rendered or something else? As a matter of policy, the answer to this question might tip the balance in close cases.

Critics claim that the "predominant purpose" test is subjective and too uncertain for consistent application. It may exclude disputes from Article 2 that should be resolved there. A possible solution is the so-called "gravamen" test, which asks whether the underlying cause of action was brought to complain about the goods or the services. For example, suppose the contract is for S to supply and install plumbing in a home under repair and a leak develops in the completed system. If the complaint was that the leak was caused by defective pipe rather than deficient installation, Article 2 would apply to the extent necessary to resolve the warranty claim. All other issues in the dispute would be resolved outside of Article 2. See *In re Trailer & Plumbing Supplies,* 133 N.H. 432, 578 A.2d 343 (1990). Similarly, if the cause of an injury was defective shampoo supplied in a beauty treatment or defective blood supplied during surgery, Article 2 would apply to the warranty claim even though services predominated in the overall transaction. Note that many states have enacted special statutes dealing with liability in transactions where blood is transferred. The effect of most is to foreclose or limit the transferor's liability (usually a medical facility) for imperfections in the blood. See, e.g., *Coffee v. Cutter Biological,* 809 F.2d 191 (2d Cir.1987) (interpreting Connecticut statute).

The disadvantage of the "gravamen" test is the resulting piecemeal application of Article 2 to what constitutes a single transaction. For example, suppose that in the sale of corporate assets, only 20% of the value involved goods. The balance involved intangibles, such as trade names, trade marks and good will. If the goods were unmerchantable and the predominant purpose of the transactions was the sale of intangibles, Article 2 would not apply to any of the transaction. Under the "gravamen" test, however, Article 2 would apply only to the warranty claim and not to any other issues involved. *Thus, a single transactions might be subject to two sources of law, depending upon the fortuity of what issue was raised in the pleadings.*

Here are some examples:

> *Example III(3):* K agrees to construct an office building for O on land owned by O. The contract is for a fixed price and there is no allocation between goods and construction services. Most courts conclude that services predominate or that there is a presumption that Article 2 does not apply unless there is a substantial justification for its use. See *Elkins Manor Associates v. Eleanor Concrete Works, Inc.*, 183 W.Va. 501, 396 S.E.2d 463 (1990). This conclusion is plausible, given the primary objective of the parties, the different practices in the construction industry, the well developed doctrines of construction contract law and the fact that the goods become fixtures or part of the realty when the project is completed. If the major dispute was over the quality of goods supplied, however, the "gravamen" test might lead to a different result.

> *Example III(4):* B contracted with S to supply and install a silo on B's farm. S contracted with A to assemble the silo from components that S had in stock. S then delivered and installed the silo. Later, the silo collapsed in a storm due to A's improper assembly. Under the "predominant purpose" test, the probabilities are that the contract for assembly between A and S is for services and the contract between S and B for supply and installation is for goods. Thus, Article 2 would apply to B's claims against S (i.e., that the silo as assembled was unmerchantable) and general contract law would apply to S's claim against A.

> *Example III(5):* P, a famous artist, orally promised to paint D's portrait for $20,000. Later, P refused to perform and D sued for breach of contract. P argued that the agreement was a transaction in goods within the scope of Article 2 and was unenforceable for failure to comply with the statute of frauds. 2–201(1). D argued that Section 2–201(1) applied only to contracts for the sale of goods and this was a contract for personal services. D is correct and the contract is enforceable because the predominant purpose of the transaction is probably services rather than a sale of goods. This outcome is also supported because the "gravamen" of the complaint is the failure to paint and the fact that courts, in close cases, tend to resolve issues against the statute of frauds.

> *Example III(6):* F granted to D a franchise to operate a restaurant. The franchise was to last 10 years, but F reserved the power to terminate

the franchise "at any time for any reason" upon the giving of 90 days notice. F terminated the franchise after three years and D argued that, under Article 2, the termination clause was either unconscionable at the time to contracting, 2–302, or the power was exercised in bad faith. 1–203 & 2–103(1)(b). Most courts have held that the dominant purpose of a franchise is services rather than the sale of goods, although the answer turns on the nature of the franchise. (An exclusive distributorship, on the other hand, is usually characterized as a contract for sale). It is, however, proper to extend the UCC's requirements of conscionability and good faith to service contracts, for these "neutral" principles are now accepted in general contract law. See, e.g., Restatement (Second) Contracts §§ 205 & 208 (1979).

Example III(7): What about the contract for computer software and hardware, noted above? In the many cases dealing with this problem, the courts purport to apply the "predominant purpose" test. At the risk of oversimplification, the transaction is treated as a contract for the sale of goods when the hardware and software, no matter how developed, are to be assembled and installed as a system at a price where no allocation is made to services. See *Advent Systems Ltd. v. Unisys Corp.,* 925 F.2d 670 (3d Cir.1991). The same result has been reached where the software in the system was licensed rather than sold. See *Step–Saver Data Systems, Inc. v. Wyse Technology,* 939 F.2d 91 (3d Cir.1991). Despite the complexity of the problem, the court's predisposition is to apply the entire Article 2 to these disputes, not just those sections dealing with warranty claims.

(f) Secured Transactions

This BLACK LETTER will explore where relevant the relationship between Article 2, Sales and Article 2A, Leases and Article 9, Secured Transactions. *Article 9 applies to "any transaction (regardless of its form) which is intended to create a security interest in personal property." 9–102(1). When the security interest is in goods, Article 2 does not apply to "any transaction which although in the form of an unconditional contract to sell or present sale is intended to operate only as a secured transaction." 2–102. Thus, if the form is a sale but the substance is security, Article 2 does not apply. Similarly, if the form is a lease of goods but the substance is a security interest, see 1–201(37), Article 9 rather than Article 2A applies.*

Under Article 2, however, goods can be the subject of both a sale and a security interest. In these cases, which article applies depends upon the nature of the dispute. If the question is whether the seller has created a security interest that is enforceable against the buyer or perfected against third parties, Article 9 applies. If the question is whether the seller has made and breached a warranty, Article 2 applies. In the middle are some overlaps of more complexity. They involve such problems as (1) security interests arising under Article 2, see 9–113, (2) priorities between sellers and buyers asserting Article 2 interests and secured parties asserting Article 9 interests, see 2–702(2), and (3) the content of good faith for a buyer of goods who claims to take free of Article 9 security interests, see 9–307(1). We will treat these overlaps in more detail in Chapter VII.

> ***Example III(8):*** B contracted to buy factory equipment from S, with the price to be paid 60 days after delivery. The parties agreed that S would retain title to the goods until the price was paid. After delivery, C, a creditor of B, obtained a judicial lien on B's assets, including the equipment. Shortly thereafter, B defaulted in its obligation to pay S the price. B also claimed that the equipment did not conform to the express and implied warranties in the contract. In this case, both Article 9 and Article 2 apply. Article 9 applies to the priority dispute between S and C because S's retention of title after delivery is treated as a security interest. See 1–201(37) & 2–401(1). Thus, C, a lien creditor, would have priority unless S filed a financing statement (perfected the security interest) before the judicial lien attached. 9–301(1)(b). Article 2 applies to the warranty dispute between S and B.

2. WHAT ARE GOODS?

The definition of goods is "all things (including specially manufactured goods) which are movable at the time of identification to the contract for sale." 2–105(1). Specifically excluded from this definition are "money in which the price is to be paid," "investment securities," and "things in action." Specifically included in this definition are the "unborn young of animals," "growing crops" and other identified things attached to and to be severed from realty by the seller, as required in Section 2–107. Goods are "identified to the contract for sale when the parties or circumstances indicate that existing goods are intended as the subject matter of the sale. See 2–501(1) & 2–105(2).

> ***Example III(9):*** S and B contracted for S to manufacture special machinery from specifications furnished by B. Shortly thereafter, S repudiated the contract and claimed that because the goods were to be specially manufactured and were not yet existing, the dispute was beyond the scope of Article 2. S is wrong. S and B have a contract for the future sale of future goods. 2–105(2). Although no interest in the machinery can pass to B until it is both existing and identified, see 2–501(1)(b), the machinery clearly would be goods when completed and identified. See 2–105(1). There is no requirement that future goods actually be existing before the remedial protection of Article 2 is available to B. See 2–106(1), 2–610 & 2–711(1).

The line between goods and interests in real estate is drawn in Section 2–107. Consider the following examples.

Example III(10): B wants to purchase a garage attached to realty owned by S. B expects to remove it from the land to his own property. A contract to sell the garage is a contract for the sale of goods if the "structure" is to be "severed by the seller." If B is to sever the structure it is a contract for the sale of land. The same rule applies to "minerals or the like (including oil and gas)." 2–107(1). If S is to sever, a contract to sell the existing, identified building or gas or minerals operates as a contract "to sell" goods until severance.

Example III(11): B, a logger, contracts with S to purchase identified standing timber on S's land. B is to cut, trim and remove the timber. Under the 1962 Official Text, this was a contract to sell land. Under the 1972 Official Text, it is a contract to sell goods regardless of who is to sever the timber. The change was made because it is easier to finance a timber sale when the subject is goods rather than land.

Example III(12): S contracted with B to sell the yield from 100 acres of soybeans to be planted by S and harvested by B. At the time of contracting, the prospective crop is future goods. The goods exist and are identified to the contract upon planting. 2–501(1)(c). The crop, upon harvesting, can be severed "without material harm" to the realty and it makes no difference whether the severance is by S or B. 2–107(2). Thus, whatever the issue, the transaction is within the scope of Article 2.

Example III(13): S, a retailer, was owed accounts receivable by customers for goods sold. See 9–106. The face amount of the accounts was $100,000. S sold (assigned) the accounts without recourse to a factor for $85,000. S also sold (transferred) a corporate stock certificate worth $10,000 to the factor. Article 2 does not apply, since the sales were of "things in action" and "investment securities." 2–105(1). Article 9, however, applies to "any sale of accounts," 9–102(1)(b), and Article 8 applies to the "sale" of investment securities.

3. WHEN ARE GOODS IDENTIFIED TO THE CONTRACT?

It is clear that Article 2 protects the interests of S and B under a contract for the future sale of future goods. The phrase "contract for sale" includes a "contract to sell goods at a future time." 2–106(1). Thus, if S repudiated a contract before the goods were either manufactured or obtained (before they were either existing or identified), B would still have appropriate remedies for breach. See 2–610(b) & 2–711. But an "interest" in the goods cannot pass to the buyer before they are both "existing and identified." 2–105(2). *Thus, it is important to know when existing goods are identified and what difference it makes. The key section is 2–501(1), which states that "identification can be made at any time and in any manner explicitly agreed to by the parties" and provides some working rules in the "absence of explicit agreement." More importantly: "The buyer obtains a special property and an insurable interest in goods by identification of existing goods as goods to which the contract refers even though the goods so identified are non-conforming and he has an option to return or reject them." 2–501(1).*

> ***Example III(14):*** B visited S, a retailer, in search of 10 air conditioners for the business. After some discussion, it was decided that Model X was appropriate. S had one Model X in stock and B said "I'll take that one." S stated that an order of 20 Model Xs was expected to arrive in "about two weeks" and B agreed to purchase 9 of them. Since the single model in stock existed and the parties agreed that it was "goods to which the contract refers," it was identified "when the contract was made," in the absence of explicit agreement otherwise. 2–501(1)(a). The balance of the order was for future goods, which became identified to the contract when "shipped, marked or otherwise designated by the seller as goods to which the contract refers." 2–501(1)(c).

As noted, Section 2–501(1) provides that the "buyer obtains a special property and an insurable interest in goods by identification of existing goods as goods to which the contract refers . . ." *This is important for at least two reasons: (1) The insurable interest gives the buyer an opportunity to insure identified goods even before they are delivered and is relevant to problems of risk of loss. See 2–509 & 510. Section 2–501(3) provides that "nothing in this section impairs any insurable interest recognized under any other statute or rule of law" and Section 2–501(2) deals with the seller's retention of an insurable interest in goods sold. (2) The special property interest, (which is not title, compare 2–401) gives the buyer a remedial advantage where there are disputes over identified goods.* In limited cases, the buyer may be able to assert claims to or recover identified goods in the hands of the seller. See 2–502 & 2–716(3).

> ***Example III(15):*** S, a breeder, contracted with B to sell a foal to be sired by a winner of the Kentucky Derby. The mare was to be bred within the month and the foal was expected to be born within 10 months after breeding. In the absence of explicit agreement to the contrary, the goods are identified when "conceived if the contract is for the sale of unborn young to be born within twelve months after contracting." 2–501(1)(c). At this point, B could insure the foal, although the risk of loss is still on S, see 2–509, and title has not passed to B. 2–401. B has only an insurable interest in the goods.

B. SPECIAL POLICIES

There are a number of approaches and policies that have a special or unique application in Article 2, Sales. They either add to or particularize the basic policies and definitions contained in Article 1 of the UCC.

1. METHODOLOGY: FROM RULES TO STANDARDS

Article 2's approach to the problems of contract formation, performance and remedy is dominated by flexible standards rather than rules. In most cases, the meaning of the standard is dependent upon relevant factors in the context of the particular dispute. To illustrate, if an offer does not unambiguously require a specific manner or method of acceptance, Section 2–206(1)(a) provides that the offer shall be construed as "inviting acceptance in any manner and by any medium reasonable in the circumstances." The relevant "circumstances" may include the subject matter of the transaction, the volatility of the market, trade usage, prior course of dealing by the parties and the like. Similarly, if the parties have intended to contract even though they have not agreed upon the price, the price is a "reasonable price at the time for delivery." 2–305(1)(a). Again, current market prices or other relevant cost data must be consulted.

On the other hand, a standard may be particularized or its effect varied, with some limitations, by agreement of the parties. 1–102(2)(b). Remember that the definition of "agreement" is also cast in the form of a standard that must be particularized: agreement means the "bargain of the parties in fact as found from their language or by implication from other circumstances including course of dealing or usage of trade or course of performance." 1–203(3). Most routes to ascertaining agreement or applying UCC performance standards, therefore, lead to relevant factors in the commercial context.

> ***Example III(16):*** B, a commercial buyer, agreed to an exclusion of liability for consequential damages in a standard form contract prepared by S. Later, B claimed that the exclusion clause was unconscionable, see 2–719(3). The court shall decide the question as a matter of law, 2–302(1), but B "shall be afforded a reasonable opportunity to present evidence" as to the commercial setting, purpose and effect of the clause to "aid the court in making the determination." 2–302(2).

2. DEEMPHASIS OF TITLE

Although title to goods must pass before a sale occurs, 2–106(1), Article 2 deemphasizes the concept of title as a problem solving device. Section 2–401(1) provides that "each provision of this Article with regard to the right, obligations and remedies of the seller, the buyer, purchasers or other third parties applies irrespective of title to the goods except where the provision refers to title."
According to the Comment to Section 2–101, this policy avoids making "practical issues between practical men turn on the location of an intangible something, the passing of which no man can prove by evidence and to substitute for such abstractions proof of words and actions of a tangible character." Thus, location of the risk of loss, 2–509, and the seller's right to the price, 2–709, which were dependent under the Uniform Sales Act upon who had title to the goods, now turn on such practical things as which party is in possession or control of the goods.

On the other hand, the power of a seller to pass better title than he or she has, 2–403, and liability for breach of a warranty of title, 2–312, do turn in part on the location of title.

Finally, the location of title as defined by Section 2–401 may be relevant to non-sales questions, such as who is the owner of goods for purposes of state and local taxation.

At this point, a contrast between title, 2–401, and the special property interest obtained upon identification of the goods, 2–501, should be made. As indicated in Chapter III(A)(3), the buyer obtains a special property and an insurable interest upon identification of the goods to the contract and these interests do have practical consequences for the buyer.

> *Example III(17):* S contracted to manufacture goods for and to ship them FOB point of shipment to B. See 2–319(1)(a). S manufactured conforming goods and, before shipment, identified them to the contract. At this point, B has an insurable interest and a special property interest in the goods. 2–501(1). S, however, has title until the "time and place of shipment," 2–401(2)(a), and the risk of loss until the goods are "duly delivered to the carrier." 2–509(1)(a). Because of the special property interest, however, B might be able to replevy the goods if S failed to deliver, see 2–716(3), and could insure them in his own name before the risk passed.

3. SCOPE OF TRANSACTION PLANNING

An important role of the lawyer is to assist the client in planning, drafting and negotiating the contract for sale. Section 1–102(3) gives the parties considerable latitude to vary the effect of the UCC by agreement, except as "otherwise provided by this Act." Article 2 implements this policy by providing maximum opportunity for the parties to define their bargain and to vary the effect of its sections and by imposing a minimum of restraints on that power. Article 2, in effect, invites planning and the "tailormade" agreement. *Subject to some limitations, therefore, the parties through agreement can control the process of contract formation, 2–204(3), spell out the terms and timing of the exchange, allocate risks through such devices as a "disclaimer" of warranties, 2–316, and clauses excusing performance under certain conditions, 2–615, define the scope and nature of remedies available upon breach, including liquidated damages, 2–718 & 2–719, and modify contracts without consideration, 2–209(1).*

(a) Limitations Upon Agreement

There are some limitations upon the power of a seller and buyer to define the terms of their bargain or vary the effect of Article 2 provisions by agreement. The types of limitations are illustrated below:

> *First,* the agreement will not affect the rights of third persons not party to the contract, unless the UCC otherwise provides;

Second, some sections state explicitly that variation by agreement is not permitted, e.g., 2–318;

Third, some sections establish core conditions for liability and remedy which, by implication, cannot be varied by agreement, e.g., the statute of frauds, 2–201.

Fourth, some sections establish overriding policies governing performance and enforcement of the contract which cannot be excluded or defined in a manifestly unreasonable way by agreement, e.g., the "duty" of good faith, 1–203 or the requirement of reasonable notice, 2–607(3)(a), see 1–102(3);

Fifth, some sections impose conditions upon the process of concluding a contract which cannot be varied by agreement, e.g., certain warranty disclaimers must be conspicuous, 2–316(2), contract modifications must be in good faith, 2–209(1), and a clause excluding consequential damages must not be unconscionable, 2–719(3).

Sixth, some sections impose retroactive controls upon agreements deemed fair at the time of contracting where new information arises or changes occur during the course of performance, and these controls cannot be varied by agreement, e.g., 2–718(1) and 2–719(2).

Here is one more example for now.

Example III(18): S sold B a large quantity of fabric to be used in the manufacture of duffle bags. B agreed to give S notice within 10 days of delivery of any defects in the fabric or be barred from any remedy. The fabric contained latent defects that could not be reasonably discovered until processing which, in the ordinary course of B's business, would not occur until 30 days after delivery. The parties have attempted to state the time of the notice required by Section 2–607(3)(a). That Section, however, requires a "reasonable time" for notice and Section 1–204(1) states that when the UCC "requires any action to be taken within a reasonable time, any time which is not manifestly unreasonable may be fixed by agreement." See 1–102(3). In these circumstances, a 10 day notice requirement is probably "manifestly unreasonable."

4. THE MERCHANT CONCEPT

The parties to a contract for sale are the seller, who sells or contracts to sell goods, 2–103(1)(d), and the buyer, who buys or contracts to buy goods, 2–103(1)(a). One or both of these parties, however, may be merchants: A "person who deals in goods of the kind or otherwise by his occupation holds himself out as having knowledge or skill peculiar to the practices or goods involved in the transaction. . . ." 2–104(1). When both parties are merchants, the transaction is "between merchants." 2–104(3). *Under Article 2, the merchant may assume different or higher responsibilities than the non-merchant. Thus, the merchant must meet a higher standard of good faith, 2–103(1)(b), the merchant seller may make an implied warranty of merchantability, 2–314(1), and in transactions between merchants, one may be bound to or affected by a writing sent by the other by failing to object to its contents. See 2–207(2) & 2–201(2). See also 2–209(2), 2–605(1)(b) & 2–609(2).* The merchant concept, which is unique to Article 2, complements an overall approach that features standards rather than rules and puts a premium upon finding the patterns of commercial behavior in the context surrounding the transaction.

> ***Example III(19):*** S and B, who were both merchants, concluded an oral contract to sell 1,000 units of goods at $50 per unit. The next day, B mailed to S a signed letter which stated, in part: "This is to confirm your agreement to sell me 1,000 gidgets at $50 per, delivery in 30 days." S received the letter but failed to respond. On these facts, S's failure to give B any notice of objection means that the statute of frauds defense is lost: between merchants, a failure to object to a written memo which is sufficient against B satisfies the statute. 2–201(2).

5.   REGULATION: UNCONSCIONABILITY AND GOOD FAITH

There are two important standards intended to permit courts to police or regulate the conduct of one or both parties to the contract for sale. One invalidates unconscionable contracts or clauses, 2–302, and the other, 1–203, requires good faith in the performance and enforcement of the contract. The first is primarily concerned about the quality of the bargaining and agreement at the time of contracting. The second is concerned about the quality of one party's conduct at the time of performance or enforcement of the contract.

(a)   Unconscionability

Section 2–302, a controversial provision, gives the court power to find as a matter of law that a contract or clause was unconscionable "at the time it was made." 2–302(1). This finding cannot be made without affording the parties a "reasonable opportunity to present evidence as to . . . (the) commercial setting, purpose and effect to aid the court in making the determination." If the contract or clause is found to be unconscionable, the court is given discretion either to "refuse to enforce the contract, . . . or enforce the remainder of the contract without the unconscionable clause, or . . . so limit the application of any unconscionable clause as to avoid any unconscionable result." Section 2–302 does not authorize the court to award damages for unconscionable conduct.

What is the content of unconscionability? One way to start is to say what it is *not:* Section 2–302 does not police against fraud, misrepresentation or duress as such. These common law defenses are still available. See 1–103. Similarly, 2–302(1) does not explicitly invalidate contract clauses which, for independent reasons, are against public policy (so-called "substantive" unconscionability.) Rather, Section 2–302 is concerned about contracts and clauses where one party has obtained a material advantage over the other that is traceable to unfair surprise or oppression at the time of contracting (so-called "procedural" unconscionability.) Both unfair surprise and oppression affect the quality of bargaining, since the person seeking relief claims to have had insufficient information to make a choice or, even with information, claims that the bargain was oppressive because of the limited choice of "take it or leave it." These conditions are more likely to occur when the buyer is a consumer dealing at retail and offered the offending clause in the fine print in a standard form contract rather than a merchant who, presumptively, has more experience, access to information and choice. As a result, Section 2–302 initially was applied primarily as a device for consumer protection rather than as a technique for regulating the bargaining process in commercial transactions. More recently, however, merchants have increasingly used 2–302 to attack allegedly unconscionable contracts and clauses.

> ***Example III(20):*** B, a consumer, purchased a stereo from S, a retailer, for $2,500. Later B tried to avoid the contract on the ground that the same system could have been purchased from another store in the area for $1,200. The contract price is not unconscionable: the contract price was clearly disclosed (no unfair surprise) and B, presumably, had the capacity to ascertain comparative prices and the opportunity to purchase elsewhere (no oppression). On the other hand, if B was a consumer of limited means and intelligence and S had sold the stereo in a home solicitation sale, the high contract price might be unconscionable.

(b) Good Faith

The general duty of good faith, imposed by Section 1–203, applies to the performance or enforcement of contracts for the sale of goods. The general, subjective definition of good faith as "honesty in fact in the conduct or transaction concerned," 1–201(19), has been supplemented by an objective definition for merchants in Section 2–103(1)(b): good faith in the "case of a merchant means honesty in fact and the observance of reasonable commercial standards of fair dealing in the trade." The burden is on the aggrieved party to prove that the other acted in bad faith. See 1–208. Thus, the aggrieved party must establish both the reasonable commercial standards of fair dealing in the trade and that the merchant failed to meet them.

There is continuing disagreement over the scope and content of the good faith obligation and the remedies available for bad faith. At this juncture, keep the following points in mind.

First, even though good faith is specifically mentioned in some sections dealing with performance, 2–306 & 2–311, enforcement, 2–706 & 2–712, and purchase, 2–403, the failure to mention it in other sections does not mean that it is inapplicable. Section 1–203 applies to "every contract or duty" within this act. Thus, a contract modification, 2–209(1), a rejection of defective goods, 2–601, and a termination of the contract, 2–309(3), must be in good faith.

Second, bad faith is dishonest or unreasonable conduct at the time of performance or enforcement. Frequently, this is manifested by exercising discretion in a way that tries to reallocate a benefit conferred upon the other or a risk allocated to the actor by the agreement. Thus, if S has agreed to supply his "output" to B at $5 per unit, the market price drops to $1.50 per unit and S substantially increases the output, the action is probably in bad faith. See 2–306(1). Similarly if S has agreed to supply 1,000 units of goods at $5 a unit, the market price drops to $1.50 and B rejects S's tender of 999 units, the rejection is probably in bad faith. In both cases, the actor has sought to exploit or avoid a bargain in the light of changed circumstances where the market risk has been allocated by the contract. This opportunistic conduct, not clearly prohibited, exceeds the bounds of honesty or commercial reasonableness and should be regulated.

Third, the remedies for bad faith must be keyed to the particular dispute. If S has increased his output in bad faith, perhaps B still should be required to take a reasonable output. If the modification is in bad faith, it should not be enforced. If the rejection is in bad faith, and thus wrongful, S should be entitled to the usual remedies for wrongful rejection, see 2–703. We will have occasion to pursue this analysis throughout this BLACK LETTER.

C. REVIEW QUESTIONS

III–A. What questions should be asked and answered to determine whether a transaction in goods is within the scope of Article 2? How does the "gravamen" test differ from the "predominant purpose" test?

III–B. What is a sale and when does it occur in the contract for sale?

III–C. *True or False:* Article 2 applies to a contract for the future sale of future goods.

III–D. Evaluate the following: "Title" and the "Special Property Interest" pass to the buyer at the same time and perform the same function under Article 2.

III–E. Which Special Policies of Article 2 are designed to facilitate or support the agreement of the parties and which are designed to regulate it?

III-F. O, the owner of a new apartment building, contracted with C, a construction contractor, to provide material and labor to complete a "hook up" with the city sewer system. C excavated a 10' deep trench some 50' long, installed cast iron pipe and specially manufactured connectors at each end and filled in the excavation. Six months later, raw sewage filled the basement to a depth of six inches. Later, it was determined that C, without negligence, installed a defective connector at the point of hook up with the city system and this defect caused the backup. O, claiming breach of an implied warranty that the connector was merchantable, see 2–314(1), sued C for damages. C asserted that Article 2 did not apply to the transaction and moved to dismiss the complaint. What should the court do?

*

IV

CONTRACT FORMATION

Analysis

A. THE IMPORTANCE OF AGREEMENT

The definition of agreement in Section 1–201(3) provides a cornerstone for two important UCC policies, namely to "permit the continued expansion of commercial practices through custom, usage and agreement of the parties," 1–102(1)(b), and to enable the parties, subject to some limitations, to vary the effect of UCC provisions. 1–102(3). Further, we noted in Chapter III(B)(1), that the broad definition of agreement complements Article 2's emphasis upon standards rather than rules. In matters of contract formation under Article 2, agreement is no less important: there must be a sufficient agreement before there can be a contract of sale. Whether the agreement is sufficient, and thus a contract, depends in large part upon Article 2, Part 2.

1. AGREEMENT DEFINED

Agreement means the "bargain of the parties in fact as found in their language or by implication from other circumstances including course of dealing or usage of trade or course of performance as provided in this Act (Sections 1–205 and 2–208)." The word "bargain" suggests that the agreement is to "exchange promises or to exchange a promise for a performance or to exchange performances," Restatement (Second) Contracts § 3 (1979), and a bargain normally would satisfy the consideration requirement that the exchange be "bargained for." See Restatement (Second) Contracts § 1(1) (1979). In addition to the "language" of the parties, note carefully that agreement can be found from "other circumstances" which include any prior course of dealing between the parties, 1–205(1), any course of performance by the parties under the agreement in dispute, 2–208, and more generally, usage of trade. 1–205(2). This broad definition simply confirms the fact that the scope and meaning of a particular bargain cannot easily be separated from the commercial setting in which it was made.

> *Example IV(1):* Under an agreement where S promised to supply B with his requirements of "chickens," a dispute arose when B claimed that "chicken" meant fryers and S claimed that it meant stewing hens. In the relevant trade, other merchants used the word "chicken" to mean fryers. If the conditions established in 1–205(3) are satisfied, the trade usage is part of the agreement and can be admitted to "give particular meaning to and supplement or qualify terms of an agreement."

2. CONTRACT DEFINED

Just because the parties have concluded some agreement that is satisfactory to them does not mean that it is enforceable as a contract. *Contract is defined as the "total legal obligation which results from the parties' agreement as affected by this Act and any other applicable rules of law."* 1–201(11). Thus, whether a contract has been formed and the scope and content of the parties' legal obligation depends upon their agreement and its legal effect under Article 2.

Example IV(2): S and B concluded an oral agreement for the sale of 1,000 widgets at $100 per widget. Payment and delivery terms were also agreed to. Later, B sent S a signed writing confirming "our widget contract." Even though the oral agreement is otherwise sufficient, it is not enforceable by either party as a contract because of the statute of frauds. 2-201. S signed no writing, 2-201(1), and B's signed confirmation contained no quantity term. 2-201(2).

B. GENERAL POLICIES

Under the classical view, enshrined in the First Restatement of Contracts, questions of contract formation were governed by clear, formal rules. At some point in the negotiations, one party made an offer that the other either accepted or rejected. Since the offer proposed a bargain, the acceptance provided consideration and, by concluding the negotiations, created the contract. A rejection terminated the negotiations and a counteroffer moved the bargaining to a different stage. In this process, a premium was put upon the timing of offer and acceptance and the rules required a high quantity and quality of agreement before any obligation arose. Thus, if a response deviated in any way from the offer or material terms were either omitted or indefinite, no contract was formed until there was further assent.

Article 2 departs from the classical view by emphasizing the broad definition of agreement rather than the concept of promise and deemphasizing the requirement of consideration. Both promise and consideration are implicit in the formation process, but do not provide the focus for analysis. In addition, Section 2-204 makes other changes of importance.

First, the contract may be made "in any manner sufficient to show agreement, including conduct of both parties which recognizes the existence of such a contract." 2-204(1). Thus, no formalities are required and the best evidence of a concluded agreement may be what the parties do rather than what they say.

Second, an agreement otherwise sufficient to constitute a contract will not fail "even though the moment of its making is undetermined." 2-204(2). Thus, the inability to pinpoint the magic moment of assent will not be fatal.

Third, and most important, is the standard expressed in Section 2-204(3): *"Even though one or more terms are left open a contract for sale does not fail for indefiniteness if the parties have intended to make a contract and there is a reasonably certain basis for giving an appropriate remedy."* Thus, the parties' intention to contract is substituted for the rules of offer and acceptance, and the question of indefiniteness goes to the enforcement rather than the creation of the contract.

Example IV(3): After negotiations, S and B conclude an agreement without agreeing on price and both commence performance. Since their conduct evidences an intent to make a contract (or, more precisely, that their agreement was concluded), a contract is created without agreement on the price term. 2–204(3). Under Section 2–305(1), the court may fill the "gap" in the agreement by inserting a "reasonable price at the time for delivery." Because a "reasonable price" can usually be determined from market or other factors, there will be a "reasonably certain basis for giving an appropriate remedy."

Fourth, as *Example V(3)* reveals, the parties' intention to contract, evidenced by their conduct, coupled with the "gap" filling provisions of Article 2, Part 3, gives the court power to supply reasonable terms and enforce the agreement to the extent that the term supplied provides a "reasonably certain basis for giving an appropriate remedy." 2–204(3).

C. OFFER AND ACCEPTANCE

Article 2's flexible approach to contract formation does not eliminate the need for the concepts of offer and acceptance. In a complex negotiation, one party may propose what purports to be an offer and withdraw it after the other purports to accept it. There is no conduct by both parties from which agreement can be inferred. The offeree claims that a contract was formed. What does Article 2 have to say about disputes of this sort?

1. THE OFFER
(a) Offer Defined
The word "offer" is used in Article 2, see 2–205, 2–206(1)(a) & 2–207(1), but not defined. This omission is an invitation to consult supplemental sources of state contract law. See 1–103. *An acceptable definition of offer, not inconsistent with UCC policies, is contained in Section 24 of the Restatement, Second of Contracts: "An offer is the manifestation of willingness to enter into a bargain so made as to justify another person in understanding that his assent to that bargain is invited and will conclude it."* If, then, this definition of offer is satisfied and the offeree has manifested assent before the offer is terminated, there is an agreement and, if other conditions are satisfied, a contract for sale is formed without the need for conduct by both parties.

Example IV(4): After negotiations where the parties have been unable to agree on price, S made a written proposal to sell described goods to B but the writing said nothing about price. B replied, "We have a deal." Before either party commenced performance, S withdrew claiming that there was no intention to conclude a bargain until there was agreement on price. Under Section 2–204(3), the question is whether the "parties have intended to make a contract" even though price was not agreed. S's intention must be ascertained from what he said and did in context. If B was "justified" in believing that S was ready to contract without agreement on price and that all B needed to do to conclude the deal was manifest assent, there is a contract. Without conduct by both parties, however, it is harder to conclude that both parties intended to contract without agreement on price.

(b) Firm Offers

Under general contract law, an offer can be revoked at any time prior to acceptance unless an enforceable option has been created. An option protects the offeree against revocation during the time specified. At common law, the option, i.e., the offer's commitment to hold the offer open for a specified time, was enforceable if it was under seal or supported by consideration. More recently, courts have created options in the interest of justice when the offer or collateral promise induced foreseeable reliance by the offeree.

Article 2 says nothing about consideration or reliance as grounds for an option and, presumably, these theories are still available. 1–103. Section 2–203, however, makes seals inoperative in contracts for the sale of goods. A substitute for the seal's formality is Section 2–205, which we examined in Chapter II(E)(2). *In essence, if a merchant buyer or seller states in a signed writing that an offer to sell or buy shall be open or "firm" for a stated period of time, the offer is "not revocable for lack of consideration during the time stated." If no time is stated, the time is a reasonable time "but in no event may such period of irrevocability exceed three months."* The primary purpose of Section 2–205 is to "give effect to the deliberate intention of a merchant to make a current firm offer binding." Comment 2. The conditions for enforcement, however, are tight and the danger of unfair surprise is reduced by the requirement that a "term of assurance on a form supplied by the offeree must be separately signed by the offeror."

> ***Example IV(4):*** S, a supplier, made an offer to furnish building materials to B, a contractor who was bidding on a project. S orally assured B that his offer was "firm until you know whether you have won the contract." B relied upon S's price in bidding on the project and, ultimately, was awarded the contract. S, claiming a mistake in bid, withdrew his offer before B accepted it. On these facts, S's firm offer was not enforceable under Section 2–205 because it was not in a signed writing. B's reliance, however, may justify the creation of an option by the court. See Restatement (Second) Contracts § 87(2). Whether S is entitled to rescind the contract for mistake is a question to be resolved under non-code law. See 1–103.
>
> ***Example IV(5):*** After negotiations, S submitted to B a signed, written proposal, dated June 1, to supply B's requirements in meat for a one year period. Among other terms, S stated that the proposal was "firm,"

proposed to charge $1.20 per pound and reserved power to increase the price after giving B 45 days notice. B neither accepted nor rejected the proposal, but over the next three months ordered and paid for over 500,000 pounds of meat at $1.20 per pound. On September 15, S announced that the price was increased immediately to $1.35 per pound. Thereafter, B ordered 100,000 pounds of meat but, after delivery, tendered the original price of $1.20 per pound. B claimed that it was entitled to price protection for 45 days. B's argument should be rejected. The written proposal, as a "firm" offer under 2–205, expired, along with its terms, after three months. Thus, agreements reached after September 1 were at S's new price, $1.50. It is unlikely that B's conduct in making separate orders under the "firm" offer amounted to a commitment (acceptance) to order all of its requirements from S for one year.

2. THE ACCEPTANCE

According to Section 50(1) of the Restatement (Second) of Contracts, an "acceptance of an offer is a manifestation of assent to the terms thereof made by the offeree in a manner invited or required by the offer." When the offer is to buy or sell goods, Sections 2–206 and 2–207 build on this general definition with interesting and sometimes puzzling results. Together, these sections make the greatest changes in the common law of acceptance.

(a) Manner and Medium of Acceptance

Section 2–206(1) provides that "unless otherwise unambiguously indicated by the language or circumstances (a) an offer to make a contract shall be construed as inviting acceptance in any manner and by any medium reasonable in the circumstances." The offeror, therefore, is still the master of his offer and can prescribe exactly how the acceptance is to be manifested and the method of communication. But unless this is "unambiguously indicated," a rule of construction is supplied that gives the offeree a broader base for acceptance.

> *Example IV(6):* S mailed a written offer to B which stated that acceptance shall be in a signed writing received before 6 PM on March 1. B manifested assent in a signed writing mailed on February 27 and received by S at 6:01 PM on March 1. There is no contract.

> *Example IV(7):* S mailed B a written offer which stated that acceptance shall be in a signed writing. The offer was received by B on February 27. On February 28, B mailed a signed, written acceptance. On March 1, S communicated a revocation of the offer to B before the acceptance was received. There was a contract when B mailed the acceptance if the mail was a "medium reasonable in the circumstances" and there were no "circumstances" unambiguously indicating otherwise. 2–206(1)(a). If the offer to sell was made in a volatile market, the circumstances might

clearly indicate to B that either actual communication to S or a more rapid manner of communication, e.g., a telex, was required.

Example IV(7) invokes the so-called "mailbox" rule, i.e., that in some circumstances an acceptance is effective when sent rather than when received. Article 2 neither explicitly displaces nor rejects that ancient rule. Presumably it can be read into 2–206 through 1–103.

In a variation on this theme, suppose that B telegraphs an offer to S which states: "Please ship within 24 hours 50 kerosene stoves at your list price." S promptly telegraphs a response in which it promises to ship within 24 hours. Before the goods are shipped, B cancels the order. Unless the language of B's offer or the circumstances unambiguously indicate otherwise, there is a contract: *"An order or other offer to buy goods for prompt or current shipment shall be construed as inviting acceptance either by a prompt promise to ship or by the prompt or current shipment of conforming or non-conforming goods. . . ." 2–206(1)(b).* B's language does not clearly indicate to S that shipment and only shipment are required for acceptance. Again, this construction broadens the ways in which an offeree can create a contract when the offeror's intention is not clear. But there is a problem or two on the edges.

> *Example IV(8):* After negotiations, B telegraphed an offer to S which stated: "Please ship within 24 hours 50 kerosene stoves at your list price." S promptly shipped 48 stoves and, while the goods were in transit, diverted them to a third party who had offered to pay a higher price than B. At common law, there would be no contract because S's shipment, which was the invited acceptance, deviated from the offer. Thus, until B accepted S's counteroffer to sell 48 stoves, S was free to deal with third parties. Within the general restrictions of 2–206(1), however, the prompt or current shipment of "non-conforming" goods creates a contract to sell 48 stoves unless S "seasonably notifies the buyer that the shipment is offered only as an accommodation to the buyer." No such notice was given here. Under this analysis, S's non-conforming shipment was an acceptance of the offer and the diversion to the third party was a breach of contract.

The student of contract law will recognize a modification of the common law doctrine that an offer requires either a bilateral contract (acceptance by promise) or a unilateral contract (acceptance by performance). Under Section 2–206(1)(b), the offeree has a choice of which method of acceptance to employ and that acceptance by performance, i.e., shipment, need not comply literally with the offer.

The last piece in the puzzle is 2–206(3), which provides that "where the beginning of a requested performance is a reasonable mode of acceptance an offeror who is not notified of acceptance within a reasonable time may treat the offer as having lapsed before acceptance." Here are two illustrations of how this principle might operate.

> *Example IV(9):* B made an offer to S which stated "please ship promptly 50 kerosene stoves." S commenced preparations to fill the order but, before the goods were shipped, B revoked the offer. There is no contract. The requested performance was the shipment of goods. S's conduct amounted to preparation to perform rather than the "beginning of a requested performance." S, however, could have created a contract by communicating a prompt promise to ship before starting preparations.

> *Example IV(10):* After negotiations over goods to be manufactured according to B's specifications, B mailed an offer to S which stated "you may accept this offer by either mailing an acceptance or commencing performance." S started to manufacture the goods but B, before learning of this conduct, canceled the order. There is a contract under Section 2–206(3). If B is notified of the acceptance within a reasonable time, B is foreclosed from revoking the offer. Arguably, this result follows even though B is notified after an attempt to cancel is made. In theory, S's part performance creates a bilateral contract, B assumes the risk of ignorance for a reasonable time and his attempt to "revoke" the offer is, in effect, a breach of contract.

(b) Additional or Different Terms

Section 2–206 alters the common law of offer and acceptance by broadening the permissible method and manner of acceptance. The burden is placed on the offeror to narrow what an acceptance can and cannot be. Section 2–207 deals with a more particularized problem: assuming that the method and manner of acceptance are reasonable, is an offer accepted when the expressed assent contains additional or different terms? At common law, the answer was no unless the offeree indicated that he or she was unconditionally accepting the offer and that the additional or different terms were simply proposals for a modification. Put differently, there was a presumption that the presence of additional or different terms rejected the offer and, in effect, proposed a counteroffer.

Section 2–207(1) reverses that presumption: a "definite and seasonable expression of acceptance or a written confirmation which is sent within a reasonable time operates as an acceptance even though it states terms additional to or different from those offered or agreed upon, unless acceptance is expressly made conditional on assent to the additional or different terms." In short, an offeree may say "yes" to the offer and propose additional or different terms without preventing the formation of a contract. Unless there is "express" language to the effect that "I won't contract at all unless you agree to my terms," a contract is formed and the additional or different terms become proposals for modification of the contract. See 2–207(2).

Section 2–207 has been justified because the common law "mirror image" rule permitted the offeree to escape liability on the basis of a minor deviation in a bargain which in commercial understanding had been concluded. More importantly, in certain transactions the offeree was perceived to have an unfair advantage in the bargaining process. Here is an example.

> ***Example IV(11):*** After negotiations, B sent a written purchase order to S for 100 barrels of specified emulsion. S sent an acknowledgement which stated "We accept your order" and shipped the goods. The acknowledgement contained standard terms drafted by S and, on the back of the form, S disclaimed all implied warranties and excluded any liability for consequential damages. B received the acknowledgement and, thereafter, accepted, used and paid for the goods without objection to the standard form terms. At common law, S's response was a counteroffer which B accepted by conduct without objection to the new terms. Thus, a contract was formed on S's terms and if the goods were defective, S's liability and remedy depended upon the effect of the disclaimer and exclusion clauses. What is S's unfair advantage? As offeree, S had the "last shot" in the transaction: S could slip favorable terms in the standard form with the knowledge that B was unlikely to read, understand and object to the terms and was likely to accept the counteroffer by using and paying for the goods. The result, arguably, was unfair surprise produced by the "mirror image" rule.

Section 2–207, then, was designed, among other things, to neutralize this form of unfair surprise. To illustrate the potential reach of this complex, controversial and frequently litigated section, here are a few examples.

> ***Example IV(12):*** How would the problem in *Example IV(8)* be decided under Section 2–207?
>
> *First,* S's language "We accept your order" is a definite acceptance with additional terms. S's conduct in shipping the goods reinforces this conclusion. See 2–204(3). If, however, the language or conduct were equivocal, no "definite" acceptance would exist. The terms are "additional" because they do not contradict or conflict with *terms* in B's written purchase order. They are "additional to . . . those offered" by B. 2–207(1).
>
> *Second,* the definite acceptance "operates as an acceptance," i.e. creates a contract under 2–207(1), "unless acceptance is expressly made conditional on assent to the additional or different terms." An early and much criticized case held that the "expressly made conditional" language

was satisfied by an additional term that was unilaterally burdensome to the offeror or materially altered the terms of the offer to the sole disadvantage of the offeror. *Roto–Lith, LTD v. F.P. Bartlett & Co.*, 297 F.2d 497 (1st Cir.1962). The prevailing (but not overpowering) view is that "expressly made conditional" requires explicit language by S. It is not to be implied from the fact that S's response may materially alter the bargain. Otherwise the language of 2–207(2), which excludes material alterations from the agreement, would be meaningless. Thus, S must say to B "we won't contract unless you agree to our additional or different terms." See *Dorton v. Collins & Aikman Corp.*, 453 F.2d 1161 (6th Cir.1972). On the facts, therefore, S's "definite" acceptance without language "expressly conditional" created a contract under 2–207(1). As a result, the "additional terms are to be construed as proposals for addition to the contract" under 2–207(2).

Fourth, if, because there was no definite acceptance or there was an express condition, no contract was formed under 2–207(1) and S's response would be treated as a counteroffer which B could accept or reject. Suppose, without more, that B simply accepted, used and paid for the goods. Does B accept the counteroffer on S's terms? The answer is no. Unless there is evidence that B negotiated over or was expressly aware of the standard form terms (thus negating unfair surprise), the dispute should be resolved under 2–207(3). There is "conduct by both parties" recognizing the existence of a contract and the terms are "those terms on which the writings of the parties agree, together with any supplementary terms incorporated under any other provisions of this Act." Since the writings did not agree on S's disclaimer and exclusion clauses and since the Article 2 standard terms permit warranties and consequential damages unless otherwise agreed, S's terms do not control. This problem is discussed again in *Example IV(14).*

Example IV(13): If, in the foregoing, a contract was formed under 2–207(1), how are we to determine whether the proposals "for addition to the contract" become part of the agreement? More specifically, suppose that B accepts and uses the goods without objecting to S's additional terms. Is that conduct which accepts the proposed addition and incorporates it into the agreement? See 2–209(1).

First, 2–207(2) provides that the "additional terms are to be construed as proposals for addition to the contract." If the transaction is *not* "between merchants," however, 2–207(2) does not say when, if ever, the proposals are accepted by B. Arguably, they should not be incorporated unless B "expressly agreed" to them. See Comment 3.

Second, 2–207(2) provides rules for inclusion when the transaction is "between merchants." See 2–104(3). In this case, the additional terms automatically become part of the contract unless: (1) B's offer "expressly limits acceptance to the terms of the offer," 2-207(2)(a); (2) B gives "notification of objection" to the terms either before they are received or "within a reasonable time after notice of them is received," 2-207(2)(c); or (3) the additional terms "materially alter" the contract. 2-207(2)(b). Assuming that (1) and (2), above, are not applicable, the key question is whether a warranty disclaimer and an exclusion of consequential damages "materially alter" the contract. If so, they do not become part of the agreement "unless expressly agreed to by the other party." Comment 3.

Third, the statute does not say when additional terms "materially alter" the contract. The comments indicate that the test is whether the result would be "surprise or hardship" if the clauses were "incorporated without express awareness by the other party." Comment 4. Assuming that the clause materially affects the agreed exchange, (a quantitative test), "unfair surprise" would arguably result if B did not see the clause in the standard form contract and it was not reasonably to be expected in the trade. Both a disclaimer and an excluder clause could satisfy this test. On the other hand, if the clause is common in the trade or has been regularly used in past transactions between the parties, the risk of unfair surprise is reduced. In these circumstances, some courts have concluded that if B knew or had reason to know that the clauses would be included in the standard form, the clauses should not be classified as material. Accordingly, they would become part of the agreement.

Fourth, if the clauses do "materially alter" the contract and, therefore, do not automatically become part of the agreement, what is the effect of B's conduct in using the goods without objection? Again, the statute does not answer this question, but the comments indicate that they will "not be included unless expressly agreed to by the other party." Comment 3. Thus, conduct without express awareness would not suffice. On the other hand, conduct of accepting and using the goods *with* express awareness is not enough, unless B is required to object at his peril to avoid accepting a proposed modification. The preferred view is that B must be aware of the additional terms and, by words or conduct, express assent to them. Anything less, arguably, impedes the objectives of Section 2-207. Clearly, the conduct of accepting and using the goods alone is not that "express agreement" necessary to neutralize the risk of unfair surprise.

Example IV(14): Suppose that no contract is formed under 2-207(1), either because there was no "definite" acceptance or B's acceptance was made "expressly conditional." S sends an acknowledgement with the additional terms and ships the goods and B accepts and uses the goods without objection. Is B bound by the additional terms?

First, note that 2–207(2) does *not* apply, for it depends upon the formation of some contract under 2–207(1).

Second, 2–207(3) appears to apply to this and any other case where there is conduct by both parties recognizing the "existence of a contract" but that no contract is formed under subsection (1). Thus, if S failed to ship the goods or B failed to accept any goods shipped, there would not be a contract at all under 2–207 or, presumably, any other section of Article 2.

Third, with conduct by both parties recognizing the existence of a contract, *some* contract is formed even though "the writings of the parties do not otherwise establish a contract." 2–207(3). But what are the terms of the contract? According to subsection (3), the "terms of a particular contract consist of those terms on which the writings of the parties agree, together with any supplementary terms incorporated under any other provisions of this Act." Thus, if mutual agreement to the disclaimer and excluder clauses was not expressed in the writings of the parties, S's terms would not be incorporated and B would be entitled to the warranties and the remedies for breach of warranty provided by Article 2. See 2–313, 2–314, 2–315, 2–714(2) and 2–715(2). Again, although the statute is not clear, the Comments suggest that B's conduct of using the goods alone will not be sufficient to show express agreement to S's additional terms.

Remember, these examples were devised in the interest of clarity. They tend to understate complexity and to simplify the analysis. Even so, there is one last question to consider. Suppose S's response contains different rather than additional terms. For example, if B's purchase order stated that S must "warrant that the goods are fit for B's particular needs and purposes" and S's acknowledgment expressly disclaims all implied warranties of fitness, there clearly are different (conflicting) terms. How should this issue be resolved?

First, the answer is relatively simple if *no* contract is formed under 2–207(1), yet there is conduct by both parties "sufficient to establish a contract for sale." 2–207(3). See 2–204(1). Section 2–207(3) should be applied, and since the writings of the parties do not agree on the warranty, the conflicting clauses drop out and the Article 2 "gap fillers" apply. See *McJunkin Corp. v. Mechanicals, Inc.,* 888 F.2d 481 (6th Cir.1989). This result would not follow, however, if B expressly agreed to the different terms in S's response.

Second, a more difficult question is posed if a contract *is* formed under 2–207(1) and the problem is how to treat the "different" terms. One approach is to conclude that B's terms (the offeror's) prevail and that S's drop out. This is supported by treating "different" terms like "additional" terms under 2–207(2) (a result supported by Comment 3) or by simply concluding that, without more, S's terms fall out. Here B's terms (the "first" shot) would prevail unless B expressly agreed to substitute S's different terms. This is highly unlikely.

The approach preferred by other courts is that the conflicting terms cancel each other. Reasoning that 2–207(2) does not apply to different terms and that neither party deserves to have their terms prevail over the other's, the courts have, in effect, applied 2–207(3) to solve the problem. See *Daitom, Inc. v. Pennwalt Corp.*, 741 F.2d 1569 (10th Cir.1984); White & Summers, Uniform Commercial Code 33–36 (3d ed. 1988). By this approach, the dispute is treated as if both parties had expressly stated that they would not be bound unless the other party agreed to the terms proposed. Although this language might preclude a contract under 2–207(1), 2–207(3) should apply if there were subsequent conduct by both parties establishing a contract for sale.

An informational note. Neither the Restatement, Second, of Contracts, the Convention on the International Sale of Goods nor Article 2A contain a provision like 2–207. What does this say about the wisdom of retaining that controversial section in any revisions of Article 2?

D. THE STATUTE OF FRAUDS

Assuming that the parties have concluded an agreement which would otherwise be a contract for the sale of goods, the statute of frauds imposes another condition to enforceability. *Section 2–201(1) provides: "Except as otherwise provided in this section a contract for the sale of goods for the price of $500 or more is not enforceable by way of action or defense unless there is some writing sufficient to indicate that a contract for sale has been made between the parties and signed by the party against whom enforcement is sought or by his authorized agent or broker."* The need for a statute of frauds for sales has been disputed. England repealed her statute of frauds for goods in 1953 and there is no statute of frauds provision in the Convention for the International Sale of Goods. Nevertheless, supporters claim that the statute prevents potential fraud and perjury in the form of claims asserted under nonexistent transactions and terms asserted that were never agreed to.

Section 2–201 is, in many ways, easy to satisfy. Section 2–201(1) provides that a signed writing is "not insufficient because it omits or incorrectly states a term agreed upon" and Comment 1 states that all that is "required is that the writing afford a basis for believing that the offered oral evidence rests on a real transaction." One important exception, however, is the quantity term. Thus, a signed writing is not enforceable "beyond the quantity of goods shown" in the writing, 2–201(1), an admission of the contract in a pleading or "otherwise in court" is not enforceable "beyond the quantity of goods admitted," 2–201(3)(b), and part-performance takes the case "out" of the statute "with respect to goods for which payment has been made and accepted or which have been received and accepted." 2–201(3)(c). *In short, if the writing is silent on quantity, it is error to admit oral evidence to supply the term.* Why this condition? Unlike the price or other performance terms, which can be supplied and monitored under standards of reasonableness, the quantity term is more vulnerable to perjury. If the parties have not agreed on quantity, who is to say what is a "reasonable" quantity? Thus, unless there is credible evidence of agreement, the risk of perjury in the proof of quantity is greater and cannot be controlled by "reasonable" terms supplied under Article 2, Part 3. This, at least, is how the argument runs.

Remember, there are other statutes of frauds that might affect a contract for the sale of goods. For example, oral agreements "not to be performed within one year" are within the scope of the general statute of frauds in most states and 1–206 provides a statute of frauds for personal property not otherwise covered.

Finally, a fast emerging problem is whether the statute of frauds can be satisfied when contracts for sale are made electronically. For example, suppose S and B, using computers, conclude the agreement by electronic transmissions and store the result on a disk. There is no printout and no handwritten signature. Some commentators have argued that the Code's definitions of "signed" and "writing" in 1–201 can be stretched to cover the new technology and that a printout clearly is a writing. See Dziewit, Graniano and Daley, *The Quest for the Paperless Office Electronic Contracting: State of the Art Possibility but Legal Impossibility,* 5 Santa Clara Computer & High Tech.L.J. 75 (1989). The uncertainties, however, suggest that appropriate revisions of Article 2 should be made to accommodate the growing use of Electronic Data Interchange. See also, Report, 45 Bus.Law. 1645 (1990).

1. **SCOPE AND REQUIREMENTS OF THE STATUTE**
    Rather than develop an elaborate textual discussion, we will cover Section 2–201 through the use of eight examples.

> ***Example IV(15):*** *Scope.* S has a contract right, valued at $100,000, for royalties from a play which she has written and is about to be produced. S made an oral, partial assignment of the right to B in satisfaction of a pre-existing $25,000 debt. Section 2–201 does not apply: the transaction is not a contract for the sale of goods. 2–201(1). At best it is a sale or assignment of an intangible. See 2–105(1). Article 9 usually applies to an assignment or sale of accounts, 9–102(1)(a), and there is a statute of frauds for Article 9. See 9–203(1). But Article 9 does *not* apply to the transfer of a single account to satisfy a preexisting indebtedness. See 9–104(f). Beware! Even though we have escaped the statute of frauds provisions of Articles 2 and 9, the residual statute of frauds for "kinds of personal property not otherwise covered" is applicable. Read 1–206(1) to see why. Thus, the oral royalty "sale" is not enforceable on these facts.

Example IV(16): Necessity for and Content of Writing. After reaching an oral agreement with S, B signed a writing which stated, "This confirms our contract to sell and buy 100 Kerosene Stoves" and handed it to S. Later, B refused to perform and raised the statute of frauds as a defense. The defense is *not* available.

First, the writing indicates "that a contract for sale has been made between the parties" and was "signed by the party against whom enforcement is sought. . . .," here B. 2–201(1).

Second, the writing is sufficient even though it omits the price and other performance terms. The important thing is that the writing affords "a basis for believing that the offered oral evidence rests on a real transaction," Comment 1, and that if conflicts in proof arise the omitted terms can be supplied under Article 2, Part 3. But the contract is not enforceable "beyond the quantity of goods shown in such writing." 2–201(1). Thus S, in enforcing the contract, may prove that the agreed price per stove was $200 but not that B agreed to buy more than 100 stoves.

Third, suppose the writing stated that B would purchase S's "output" of goods. This is a quantity term the content of which is regulated by the limitation that the quantity must be S's "actual output in good faith." 2–306(1). "Output" and "requirement" and similar flexible quantity terms satisfy 2–201(1), provided that the court can determine their meaning with reasonable certainty. See, for example, *Barber & Ross Co. v. Lifetime Doors, Inc.,* 810 F.2d 1276 (4th Cir.1987).

Example IV(17): Confirmatory Memoranda. After reaching an oral agreement with S over the telephone, B mailed and S received the following letter: "This is to confirm our contract to sell and buy Kerosene Stoves at $200 each." S threw the letter in the wastebasket and, later, denied the oral contract for sale. B sued for breach of contract and alleged an agreement to sell 1,000 stoves. The contract is *not* enforceable under Section 2–201(2), but two steps are essential to that conclusion.

First, if this transaction is "between merchants," see 2–104(3), the failure of S to respond or object to B's letter "in confirmation" of the contract *may* mean that S loses the statute of frauds defense, even though S signed nothing. Silence by a merchant in the face of a confirmation is tantamount to a signature. 2–201(2). Note that subsection (2) is hedged with conditions: B must send the confirming letter within a reasonable time; S must receive it and have reason to know of its contents; and S must give written notice of objection "to its contents" within 10 days after it is received. Also, the courts have disagreed on who is a merchant under this subsection. See 2–104(1). For example, some, but not all, courts have held that a farmer is not a merchant even though the broad definition of merchant applies and the farmer is experienced in growing and selling crops.

Second, assuming that all other conditions are satisfied, the letter or confirming memo must be "sufficient against the sender." B's letter, although otherwise satisfying Section 2–201(1), fails to state a quantity term. Thus, if S sued B for breach, the contract would not be enforceable because no quantity was shown in the writing. Since the writing is not sufficient against B, the sender, it is not enforceable against S, who received it and did not object. One final note. Even if the writing shows a quantity term, S, by failing to answer, has simply lost the statute of frauds defense. B must still prove the agreement and breach and, of course, is limited by the quantity of goods shown in the writing.

Example IV(18): Multiple Writings. Suppose, in *Example IV(17),* that there was, in addition to the written confirmation, a written, unsigned memo in S's possession which stated: "We have agreed to the sale of 1,000 kerosene stoves." Would this memorandum satisfy the quantity requirement? The probable answer is yes, although Sections 2–201(1) & (2) are far from clear. The first question is whether all of the writings can be related to the same transaction without the use of extrinsic evidence. Here the content of the writings without more suggests that the answer is yes and the phrasing of the unsigned memo indicates that a quantity term was agreed upon. The next question is whether the writing containing the quantity term must be signed by one or both parties. The answer appears to be no. Section 2–201(1) states that there must be "some" signed writing sufficient to indicate that a contract for sale has been made between the parties and this condition has been for both parties satisfied by B's confirmatory memo, to which S made no objection. Section 2–201(1) then provides that "A writing" is not insufficient because it "omits or incorrectly states a term agreed upon but the contract is not enforceable under this paragraph beyond the quantity of goods shown in such writing." A strict reading of this language supports the conclusion that the signed writing must contain the quantity term. An unsigned memorandum simply will not do. But if the contents of all writings clearly link them as part of the same transaction, if both parties have authenticated "some" writing that indicates a contract for sale has been made and if "a" writing of which S was aware in the total agreement shows that a quantity was agreed upon, the requirements of the Statute of Frauds would seem to be satisfied. Put another way, the danger of fraud and perjury has been averted if S knows of or is in possession of the unsigned writing and the plaintiff should be permitted to prove the agreement.

2. AGREEMENTS "TAKEN OUT" OF THE STATUTE

To summarize, the statute of frauds applies to contracts "for the sale of goods for the price of $500 or more." 2–201(1). If the contract is within the scope of Section 2–201, it must satisfy the requirement of a signed writing to be enforceable. These *requirements are less stringent than those exacted by pre-code law, except for the quantity term.* But suppose the agreement is within the statute and does not satisfy the requirement of a signed writing. Are there other ways to take the contract "out of" or to satisfy the statute? The answer is yes and these "outs" are contained in Section 2–201(3).

Example IV(19): B, a 450 pound man, made an oral agreement with S, a tailor, to buy an orange suit to be specially created for $500. S took B's measurements and promised delivery in three weeks. The next day, S purchased cloth worth $300 and commenced work. One week later, B repudiated the agreement. If S were to sue B for breach, the statute of frauds defense would not be available. Although the agreement does not satisfy the "requirements of subsection (1)," it falls squarely within the exception created by subsection (3)(a): the goods were to be "specially manufactured" for B, they were not "suitable for sale to others in the ordinary course of the seller's business," and S made a "substantial beginning on their manufacture" "before notice of repudiation is received and under circumstances which reasonably indicate that the goods are for the buyer." Put another way, the circumstances indicate that S probably acted in response to an order from B and this neutralizes the risk of fraud and perjury.

Example IV(20): S and B reached an oral agreement to sell 1,000 kerosene stoves at $200 each. B drew and S accepted a check for $5,000 as a down payment. Later, S refused to deliver any stoves and B sued for breach of contract. The contract is enforceable "with respect to goods for which payment has been made and accepted or which have been received and accepted." 2–201(3)(c). Because the conduct of part payment indicates that a contract for sale has been made, oral evidence is admissible to establish the agreed price per stove and a simple exercise in long division determines the quantity to be enforced, here 25 stoves. The contract, therefore, is enforceable up to but not beyond 25 stoves. Note that if the payment accepted is less than the agreed price for a particular unit, the contract is enforceable for the full unit involved. Thus, if, in *Example IV(17)*, B had tendered and S had accepted $50 down on the orange suit to be made, the part payment would justify enforcing the contract to sell a whole suit, not just $50 worth of the trousers. See 2–201, Comment 2.

Example IV(21): S and B concluded an oral agreement to sell 1,000 kerosene stoves at $200 each. B repudiated the agreement and, when S sued for breach of contract, B, through appropriate pleadings, raised the statute of frauds defense without admitting that a contract for sale had been made. In a pre-trial deposition, B, under oath, was asked by S's lawyer: "Did you agree to buy the kerosene stoves." B replied "Yes." B then was asked, "how many stoves did you agree to purchase," and replied, "I don't remember." Relying on Section 2–201(3)(b), S's lawyer then asked the court to deny the statute of frauds defense.

B's first answer, elicited under oath, "admits . . . that a contract for sale was made" and the contract, if valid in other respects, "is enforceable." But it is not enforceable "beyond the quantity of goods admitted." Since B admitted no quantity, the contract, in practical effect, is not enforceable. Whether B committed perjury is a matter for separate consideration. Remember, 2–201(3)(b) is a particularized application of the principle that either party can waive the statute of frauds defense. The courts and commentators have disagreed over the scope of the phrase "admits in his pleading, testimony or otherwise in court," but most courts have accepted an expansive reading. See, generally, *DF Activities Corporation v. Brown*, 851 F.2d 920 (7th Cir.1988).

Example IV(22): On March 1, S, a farmer, made an oral contract with B, a grain dealer, to sell 5,000 bushels of corn at $2.40 per bushel, delivery after harvest. B, as was customary in the trade, resold the corn to M, a flour mill, for $3.00 per bushel. Later, the market price of corn advanced to $5.00 per bushel. S repudiated and, in a subsequent suit by B for breach of contract, S raised the statute of frauds defense. B, conceding that none of the statutory exceptions in 2–201(3) applied, argued that the statute of frauds did not apply because B had relied upon S's promise to deliver. The courts are split on whether B's foreseeable and substantial reliance on the oral agreement takes the case out of the statute. Some deny B's argument on the ground that Section 2–201 is the exclusive statement of exceptions to the statute and that allowing reliance as a nonstatutory exception would undercut basic policies. Other courts have concluded that Section 2–201 was not intended to be an exclusive listing of exceptions and that under Section 1–103 a resort to more general principles of estoppel is available. See, e.g., Restatement (Second) Contracts 139 (1979). These courts are motivated in part by a conclusion that B's reliance corroborates the making and terms of S's promise and in part by a concern lest the statute of frauds be used as an instrument of fraud.

What is the effect of deciding that B's reliance takes the case "out" of the statute? The preferred answer is simply that S is precluded from raising the statute of frauds defense and that B, if the contract can be proved, is entitled to pursue normal remedies for breach. Some have argued, however, that B's recovery should be limited to reliance rather than expectation damages, since the theory used to avoid the statute is rooted in promissory estoppel. What do you think? (One of your co-authors feels strongly that the argument is fallacious.)

E. REVIEW QUESTIONS

IV-A. *True or False:* Article 2 does not require consideration for contract formation.

IV-B. After negotiations, S and B could not agree on either the quantity of goods or the price to be paid. Later, B sent S an offer to purchase 1,000 units at $15 per unit and S sent B an offer to sell 1,200 units at $15 per unit. The "offers" crossed in the mail. Later, S shipped and B rejected 1,000 units.

    1. Was there a contract? See 2–204.

    2. Suppose S had shipped and B had accepted the 1,200 units. Contract?

IV-C. Suppose S and B conclude negotiations and reach agreement on a proposed exchange. They intend to contract but leave the quantity term "to be agreed upon." Later, B refuses to negotiate over quantity and repudiates the bargain. S sues for damages. What result?

IV-D. After negotiations where some terms were agreed, B telegraphed S: "Please telegraph your best price per 1,000. Must act fast. Need 5,000." S responded: "Best price is $22.50 per thousand, up to 5,000. Shipment follows." S shipped 5,000 units and B, who had just purchased 5,000 units from C at $21 per, refused to accept them. Contract?

IV-E. After negotiations, B ordered 1,000 units of goods from S at $20 per. S responded that she was "pleased" to have the order, that the goods would be "shipped promptly" but that she could not sell them for less than $25 per 1,000. S shipped and B accepted the goods without objection. Later, a bill for $25,000 arrived and B refused to pay. B argued: (1) I intended to pay $20,000 and there is a contract at that price; and, in the alternative, (2) Under Section 2–207(3), there was conduct by both parties indicating that a contract was formed, the writings do not agree on price and a reasonable market price for the goods is $21.50. S argued that B's response and shipment was a counteroffer to sell at $25 and B accepted it by taking the goods without objection. Who should prevail?

IV-F. S and B, both merchants, concluded an oral agreement for the sale of 1,000 units of goods at $15 per unit. Later, B mailed to S a letter which stated, in part: "This is to confirm our contract for Blips at $15 per unit, you to ship promptly FOB point of shipment." B signed the letter. S responded with a short, signed note which read: "Will ship Blips by end of week." At the same time, S dictated an unsigned memo to his plant manager which stated: "Select 1,000 Blips and ship to B by end of week." Later, S received an offer from C to buy all of his Blips for $18 per unit. S then repudiated the agreement with B over the telephone and, in a subsequent law suit by B, raised the statute of frauds defense. Should S prevail?

*

V

PERFORMANCE OF THE CONTRACT FOR SALE

Analysis

A. INTRODUCTION

After the parties have concluded their agreement, questions about the order and content of performance may arise. *The starting point for analysis is Section 2–301, which provides that the "obligation of the seller is to transfer and deliver and that of the buyer is to accept and pay in accordance with the contract."*

Since "contract" is defined as the "total legal obligation which results from the parties' agreement," 1–201(11), the next step is to determine what, if anything, the parties have agreed on the point at issue. Review Chapter IV(A). With this step in mind, Chapter V will first examine how to determine the scope and meaning of agreement under Article 2. At this point you should review Chapter III(B)(3) on the "scope of transaction planning" and Chapter III(B)(5) on the role of "unconscionability" and "good faith" as regulators of the parties' agreement in fact.

If the parties have failed to reach complete agreement on all terms but still "have intended to make a contract," 2–204(3), the next step is to determine the extent to which Article 2, Part 3 supplies sufficient performance terms to fill the gap and preserve enforceability. Chapter V will explore this methodology and analyze obligations which are common to the parties and obligations which are distinctive to the seller and to the buyer.

Finally, Chapter V will examine two specialized problems of filling gaps in agreed risk allocation, risk of loss, see 2–509 & 2–510, and excuse for non-performance due to changed circumstances, see 2–613 through 2–616. *Throughout this discussion, remember that Article 2: (1) gives the parties considerable power to specify the order and content of performance by agreement; (2) preserves the contract in the face of a failure to agree if the parties have "intended" to make a contract; and (3) supplies a term judged to be reasonable or fair in the commercial setting to fill the gap in agreement. But if these efforts cannot provide a "reasonably certain basis for giving an appropriate remedy," the contract will "fail for indefiniteness." 2–204(3)*

B. SCOPE AND MEANING OF AGREEMENT

We have already considered the content of agreement and its importance in the scheme of Article 2. See Chapter IV(A). We will now examine how to resolve disputes over the scope and meaning of agreement. Issues of "scope" normally involve the parol evidence rule. 2–202. See also Section 2–207 and the discussion in Chapter IV(C)(2)(b). Problems of "meaning" invariably involve the process of interpreting the agreement to determine whether the seller's or buyer's asserted meaning should prevail in disputed cases.

1. SCOPE: THE PAROL EVIDENCE RULE

Suppose that S and B, after extensive negotiations, concluded an agreement that was *not* reduced to a final writing and commenced performance. Later, S refused to tender delivery on the ground that its duty was expressly conditioned upon the occurrence of a specified event and that the event had not yet occurred. S claims and B does not deny that the parties agreed to the condition mid-way in the negotiations. That fact is not in dispute. B, however, argues that the condition "dropped out" of the agreement because it was agreed to early in the negotiations and followed by oral and written agreement to other terms which were, on the whole, inconsistent. Therefore, S's evidence on agreement to the express condition should be excluded.

On the facts as stated, B's argument is unsound. The express condition, regardless of when agreed to, is part of the parties' total agreement and, therefore, must be considered along with other evidence of the agreement. The resolution of apparent inconsistencies is for the trier of fact. Why? *In the absence of a writing adopted by the parties with the intention that it be a "final expression" of their agreement with regard to some terms or a "complete and exclusive statement" of all terms, see 2–202, there is no basis (except relevance) for excluding evidence introduced by S to establish the agreement. The parol evidence rule operates to exclude that evidence only when the term contradicts a term in a writing "intended by the parties to be a final expression of their agreement with respect" to that term or where the parties have adopted a "total" integration, i.e., a writing "intended . . . as a complete and exclusive statement of the terms of the agreement." 2–202. There was no such "integrated" writing in this case.*

Now, read Section 2–202 carefully and consider the following analysis.

First, the rationale of the rule explains why it does *not* apply to certain kinds of parol evidence. Where parties have intended the writing to be a final and exclusive statement of the terms, it makes sense to exclude prior or contemporaneous evidence that would contradict or supplement the written agreement. But the rule presupposes an *enforceable* written contract. Therefore it would not exclude evidence introduced to establish fraud, mistake, duress, or an express condition which was to occur *before* a contract was to come into existence. Likewise, the reason for the rule makes it inapplicable to evidence introduced to establish that the parties *subsequently* modified the original agreement. In short, the parol evidence rule is limited to disputes over the scope of an unmodified agreement which is otherwise enforceable as a contract.

Second, application of the parol evidence rule depends upon the intention of the parties. Whether the parties have intended a writing to be a partial or total integration can be complicated. The easiest case is where both parties have assented to a writing containing a "merger" clause, which provides in essence that "this writing is the final and exclusive statement of the terms and conditions of the agreement." On the face of it, the parties intend a total integration. Even here, however, some courts permit evidence to show that the parties really did not intend the integration or that the integration clause was unconscionable due to unfair surprise. In commercial cases, this evidence is rarely sufficient to overturn a clear and conspicuous "merger" clause to which both parties have assented.

A more complicated case is where the parties have adopted a writing which is clear and complete on its face but does not contain a merger clause. Here there may be a presumption that the writing was intended at least to be a partial integration, but any credible evidence offered to rebut that presumption should be admitted. The court must decide the question, and must infer the parties' intention from the probabilities. A suggested test is whether the term in "any prior agreement" or in "a contemporaneous oral agreement" would, if agreed upon, "certainly have been included" in the writing. Comment 3. If not, the writing is not integrated with regard to that term and the evidence is admissible to prove the agreement.

> *Example V(1):* S and B commenced negotiations over the proposed sale of machinery. Early in the process, the parties agreed in writing on a $50,000 price. Later in the process, the parties orally agreed that B's duty to pay was conditioned upon getting financing from a bank. At the conclusion of negotiations, the parties signed a writing which was complete on its face and did not contain a merger clause. The contract price was stated to be $60,000 and the financing condition did not appear in the writing. Later, B claimed that the price was $50,000 and that this duty to pay was conditioned and sought to introduce evidence to that effect.
>
> The court should hold a preliminary hearing on the question of intention.
>
> (1) It is probable that the parties intended the writing to be a "final expression of the agreement" with regard to price: the conflict between the earlier and later price agreement suggests that the earlier term *certainly* would have been included in the writing if intended to bind the parties. Since there is a "partial" integration, the price term "may not be contradicted by evidence of any prior agreement or of a contemporaneous oral agreement. . . ." 2–202(a).
>
> (2) Assuming that the agreement is partially integrated, should evidence of the financing condition be admitted? The answer depends upon whether the condition is classified as a "consistent additional term." 2–202(b). Early cases concluded that if the condition supplemented or limited but did not directly contradict the term, the proferred term was consistent and additional. Recent cases have rejected this anti-parol

evidence approach and, instead, have asked whether there was "reasonable harmony" between the proferred term and the language and respective obligations of the parties. This question requires evidence of the circumstances surrounding the negotiations, including trade usage. If not, the proferred term can be excluded on the grounds that it either contradicts the price term or it would "certainly" have been included in the writing if agreed to. See *Alaska Northern Development, Inc. v. Alyeska Pipeline Service Co.,* 666 P.2d 33 (Alaska 1983), cert. denied, 464 U.S. 1041, 104 S.Ct. 706, 79 L.Ed.2d 170 (1984).

Third, the legal effect of the parol evidence rule depends upon whether the writing was intended to be a "partial" or a "total" integration of the agreement. In a "partial" integration, the writing is intended to be a final expression of agreement with respect to some of the included terms. *In this case, "such terms . . . may not be contradicted by evidence of any prior agreement or of a contemporaneous oral agreement but may be explained or supplemented (a) by course of dealing or usage of trade . . . or by course of performance . . .; and (b) by evidence of consistent additional terms. . . ."* 2–202. In a "total" integration, the writing is intended as the "complete and exclusive statement of the terms of the agreement." As such, it may not be contradicted by evidence of any prior agreement or contemporaneous oral agreement or supplemented by evidence of consistent additional terms.

Fourth, whether the integration is total or partial, the writing may be explained or supplemented by "course of dealing or usage of trade . . . or by course of performance. . . ." 2–202(a). Unless carefully negated, it is assumed that practices and meanings derived from trade practice or from the parties' prior course of dealing are incorporated into their current agreement. See Comment 2. See also, 1–201(3) & 1–205.

> *Example V(2):* S and B concluded a five year contract for the sale of phosphate at a fixed price of $20 per ton. Employing a general merger clause, they adopted a writing intended to be a "total" integration. After two years, the market price for phosphate dropped 60% below the contract price to $8 per ton. B claimed that a trade usage required that the parties engage in good faith negotiations toward a price adjustment. If the practice was based upon a trade usage and the conditions of Section 1–205(2) are met, it may be proved to supplement the writing unless the practice has been carefully negated in the writing. A general merger clause is not such a careful negation.

Fifth, when a term is found to be part of the agreement, the parol evidence rule does not exclude evidence intended to explain or interpret that term. In short, the parol evidence rule does not exclude evidence offered to interpret terms that are part of the agreement, provided that the evidence advances an interpretation to which the language is reasonably susceptible. The language, however, does not have to be ambiguous before interpretive evidence is admissible. See 2–202, Comment 1.

2. INTERPRETATION

Interpretation is the process by which the meaning of an agreement is ascertained. If that meaning is disputed, interpretation either prefers the meaning asserted by one party over the other or suggests that, because such a preference is not possible, the agreement is either fatally defective and cannot be enforced or that the gap in the agreement should be filled by some reasonable term. The UCC, although defining the elements of agreement and their relative priority, provides no clear test of preference in the process of interpretation. Thus, resort must be had to general contract law for guidance on this question.

(a) The Restatement, Second Test

Section 201 of the Restatement, Second of Contracts provides a general test to determine whose meaning prevails in an interpretation dispute. If both parties attach the same meaning to a "promise or agreement," it is interpreted in accordance with that meaning even though a different and arguably more reasonable meaning may exist. If they attach different meanings to the term, the meaning of one party is preferred over that of the other if: (1) "that party did not know any different meaning attached by the other, and the other knew the meaning attached by the first party," or (2) that party had no reason to know of any different meaning attached by the other, and the other had reason to know the meaning attached by the first party." The test is stated in terms of what the parties knew or had reason to know at the "time the agreement was made" and does not turn on whether the prevailing party's meaning was reasonable. Rather, if the other party knew or had reason to know that meaning and failed to object or to clarify the situation, he cannot later be heard to complain about any differences in meaning. This general test is supplemented in the Restatement by rules in aid of interpretation, Section 202, and standards of preference in interpretation, Section 203. An example of a "rule" in aid of interpretation is that "words and other conduct are interpreted in the light of all the circumstances, and if the principal purpose of the parties is ascertainable it is given great weight." Section 202(1). An important "standard" of preference is that an "interpretation which gives a reasonable, lawful, and effective meaning to all the terms is preferred to an interpretation which leaves a part unreasonable, unlawful, or of no effect." Section 203(a). See A. Farnsworth, Contracts Ch. 7(D) (2d ed. 1991).

(b) The Code Approach to Interpretation

Suppose that S agreed to supply steel beams to B which were described as "36 inches wide." S tendered and B rejected beams which were 37 inches wide. Over B's protest, S claimed that the description "36 inches wide" meant that steel of a width not less than 36 inches or more than 37 inches conformed to the contract. How should this dispute be resolved?

In general, the Code rejects the "plain meaning" rule: S may introduce evidence relevant to his claimed meaning without an "original determination by the court that the language used is ambiguous." 2–202, Comment 1. But what evidence is relevant? In general, it is evidence relevant to a meaning of language "which arises out of the commercial context in which it was used" rather than that "attributable . . . by rules of construction existing in the law." 2–202, Comment 1(b). Again, the "meaning of the agreement . . . is to be determined by the language used by them and by their action, read and interpreted in light of commercial practices and other surrounding circumstances." 1–205, Comment 1. For S, the most promising sources of this evidence may be course of performance and course of dealing between the parties and usage of trade.

(1) Course of Performance
   Section 2–208(1) provides that where the contract "involves repeated occasions for performance by either party with knowledge of the nature of the performance and opportunity for objection to it by the other, any course of performance accepted or acquiesced in without objection shall be relevant to determine the meaning of the agreement." Thus, if S had tendered and B had accepted without objection some 36 inch and some 37 inch steel, this course of performance might support S's claimed interpretation. At the very least, it tends to establish that the parties thought that the term "36 inches wide" was flexible. If so, the "express terms of the agreement" and the course of performance can be reasonably construed "as consistent with each other." Note that if a construction of consistency is not reasonable, "express terms shall control course of performance . . . " 2–208(2). But the course of performance, in any event, may constitute a waiver of the express term or an agreed modification of the contract. See 2–208 & 2–209. In this case, B promptly objected to a tender of 37 inch steel, thereby foreclosing any claims derived from course of performance.

(2) Course of Dealing
   Section 1–205(1) provides that a "course of dealing is a sequence of previous conduct between the parties to a particular transaction which is fairly to be regarded as establishing a common basis of understanding for interpreting their expressions and other conduct." A course of dealing between parties can "give particular meaning to and supplement or qualify terms of an agreement." 1–205(3). If, however, the express terms of the agreement and the course of dealing cannot reasonably be construed as consistent with each other, the express terms control. 1–205(4). Thus, if in six prior contracts, B had accepted without objection both 36 inch and 37 inch steel under a contract description of "36 inch steel," this course of dealing would support S's claim under the seventh contract that "36 inch steel" permitted the tender of 37 inch steel. B, to change the

particular meaning derived from the course of dealing, should have spelled out his intention more clearly in the seventh contract.

> ***Example V(3):*** In six previous contracts, S had tendered and B had accepted without objection both 36 inch and 37 inch steel under a contract description calling for 37 inch steel. In the seventh contract, the description called for 36 inch steel and B rejected S's tender of 37 inch steel. The rejection was proper. The course of dealing in the prior contract evolved under a contract description calling for 37 inch steel. The seventh contract used different language which, without more, has an express meaning. That express term controls the course of dealing unless they can be reasonably construed as consistent with each other. That is unlikely on these facts.

(3)   Usage of Trade
       Section 1–205(2) provides that a "usage of trade is any practice or method of dealing having such regularity of observance in a place, vocation or trade as to justify an expectation that it will be observed with respect to the transaction in question." Any "usage of trade in the vocation or trade in which" the parties are "engaged or of which they are or should be aware" can be proved as a fact to "give particular meaning to an supplement or qualify terms of an agreement." 1–205(3). It is possible, then, that trade usage supports S's interpretation of the contract term, that B is either in the trade or should be aware of the usage, and that B's failure explicitly to negate the usage in the agreement means that B is bound by S's interpretation. Put another way, S's meaning is consistent with a trade usage the content of which B knows or has reason to know. The failure to object means that the usage is incorporated to give particular meaning to the terms used in the agreement.

> ***Example V(4):*** S, a steel manufacturer, sold goods described as "36 inch steel" to B, a steel fabricator. In the steel trade, of which S was a regular participant and B was not, "36 inch steel" was understood to permit a variation of not less than 36 inches or more than 37 inches. Outside of the steel trade, a reasonable meaning of the description was steel exactly 36 inches in width. B is not bound by the usage unless he should have been aware of it. 1–205(3). Even if B should have been aware, Section 1–205(6) provides that evidence of the usage is "not admissible unless and until he has given the other party such notice as the court finds sufficient to prevent unfair surprise. . . ." In addition, it is presumed that a usage proved as a fact is reasonable until the contrary is shown. See 1–205, Comment 6.

(c) Effect of Failure to Agree

In our "36 inch steel" case, the failure of S to prove from course of performance, course of dealing, trade usage or other circumstances that there was another meaning of the term of which B had reason to know results in a victory for B: B's interpretation, if reasonable, prevails. In some cases, however, the parties may attach equally reasonable meanings to the same term or, because of ambiguity, no reasonable meaning can be found. Here there is no basis for preferring one party over the other. The parties have failed to agree on the term. The court has three alternatives at this point: (1) The "tie" might be broken by interpreting the language against the draftsperson or imposing an interpretation that favors some public interest, see Restatement (Second) Contracts §§ 206 & 207; (2) The Court might conclude that the failure to agree on a material term means that no enforceable contract was concluded, either because of the parties' presumed intention or indefiniteness; or (3) The court might conclude that despite the failure of agreement, the parties intended to contract and that the gap should be filled by some reasonable term supplied from the commercial context. The Code is not clear on which alternative should be preferred. *Section 2–204(3), however, supports the third alternative and suggests that the contract for sale "does not fail for indefiniteness if . . . there is a reasonably certain basis for giving an appropriate remedy."* Given this general policy, we will now consider how a court should fill gaps under Article 2, Part 3.

C. GENERAL OBLIGATIONS OF THE PARTIES

The general obligation of the seller is to "transfer and deliver" and that of the buyer is to "accept and pay for" the goods "in accordance with the contract." 2–301. The agreement may specify such things as the time for performance, duration of the contract, the quantity and quality of the goods the seller is to deliver, the method and time for delivery, the price to be paid, and so forth. If the agreement fails to cover one or more of these terms and the parties still intended to conclude a contract, the court may then utilize the appropriate "gap" filling provisions in Article 2, Part 3 and enforce the contract. To illustrate this process, we will first discuss the "gap" fillers that are common to both parties and help to structure the exchange. Next we will treat obligations which are distinctive to the seller and then, those which are distinctive to the buyer.

1. WAS CREDIT EXTENDED?

Unless otherwise agreed, neither party is entitled to demand performance by the other before it has tendered performance. Thus, the buyer is not entitled to demand delivery of the goods before a tender of payment is made. *Section 2–511(1) states that "tender of payment is a condition to the seller's duty to tender and complete delivery."* Similarly, the seller may not demand payment before the goods are tendered to the buyer. In fact, *"tender of delivery is a condition to the buyer's duty to accept . . . and . . . to pay"* for the goods. 2–507(1). The agreement, of course, may require one party to extend credit to the other. But in the absence of agreement, the Code imposes what contract lawyers call "concurrent" conditions of exchange.

> ***Example V(5):*** S agreed to sell goods to B for $1,000. The time for performance was fixed for July 1. On July 1, S drove to B's place of business with the goods in a loaded truck. S said: "You have to pay me the $1,000 before you get the goods." B refused to tender payment and S refused to tender the goods. There is a stalemate. Until one party actually tenders performance there can be no breach of contract. In the absence of agreement, the code does not say who must tender first. But whoever tenders first puts the other in default if she then fails to tender the promised performance.

2. TIME AND ORDER OF PERFORMANCE

The agreement may provide for the time and order of performance. Thus, if the agreement states that S is to deliver goods on April 1 and B is to pay for them on August 1, we know that S has extended credit to B and when the parties are to perform and who is to go first. But suppose the agreement is silent on these terms? *Section 2–309(1) provides that the "time for shipment or delivery or any other action under a contract if not provided in this Article or agreed upon shall be a reasonable time." What is a reasonable time is a question of fact and "depends upon the nature, purpose and circumstances" of the action to be taken. 1–204(2).* Thus, the time for delivery or payment might turn on such things as the nature of the goods (are they durable or perishable), market conditions, B's needs, relevant trade usage or any prior course of dealing or course of performance between the parties.

> ***Example V(6):*** On June 1, S contracted to sell goods to B, to be picked up at S's place of business after notice of their availability was given. On July 1, S telephoned B and stated that the goods were ready and requested that they be taken. By August 1, B had not picked them up and S, disgusted, canceled the contract and resold the goods to C. In S's action for damages against B, the factual questions will be whether S tendered delivery within a reasonable time after the contract, see 2–503(1), and whether B's failure to accept and pay for the goods by August 1 was unreasonable. If the answer to either question is no, then S's conduct is a breach of contract.

What about the order of performance in the absence of agreement? As *Example V(5)* suggests, the Code seems to impose concurrent conditions of exchange and, by uncertainty as to who must tender first, prompts the party with the greatest incentive to complete the exchange to tender first and put the other party in danger of default. The following scenario is not unreasonable: *First,* in a case where shipment of the goods is not required, S telephones B and tenders delivery by stating that the goods are available at S's place of business. See 2–503(1). *Second,* B arrives at S's place of business within a reasonable time and, after exercising his right to inspect, see 2–513(1), demands possession of the goods. S, quite properly, refuses to complete the delivery until B has tendered payment. 2–511(1). *Third,* B tenders payment (a check is usually OK) and, according to the Code's script, a simultaneous exchange of check for goods occurs. *But note that the longer it is expected to take for S to obtain or to manufacture the goods, the greater is the inference that S must tender delivery within a reasonable time before B has a duty to pay. If the inference is sound, we have what contract lawyers call a constructive condition precedent: S must tender delivery before B must tender payment and the failure to do so is a breach.*

3. GOOD FAITH IN PERFORMANCE

Section 1–203 provides that "every contract or duty within this Act imposes an obligation of good faith in its performance or enforcement." As we have seen, the effect of this duty cannot be "disclaimed by agreement." 1–102(3). Further, the basic definition of good faith as "honesty in fact in the conduct or transaction involved," 1–201(19), is augmented in Article 2 when either party is a merchant by an objective standard: in addition to honesty in fact, a merchant must observe "reasonable commercial standards of fair dealing in the trade." 2–103(1)(b). The function of good faith in performance is twofold: *first,* the obligation furnishes consideration when one party has reserved discretion in performance; and *second,* the obligation guarantees that the parties' conduct must satisfy minimum standards of honesty and commercial reasonableness. Here are some examples.

> ***Example V(7):*** B purchased 1,000 units of goods under an agreement reserving to S the power to specify a per unit price between $18 and $20. Later, the market price of the goods dropped to $12 per unit and B, claiming that S's reserved discretion made the bargain illusory, terminated the contract. The cancellation was a breach. Section 2–311(1) provides that a contract "is not made invalid by the fact that it leaves particulars of performance to be specified by one of the parties" and that "any such specification must be made in good faith and within limits set by commercial reasonableness." These limitations on S's discretion furnish consideration to B. If, however, the market price was $12 and S set the per unit price at $20, the burden is on B to show that the specification was made in bad faith.

> ***Example V(8):*** B purchased 1,000 units of goods from S at $20 per unit, subject to obtaining financing from Bank, upon whose board of directors S served. When the market price rose to $25 per unit, S advised Bank to deny B's application for a loan. The application was denied and S refused to deliver on the grounds that the contract was discharged by the failure of an express condition precedent. S's conduct in preventing the condition was a breach of an implied duty of cooperation. See 2–311(3) and Restatement (Second) Contracts § 205. A failure to cooperate motivated by a desire to avoid an unprofitable bargain is bad faith and B is entitled to pursue remedies for breach of contract.

> *Example V(9):* B, a distributor, agreed to purchase its "requirements" of goods from S, a manufacturer, over a five year duration at $10 per unit. B is obligated to purchase its "actual . . . requirements as may occur in good faith" and its discretion is limited in that the "requirements" cannot be unreasonably disproportionate to any stated estimate "or in the absence of a stated estimate to any normal or otherwise comparable prior . . . requirements." 2–306(1).

It is one thing to determine when one party's performance obligation is subject to a good faith duty and quite another to determine what is "bad faith" and what remedies are available for bad faith conduct. We will deal with these questions in the materials that follow.

4. DURATION AND TERMINATION OF THE CONTRACT
(a) Duration

The agreement of the parties can fix the duration of the contract. Thus, the parties may validly agree that the duration of a "requirements" contract shall be 10 years. In this situation, either party may cancel the contract upon breach by the other, see 2–106(4), 2–703(f) & 2–711(1), or either party can terminate the contract if, for example, their performance is made commercially impracticable under Section 2–615. See 2–106(3). But unless power to terminate is reserved to one or both parties by the agreement, attempts to avoid an unprofitable bargain by termination without a breach by the other or some other legal excuse may amount to a repudiation by the terminating party. If no duration is agreed, the time for performance when a single tender is required "shall be a reasonable time." 2–309(1). When the contract "provides for successive performances but is indefinite in duration it is valid for a reasonable time." 2–309(2). Thus, some variation on the "reasonable time" standard is supplied when the parties have failed to agree upon duration.

> *Example V(10):* B, a distributor, agreed to purchase requirements from S, a manufacturer, for $10 per unit. A ceiling of 50,000 units per year was established but no duration was agreed. For two years, B, in good faith, ordered 50,000 units per year in a market where the average price per unit was $12. At the end of two years, S refused to deliver and claimed that the contract was terminated by lapse of time. It is a question of fact whether two years was a reasonable time. If not, then S's termination is arguably premature and constitutes a breach. If so, S, unless otherwise agreed, may terminate the contract "at any time." 2–309(2). Despite some uncertainty, a preferable reading of Section 2–309(2) is that a reasonable time must elapse before either party can terminate. See Comment 7.

(b) Termination

There are at least three situations where one or both parties have power to terminate without liability for breach.

The *first,* noted in *Example V(10),* above, is after a contract for successive performances has existed for a reasonable time. After that, the contract may be "terminated at any time by either party." 2–309(2).

The *second* is where the agreement states that the contract shall terminate upon the happening of some specified event, e.g., when the "market price per unit exceeds $15."

The *third* is where the agreement reserves to one or both parties the power to terminate, with or without conditions. In the second situation, above, termination is automatic when the specified event occurs. It does not depend upon the exercise of discretion. In the first and third situations, a choice to terminate must be exercised.

An important issue is what, if any controls, are imposed upon the exercise of the choice to terminate? *Section 2–309(3) provides that "termination of a contract by one party except on the happening of an agreed event requires that a reasonable notification be received by the other party. . . ."* Thus, in our three situations above, notice is required in situations one and three but not in situation two.

"Reasonable" notification in this setting requires that the terminating party give the other "reasonable time to seek a substitute arrangement." Suppose that the parties agree to dispense with notice. Section 2–309(3) provides that such an agreement is "invalid if its operation would be unconscionable." Similarly, an agreement limiting the time after notice in which the termination will occur cannot be "manifestly" unreasonable." See 1–204(1) and 2–309, Comment 8. Again, the question is whether the terminated party has had a fair chance to salvage and relocate his business operation before the contractual relationship is ended.

> *Example V(11):* S granted B an exclusive right to distribute products within a defined market area. No duration was agreed. The agreement provided that after two years, either party could terminate the contract at any time without cause upon the giving of ten days notice in writing. Over a two year period, B invested $500,000 in the distributorship, primarily in a lease, equipment and capital improvements. S elected to terminate the contract and informed B that deliveries would cease ten days after notice. The question is whether ten days is manifestly unreasonable, given the magnitude of B's investment and the difficulty involved in locating another supplier before the contract is terminated. It

is assumed that two years is a reasonable time within which to develop the business opportunity and recoup the investment.

A final problem involves the relationship of the termination power and the duty of good faith performance. Suppose that the agreement provides that S, the manufacturer, can terminate "at any time for any reason" upon the giving of six months notice. Assume further that a six months notice is reasonable in the termination of a distributorship. Are there any controls upon S's decision to terminate where the agreement states that it can be "at any time for any reason?"

Unless the termination clause is deemed to be unconscionable at the time of contracting, some courts have concluded that the power can be exercised without regard to good faith. *The better view, however, is that exercise of the reserved power is subject to the duty of good faith and that bad faith may exist where S's motives have little to do with the quality of B's performance and much to do with S's self interest.* Thus, if the reason for termination is S's desire to take over a highly profitable distributorship rather than B's substandard performance, a persuasive case for bad faith has been established. In summary, it appears that imposing a good faith duty on the exercise of the power prevents S from stealing a profitable opportunity that B has developed and the reasonable notice requirement protects B in transition after an otherwise honest termination decision has been made. A leading case involving these issues is *Zapatha v. Dairy Mart, Inc.*, 381 Mass. 284, 408 N.E.2d 1370 (1980), holding that the contested termination was in good faith.

D. SELLER'S OBLIGATIONS

We have just considered some obligations common to both parties to the contract for sale. In this section we will treat some aspects of the seller's obligation "to transfer and deliver . . . in accordance with the contract." 2–301. Later, we will have occasion to examine the buyer's remedies when the seller's performance fails to conform to the contract. See, e.g., 2–711.

1. DELIVERY OF THE GOODS
When the time for "transfer and delivery" arrives, the seller must answer three questions: (a) What part of the total quantity sold must be tendered; (b) Where is the place for tender and delivery; and (c) What is the required tender of delivery?

(a) Quantity Tendered
The agreement may require S to deliver all of the promised goods at once or may authorize delivery in installments. See 2–612(1). *In the absence of agreement, Section 2–307 states that "all goods called for by a contract for sale must be tendered in a single delivery and payment is due only on such tender*

. . . ." Thus, if S agreed to sell 1,000 kerosene stoves and the time for delivery was March 1, S must tender all 1,000 stoves on that date unless there is agreement to the contrary.

Section 2–307(1), however, also states that the "circumstances" may "give either party the right to make or demand delivery in lots" and that the "price if it can be apportioned may be demanded for each lot." The "circumstances" justifying a tender of something less than 1,000 units may involve the feasibility of shipping the entire lot, such as where there is a temporary shortage of rail cars. See Comment 3. B's temporary loss of storage space may also justify a demand for less than the full lot. The demand is for short-term accommodation, with the understanding that the balance will be tendered and accepted within a reasonable time. *In effect, the "circumstances" convert a "single lot" delivery into an installment contract, where the agreement authorizes the "delivery of goods in separate lots to be separately accepted." 2–612(1).*

(b) Place of Delivery

Unless otherwise agreed, the place of delivery is the "seller's place of business or if he has none his residence." 2–308. Where the goods are identified at the time of contracting and both parties know that they are "in some other place, that place is the place for their delivery." 2–308. Thus, if identified goods are stored in a warehouse at the time of contracting, the warehouse is the place of delivery. In these cases it is said that the goods are to be delivered "without being moved:" The buyer must go to the seller or the bailee to take delivery.

The seller, of course, may agree to deliver the goods to the buyer or to ship them via a common carrier. Where the goods are to be sent by carrier, the terms of the contract determine whether it is a "shipment" contract with delivery taking place at the point of shipment, see 2–319(1)(a), or a "destination" contract, with delivery taking place at the point of destination, see 2–319(1)(b). Determining the place of delivery is an important first step to ascertaining what the seller must do to tender delivery.

(c) Tender of Delivery

The tender of delivery is a critical part of S's obligation to "transfer and deliver" the goods. The failure to or an improper tender is a breach of contract. See 2–711(1). Tender, a technical concept, has requirements that vary with who has possession of the goods, whether S has an obligation to ship them to B and, if so, whether S has agreed to ship them "FOB point of shipment" or "FOB point of destination." 2–319(1). Section 2–503 provides the key ingredients for this technical exercise.

(1) Seller in Possession: No Duty to Ship
If the goods are to be delivered at S's place of business or a place controlled by it, S's tender of delivery must conform to Section 2–503(1). S must "put and hold conforming goods at the buyer's disposition and give the buyer any notification reasonably necessary to enable him to take delivery." The tender must be at a reasonable hour, the goods must be held for the period "reasonably necessary to enable the buyer to take possession" and the buyer must "furnish facilities reasonably suited to the receipt of the goods." 2–503(1)(b).

(2) Bailee in Possession: No Duty to Ship
If the goods are in the possession of a bailee, usually a warehouseman or a carrier, and are to be delivered "without being moved," S's tender requirements are governed by Section 2–503(4).

If the bailee has issued a negotiable document of title (more on this later), S must tender that document to B or procure "acknowledgment by the bailee of the buyer's right to possession of the goods." 2–503(4)(a). Either event is an important first step to authorizing the bailee to deliver to B without breaching its contract of storage with S. (The rights and duties under that contract are governed, in the main, by Article 7.) In addition, S could tender a non-negotiable document (more on this later) if one has been issued or a written direction to the bailee to deliver to B, but B can seasonably object to this tender. 2–503(4)(b). As a practical matter, S must give B sufficient authority to take possession of the goods without objection from the bailee, and Section 2–503(4) provides the necessary guidance.

> ***Example V(12):*** S, in New York, sold B 60,000 gallons of wine which was stored in vats at S's vineyard in California. The vats were padlocked and monitored by W, a warehouseman, who was operating a field warehouse to protect the security interest of SP, a secured creditor of S's. W had issued non-negotiable warehouse receipts and, under the bailment contract with SP, was to release goods only when payment for their sale had been received either by SP or W.
>
> In this case, B should object to a tender by S of either the non-negotiable document or a written direction to W to deliver to B. Although B is technically entitled to the goods under these documents, W need not deliver them until payment is made. Thus, a tender of delivery requires that S "procure acknowledgment by the bailee of the buyer's right to possession," 2–503(4)(b), and B will not give that acknowledgment until the payment condition is met.

(3) Shipment and Destination Contracts

If S agrees or is authorized to ship the goods to B, the place for and the requirements of the tender of delivery will depend upon whether the shipment is to be FOB "point of shipment" or FOB "destination." These are delivery terms.

In an FOB "point of shipment" contract, the seller must "at that place" ship the goods "in the manner provided" in Section 2–504 and "bear the risk and expenses of putting them into the possession of the carrier." 2–319(1)(a). Section 2–504 requires that S put the goods in the carrier's possession, make a reasonable contract for their shipment, obtain and promptly tender or deliver any documents necessary for B to obtain possession and promptly notify the buyer of the shipment. When these events have occurred, S has tendered delivery. See 2–503(2).

In the exceptional case of an FOB "destination" term, S is required to deliver the goods to their destination point, probably the place where B does business. S must "at his own expense and risk transport the goods to that place and there tender delivery of them in the manner provided . . ." in Section 2–503. 2–319(1)(b). Thus, when the goods arrive, S must tender as required by Section 2–503(1) and, where appropriate, tender any necessary documents in proper form. 2–503(3). This means that S must give B reasonable notice at a reasonable hour of their arrival and arrange with the carrier to keep them available for a reasonable time to enable B to take possession.

> **Example V(13):** S, in California, sold lumber to B, in Oregon, and agreed to ship it to B "FOB delivered." At the time of shipment, S complied with 2–504 except that it failed to promptly notify B of the shipment. When the goods arrived, S attempted to tender delivery as required by 2–503(3) and 2–503(1), but B rejected the goods on the grounds that tender of delivery should have taken place at the point of shipment and S failed to give notice of shipment. B's argument is sound. Although the term "FOB delivered" required that S pay the freight to the destination point, it is not sufficient to impose a requirement that S deliver to the destination. As a matter of practice a "shipment" contract is regarded as normal and a "destination" contract is regarded as an exception. As a matter of policy, S is not required to deliver to the destination "unless he has specifically agreed so to deliver or the commercial understanding of the terms used by the parties contemplates such delivery." 2–503, Comment 5. The "FOB delivered" term is not such a specific agreement. B, however, cannot reject the goods unless S's failure to notify of the shipment causes "material delay or loss." 2–504.

(d) Documentary Sales: Article 7

As previously noted, in some contracts for sale the goods may be in a warehouse at the time of contracting or S may be required to ship them to B by carrier. In either situation, documents of title will be issued, a warehouse receipt in W's case and a bill of lading in C's case. These documents acknowledge the bailee's possession of described goods and promise to deliver them to the person "entitled" under the document. See 7–102(2) and 7–403(4). For key definitions, see 1–206(6), (15) and (45). Obviously, B may need these documents or their equivalent to obtain possession of the goods.

If the document is *not* negotiable, the person entitled under the document is the "person to whom delivery is to be made by the terms of or pursuant to written instructions. . . ." 7–403(4). If that person, usually called the "consignee," presents proper identification, it may obtain possession of the goods without surrendering the document.

If the document *is* negotiable, i.e., "by its terms the goods are to be delivered to bearer or to the order of a named person," 7–104(1)(a), the person entitled under the document is the "holder." 7–403(4). See 1–201(2). The holder is the person to whom the document has been issued or a person to whom it has been "duly negotiated," by delivery if issued to bearer and by indorsement and delivery if issued to the order of a named person. See 7–501. In order to obtain possession of the goods from the bailee, the "holder" must surrender the negotiable document of title for cancellation. 7–403(3). Until the document is surrendered, therefore, claims to the goods are "locked up" in the document. As the legal embodiment of the goods, the negotiable document can be transferred for value, see 7–502, and used as collateral to secure an extension of credit. See 9–102(1).

We have already explored the seller's obligation to tender delivery when the goods are in the possession of a bailee and documents have been issued. See Ch. 5(D)(1)(c)(2). Similarly, we have examined the tender obligation when the goods are to be shipped and a document of title will be issued by the carrier. Tender in both cases may involve the tender by S of appropriate documents to enable B to obtain possession. See 2–504(b) & 2–503(4)(a).

If the contract or the rules of tender require the delivery of a document, it must be in proper form, 2–503(5), and may be tendered through "customary banking channels." 2–503(5)(b), 2–308(c). If the documentary tender does not conform to the contract, B may reject it. 2–601, 2–512(2). If the tender conforms, S will deliver or negotiate the document to B who, in turn, will take appropriate steps to obtain possession from the carrier.

> **Example V(14):** S sold B factory equipment for $50,000. S agreed to ship the goods to B, but insisted on "payment against documents of title." In essence, B agreed to pay the price upon demand by S's agent

at the place of delivery but before delivery of the goods. S's agent, in turn, agreed to duly negotiate a document of title issued by the carrier to "S or S's order." Under this arrangement, B defaults if payment is not made on demand. But if payment is made, S's agent must duly negotiate the document to B or fail to comply with the requirements for a proper tender of delivery. 2–503(5)(a).

2. QUANTITY

In the well planned, carefully drafted contract, the seller's obligation with regard to quantity should be clearly spelled out in writing. There are two risks in failing to heed this advice.

First, a court might conclude that the parties have failed to agree on the quantity term. Even if they have intended to conclude a contract, the "gap" in agreement cannot easily be filled by some "reasonable" quantity term and the probability is that there is no "reasonably certain basis for giving an appropriate remedy." 2–204(3).

Second, even if there is some agreement on quantity, the statute of frauds provides that the writing signed by the party against whom enforcement is sought is not enforceable as a contract "beyond the quantity of goods shown in such writing." 2–201(1). The risk of perjury over the quantity term prompted the Code drafters to limit enforcement to quantity terms, fairly interpreted, that appear in the signed writing. This sharply limits the admissibility of evidence intended to show a different agreement.

> *Example V(15):* Over the past 10 years, S and B have had successive written contracts for the sale of corn. In no case did the writing state a quantity term. In each case, S tendered and B accepted an amount ranging between 10,000 and 12,000 bushels, approximately 50% of S's output. The same pattern continued in the 11th year, except that S tendered and B rejected 11,000 bushels. B contended that the lack of a quantity term made the contract fatally indefinite or, in the alternative, that the contract was unenforceable under the statute of frauds.
>
> This is a close case, but B is probably wrong on the indefiniteness issue but right on contending that the contract is within the statute of frauds. On the one hand, the course of dealing between the parties provides a basis for interpreting their expressions and conduct, 1–205(1). Course of dealing is normally used to "give particular meaning to and supplement or qualify terms of an agreement." 1–205(3). From this angle, if there is no quantity term in the writing, there is nothing to interpret or supplement. On the other hand, agreement is defined as the "bargain of the parties in fact as found . . . by implication from other circumstances including course of dealing . . ." 1–201(3). Further, "term" means that "portion of an agreement which relates to a particular matter." 1–201(42). The implication

from the course of dealing is that B agreed to buy S's output between 10,000 and 12,000 bushels. This was an implied term. Nevertheless, even though there was agreement, because the quantity term was not "shown in such writing," it appears to be subject to the statute of frauds. 2–201(1).

Of course, if S and B have agreed in writing that S shall sell its "output" to B, 2–306(1), or S is to have discretion to specify quantity, see 2–311(1), the writing contains a quantity term and the statute of frauds is satisfied.

(a) Requirements and Output Contracts

Frequently, the contract will require that the seller supply its "output" or that S meet B's "requirements" over a stated period of time at an agreed price. *Do these contracts fail for indefiniteness? No, because the quantity is measured by the "actual output or requirements as may occur in good faith." 2–306(1). The parties either have actual output or requirements or they don't. If they do, the quantity is measurable and discretion is controlled.*

One can pose and answer three questions about 2–306(1). (1) Does the discretion reserved to seller or buyer to vary actual requirements or output mean that the contract is unenforceable for lack of consideration? No, because the parties must act in "good faith." 2–306(1). Some courts, however, have concluded that an "output" or "requirements" contract is not enforceable unless there is an exclusive dealing feature for all or part of the indefinite quantity. This condition is satisfied if there is a commitment to take from or to supply to the other party all or a definite part of the quantity. For example, B might agree to order 10% of its actual requirements from S.

(2) Does this reserved discretion mean that one party, acting in good faith, can increase or decrease output or requirements to the disadvantage of the other? The answer is no. *In addition to the good faith requirement, Section 2–306(1) also provides that "no quantity unreasonably disproportionate to any stated estimate or in the absence of a stated estimate to any normal or otherwise comparable prior output or requirements may be tendered."* Thus, if the contract estimated S's output at 100,000 units per year and S's actual output in good faith was 200,000 units, B could object to a tender of the larger amount as "unreasonably disproportionate."

(3) Can S or B cease having output or requirements in good faith, even though this action is "unreasonably disproportionate" to prior levels of performance. The answer is yes. If disproportionate output or requirements are neither "tendered or demanded" (because there is nothing to tender or demand), the "unreasonably disproportionate" limitation does not apply and the case rests solely on whether the party acted in good faith. A case so holding is *Empire Gas Corp. v. American Bakeries Co.*, 840 F.2d 1333 (7th Cir.1988).

Here are some additional examples.

Example V(16): B agreed to buy S's output for 5 years at a fixed price. After two years, S ceased manufacturing the goods because the operation was unprofitable. The shut down was probably in bad faith. See Comment 2.

Example V(17): B, a government contractor, agreed to buy its requirements of engine parts from S for 3 years at a fixed price. After the first year, the government terminated B's contract for government convenience (yes, there is such a clause in the standard government contract) and B had no more requirements for parts. B's failure to have actual requirements is in good faith.

Example V(18): B agreed to purchase its annual requirements of fuel oil, but not less than 10,000 gallons, from S for 5 years at a fixed price. In the first year, B ordered 20,000 gallons and in the second year 22,000 gallons were required. During the third year, the market price for fuel oil increased by 75% and B ordered 40,000 gallons. Of that amount, 25,000 gallons were used in B's plant and the balance was sold on the spot market. The quantity demanded was "unreasonably disproportionate" to the prior requirements and S need not comply. Even if B have acted in good faith (a close question), the risk of this disproportionate order should not be imposed on S.

Example V(19): S contracted to supply B, a public utility, with 50% of its output of uranium oxide for 10 years at a fixed price subject to escalation. Three other buyers had contracts for the rest of the output. S's plant had a capacity to produce 300,000 pounds of uranium oxide per year. After 4 years, the market price of UO had dropped to 50% below the fixed floor of contract price. In addition, S had lost its three other buyers and could not replace them. In the fifth year, S tendered and B refused to accept 150,000 pounds of UO, S having produced 300,000 pounds as in prior years. S argued that the amount was not disproportionate to prior years and that the excess UO would be stockpiled until demand increased. B argued that S was unreasonable in operating at full capacity in a collapsed market and that, in any event, the reason for S's conduct was to exploit B, who had agreed to pay the fixed price. According to B, this is bad faith. How should this case be resolved under Section 2–306(1)?

If B still has a need for the quantity tendered and is seeking to avoid the unfavorable price, S, perhaps, should prevail. But suppose B has less requirements. Can S, by maintaining an arguably unreasonable level of output, exploit both the price term and B's declining need for the balance of the contract? Is this conduct bad faith? Such an argument is plausible, but the answer is far from clear under the UCC.

E. SELLER'S OBLIGATION OF QUALITY: HEREIN OF WARRANTY

1. WARRANTY IN GENERAL

A warranty, in general, is the seller's agreement or representation, express or implied, about what the goods or their basic attributes are or for what uses the goods are suitable. Normally, warranties relate to conditions or events beyond the seller's control. Thus, when S says to B, "This race horse is in sound condition," or "This racehorse is especially good on a slow track," she is representing facts that may or may not be true and over which she has little or no control. If the sale is concluded and the delivered horse is not a "racehorse" or has a thrombosis or can't run in the mud, B's expectations will be disappointed and he will want to put the risk of that disappointment on S. Put another way, B will claim that the representations became part of S's legal obligation to B and that the non-conformity entitles B to pursue remedies for breach of warranty.

Whether these representations are part of a seller's contract is a recurring question in commercial and consumer transactions and the matter is frequently litigated. Keep the following points in mind:

First, the Code recognizes three kinds of warranties, an express warranty, 2–313, an implied warranty of merchantability, 2–314, and an implied warranty of fitness for particular purpose, 2–315. There is considerable overlap and frequently all three warranties will be made in the same case.

Second, a general policy is that warranties, whether express or implied, "shall be construed as consistent with each other and as cumulative, but if such construction is unreasonable the intention of the parties shall determine which warranty is dominant." 2–317. Rules for ascertaining that intention are also provided, the most important of which is that "express warranties displace inconsistent implied warranties other than an implied warranty of fitness for a particular purpose." 2–317(c).

Third, the Code recognizes that a warranty made in a particular transaction may be disclaimed or limited by agreement with the buyer, but attempts to regulate the disclaimer process in Section 2–316. Thus, a disclaimer of express warranties is prohibited, 2–316(1), and efforts to disclaim implied warranties must, at the very least, be CONSPICUOUS. 2–316(2). See 1–201(10), defining "conspicuous."

Finally, whether or not a seller's warranty extends beyond its immediate buyer to remote buyers of or persons affected by the goods depends upon the version of Section 2–318 enacted by the state, the willingness of courts to extend warranty liability without the benefit of statute and the scope of strict products liability in the particular jurisdiction.

We will consider some aspects of warranties of quality in this Section. Warranties of title will be considered in Chapter VII(D). *Remember that the "whole purpose of the law of warranty is to determine what it is that the seller has in essence agreed to sell." Section 2–313, Comment 4.*

2. BUYER'S REMEDIES FOR BREACH OF WARRANTY: AN OVERVIEW

If S has made a warranty to B and the tendered goods fail to conform to the contract, the "breach of warranty occurs when tender of delivery is made," 2–725(2), and the Code's four year statute of limitations begins to run. 2–725(1). Upon tender by S, B has a right to inspect the goods. 2–513(1). If the breach is discovered, B may reject the goods under Section 2–601 and pursue the remedies provided for "rightful" rejection in Section 2–711(1). If B accepts the goods, 2–606, with or without discovering the defect, the remedial picture changes. B is liable for the price of the goods accepted and cannot reject them. See 2–607(1) & (2). Furthermore, the "burden is on the buyer to establish any breach with respect to the goods accepted." 2–607(4). But B may be able to revoke his acceptance under Section 2–608. The Section 2–608 pitfalls are infamous, and we will wrestle with them later on. For now remember that if B can successfully revoke acceptance, it has the "same rights and duties with regard to the goods involved as if he had rejected them." 2–608(3). In short, it may pursue the remedies available for justifiable revocation of acceptance under Section 2–711(1).

But suppose B has accepted defective goods and is unable or unwilling to revoke acceptance. Is B barred from any remedy? The answer is no, provided that B has "within a reasonable time after he discovers or should have discovered any breach" notified "the seller of breach." 2–607(3)(a). The measure of damages for a breach with regard to accepted goods is set forth in Section 2–714 and any damages established may be deducted from the contract price. See 2–717. The main point is this: B's remedial options where direct damages are involved vary with whether the goods have been rejected or the acceptance revoked or not. The later the defect is discovered, the less flexibility is found in the remedies. But in any case, the buyer may claim incidental damages under Section 2–715(1) and consequential damages under Section 2–715(2). We will have much more to say about all of this in Chapter VI(D) & (E).

3. EXPRESS WARRANTY
(a) Nature and Scope
The seller may create express warranties in three ways: (1) by affirmations of fact or promises made to the buyer which relate to the goods, 2–313(1)(a); (2) by a description of the goods, 2–313(1)(b); and (3) by displaying a sample or model of the "whole" of the goods. 2–313(1)(c). In each case, the affirmation, description or sample must become "part of the basis of the bargain." It is not necessary that S use "formal words such as 'warrant' or 'guarantee'" or

that it have a "specific intention to make a warranty." 2–313(2). Nor is it necessary that B prove that it relied upon the affirmation, promise, description or sample. The assumption is that the affirmations, descriptions or samples, if made, become part of the basis of B's bargain unless S produces "clear affirmative proof" to the contrary. Comment 3.

However, an "affirmation merely of the value of the goods or a statement purporting to be merely the seller's opinion or commendation of the goods does not create a warranty." 2–313(2). Nevertheless, the assumption is that such affirmations or opinions, if made, become part of the basis of the bargain unless S excludes them by clear evidence. See 2–313, Comment 8.

Here are some examples of these seemingly simple principles in action.

Example V(20): S, a dealer, owned a storage tank containing 50,000 bushels of yellow corn. S, in a signed writing, agreed to sell B 10,000 bushels of "corn" for $2.40 each. Before the contract was signed, S said to B: "This corn is # 1 grade Iowa yellow with no more than 2% mildew." After the contract was signed, S said to B: "This corn will improve the potency of any bull that eats it." S tendered # 2 grade Iowa yellow with 4% mildew and B rejected it. The rejection was proper. S's description of the goods (# 1 grade Iowa yellow) and the affirmation of fact about mildew (no more than 2%), made before the contract was signed, became "part of the basis of the bargain" and created express warranties that the goods would conform to the description and affirmation.

The statement about what the corn would do for bulls, made after the contract was signed, was presumptively part of the basis of the bargain, see 2–313, comment 7. It could be treated as a modification. Ultimately, however, S could exclude it because B should have understood that it was an "affirmation merely of the value of the goods or a statement purporting to be merely the seller's opinion." 2–313(2). In short, the affirmation is a classic example of "puffing" and B would be unreasonable to include it as part of the agreement.

Example V(21): Suppose, in *Example V(20),* that S, before the writing was signed, showed B a bushel of # 1 Yellow corn and stated that "this corn came from my silo." B then purchased 10,000 bushels of "yellow corn from S's silo." S tendered and B rejected a tender of # 2 yellow corn. The rejection was proper. The sample was made "part of the basis of the bargain" and created an "express warranty that the goods shall conform to the description." 2–313(1)(c).

When made, therefore, express warranties place the risk of quality on S even though S was unaware of and had no control over the actual condition of the goods. The more that S says to induce the sale in a context where he speaks as if he had actual knowledge, the greater the probability that the affirmations will become part of the basis of the buyer's bargain. The more general the statements where both are equally ignorant or where B has a superior opportunity to determine quality of the goods, the greater the probability that no express warranty was made. The question is one of fact to be determined in each case.

> ***Example V(22):*** S, a breeder, and B, a dealer, negotiated over the sale of a black angus cow. S stated that, in her judgment, the cow was "with calf." B, after examining the cow and consulting his vet, concurred. The written contract described the goods as a "black angus cow with calf" and B agreed to pay $15,000. After delivery, B discovered that the cow was not with calf and was in fact, barren and worth only $7,500. On the facts, it is doubtful that S's judgment and the contract description became "part of the basis of the bargain:" B had equal information and experience and may have relied upon the judgment of his vet. See 2–313(1). But since both parties assumed that the cow was with calf and both were mistaken, B may be able to avoid the contract on the grounds of "mutual" mistake. See 1–103 and Restatement (Second) Contracts 152 & 154. If and no warranty was made and no mistake can be established, B owes S the full contract price. See 2–709(1)(a).

(b) Disclaimer of Express Warranty

Suppose that S and B entered negotiations for the manufacture of a machine designed to drill a tunnel 17 feet wide in the side of a mountain. A critical question was how fast the machine would drill into the mountain. S's agent, an engineer, stated unequivocally that the machine would drill "at a speed of 2.5' per hour" and this affirmation was repeated in a letter to B from S. Later, B signed a written contract drafted by S which contained, *inter alia,* a warranty that the machine was free from defects in material and workmanship and a statement that the warranty was the "exclusive" express warranty and all other express warranties were "disclaimed." The written contract also contained a "merger" clause, stating in effect, that the writing was the final and exclusive statement of the terms of the agreement. B signed the writing without objection. Later, B discovered that the machine drilled at a rate of 1' per hour and S, despite reasonable efforts, was unable to increase the speed. B now claims that S breached an express warranty that the machine would drill at 2.5' per hour.

In analyzing this problem, the probable solution is as follows.

First, S made orally and in writing an express warranty by affirmation that the machine was suitable for a particular purpose and would perform in a special way. 2–313(1)(a). As such, the affirmation complements the subsequent statement that the machine was free from defects in material and workmanship. See 2–317. Without more, the express warranties are cumulative.

Second, the attempt to disclaim the earlier express warranty by language in the subsequent written contract is arguably not effective. *Section 2–316(1) provides that "words or conduct relevant to the creation of an express warranty and words or conduct tending to negate or limit warranty shall be construed wherever reasonable as consistent with each other; but . . . negation or limitation is inoperative to the extent that such construction is unreasonable."* Thus, if the earlier affirmation became part of the basis of B's bargain, a later negation or disclaimer, no matter how clear or conspicuous, is effective only if consistent with the warranty. There is no consistency here.

Third, the anti-disclaimer policy of 2–316(1) is "subject to the provisions of this Article on parol or extrinsic evidence (Section 2–202) . . . ." *Thus, if the parties intended the writing to be a total integration of the agreement, the earlier express warranty drops out, not because the seller disclaimed it but because both parties intended that the final writing supersede it.* In practice, most courts have upheld the merger clause in commercial cases, suggesting that here the earlier express warranty is outside the scope of the final agreement. Review Chapter V(B)(1), the Parol Evidence Rule.

4. IMPLIED WARRANTY OF MERCHANTABILITY
(a) Scope and Content

Suppose that in a written contract between S and B, the goods are described as "yellow corn." S tendered and B rejected corn 15% of which was mildewed. It is conceded by both parties that the corn conformed to the general contract description, "yellow corn." See 2–313(1)(b). Did S make and breach any other warranty under the Code? The answer is that S probably made and breached an implied warranty of merchantability under Section 2–314. What steps must be taken to support this conclusion?

First, the seller must be a "merchant with respect to goods of that kind." 2–314(1). If S is not a merchant, see 2–104(1), (courts have held that some farmers are not merchants), no implied warranty of merchantability is made. Thus, casual sales are not subject to the requirements of 2–314(1), although any seller can make an express warranty under Section 2–313 or an implied warranty of fitness under Section 2–315.

Second, there must be a contract for the sale of the goods and no effective clause excluding or disclaiming the implied warranty. 2–314(1).

Third, the goods must be unmerchantable. 2–314(2). This is a factual determination that turns on the contract description and circumstances in the commercial setting, including trade usage and the price, and is aided by the guidelines in Section 2–314(2). In our case, yellow corn with 15% mildew would be unmerchantable if it: (1) failed to pass "without objection in the trade under the contract description," 2–314(2)(a); (2) was not, as fungible goods, of "fair average quality within the description," 2–314(2)(c); or (3) was not "fit for the ordinary purposes for which such goods are used." 2–314(2) (c). Section 2–314(2) states what goods "must be" to be merchantable and the burden is on B to prove that they were not at the time of tender. Here are more examples.

Example V(23): Under a contract calling for "10,000 bushels of # 1 yellow corn," S tendered and B rejected 10,000 bushels of # 2 yellow. S made and breached both an express warranty and, if a merchant, the implied warranty of merchantability: the # 2 corn failed to conform to a contract description made part of the basis of the bargain, 2–313(1)(b), and would not "pass without objection in the trade under the contract description." 2–314(2)(a).

Example V(24): S tendered and B accepted yellow corn with 15% mildew under a contract calling for "yellow corn." B, without discovering the mildew, fed the corn to his hogs, some of which became sick and died. To establish breach of the implied warranty of merchantability, B must prove, (a) that feeding hogs was an ordinary purpose for the use of yellow corn, and (b) that yellow corn with 15% mildew was not "fit" for that ordinary purpose.

Example V(25): S, a dealer, sold B, a consumer, a used 1988 automobile described as a "Green Tornado." Beyond the description, no express warranties were given. B immediately drove the car on vacation where, two weeks later, the axle broke on a mountain road. Even though the car was used, S made an implied warranty of merchantability. The standard of fitness, however, is determined by both B's use and what is reasonable to expect for used goods of that age and description.

(b) Disclaimer and Exclusion

The warranty of merchantability is implied from the nature and .description of the goods and "circumstances" in the commercial setting in which they are sold and used. See also, 2–314(3). It establishes what might be called a "bottom line" of quality which a buyer who pays a fair price can reasonably expect. Unlike express warranties, however, there is more room for the disclaimer or exclusion of this warranty under the Code. *The implied warranty of merchantability may be excluded or disclaimed by: (1) B's examination of the goods before entering the contract, 2–316(3)(b); (2) language in the contract for sale, see 2–316(2) & (3)(a); and (3) "course of dealing or course of performance or usage of trade." 2–316(3)(c).*

Example V(26): B, a racehorse owner, examined a horse about to be put up for auction. B found no infirmities and subsequently bought the horse for $5,000. After the sale, B discovered that the horse was lame and, therefore, unmerchantable. If B, before the sale, examined the goods "as fully as he desired," there was "no implied warranty with regard to defects which an examination ought in the circumstances to have revealed to him." 2–316(3)(b). It is a question of fact whether B ought to have discovered the infirmity.

Example V(27): B purchased a new engine for his fishing boat from S. B signed a written contract which, on the front, stated in CONSPICUOUS LANGUAGE that the agreement consisted of the terms on the front and back of the writing. On the back, S, again in CONSPICUOUS LANGUAGE, disclaimed the "implied warranty of merchantability." B later discovered that the engine was not fit for ordinary purposes, and sued S for breach of the implied warranty of merchantability. S argued that the warranty was effectively disclaimed, in that it met the requirements of Section 2–316(2). S may be wrong. Although the language on the back of the writing was CONSPICUOUS and mentioned the word "merchantability" as required by 2–316(2), some courts have required that language or a clearer indication of the disclaimer to be on the front of the writing. Thus, a conspicuous but general reference on the front to the back of the contract, may be inadequate to inform B (and thus avoid unfair surprise) that the "bottom line" warranty of quality has been disclaimed. Other courts have disagreed, however.

Example V(28): S, a used car dealer, sold a used pick-up truck to B, a farmer. The contract for sale stated conspicuously on the front: "THERE ARE NO IMPLIED WARRANTIES. THIS SALE IS 'AS IS, WHERE IS.' " Later, the truck broke down and could not be repaired. The language of the disclaimer does not satisfy the requirements of 2–316(2): it does not mention MERCHANTABILITY." The "AS IS, WHERE IS" language, however, may disclaim the warranty under 2–316(3)(a) if the language "in common understanding calls the buyer's attention to the exclusion of warranties and makes plain that there are no implied warranties." This is most likely to occur in the commercial sale of used goods where there is an established trade usage of which B is aware. See Comment 7. If B is relatively inexperienced or unaware of any usage, a court should be sensitive to the risk of unfair surprise.

Except for the requirements of 2–316(2), there is no special protection in Article 2 for consumers against disclaimers of the implied warranty of merchantability. Consumer buyers are expected to know from the CONSPICUOUS language of 2–316(2) that they assume the risk of unmerchantability. Section 108(a) of the Magnuson–Moss Warranty Act, 15 U.S.C. § 2308(a), however, provides that a supplier who makes a written warranty to a consumer regarding a consumer product cannot "disclaim or modify . . . any implied warranty to a consumer with respect to such consumer product. . . " It is conceivable that § 108 will provide a model for the revision of Article 2.

5. IMPLIED WARRANTY OF FITNESS FOR PARTICULAR PURPOSE
(a) Basis for Implication

The implied warranty of fitness, see 2–315, is the most difficult to establish. Suppose that B, a contractor, needs an industrial glue with sufficient strength to meet a particular set of circumstances. B goes to S, a dealer, and states his requirements in some detail. He asks S: "Can you supply an adhesive strong enough to meet my needs?" S produces a gallon of adhesive, described as E–424, and states: "This will do the trick." If B purchases E–424 and it does not adhere, the probabilities are that S has made and breached an *express* warranty of fitness for particular purpose. 2–313(1)(a). Even though B's needs were unique, there is no need to imply that S agreed to meet them: S has affirmed or promised that the goods will work and these affirmations have become part of the basis of B's bargain.

To vary our example, suppose that after B described his needs and asked whether S had an adhesive strong enough, S simply tendered a gallon of E–424 and said: "Here." There is no express warranty of fitness here and it is probable that the goods conformed to the contract description. See 2–313(1)(b) & 2–314(2)(a). If the glue does not adhere, B's only hope is to establish that S made and breached an implied warranty of fitness for a particular purpose under Section 2–315:

> *Where the seller at the time of contracting has reason to know any particular purpose for which the goods are required and that the buyer is relying on the seller's skill or judgment to select or furnish suitable goods, there is unless excluded or modified under the next section an implied warranty that the goods shall be fit for such purpose.*

On these facts, Section 2–315 has been satisfied: B has communicated sufficient facts about his particular needs to B and S knows that B is relying on his skill and judgment. It is reasonable to imply an undertaking by S to meet those particular purposes from his conduct of furnishing goods without disclaiming or modifying the warranty.

> *Example V(29):* B, a contractor, needs an industrial glue strong enough to meet the demands of a construction project. After consulting a trade journal, B went to S, a glue merchant, and ordered 3 barrels of E–424. The glue did not adhere and B suffered direct and consequential damages. There was no implied warranty of fitness, because B did not rely on S's skill and judgment. Further, S had no information about B's particular needs. If, however, B's needs were the ordinary ones for which E–424 was used, S made and breached and implied warranty of merchantability. 2–314(2)(c). Whether B's needs were "ordinary" or

"particular" and whether the product was fit for those needs are questions of fact to be established by B. 2–607(4). See *Trans–Aire International, Inc. v. Northern Adhesive Co.*, 882 F.2d 1254 (7th Cir.1989), where similar questions were involved.

Example V(30): B installed a new hydraulic system in her sawmill and needed an appropriate lubricant. She described the system to S, an oil dealer, and asked for a recommendation. S asked a few more questions and, without conducting an independent investigation of the system, furnished B with a lubricant without additives. The oil did not work and B suffered direct and consequential damages. Later, it was discovered that the hydraulic system contained a special pump of which neither party was aware and that an oil with a special additive should have been furnished. B clearly relied on S's skill and judgment, but the question is whether S had "reason to know any particular purpose for which the goods are required." 2–315. If, from the information supplied B, S had no reason to know about the special pump in the described system, there is no implied warranty of fitness unless the court imposes the risk of failing to make a further investigation on S. Where S is a merchant and B is not and B is relying on S's skill and judgment, some courts have imposed the risk of imperfect information on S. See *Lewis v. Mobil Oil Corp.*, 438 F.2d 500 (8th Cir.1971).

(b) Exclusion or Disclaimer

The sources of possible exclusion or disclaimer of the implied warranty of fitness are generally the same as the implied warranty of merchantability. Review Chapter V(E)(4)(b). One difference is in the content of the disclaimer language.

Section 2–316(2) provides that to "exclude or modify any implied warranty of fitness the exclusion must be by a writing and conspicuous." Language to exclude all implied warranties of fitness "is sufficient if it states, for example, that 'There are no warranties which extend beyond the description on the face hereof.'" 2–316(2). This language is effective even though it does not mention the word fitness but, of course it would be insufficient to disclaim the implied warranty of merchantability.

Example V(31): S sold B paint which was to be applied to metal through a process involving electrolysis. B explained the process and the need for the paint to be applied evenly and to a specified depth. In the written contract, S expressly warranted that the paint, if applied properly, would achieve results X and Y. Results X and Y were achieved, but result Z, which B wanted most of all, was not. S conceded that there was an implied warranty that the paint was fit to achieve result Z under Section 2–315, but argued that the implied warranty was excluded by the written express warranty as to results X and Y. S is wrong: under

Section 2–317, warranties "whether express or implied shall be construed as consistent with each other and as cumulative, but if such construction is unreasonable the intention of the parties shall determine which warranty is dominant." Arguably, the express warranty and the implied warranty of fitness are consistent and cumulative here. If that interpretation is unreasonable, the intention of the parties is to be determined by the following rule: "Express warranties displace inconsistent implied warranties other than the implied warranty of fitness for a particular purpose." 2–317(c). Clearly, the implied warranty of fitness, if made, survives.

(c) A Final Review Example

Example V(32): S, a manufacturer of steel products, was approached by B, the operator of a large Christmas tree farm, and asked to design a metal collar for a "hoedad," a tool designed to dig a hole to plant a pine seedling. B stated that the tool consisted of a blade, a collar and a wooden handle and that the collar had to be strong enough to withstand the stress of hitting roots, rocks and hard soil. S agreed to the project and, in a short time, had completed a casting, tested a few collars and completed the order, some 5,000 collars. B accepted delivery and distributed the hoedads, with collars, to her three tree farms in the state. In Farm # 1, where the soil was mainly sand and clay, the collar breakage rate was 5%. In Farm # 2, where the soil was mainly hard clay, interspersed with roots and some rocks, the breakage rate was 15%. In Farm # 3, where the soil was hard and rocky, the breakage rate was 30%. B maintains that the breakage rate for collars should never exceed 5%, regardless of the type of soil, and claims that S made and breached express and implied warranties concerning the durability of the collars. What do you think?

6. SCOPE OF WARRANTY PROTECTION

The scope of warranty protection under the Article 2 involves a determination of: (1) the type of warranty, express or implied, made by the seller, (2) the person to whom that warranty is made; and (3) the remedies available for breach of warranty. Thus, S may make an implied warranty of merchantability to its immediate buyer for the breach of which B may recover direct, 2–714(2), incidental, 2–715(1), and consequential damages, which include both damages for loss of bargain, 2–715(2)(a), and damage to person or property "proximately" caused by the breach, 2–715(2)(b).

There are, however, limitations upon the scope of warranty protection built into the Code.

First, as we have seen, a warranty made may be limited or disclaimed by agreement. See 2–316.

Second, as we will see, *infra* at Ch. VI(D)(5), the remedies available for breach of warranty may also be limited by agreement. Thus, damages caused by the breach may be liquidated in advance, 2–718(1), and consequential damages may be excluded altogether. See 2–719(3).

Third, the buyer's claim for breach may be lost because of three failures: (1) failure to prove a breach at the time the goods were tendered, 2–607(4); (2) failure to give notice of breach within a reasonable time after the breach was or should have been discovered 2–607(3)(a) and (3) failure to file the action before the statute of limitations has run, see 2–725.

Fourth, the claim may fail because of lack of privity of contract between the seller and the plaintiff. Put another way, S may persuade the court that its warranty ran only to the immediate buyer of the goods, not a remote buyer down the distributive chain or some other person who used or was affected by them. These limitations, which Dean Prosser called the "intricacies of the law of sales," can undercut the scope of warranty protection.

For now, we will focus upon one "scope" problem, the requirement of privity under the Code, and examine the tension between warranty theory and the developing doctrine of strict products liability.

(a) Extension of Warranties: Section 2–318

Suppose S, a retailer, sold B, a consumer, carpeting manufactured by M. After six months, heavy lines and folds had developed in the carpet and B, without negligence, tripped over a fold and was seriously injured. Under the Code, if the carpeting was unmerchantable and the retailer, S, was a merchant, B would have a breach of warranty claim. B would be able to recover both economic loss, measured by the difference in value between the carpeting as warranted and the carpeting actually received, 2–714(2), and for injury to person "proximately caused" by the breach of warranty, 2–715(2)(b). B might also have a claim in strict products liability for the personal injuries suffered. See Restatement, Second, Torts § 402A.

But suppose that B's friend, C, tripped on the rug and was injured. Would C be able to sue S for breach of warranty and recover for injury to person? Or, suppose that S, the retailer, had gone out of business. Would B be able to sue M, the rug manufacturer, and recover for breach of warranty?

The answer turns in part on which of the three alternative versions of 2–318 the state whose law controls has enacted. If 2–318 extends warranty protection to the plaintiff, the answer is yes. If 2–318 does not extend protection, the answer turns on whether the court is willing to extend warranty protection without the benefit of legislation. Comment 3 states that 2–318 is neutral beyond its scope and is "not intended to enlarge or restrict the developing case law on what the seller's warranties, given to his buyer who resells, extend to other persons in the distributive chain."

Here is how our simple problems would be resolved under the three alternatives to Section 2–318. Assume that M is the manufacturer, S is the retailer, B is the buyer from S and C is a guest in B's home. Assume also that B was not injured in person. Rather, B suffered only economic loss from the unmerchantable carpet. Please read the three Alternatives to 2–318 now. *Remember, even though the particular Alternative may not extend warranty protection, the courts in a particular state may extend it anyway.*

Alternative A: Under Alternative A, M is insulated from liability. M's warranty, if any, extends only to S. Neither B nor C can sue M for breach of warranty. S, however, is vulnerable to both B and C. B, the buyer from S, and C, a natural person, can recover from S for injury to person caused by breach of the implied warranty. C is within the group protected and it is "reasonable to expect that such person may use, consume or be affected by the goods." Note that C can sue S only for injury to person and that S's warranty liability is extended horizontally (to C) not vertically (to a possible subpurchaser from B).

Alternative B: Under Alternative B, C but not B may sue M, a seller, and S, a seller, for breach of implied warranty. B is precluded because he was not "injured in person by breach of warranty." He suffered only economic loss. C, however, is a natural person who could "reasonably be expected to use, consume or be affected by the goods" and was "injured in person by breach of the warranty." Thus, M's warranty is extended directly to C, a non-buyer who was injured in person, but not to B, a buyer from S who suffered only economic loss. B's remedies are exclusively against S.

Alternative C: There are two major expansions of liability under Alternative C: M's warranty extends to (1) "any person" (not any "natural" person) who is (2) "injured by breach of the warranty" (not who is "injured in person" by the breach.) The definition of "person" includes both an "individual and an organization," 1–201(30), and the concept of injury is broad enough to include damage to property and, with some stretching, loss of bargain. Thus B, whether an individual or a corporation, should be able to sue M (or S) for economic losses caused by breach of implied warranty even though there was no privity of contract. Less than 15 states have enacted some version of Alternative C. In other states, Article 2 provides no explicit support for a suit by B against M for economic loss without privity of contract.

Under all Alternatives, 2–318 provides that a seller "may not exclude or limit the operation of this section" where injury to the person of an individual is concerned. Under Alternative C, however, the inference is that the seller can exclude or limit its operation with respect to other types of loss.

Finally, if the plaintiff is within the protection of 2–318 and asserts a claim against a remote seller for breach of warranty, the claim is subject to the normal limitations upon liability imposed by the Code. Thus, the plaintiff must give reasonable notice of the breach, assert the claim before the statute of limitations expires and, if he has agreed, is subject to valid disclaimers and limitations upon remedies.

> *Example V(33):* On July 1, 1990, M, a manufacturer, sold a component for factory equipment to D, a distributor. On August 1, 1990, D resold the component to B, a corporation, and it was installed in B's equipment. The component contained a latent defect that was not reasonably discoverable until September 1, 1994. It is stipulated that the component was unmerchantable and that B has suffered economic loss (but not damage to property) in the amount of $100,000. D, who sold the component to B, has gone out of business. B sued M in warranty and in tort for economic loss, claiming both loss of bargain and consequential damages.

> Depending upon the law of the particular state, the following results are predictable:

> > (1) If Alternative C has *not* been enacted, the warranty claim should be dismissed for lack of privity, unless the court decides to extend it without the benefit of legislation. Most states, however, preserve the privity defense in these cases, reasoning that B should bargain with D for protection. Note that B, a corporation, is a "person" under the UCC. 1–201(30).

> > (2) If Alternative C *has* been enacted or the court extends warranty protection to B, the claim is arguably barred because B failed to give M timely notice, 2–607(3)(a) or because the statute of limitations has run, 2–725(1). M will argue with some plausibility that the cause of action accrued when the component was tendered to D, see 2–725(2), and that M failed to sue within four years of that time.

> > (3) If the court imposes strict liability in tort for economic loss and the tort statute of limitations has not run, the tort claim may succeed. But even though the tort statute of limitations begins to run when the defect was discovered rather than when the goods were tendered, most states have refused to extend the doctrine of strict tort liability to claims for economic loss. An influential case is *East River S.S. Corp. v. Transamerica Delaval, Inc.*, 476 U.S. 858, 106 S.Ct. 2295, 90 L.Ed.2d 865 (1986). The problem with these outcomes is analyzed and a plea for the abolition of the privity defense in economic loss cases is made in Speidel, *Warranty Theory,*

Economic Loss, and the Privity Requirement: Once More Into the Void, 67 B.U.L.Rev. 9 (1987).

(b) The Scope of Strict Tort Liability

The law of strict products liability, influenced by Section 402A of the Restatement (Second) of Torts, imposes liability without regard to privity on the manufacturer or seller of a defective or dangerous product which causes damage to the person or property of a reasonably foreseeable buyer, consumer or person affected by the goods. Again, privity of contract is not required, the plaintiff need not give reasonable notice of the injury, disclaimers and agreed remedies are generally against public policy and the tort statute of limitations applies. Thus, the "intricacies" of the law of sales are not applicable to claims in strict products liability.

The overlap between warranty theory and strict tort arises when the goods sold are unmerchantable and the nonconformity creates a risk of injury to person and property. For example, canned spinach containing ground glass would be both unmerchantable and dangerous. From the plaintiff's standpoint, the claim may sound in warranty (contract), strict products liability (tort), both or neither. Here are some examples that highlight some choices that the plaintiff must make and the tension between the Code and developing tort law. In all cases, assume that the defendant has sold goods which are unmerchantable under Section 2–314 and are dangerously defective under Section 402A.

Case # 1: The state has enacted Alternative A. P, a bystander, is injured when a product manufactured by M, sold to R, a retailer, and resold to C, a consumer, explodes. P does not have a warranty claim under the Code (P is not a person "in the family") but does have a claim in strict tort liability against M and, possibly, R.

Case # 2: Assume, in Case # 1, that the state has enacted Alternative B to Section 2–318 and P, who was injured in person, was either a purchaser from the retailer or a bystander. P's claim is cognizable in both warranty under the Code and strict tort liability. Suppose that the statute of limitations has run under 2–725. If this UCC limitation bars warranty liability, many courts avoid the limitation by applying strict tort theory. The reasoning is that unless the legislature clearly intended to preempt tort law in cases of overlap by enactment of the Code, the plaintiff should be permitted to pursue the theory that offers the greatest protection.

Case # 3: Assume, in Case # 1, that the state has enacted Alternative B to Section 2–318, the plaintiff is a purchaser from the retailer, the dangerous defect has caused only consequential economic loss and P has assented to a clause excluding consequential damages from the scope of either M's or R's liability. P does have a warranty claim against R under the Code but the exclusion clause is probably enforceable. See 2–719(3). P does not have a warranty claim against M (no privity) under Article 2. P does not have a strict tort claim in most states. Even though the defect was dangerous, the only damage was to P's expected profits. The courts have reasoned that this interest is more appropriate for resolution by contract rather than tort principles and, consequently, the Code should apply. If neither Code nor Tort law permits relief, P assumes the risk in the transaction.

Here by way of summary is a final example.

Example V(34): M, a manufacturer, sold goods to D, a distributor. D resold the goods to B as equipment for use in its factory. The goods were unmerchantable and caused damage to B's property, lost profits while repairs were being made and personal injuries to E, an employee.

(1) In most states, B can recover the property damage but not the lost profits in tort. In a few states, however, the combination of property damage and loss profits justifies a tort claim.

(2) Under the UCC, B can recover nothing from M under Alternatives A and B to Section 2–318 (B was not injured in "person"), but can recover all losses if Alternative C were enacted and the word "injury" is given a broad meaning.

(3) E, the employee, could recover damages against M in strict tort or damages for personal injuries in warranty under Alternatives B and C to Section 2–318. See 2–715(2)(b), which permits the recovery of "injury to person or property proximately resulting from any breach of warranty."

How and why these somewhat arbitrary lines are drawn is a matter of some academic debate and varies from state to state.

F. BUYER'S OBLIGATIONS

The general obligation of the buyer is to "accept and pay in accordance with the contract." 2–301. Unless otherwise agreed, the duty to accept and to pay arises upon tender of delivery by the seller: "Tender entitles the seller to acceptance of the goods and to payment according to the contract." 2–507(1). We will organize the discussion of the timing and content of these duties around three headings, Price, Acceptance and Payment.

1.   PRICE TO BE PAID

(a)   What Is the Price?

The price to be paid by B is, in essence, the consideration for S's transfer and delivery of the goods. 2–106(1). The price can be made payable in money, see 1–201(24), goods or an interest in realty. 2–304. *Normally, the price will be payable in money and the amount will be fixed in the agreement. Depending on the circumstances, B may agree to pay a fixed price, a price to be determined by some external standard or agency, a fixed-price subject to escalation or a price to be fixed by S. Occasionally, the parties will conclude the agreement and intend to be bound without fixing the price.* In "such a case the price is a reasonable price at the time for delivery if (a) nothing is said as to price. . . ." 2–305(1)(a). Unlike the quantity term, a gap in the agreement on price can be filled by resort to reliable market prices or other evidence of reasonable costs and profit.

(b)   Risk Allocation

The price is one method by which the parties allocate the risks of market change over the term of the contract. In a fixed price contract, B must pay the agreed price even though the market price has dropped or S's production costs have decreased. In an "open-price" contract, B pays the going rate at the time of delivery and in escalation contracts, B's price may vary around a fixed amount depending upon S's production costs or other cost indices. These pricing techniques benefit S as well, and are frequently the subject of intense bargaining.

> ***Example V(35):*** S and B entered into a five year contract under which S was to supply 1,000 units per year and B was to pay $50 per unit. In the third year of the contract, a mild recession developed. S's production costs dropped to $25 per unit and B could purchase the same goods on the open market for $22 per unit. The fixed-price allocated the risk of these changes to B and, unless both parties agree to a modification, B must pay for 1,000 units at $50 per for the balance of the contract. See 2–615(a).

Another risk is that the pricing technique agreed at the time of contracting may fail during performance. Suppose that the price was to be determined by a formula based upon data contained in indices published by X, a trade publication. Suppose, further, that X suspended publication and the agreement did not provide an alternative price. *If the parties did not intend to be bound "unless the price be fixed or agreed and it is not fixed or agreed there is no contract." 2–305(4). The relationship is terminated, subject to liability for goods already delivered. If the parties intended to contract "even though the price is not settled," the price is a "reasonable price at the time for delivery." 2–305(1)(c).* In this situation, Section 2–305(1) fills the gap with a price that balances the supply-demand risk between the parties. Whether the market goes up or down, a "reasonable price at the time for delivery" follows the fluctuations without giving either party an advantage. An important case involving these issues is *Oglebay Norton Co. v. Armco, Inc.,* 52 Ohio St.2d 232, 556 N.E.2d 515 (1990).

Example V(36): In a contract for sale of manufactured goods, the price was to be "fixed by the buyer" between an agreed minimum and maximum from production cost data to be supplied by the seller. If S fails to supply the data, B may, at his option, either cancel the contract for breach or fix a reasonable price. 2–305(3). If S supplies the necessary data, B must fix the price in good faith. 2–305(2). See 2–311.

Example V(37): S and B, with intent to contract, conclude a contract for sale and leave the price "to be agreed in the future." Both parties are obligated to negotiate in good faith to reach an agreed price. If, after good faith negotiations, they fail to agree and both intended to be bound even though the price was not agreed, the price is a "reasonable price at the time for delivery." 2–305(1)(b). The parties' intention is a question of fact to be determined from their words, conduct and other commercial circumstances.

2. ACCEPTANCE OF THE GOODS

Three problems arise in connection with the buyer's duty to accept the goods: (1) how broad is B's right to inspect the goods, 2–503; (2) what is an acceptance, 2–606; and (3) what is the effect of acceptance, see 2–607.

(a) Right to Inspect the Goods

Suppose that S, after making a proper tender of delivery, demands that B accept and pay for the goods. This demand is premature, for unless otherwise agreed, B has a "right before payment or acceptance to inspect them at any reasonable place and time and in any reasonable manner." 2–513(1). Inspection expenses are to be borne by B unless the goods are nonconforming and B rejects them, whereupon they may be recovered from S. The parties may fix the scope, place or method of inspection by agreement and this is "presumed to be exclusive." 2–513(4). But unless otherwise expressly agreed, this "fixing" does not postpone identification or shift the place of delivery or for passing the risk of loss." 2–513(4).

The right of inspection is important, for if a nonconformity is discovered, B has an opportunity either to seek a "cure" of the defect from S, 2–508, or to reject the goods, 2–601, and pursue remedies for breach of contract under 2–711(1). Although the time and place for inspection are normally when and where the tender of delivery is made, Section 2–513(1) provides that when the seller is "required or authorized to send the goods to the buyer, the inspection may be after their arrival."

> *Example V(38):* S agreed to ship the goods to B, FOB the point of shipment. See 2–319(1)(a). S delivered nonconforming goods to the carrier and, when they arrived, B inspected, found the defect and rejected them. S argued that B should have inspected the goods at the point of shipment and that by failing to exercise its right of inspection, B accepted the goods. 2–606(1)(b). S is wrong: B may inspect the goods "after their arrival." 2–513(1).

The agreement could provide that B had no right to inspect the goods *before* the duty to pay for them arose. Typical clauses with this effect provide for "delivery C.O.D." or for "payment against documents of title." 2–513(2). In these cases, B must pay first and inspect later. If the later inspection reveals nonconformities, B may still reject the goods and pursue remedies for breach under Section 2–711. See 2–512(2). But the advantage of withholding payment until quality is ascertained has been lost. If, however, the nonconformity of the goods "appears without inspection," the buyer may refuse to make payment. 2–512(1)(a).

> *Example V(39):* S, a fruit grower, shipped a box of pears to B by United Parcel Service "Cash on Delivery." Upon delivery, UPS demanded payment before inspection. The box, however, was stained with juice and the air reeked of spoiled pears. B may refuse to pay without breaching the contract, for the nonconformity of the goods "appears without inspection." 2–512(1)(a).

One last point. If the contract requires the seller to deliver documents, such as a warehouse receipt, S must "tender all such documents in correct form." 2–503(5)(a). Presumably, B may inspect the documents and reject the tender if it fails to conform to the contract. See 2–601.

(b) **What Is an Acceptance?**
Section 2–606 governs the question, "when does the buyer accept tendered goods?"

Two forms of acceptance depend upon affirmative conduct by B. Thus, if B has had a reasonable opportunity to inspect and "signifies to the seller that the goods are conforming or that he will take or retain them in spite of their nonconformity," B has accepted them. 2–606(1)(a). Or if B, with or without inspection, destroys the goods with an ax, that act, which is "wrongful against the seller," is an acceptance "only if ratified by the seller." 2–606(1)(c). Otherwise, S may pursue remedies for tort.

The third and most prevalent form of acceptance turns upon inaction by B. Thus, if B, after a "reasonable opportunity to inspect," "fails to make an effective rejection," an acceptance has occurred. 2–606(1)(a). An "effective rejection" occurs when B has notified S of the rejection "within a reasonable time after their delivery or tender." 2-602(1). In this situation, B has little middle ground between rejection and acceptance after it has had a reasonable opportunity to inspect. Failure to reject is an acceptance, whereupon the duty to pay for the goods under the contract arises. 2-607(1).

> *Example V(40):* B purchased a race horse warranted by S to be "sound" at an auction and, without inspecting the goods, shipped the horse by van to his stables. The next morning B and his trainer inspected the horse and found a broken shin bone. B attempted to reject the horse in a telephone call to S, but S insisted that B had accepted the horse and must pay. S is correct on the acceptance issue if it is determined, as a matter of fact, that a reasonable time for inspection occurred between the time the horse was tendered to B and the time it was put on the van. The failure to reject the goods at the end of that time amounts to an acceptance. 2-606(1)(b). B, however, might still revoke acceptance and avoid liability for the price if timely notice of breach was given, 2-607(3)(a), and the conditions for revocation in 2-608 are satisfied.

> *Example V (41):* B, a corporation, purchased 25 pieces of furniture from S for a newly refurbished conference room. The suite was regarded as a "commercial unit" in the trade, i.e., a "unit of goods as by commercial usage is a single whole for purposes of sale and division of which materially impairs its character or value on the market or in use." 2-105(6). S tendered the suite and B, after inspection, indicated that it would take 10 of the pieces and reject the rest for nonconformity. B has accepted the entire suite of furniture: "Acceptance of a part of any commercial unit is acceptance of that entire unit." 2-606(2). See 2-601(c).

(c) Effect of Acceptance

What effect does acceptance of the goods have on B's rights and remedies. A brief listing of these important consequences will suffice for now.

> *First,* B must "pay at the contract rate for any goods accepted." 2-607(1). This result is confirmed in 2-709(1)(a).

> *Second,* risk of loss passes from S to B even though the goods are nonconforming. 2-510(1).

> *Third,* B can no longer reject the goods. 2-607(2).

> *Fourth,* B must "within a reasonable time after he discovers or should have discovered any breach notify the seller of breach or be barred from any remedy." 2-607(3)(a).

Fifth, the burden is on B to "establish any breach with respect to the goods accepted." 2-607(4).

Finally, B's remedies will be more limited. It is, for example more difficult for B to revoke acceptance under 2-608 than to reject a nonconforming tender under Section 2-601. Further, if revocation of acceptance is not possible, B is limited to damages for breach with regard to accepted goods under Section 2-714 rather than the broader remedial options available upon rejection or revocation of acceptance. See 2-711(1). Finally, B could be barred from any remedy for failing to give prompt notice under 2-607(1)(a).

Example V(42): In *Example V(40),* if B accepted the horse by failing to reject within a reasonable time, the burden of proving "any breach with respect to the goods accepted" is on B, 2-607(4), and the breach of warranty, if any, occurred at the tender of delivery. 2-725(2). If B is unable to produce sufficient credible evidence on the condition of the horse at that time, the breach of warranty claim will fail.

3. PAYMENT

The time, place and method of payment are important to the allocation of credit risks and the determination of transaction costs. In the usual case, S tenders the goods to B, B tenders payment in cash or by check to S and the exchange occurs. Neither party extends credit to the other and the exchange costs are minimal.

The agreement, of course, can provide that payment will be made before or after the tender of delivery and specify how payment is to be made, i.e., in cash, by check, by letter of credit or "against documents of title." Agreements of this sort provide that one party will extend credit to the other and, depending upon delays and the complexity of payment arrangements, increase costs. In this subsection, we will examine, briefly, when and where payment is due and some common methods of payment.

(a) When and Where Due

In the absence of contrary agreement, when and where payment is due is determined by Section 2-310. *The general rule is that payment is "due at the time and place at which the buyer is to receive the goods even though the place of shipment is the place of delivery." 2-310(a).* Thus, if the shipment is FOB place of shipment and S has delivered the goods to the carrier under Section 2-504, payment is due when the goods arrive at their destination. *If delivery is "authorized and made by way of documents of title . . . then payment is due at the time and place at which the buyer is to receive the documents regardless of where the goods are to be received." 2-310(c).* Thus, if the goods are in a warehouse in Pittsburgh and B is to receive a negotiable warehouse receipt in Cincinnati, payment is due when the document is tendered in Cincinnati. See also 2–310(b) and 2–505, dealing with shipments under reservation.

> ***Example V(43):*** B agreed to pay $10,000 for goods which S promised to ship FOB point of shipment before October 1. Later, S demanded that B tender payment at the point of shipment. S is wrong. Even though S must tender delivery at the point of shipment, see 2–504, B need not tender payment until the goods have arrived at their destination and B has inspected them. See 2–513(1). Whether B must pay before getting the goods depends upon the arrangement between S and the carrier.

(b) Method of Payment

Questions concerning the method of payment are distinguishable from questions of when or where payment is to be made. Method involves two aspects, (1) what is tendered in payment, e.g., money or a check, and (2) the arrangement facilitating that payment, e.g., a letter of credit. We will briefly treat three methods of payment: by check; against documents of title; and by letter of credit.

(1) By Check

B's tender of payment is "sufficient when made by any means or in any manner current in the ordinary course or business." 2–511(2). This normally would include a check, which is a "draft drawn on a bank and payable on demand," 3–104(f) (1990 Official Text), and might include drafts drawn on corporations or individuals. S, however, may demand payment in legal tender and must give B "any extension of time reasonably necessary to procure it." 2–511(2). The check, however, is conditional payment. If the check is paid by the drawee bank when presented by S for payment, B's obligation on the check (and the underlying obligation) is discharged. If the check is dishonored (not paid) by the drawee bank, then payment is "defeated as between the parties." S, at a minimum, can then sue B on either the check or the underlying obligation. 2–511(3). See 3–310 (1990 Official Text).

(2) Against Documents of Title

Payment "against documents of title" is a method required by the agreement which enables S, in shipment contracts, to get payment when the documents are tendered rather than when the goods arrive at the destination. To this extent, B extends credit to S because it must pay before the goods arrive and it has a chance to inspect them. See 2–513(3). By this device, or some reasonable variation, S delivers the goods to the carrier and obtains a negotiable bill of lading to "S or his order." S then draws a draft on B which orders B (who owes S the price) to pay "S or his order" the agreed price on presentation of the draft ("on sight"). S then empowers a bank or other agent to act on its behalf and sends both the bill of lading and sight draft to B through usual banking channels. On presentation of the draft by the agent, B is expected to pay the stated amount (by check or cash). At this point, the agent negotiates the bill of lading to B, who then becomes the person entitled under the document. When the goods arrive, B goes to the carrier with the document and surrenders it for the goods. If B fails to pay the draft upon "sight" it breaches the contract and S, in theory, can stop delivery. See 2–705. If S attempts to obtain payment against documents without authorization in the contract, S is in breach.

(3) By Letter of Credit

Letters of credit, which are governed by Article 5 of the UCC, are important documents in transactions where credit is extended and in contracts for the sale of goods where S desires to obtain payment for goods shipped to a distant B at or shortly after the time of shipment. Review the transaction described in Chapter II(D)(4). Note that the issuing bank and its correspondent are committed to B, who has given value, to make the payment to S upon presentation of the documents in proper form as required by the letter of credit. With limited exceptions, the bank must pay when the documents conform to the contract even though it knows that the goods are nonconforming or that B's financial situation is deteriorating.

G. RISK OF LOSS

The problem can be simply stated. S contracts to sell described goods to B. After identification to the contract, the goods are totally or partially destroyed without the fault or negligence of either party. S, claiming that the risk of loss has passed to B, seeks to recover the price. 2–709(1)(a). If this claim is valid, B must pay S and seek indemnification from its insurance company. If the risk has not passed, S must seek indemnification from his insurance company and may still have an obligation to deliver conforming goods to B. See 2–613. If the party upon whom the risk falls is not insured (but could or should be) the economic impact is severe. The value of the goods is lost, yet contractual obligations are, in most cases, not discharged. How are these questions resolved under Article 2?

The answers, which are found in Sections 2–509 and 2–510, do not depend upon which party has title to the goods. See 2–401. Nor does the answer turn on whether B has a special property interest in the goods, although there is an insurable interest in them upon identification. 2–501(1). Rather, the Article 2 answer turns upon two practical considerations: (1) Which party, S or B, is in control of the goods and thereby in the "best" position to prevent the loss, and (2) Which party, S or B, is in the "best" position, cost considered, to insure against the loss? Presumably, the answer to both questions turns on who has possession or access to possession of the goods and this is the undergirding principle of 2–509. Put differently, Article 2's risk of loss rules turn, in most cases, upon which party has possession of the goods unless the parties have agreed to the contrary. 2–509(4).

The risk of loss rules are not unduly complicated and can be illustrated by considering, (1) the risk of loss in the absence of breach, 2–509, and, (2) the effect of breach on risk of loss, 2–510.

1. RISK OF LOSS IN THE ABSENCE OF BREACH

Section 2–509 contemplates three risk of loss patterns: (1) the contract "requires or authorizes the seller to ship the goods by carrier," 2–509(1); (2) the goods are "held by a bailee to be delivered without being moved," 2–509(2); and (3) other cases not within the first two patterns. As we shall see, risk of loss in the absence of breach by S will normally pass before B has accepted the goods. Compare 2–510(1). See 2–709(1)(a). Also, the provisions of Section 2–509 are "subject to contrary agreement of the parties." 2–509(4).

(a) Shipment Contracts

Where the contract requires or authorizes the seller to ship the goods by carrier, when the risk passes turns on whether the contract requires S to "deliver them at a particular destination" or not. 2–509(1)

If so, and this would normally be indicated by the term "F.O.B. the place of destination," see 2–319(1)(b), risk passes "when the goods are there duly so tendered as to enable the buyer to take delivery." 2–509(1)(b). Due tender, in turn, depends upon whether S has met the requirements of Section 2–503(3).

If not, and this would normally be indicated by the term "F.O.B. the place of shipment," 2–319(1)(a), risk passes "when the goods are duly delivered to the carrier even though the shipment is under reservation . . . ." 2–509(1)(a). Due delivery, in turn, depends upon whether S has "put the goods in the possession of . . . a carrier" and otherwise complied with Section 2–504.

These delivery terms in 2–319, along with those in 2–320 through 2–322, are customarily understood to define whether S must deliver the goods at a particular destination or not. *The "point of origin" contract, however, is regarded "as the 'normal' one and the 'destination' contract as the variant type." 2–503, Comment 5. In the absence of a well understood delivery term which obligates the seller to deliver to a particular destination, S must specifically agree to undertake that obligation and, thereby, retain the risk of loss beyond delivery to the carrier.*

> ***Example V(44):*** S agreed to ship the goods to B "FOB point of destination." Conforming goods were delivered to the carrier and, upon arrival at the destination, Carrier, upon instructions from S, notified B at 4 PM that the goods had arrived and could be picked up at C's place of business. B arrived at 9 AM the next morning to take delivery and

discovered that the goods had been destroyed by fire during the night. Assuming that S has duly tendered so to enable B to take delivery of the goods, see 2–509(3), risk of loss passed to B at 4 PM before actual delivery. B, therefore, is liable to S for the price, 2–709(1)(a). B's insurance company, upon paying B, may have a claim by subrogation against C if C is liable to B for the loss.

Example V(45): S agreed to ship the goods to B "C.I.F.," which means that the price "includes in a lump sum the cost of the goods and the insurance and freight to the named destination." 2–320(1). S duly delivered the goods to the carrier under Section 2–320(2) but before they arrived at the destination they were destroyed by fire while still in the possession of the carrier. The risk of loss is on B: The "C.I.F." contract, although imposing greater obligations on S regarding shipment, is a point of origin rather than a destination contract. Comment 1, 2–320.

Example V(46): In the contract for sale, S agreed to "ship the goods to B" and to pay the "cost of shipment." Without more, this is not a destination contract. S must specifically agree to deliver the goods to a particular destination and, thus, retain the risk until that time, and an agreement to pay the cost of shipment to B is not such a specific agreement. Comment 5, 2–503.

Although the word "carrier" in 2–509(1) is not defined, it is commonly understood that it does not include transport facilities, such as delivery trucks, operated by the parties. The term clearly includes independent carriers, whether on land, sea or in the air, and, perhaps even the U.S. Mail. See White & Summers, Uniform Commercial Code 220 (3d ed. 1990).

(b) Goods in Possession of Bailee

At the time of contracting, the goods may be in the possession of a warehouseman who has issued a document of title or some other party who holds them as a bailee. If the goods are to be delivered "without being moved," that is, B is to go to the bailee and take delivery, risk of loss is determined under Section 2–509(2). To put the matter more concretely, suppose the goods are destroyed between the time of contracting and the time when B was to take delivery. Who bears the risk? Consider these examples.

Example V(47): At the time of contracting, the goods are in the possession of a carrier who has issued a negotiable warehouse receipt to "S or order." Here risk of losses passes to B "on his receipt of a negotiable document of title covering the goods," 2–509(2)(a), or "on acknowledgment by the bailee of the buyer's right to possession of the goods." 2–509(2)(b). Although it is not clearly stated, one would expect B to receive a negotiable document "duly negotiated" to B or his order and C to be reluctant to acknowledge B's right to possession before the negotiable document, properly indorsed, is presented by B.

Example V(48): At the time of contracting, the goods are in the possession of a warehouse which has issued a non-negotiable warehouse receipt. Here risk of loss passes to B either upon "acknowledgment by the bailee of the buyer's right to possession of the goods," 2–509(2)(b), or "after his [B's] receipt of a non-negotiable document of title or other written direction to delivery. . . ." 2–509(2)(c).

In the former case, 2–509(2)(b) does not explicitly say that the bailee's acknowledgment must be made to B. This is the clear implication, however, and at least one well-reasoned case has so held. See *Jason's Foods, Inc. v. Peter Eckrich & Sons, Inc.,* 774 F.2d 214 (7th Cir.1985).

In the latter case, risk of loss remains on S until B "has had a reasonable time to present the document or direction and a refusal by the bailee to honor the document or to obey the direction defeats the tender." 2–503(4)(b).

Example V(49): S sold his horse Bozo to B for $500. At the time of the sale, Bozo was at the blacksmiths getting a new pair of shoes. (By Gucci, no doubt.) S telephoned the blacksmith, and stated: "Leon, I've just sold old Bozo to my friend Bill. When he comes by to get the horse, you give her to him. OK?" Leon, who had already been paid for his services, replied: "I reckon so." Later, before Bill took possession, Bozo was killed when kicked in the head by another horse. The risk remains on S. Although Leon, a bailee, acknowledged B's right to possession of the goods, the acknowledgment was made to S, not B. As such, B had no opportunity to take possession or to obtain insurance before the loss.

In *Example 48,* the warehouseman is a "bailee" within the definition in Article 7. See 7–102(1)(a). In *Example 49,* Leon is a common law bailee. There is no other Code definition of bailee.

(c) Other Situations

Section 2–509(3) provides that in "any case not within subsection (1) or (2), the risk of loss passes to the buyer on his receipt of the goods if the seller is a merchant; otherwise the risk passes to the buyer on tender of delivery." Thus, if S is in control of the goods and is *not* to ship or send them to B, the first question is whether S is a merchant. See 2–104(1). If so, the risk passes when B receives the goods, i.e., takes physical possession of them. See 2–103(1)(c). If not, the risk passes when S tenders delivery by complying with Section 2–503(1). According to Comment 3 to 2–509, the "underlying theory of this rule is that a merchant who is to make physical delivery at his own place continues meanwhile to control the goods and can be expected to insure his interest in them. The buyer, on the other hand, has no control of the goods and it is extremely unlikely that he will carry insurance on goods not yet in his possession."

> *Example V(50):* S, a manufacturer, contracted to sell machinery to B, delivery by October 1. It was understood that when the goods were ready, S would notify B and B would send an agent to pick them up at S's plant. On September 24, S tendered delivery as required by Section 2–503(1). On September 25, B arrived with a truck to take possession and was informed that the goods, which had been identified to the contract, were destroyed by fire the night before. Since S is a merchant, the risk of loss had not passed to B even though a tender of delivery had been made. B, therefore, is not liable for the price.
>
> If, however, S is not a merchant, the risk passes to B upon tender of delivery on September 24. This result is questionable, since S, merchant or not, is still in control of the goods and is more likely to have insurance than B.

Another case where special rules for risk of loss apply is the "sale of approval" and "sale or return." See 2–509(4). In the former case, the goods are delivered "primarily for use" by B and, if not approved, may be returned "even though they conform to the contract." 2–326(1)(a). In this case, the risk of loss does not pass to B until the goods are accepted. 2–327(1)(a). In the latter case, the goods are delivered "primarily for resale" and, if not resold, can be returned even though they conform to the contract. 2–236(1)(b). Section 2–327(2)(b) provides that in a sale or return, the "return is at the buyer's risk and expense" and Comment 3 to Section 2–327 provides that "in a sale or return the risk remains throughout on the buyer."

A consignment, however, is neither a sale on approval nor a sale or return. Rather, S delivers goods to an agent with power to sell them in the ordinary course of business to B. The consignment, however, is treated as a sale or return when claims are asserted to the goods by the agent's creditors. See 2–326(3). It is not clear whether the consignment should be treated as a sale or return for purposes of risk of loss. As a matter of policy, the answer should be yes: the agent has possession and an insurable interest and can readily insure to protect his and S's interest. As a matter of practice, who should insure what interests and who has what risk of loss are usually worked out in the consignment agreement.

(d) Effect of Agreement

The risk of loss rules in Section 2–509 are based upon a practical judgment about who is in the best position or is most likely to insure and, where common delivery terms are employed, commercial understanding about who is required to bear the risk. *Section 2–509(4) provides, however, that the*

*"provisions of this section are subject to contrary agreement of the
parties. . . ." According to Comment 5, the word "contrary" should be
equated to the phrase "unless otherwise agreed" and the parties are "free to
readjust their rights and risks as declared in this section in any manner
agreeable to them."* Thus, the parties might agree that in an "FOB
shipment" contract S bears the risk until B takes possession at the point of
delivery, or that risk passes to B upon tender of delivery in a sale or return.
Similarly, the parties might agree that the risk of loss on goods in the
possession of a bailee passes at the time of contracting, even though the
bailee has issued a negotiable document of title. If the agreement is clear and
the party with the risk has an insurable interest and can purchase adequate
insurance coverage, it should be enforced.

The limitations on agreement, not clearly spelled out in Section 2–509, must
be inferred from the underlying policies. Thus, if B agrees to assume the risk
of loss of goods in which he has no insurable interest or in a case where B
must pay a prohibitive cost for insurance while S can obtain it with ease, a
court might be justified in denying enforcement, especially if there were
elements of unconscionability at the time of contracting.

2. EFFECT OF BREACH ON RISK OF LOSS

(a) Breach by Seller

The risk of loss rules in Section 2–509 are also subject to Section 2–510,
which deals with the effect of breach by either party on who bears the risk.
2–509(4). Suppose that S agreed to sell B #1 grade yellow corn and to ship
it "FOB point of shipment." S ships in compliance with Section 2–504 but
the corn delivered to the carrier is unmerchantable. During shipment, the
corn is destroyed in a derailment. Does B have the risk of loss? The answer
is no. *Section 2–510(1) provides that where a "tender or delivery of goods so
fails to conform to the contract as to give a right of rejection the risk of their
loss remains on the seller until cure or acceptance."* Thus, if the corn was
unmerchantable at the time of tender of delivery and if B could have rejected
it under Section 2–601, the risk remains on S.

Suppose, however, that B had accepted the unmerchantable corn at the point
of shipment and the loss occurred before arrival. Here the risk of loss is on
B, 2–510(1), unless B has rightfully revoked the acceptance under Section
2–608 before the loss occurs. *In this case, he may, "to the extent of any
deficiency in his effective insurance coverage treat the risk of loss as having
rested on the seller from the beginning." 2–510(2). According to Comment 3,
"deficiency" means "such deficiency in the insurance coverage as exists
without subrogation." Section 2–510 "merely distributes the risk of loss as
stated and is not intended to be disturbed by any subrogation of an insurer."*

Example V(51): S delivered unmerchantable corn to a carrier in an
FOB Shipment contract. The contract price was $10,000 and the value of

the non-conforming corn delivered was $7,500. B, through an agent, accepted it at the point of shipment.

(1) Upon acceptance of non-conforming goods, the risk of loss passes to B. 2–510(1). If the goods are later destroyed, B must pay S the contract price, $10,000, adjusted for the difference in value between the goods as warranted and the goods received, some $2,500, for S's breach of warranty. See 2–714(2) & 2–717. If B is insured, it should collect the value of the goods lost from Insurer, who might then pursue a subrogation claim against Carrier. Note that B's damage remedies are preserved even though risk of loss has passed.

(2) If B rightfully revoked acceptance before but was still in possession when the goods were lost, the question under 2–510(2) is whether there is any "deficiency in his effective insurance coverage." If not, he must pay the adjusted contract price of $7,500 to S. If so, then B may, "to the extent of any deficiency . . . treat the risk of loss as having rested on the seller from the beginning." Put differently, the deficiency, if any, is a further offset from the value of the goods. Thus, if B had no insurance there would be no liability for the value of the goods (the deficiency is $7,500) and if the insurance covered 50% of the loss ($3,750) the adjusted value would be reduced by 50%.

(3) If B has a deficiency and S was not insured, the loss stops there. If S is insured, Insurer must pay S to the extent required by the policy. But Insurer has no claim by subrogation against B: once the risk of loss is determined under Section 2–510, it cannot be reallocated or "disturbed" through subrogation.

In sum, if the destroyed goods with defects were worth $7,500 (B's liability to S) and B's deficiency in insurance was 50%, B should pay S $3,750. Since S has the risk of loss for the deficiency, S's insurer should also pay S $3,750. That payment makes S whole and leaves the loss on the insurer.

(b) Breach by Buyer

What about breaches by B? *Section 2–510(3) provides that where B repudiates or is otherwise in breach "as to conforming goods already identified to the contract for sale" before "risk of loss has passed to him," the seller may "to the extent of any deficiency in his effective insurance coverage treat the risk of loss as resting on the buyer for a commercially reasonable time."* The classic cases here involve situations where S, still in possession of identified goods, has tendered delivery under Section 2–503(1) and B either repudiates the contract or delays unreasonably in taking delivery. If the loss occurs within a commercially reasonable time thereafter and S is not fully insured, S, apparently, can recover the deficiency from B and B's insurer, if B was insured, is denied subrogation. In this case, at least, there is some causal connection between B's delay and the risk of loss.

In sum, Section 2–510 is distressingly vague when the questions of remedy and subrogation arise and does not seem to have had much impact on insurance practice. More importantly, if Section 2–509 has developed risk of loss rules based upon assumptions about who is in the best position to insure, one wonders why the risks are reallocated because a breach by one party reveals a deficiency in coverage by the other. Unless the purpose is to punish or to deter breach, with the ultimate costs allocated to insurers who are denied subrogation, the fact of breach alone is not a key factor in assessing relative capacities to insure. A possible solution is to provide that the fact of breach is irrelevant to risk of loss unless the breach is some way contributed to the loss. If there is no casual connection, the risk of loss rules in 2–509 should apply and the remedies of S and B for breach should not be impaired. Compare Article 70 of CISG.

3. RISK OF LOSS AND INSURANCE

An underlying assumption is that when the risk of loss is allocated by Section 2–509 or agreement to S or B, that party will be able to purchase insurance against the risk. Put another way, the burden is on the party with the risk of loss to insure and the failure to do so means that the loss must be met from corporate rather than insurance company assets. Thus, the party with the risk of loss and an insurable interest in the goods must purchase a policy which effectively covers the risk, whether that be a standard fire policy or more particularized contracts, such as a Manufacturer's Output Policy or an "All Risks" transportation form.

If a policy is purchased and a risk occurs within its scope, the insurance company, assuming that all other conditions are satisfied, must pay that loss and no more. The policy indemnifies the insured against actual loss. The proceeds of the policy, therefore, replace the lost interest in the goods. If the risk was on B, the proceeds might be used to pay the contract price. If the risk was on S, the proceeds might be used to purchase replacement goods to be delivered to B under the contract.

The more complicated questions involve the rights of Insurers after they have paid the actual losses suffered by their insureds. To what extent can Insurer, by being subrogated to the claims of the insured against third parties, recover all or part of the payment made? Suppose there are two or more insurance companies which have insured the same loss. If they are not parties to the same contract, how are problems of excess insurance (the avoidance of windfalls) to be worked out?

Finally, what about the relationship between the insurer of S or B and the insurer of a carrier who is liable for the loss to either the consignor or consignee? The answers to these questions, which involve principles of insurance law, and the state and federal statutes governing carrier liability, are beyond the scope of this

BLACK LETTER. For discussion, see R. Keeton & A. Widiss, Insurance Law (2d ed. 1988); Sorkin, *Allocation of the Risk of Loss in the Transportation of Freight—The Function of Insurance*, 40 Fordham L.Rev. 67 (1971).

H. EXCUSABLE NON-PERFORMANCE

A breach of contract occurs when one party, without justification, repudiates the contract or fails to perform obligations that have become due. The forms of breach and the remedies available to aggrieved parties will be considered in Chapter VI. Here we treat one form of justification or excuse for non-performance—a form variously described as "impossibility" of performance or "commercial impracticability." In essence, the key question is when, if ever, can S or B escape liability for breach because of the adverse impact of post-contract changed circumstances.

If the agreement clearly allocates the risk of these changes, it will normally control. But in most litigated cases, the parties may not have foreseen the changes as likely to occur, much less dealt with them in the agreement. Thus, excuse, if granted, must satisfy a legal standard imposed to fill a gap in the parties' agreed risk allocation. These standards are expressed in Section 2-613, 2-614, 2-615 and 2-616.

When excuse is claimed, notice must be given to the other party, see 2–615(c), and Section 2–616 establishes a procedure to be followed on "notice claiming excuse." If excuse is granted with regard to the total unperformed contract, the contract is discharged, subject to any claims for partial performance or restitution. If excuse is granted with regard to part of the unperformed contract, those obligations are discharged but the excused party may have a duty to perform the part not discharged. See, e.g., 2–613(b) & 2–615(b). Within this general framework, let us consider some of these questions in more detail.

1. CASUALTY TO IDENTIFIED GOODS
Section 2–613 states that where the contract "requires for its performance goods identified when the contract is made and the goods suffer casualty without fault of either party before the risk of loss passes to the buyer, then (a) if the loss is total the contract is avoided. . . ." Suppose that B has agreed to pay $25,000 for a prize bull named Eros, which is owned by S. S, a merchant, tendered delivery but before B could take possession, Eros died. The contract is avoided under Section 2–613, because Eros was identified at the time of contracting, the contract required Eros and none other for performance, and the casualty occurred without S's fault before risk of loss passed. See 2–509(3). Thus, S had the risk of loss but was excused from the contract by 2–613. If the risk of loss had passed to B before Eros died, B, as we have seen, would be liable for the contract price. See 2–709(1)(a).

> ***Example V(52):*** S contracted to sell B his prize bull, Eros, for $25,000 and a bull calf to be selected later. Unknown to both parties, Eros was dead in

the field at the time of contracting. Later, S identified a calf to the contract but, before delivery, the calf was killed in an accident. With regard to Eros, a fair reading of Section 2–613 will justify excuse. Comment 2 states that 2–613 applies whether or not "the goods were already destroyed at the time of contracting." Even so, most courts treat casualty to the required subject matter before rather than after contract formation as a mutual mistake of fact and would avoid the contract. See 1–103.

With regard to the calf, Section 2–613 does not apply because the goods were not identified at the time of contracting. The contract, however, may be discharged if the conditions of Section 2–615(a) are satisfied.

Example V(53): S, a farmer, sold B, a grain dealer, his "output" of # 1 yellow corn, already planted in a 100 acre field. Thereafter, the crop was totally destroyed by drought. S is excused under Section 2–613. Assuming that S did everything reasonable to save the crop, the goods were identified at the time of contracting, 2–501(1)(c), and the "output" of the particular 100 acre field was required for performance of the contract. Where the contract specifies crops to be grown from a particular field and it is not expected that the farmer will obtain crops from other sources, the common assumption is that the crop is "required" for performance and will continue to exist.

Suppose, however, that S was a grain dealer who sold B 50,000 bushels of # 1 yellow corn and identified the corn as coming from a silo containing 100,000 bushels of # 1 yellow. If that silo and its contents are destroyed before risk of loss passes, S is probably not excused under Section 2–613. Although the corn was identified, there is no evidence that it was required for performance. B could not object if S produced 50,000 bushels of the fungible goods from another silo and, given the nature of S's business and his access at low cost to multiple sources of supply, a common assumption is that S must resort to other sources when goods under his control at the time of contracting are destroyed. If, however, the parties expect that the dealer will obtain corn from a limited geographical area and a severe drought hits the region, partial excuse may be granted. See *Alimenta (U.S.A.), Inc. v. Gibbs, Nathaniel (Canada) Ltd.,* 802 F.2d 1362 (11th Cir.1986).

Section 2–613(b) gives the buyer power to adjust the contract if the "loss is partial or the goods have so deteriorated as no longer to conform to the contract." Even though the partial loss is material, the buyer may "nevertheless" demand inspection and at his option either treat the contract as avoided or accept the goods with due allowance from the contract price for the deterioration or the deficiency in quantity but without further right against the seller.

Example V(54): S, a farmer, contracted to sell B 1,000 bushels of # 1 yellow corn to be grown on a particular tract of land owned by S. Due to a drought,

S was able to harvest only 500 bushels of corn and only 200 bushels of that qualified as #1 yellow. S notified B of the situation and stated that the entire contract was avoided. B, however, may elect to take the 200 bushels of #1 yellow at the contract price and the 300 bushels of nonconforming corn at its market price. If so, the balance of the contract is discharged and B has no further claims against S.

2. FAILURE OF PRESUPPOSED CONDITIONS

(a) Test of Excuse

Suppose that S, a manufacturer, sold B three pieces of factory equipment, with a delivery date of October 1. Shortly thereafter, an unexpected Teamsters strike was called and S was unable to get ordered components necessary to complete the equipment. Consequently, S failed to meet the delivery date and, after giving notice of the non-delivery, see 2–615(c), claimed excuse.

Note that there was no casualty to identified goods: rather, the strike interfered with S's capacity to perform the contract on time. Assuming that S did not cause the strike and took all reasonable steps to obtain the components, should excuse be granted? *Section 2–615(a) reads as follows: "Delay in delivery or non-delivery in whole or in part by a seller who complies with paragraphs (b) and (c) is not a breach of his duty under a contract for sale if performance as agreed has been made impracticable by the occurrence of a contingency the non-occurrence of which was a basic assumption on which the contract was made or by compliance in good faith with any applicable foreign or domestice governmental regulation or order whether or not it later proves to be invalid." The answer is yes if three conditions required by 2–615(a) are met.*

First, the risk must *not* be allocated to S by the agreement. Assuming that excuse would otherwise be granted, S must not have assumed "a greater obligation" by agreement. More probably, if there is any agreement at all it will tend to excuse S from strikes, bad weather, acts of the public enemy and other catastrophies—under a standard *force majeure* clause.

Second, the contingency preventing performance, a strike, must have been a "contingency the non-occurrence of which was a basic assumption on which the contract was made." Put another way, the court must conclude that at the time of contracting both parties assumed that the strike would not occur. This result is not likely if both parties discussed the possibility and S still made an unconditional promise or the strike was foreseeable as likely to occur. The more the contingency is foreshadowed in the bargaining process, the greater the inference that if the parties did not expressly provide against it, the promisor must have assumed the risk of its occurrence. The basic assumption test is most likely to be satisfied when the contingency, although foreseeable in general, was not foreseen as likely to occur. Where the probability of the event and its impact on performance is remote, it is permissible to conclude that neither party assumed the risk.

Third, the occurrence of the contingency the "non-occurrence of which was a basic assumption on which the contract was made" must make "performance as agreed . . . impracticable." Thus, if S did not assume the risk of the strike and the strike made "performance as agreed" impracticable, the non-delivery is excused. The content of "impracticability" has been hotly debated and there is no clear consensus on what it means. In our case, however, performance as agreed would be impracticable if the strike prevented S from obtaining essential components; there was no available source and the various costs, economic and otherwise, of attempting to run the picket line are too heavy to incur.

Applying our three step test, here are some routine examples.

> *Example V(55):* S, a grower, agreed to sell B, a dealer, its output of cotton for Fall delivery at $.33 per pound. During the Summer, the market price of cotton rose to $.90 per pound. S failed to deliver and claimed excuse under Section 2–615(a). Excuse should be denied. Most courts have concluded that the fixed price is an agreement which allocates the risk of price fluctuations during the term of the contract. Further, the price increase does not make performance as agreed impracticable. S is simply deprived by his agreement of an opportunity to obtain a greater yield on his investment. See 2–615, Comment 4.

> *Example V(56):* S, a manufacturer, agreed to supply B with a fixed quantity of manufactured goods over a five year period. B agreed to pay a fixed price, subject to escalation based upon an established production cost index. After two years, unanticipated inflation and production cost increases outstripped the index. In fact, S was incurring actual costs of $500 for every unit manufactured and was paid under the price escalation clause only $200 per unit. At the same time, B would have to pay $550 to get the same goods on the open market. S argued that the escalation clause was not intended to deal with such an unanticipated surge in costs, that both parties assumed that contingencies of this magnitude would not occur and that the projected loss over the entire contract, some $3,000,000, made performance as agreed impracticable.

> For various reasons, most courts have rejected the excuse claim in cases of this sort. Implicit in these decisions is the view that S, at the time of contracting, was in the best position to anticipate the contingency and its impact and to manage the risk through contract clauses or other risk spreading techniques. The rare case granting excuse will stress that the contingency was not foreseeable as likely to occur and that performance under the contract terms would be commercially senseless. See

Aluminum Co. of America v. Essex Group, Inc., 499 F.Supp. 53 (W.D.Pa.1980). The message however is clear: Section 2–615(a) promises more excuse than has actually been delivered by the courts. The parties are well advised to bargain for terms that grant relief in case of extreme changed circumstances.

Example V(57): B, a public utility, agreed to purchase 50% of S's output of uranium oxide over a 10 year period at a fixed price subject to escalation. The purpose was to fuel a nuclear power plant under construction. After three years, the demand for uranium oxide collapsed: the market price for UO was $.20 per pound and B was paying S $.50 per pound under the escalation clause. Further, the state in which B operated imposed an indefinite moratorium on the construction of nuclear reactors, thereby frustrating B's primary purpose for entering the contract. B refused to accept and pay for the next tender of delivery and claimed excuse under Section 2–615(a).

Although excuse for buyers is not mentioned in Section 2–615(a), the same principles are inferentially applicable. See Comment 9. See also, Restatement (Second) Contracts, Chapter 11. B, however, will have no better luck than S in claiming excuse because the market broke the wrong way: the escalation clause allocated the price risk to B. See *Northern Indiana Public Service Co. v. Carbon County Coal Co.*, 799 F.2d 265 (7th Cir.1986).

Furthermore, the moratorium, in general, impairs B's incentive to perform the contract rather than its capacity to perform. B can take and pay for the UO, it just doesn't want to. *Most courts are unwilling to hold that a failure of B's purpose was a contingency the "nonoccurrence of which was a basic assumption on which the contract was made," and even so, the impracticability argument is less appealing where B can buy the UO and resell it for some value on the open market.* B's strongest argument may be that excuse is justified, because it complied in "good faith with [an] applicable . . . domestic governmental regulation or order whether or not it later proves to be invalid." 2–615(a). But this argument restates rather than answers the question: was the government regulation a contingency which both parties assumed would not occur? If not, B assumed the risk of the moratorium and is not excused from the contract.

(b) Failure of Agreed Method or Manner of Performance

Sections 2–613 and 2–615 deal with events which substantially impair the capacity or incentive to perform. They go to the "very heart of the agreement." 2–614, Comment 1. *Section 2–614 deals with contingencies that are not basic assumptions of the parties but, nevertheless, make performance of incidental aspects of the bargain difficult if not impossible.* Thus, if the agreement provides for a certain type of loading facility or carrier, the facility or carrier are not available and Section 2–615(a) does not justify excuse, Section 2–614(1) provides a more limited remedy: *if "a commercially reasonable substitute is available, such substitute performance must be tendered and accepted."*

But Section 2–614 does not tell us what happens when the agreed loading facility fails and there is no commercially reasonable substitute. The options appear to be these: (1) If the other party promised the facility or caused the failure, the aggrieved party can, at a minimum, suspend performance without liability until a facility becomes available; (2) If the failure involves a basic assumption of the contract, excuse might be available under Section 2–615(a); and (3) If neither (1) nor (2) is applicable and a commercially reasonable substitute is not available, the promisor, apparently, must muddle through as best he can without any relief.

> *Example V(58):* B, an American corporation, bought goods from S, a Mexican corporation, and agreed to pay the price in Mexican pesos by a check drawn on Bank X. Later, Bank X failed and was closed by order of the Mexican government. At the same time, the Mexican peso was devalued by 25%. Here the "means or manner of payment" have failed because of government regulations, and S may "withhold or stop delivery" of the goods unless B "provides a means or manner of payment which is commercially a substantial equivalent." 2–614(2). Thus, B might tender the pesos in cash, arrange for a letter of credit, or tender a check drawn on another, reputable bank. The devaluation of the peso, however, is not a failure of the "agreed means or manner of payment" and, without agreement, is a risk which S assumes.

3. POST–CONTINGENCY ALLOCATION AND ADJUSTMENT

So far, we have seen two example of what might be called post-contingency adjustments, namely, B's options under Section 2–613(b) when the casualty to identified goods is "partial" and the commercially reasonable substitute required when available by Section 2–614.

Another form of adjustment arises under Sections 2–615(b) and 2–616. Suppose that S's factory has the capacity to produce 5,000 units per year and that it has contracted to sell 2,500 units to B. Assume that a strike reduces its capacity to 3,000 units per year and that S can claim excuse under Section 2–615(a) for that part of capacity affected by the strike. Finally, assume at the time of the strike, S had contracted with B to sell 2,500 units, with C to sell 1,500 units and with D to sell 1,000 units. How is this situation to be handled under the Code?

> *First,* where only part of its capacity to perform is affected, S "must allocate production and deliveries among customers" and "may so allocate in any manner which is fair and reasonable." 2–615(b). Assume that after due

consideration, S makes a pro rata allocation and decides to deliver 1,250 units to B.

Second, S must notify B "seasonably" that an allocation is required and "of the estimated quota . . . made available for the buyer." 2–615(c).

Third, upon receipt of notice of an allocation, B is given a choice by Section 2–616(1): (1) if the deficiency is material, B may "terminate" the contract and "discharge any unexecuted portion," 2–616(1)(a), or (2) B may "modify the contract by agreeing to take his available quota in substitution." 2–616(1)(b). If B fails to modify the contract "within a reasonable time not exceeding thirty days the contract lapses with respect to any deliveries affected." 2–616(2).

> *Example V(59):* Suppose, in *Example V(56),* that after the inflation and cost increases had occurred S said to B: "I will lose $3,000,000 by performing this contract according to its terms. Unless you agree to modify the escalation clause to reflect changed costs, I will terminate the contract." B refused either to negotiate or to agree to a modification, and S terminated the contract. B sued for breach. Even though S may claim excuse under Section 2–615(a), the procedure on "notice claiming excuse" in Section 2–616 is not applicable: S is not claiming an excused delay or proposing an allocation of goods. Furthermore, outside of statutory adjustment procedures or an agreement, the courts have held that B has no duty either to negotiate in good faith or to agree to an adjustment, no matter how fair. But see 2–615, Comments 6 and 7. Thus, if S is not excused under 2–615(a), he is liable for breach of contract and cannot fault B's conduct. If S is excused, the contract is discharged and unless the parties actually agreed on a modification and continued performance, the primary remedy is restitution.

I. MODIFICATION OF THE CONTRACT

As noted in *Example V(59),* unless a statute requires it or the parties have agreed, neither party has a duty to negotiate over or to accept a proposed modification by the other. To date, the courts have refused to impose the general duty of good faith in performance on this situation. Thus, the focus has been upon the legal effect of actual agreements purporting to modify an existing contract or conduct by one party which the other claims "waived" terms or an executory part of the contract. Section 2–209 deals with these problems of adjustment as contract performance unfolds.

1. MODIFICATION BY AGREEMENT
Section 2–209(1) provides that "an agreement modifying a contract within this Article needs no consideration to be binding." On its face, this appears to change the common law "preexisting duty rule," which declared that a modification without

new consideration was unenforceable. According to Comment 2, a modification must now "meet the test of good faith imposed by this Act." Thus, a "bad faith" modification is not enforceable and bad faith here includes the "extortion" of a modification "without legitimate commercial reason." On the other hand, a good faith modification may rest upon an unexpected change during performance which although not justifying excuse under Section 2–615(a) seriously affects one party's ability to perform or its cost of performance. In each case, the court must draw the line between the good faith and the bad faith modifications under Section 2–209(1).

> *Example V(60):* During negotiations over the sale of a cow which B hoped was pregnant, S refused to affirm whether she was or was not. The contract was concluded, but when the time for delivery and payment arrived, B said to S: "Is this cow pregnant or not?" At this point S affirmed that the cow was indeed pregnant and B paid the price. Later, B discovered that the cow was not pregnant. S has made and breached an express warranty, even though the affirmation was made after contract formation: the "additional assurance . . . becomes a modification, and need not be supported by consideration if it is otherwise reasonable and in order." 2–313, Comment 7. See 2–209(1).

> *Example V(61):* S agreed to meet B's requirements of specialized goods for use in a government prime contract at a fixed price of $100 per unit. Later, S discovered that the contract was unprofitable and threatened to breach the contract unless B agreed to pay $150 per unit. B was under time pressure from the Government and there was no readily available alternate source of supply for the goods. After some discussion, B was compelled to accept the modification or be defaulted by the government. The modification was in bad faith (if not under duress) and is not enforceable. Although S may honestly believe that his self interest dictates the higher price and holds no malice toward B, S has exploited B's tight position to reallocate a risk originally assigned to S by the contract. S, under the circumstances, could not reasonably request a modification simply because the contract was unprofitable and has, in addition, threatened to breach the contract. As such, the modification is in bad faith, 2–103(1)(b), and would not be saved by the addition of a "mere technical consideration." 2–209, Comment 2. See *Roth Steel Products v. Sharon Steel Corp.*, 705 F.2d 134 (6th Cir.1983). The modification may also be invalid for duress, since S made a "wrongful threat" to withhold delivery and B neither could find substitute goods from another source nor had an adequate remedy for breach.

> *Example V(62):* During contract performance, S encountered unanticipated difficulties which increased his cost under a fixed price by 500%. At the same time, the market price for similar goods rose some 300% from the time of contracting. Without threatening to terminate, S explained its difficulty to B, reaffirmed the commitment to the contract and proposed a modification

which was reasonable in light of the changed circumstances. B accepted the proposal but, after performance was completed, refused to pay the higher price. The modification is enforceable even though S would not be excused under Section 2–615(a): the changed circumstances caused unanticipated loss to S and an unanticipated gain to B; S did not threaten to breach the contract; the proposed modification was reasonable in light of the changed circumstance; and B's assent was motivated more by a desire to preserve the contract than market compulsion.

2. MODIFICATION BY WAIVER

(a) In General

A "waiver" is voluntary conduct by one party which modifies an existing contract. Suppose S's duty to deliver goods is expressly conditioned upon B giving notice of the delivery point by a specified date. If notice is not given or is given late, S has no duty to deliver and the contract is discharged. S, however, may elect not to insist upon the condition. Thus, if B's notice is six days late and S still ships the goods, the election "waives" the condition and modifies the contract. On the other hand, suppose, before the condition fails, S tells B: "Don't worry about the time of notice. You can be a few days late and I won't mind." B is a few days late and S refuses to ship the goods. *Here, the condition is waived because S induced B to materially change his position "in reliance on the waiver." 2–209(5). The waiver was of an executory part of the contract rather than by an election not to insist upon a condition that has already failed. In the executory waiver, S could retract the waiver by "reasonable notification" received by B that strict performance will be required "unless the retraction would be unjust in view of a material change of position in reliance on the waiver." 2–209(5).* Note that consideration is not required when the waiver is by "election" or through induced reliance.

(b) The Statute of Frauds

The statute of frauds, 2–201, or an agreement of the parties may impose some limitation upon the form of a modification. Section 2–209(3) provides that the "requirements of the statute of frauds . . . must be satisfied if the contract as modified is within its provisions." Section 2–209(2) provides that a "signed agreement which excludes modification or rescission except by a signed writing cannot be otherwise modified or rescinded, but except as between merchants such a requirement on a form supplied by the merchant must be separately signed by the other party." Finally, Section 2–209(4) provides that "although an attempt at modification or rescission does not satisfy the requirements of subsection (2) or (3) it can operate as a waiver."

> *Example V(63):* S and B entered a written contract to sell an airplane for $20,000. For additional consideration, S orally agreed to sell B some radar equipment for the plane for $1,500 and the parties orally agreed to increase the contract price to $21,500. Since the oral modification is within the statute of frauds, 2–201(1), it is not enforceable. 2–209(3).

The statute could be avoided, however, if B accepted the radar equipment or paid the modified price, 2–201(3)(c), but neither party can by agreement or waiver otherwise escape the statute.

Example V(64): S agreed to manufacture complicated machinery for B according to B's specifications. The written contract provided that "no change orders shall be effective unless made in a writing signed by B and no compensation will be paid for extra work without a written change order." An oral change order relied upon by S does not create an enforceable modification, 2–209(2), but B could, by election or by an oral statement abandoning the requirement of a writing, "waive" the requirement. See 2–209(2) & (3). There is a dispute over whether B's "waiver," however defined, must induce S to rely. At least one carefully considered opinion has held that reliance is required. *Wisconsin Knife Works v. National Metal Crafters,* 781 F.2d 1280 (7th Cir.1986) (Posner, J. with a strong dissent by Easterbrook, J.)

J. REVIEW QUESTIONS

V–A. Under what circumstances does the parol evidence rule apply? What is the test of when a writing is "integrated?"

V–B. What is the legal effect of a "total" integration?

V–C. *True or False:* A term in a writing must be ambiguous on its face before extrinsic evidence to aid in interpretation can be admitted.

V–D. Under what circumstances and with what legal effect can evidence of trade usage be admitted?

V–E. *True or False:* If the parties disagree on the meaning of a term and that disagreement cannot be alleviated through the process of interpretation, the contract is unenforceable.

V–F. S and B entered a written agreement to sell "chickens" at $1.56 per pound. At that time, S intended to deliver stewing hens and B intended to buy fryers. Neither said anything to the other about their intentions. S tendered and B rejected stewing hens. S sued B for damages based upon a contract to sell stewing hens and B argued that the contract was too indefinite to enforce: the word "chicken" had no objective meaning and, since the parties subjective intention did not coincide, there was no contract. How should S respond to this argument?

V–G. *True or False:*

1. Unless otherwise agreed, neither party is obligated to extend credit to the other.

2. Where S and B are to exchange performances at the same time, S must tender first or be in default.

3. The duty of good faith applies to pre-contract negotiations.

4. A primary function of the good faith duty is to control the exercise of discretion reserved to one or both parties by the agreement.

V-H. Evaluate the following: If, in a ten year exclusive distributorship, the parties agreed that after three years S can "terminate at any time and for any reason upon the giving of six months notice" and if this clause is conscionable at the time of contracting, the termination power can be exercised by S without regard to the duty of good faith.

V-I. In the absence of agreement:

1. How much of the total amount of goods promised must be delivered at the agreed time?

2. Where is the place for delivery?

3. What must S do to tender delivery?

V-J. If a bailee is in possession of goods sold to B and no documents have been issued, what must S do to tender delivery? Is it sufficient that the bailee acknowledges to S that B may take delivery?

V-K. In shipment contracts, what is the difference between an FOB point of shipment and an FOB point of destination term when S's delivery obligations are considered? What is the difference when risk of loss is considered?

V-L. In a shipment contract, what is the advantage to S of taking a negotiable bill of lading to his own order from the carrier and drawing a draft for the contract price on B payable "on sight?" Under what circumstances can this be done?

V-M. S and B concluded a 10 year exclusive dealing contract under which S was to furnish B's requirements at a fixed price with escalation. For the first five years, B's requirements averaged 100,000 units per year. In the middle of the sixth year, B shut down its business operation in good faith: new technology had been developed that required complete retooling in order to stay competitive. B's actual requirements for the sixth year were 40,000 units. For the balance of the contract it was clear that B would have no requirements for S's goods. S claims damages based upon 60,000 units for the sixth year and 100,000 units for the remaining four years on the contract. He argues that the first five years established B's reasonable requirements and that the orders in the sixth year and thereafter were "unreasonably disproportionate." Assuming that B is in good faith, is S correct?

V–N. What are the major similarities and differences among the three UCC warranties? Think of a case where all three warranties would apply to the same sale.

V–O. How can one tell whether an alleged express warranty has become part of the basis of the bargain?

V–P. *True or False:* The implied warranty of fitness for particular purpose is the hardest for B to prove and the easiest for S to disclaim.

V–Q. What is the answer to the question posed in Example V(32)?

V–R. Evaluate the following: The unprotected gap between warranty and strict tort law involves economic loss caused by defective products where there is no privity of contract: there is no basis for recovery under either body of law.

V–S. On July 1, 1986, S sold to B and installed 100 storm windows in B's apartment building. The contract provided that the glass was "guaranteed for a period of ten years from the date of acceptance" and that S would "furnish and replace free of charge any unit which develops material obstruction of vision between the interglass surfaces." In January, 1992, visual obstructions developed in 40 windows due to a defect which was inherent but not discoverable at the time of installation. B requested S to replace the windows. S refused, claiming that the statute of limitations on B's claim had run. S cited Section 2–725. Is S correct?

V–T. How does an "open" price term allocate risks between seller and buyer? How does a fixed price term allocate risk?

V–U. When will B have no right to inspect the goods before acceptance and payment?

V–V. What is the legal effect of acceptance?

V–W. S sold goods to B, FOB point of shipment. B denied the rumors and refused S's demand to pay before shipment. S then shipped the goods "under reservation," i.e., procured from the carrier a negotiable bill of lading to S's order, and refused to duly negotiate the document until B had paid. B refused to pay and claiming breach, sued S for damages. Should B prevail?

V–X. S sold B goods for $10,000, shipment FOB point of shipment. S shipped nonconforming goods which B, if the defect was discovered, could have rejected. B however, accepted the goods and did not discover the defect until later. B promptly telephoned S and revoked his acceptance. That night the goods were destroyed by fire while in B's possession. B's insurance covered $5,000 of the loss. S has now sued B for the price of goods accepted, $10,000. What result?

V-Y. B asked S to manufacture special equipment for B's plant. During negotiations, both parties knew that an important component had to be imported from Japan and that Congress was considering new trade restrictions that might affect the component. Nevertheless, S agreed to manufacture the goods for a fixed price, $50,000, and the agreement said nothing about the component. Later, the United States government prohibited the import of the component, among other things. As a result, S incurred additional costs of $200,000 in obtaining a substitute and was 120 days late in delivery. S claims that the delay was excused by an act of government. More importantly, S argued that the price term should be deleted and B should pay the reasonable costs incurred to manufacture the goods.

1. What result on these facts?

2. Suppose that S and B, shortly after the embargo, agreed to a modification of the contract: S was given a 120 day extension on the delivery date and B agreed to pay 75% of any additional costs incurred. Is this modification enforceable?

V-Z. One last problem for Chapter V. B contracted with S to supply 10,000 pairs of combat boots. S knew that B had a contract for resale to buyers in Africa and B knew that S would have the boots manufactured in Korea. The date of the contract was April 1 and S agreed to deliver the boots to B in New York on or before September 1. S ordered the boots from a reliable Korean manufacturer and they were delivered by ship to S in San Francisco on August 1. The boots conformed to the contract but had no markings of identification. S then shipped the boots by rail to his agent in New York for delivery to B. En route, the boots were totally destroyed by fire while in the carrier's possession. S was unable to deliver conforming boots to B on September 1. Which of the following accurately describes the legal result in this case:

1. Risk of loss had passed to B, who owes the full contract price;

2. S is excused under Section 2–613;

3. S is excused under Section 2–615;

4. Risk of loss was on S and he was not excused from contract performance;

5. None of the above;

6. All of the above.

*

REMEDIES FOR BREACH OF CONTRACT FOR SALE

Analysis

A. *In General*
B. *Breach of Contract*
   1. *Right to Adequate Assurance: Section 2–609*
   2. *Repudiation*
   3. *Other Types of Breach*
C. *Seller's Remedies*
   1. *Self-Help*
     (a) Withholding or Stopping Delivery
     (b) Cancellation of the Contract
   2. *Recovery of the Price: Section 2–709*
   3. *Resale: Section 2–706*
     (a) Availability and Effect
     (b) The Lost Volume Problem
   4. *Damages: Section 2–708*
     (a) The Damage Formula: Section 2–708(1)
     (b) The "Components" Analysis: Section 2–708(2)
       (1) Applicability
       (2) Application
   5. *Other Problems*
     (a) Mitigation of Damages
     (b) Incidental Damages
     (c) Consequential Damages
D. *Buyer's Remedies*
   1. *In General*

A. IN GENERAL

Even though the contract obligations are clear and complete, trouble may arise as performance unfolds. One party may be insecure about whether the other will perform as agreed. One party may repudiate the contract. The seller may breach by failing to make any delivery or by tendering goods that do not conform to the contract. The buyer may breach by wrongfully rejecting a conforming tender or failing to make a payment when due.

One response to trouble should be an effort by both parties to determine the cause and, if possible, to resolve the dispute by agreement. The Code, with its overriding obligation of good faith, facilitates these efforts. See 2–209(1) and Chapter V(I). Also, the parties may have agreed to arbitration or some other method of dispute resolution.

If the dispute cannot be resolved, the aggrieved party may claim that the other has breached the contract and pursue appropriate remedies. *For the seller, the buyer's breaches are listed and the remedial options are described in Section 2–703. Section 2–711(1) lists the seller's breaches and states the buyer's remedial options. A basic remedial policy, however, is stated in Section 1–106(1)*

> *The remedies provided by this Act shall be liberally administered to the end that the aggrieved party may be put in as good a position as if the other had fully performed but neither consequential or special nor penal damages may be had except as specifically provided in this Act or by other rule of law.*

Note that 1–106(1)'s object is to protect the so-called expectation interest. There is no explicit recognition of the reliance or restitution interests in contract damages. Also, 1–106(1) excludes both punitive and consequential damages unless "specifically provided in this Act or by other rule of law." There is no provision for punitive damages in Article 2. Moreover, there is a provision for buyer's consequential damages in 2–715(2) but no corresponding provision for the seller.

Thus, the Code seeks to compensate the aggrieved party by protecting the expectation interest rather than by punishing the other party for breach. As we shall see, there are other policies associated with the compensation objective and implicitly recognized by Article 2, namely: (a) the breach must cause the loss; (b) the plaintiff must prove damages with reasonable certainty; (c) the plaintiff must take reasonable steps after the breach to avoid its consequences; and (d) the recovery of consequential damages is regulated by Section 2–715(2).

Finally, there are special policies associated with the enforcement of contracts for the sale of goods, e.g., that the remedial choices in 2–703 and 2–711(1) are cumulative and that neither party should be forced into a premature election.

With this background, let us proceed.

B. BREACH OF CONTRACT

Code remedies are invoked in response to conduct that constitutes a breach of the contract for sale. Thus, either S or B might repudiate the contract, S may tender non-conforming goods or B may wrongfully revoke acceptance. In addition, the conduct of one party may not amount to a breach but still give the other party reasonable grounds to believe that due performance will not be forthcoming. In this section, we will briefly examine the concept of breach and explore what the aggrieved party should do to maximize remedial options.

1. RIGHT TO ADEQUATE ASSURANCE: SECTION 2–609

Suppose that S has agreed to deliver manufactured goods to B by October 1. Time is of the essence and S knows it. On September 1, B learns that a union has picketed S's plant and that S's bank has terminated its line of credit. B doubts whether S can perform on time, but S has not yet breached the contract. Moreover, S's president has assured B that "everything will be O.K." Must B wait until October 1 to learn its fate?

The answer is no. *Section 2–609(1) imposes an "obligation on each party that the other's expectation of receiving due performance will not be impaired." When "reasonable grounds for insecurity arise with respect to the performance of either party the other may in writing demand adequate assurance of due performance and until he receives such assurance may if commercially reasonable suspend any performance for which he has not already received the agreed exchange."* This language is open-ended and difficult to particularize. But there are some steps that are helpful in understanding what must be done.

First, S's duty not to impair B's "expectation of receiving due performance" is imposed by the contract for sale. 2–609(1).

Second, B must have "reasonable grounds for insecurity" and, between merchants, the reasonableness of these grounds shall be "determined according to commercial standards." 2–609(2). Would the strike or terminated line of credit qualify? Probably so, if they tended to affect the capacity of S to perform where time was of the essence.

Third, the demand for assurance must be in writing and B may suspend its performance until the assurance is received. In a close case, B can demand adequate assurance without suspending performance, for the risk of being wrong is that suspension by B might be a breach of contract.

Fourth, if S responds, the adequacy of his assurance, between merchants, shall be determined according to "commercial standards." 2–609(2). S must demonstrate that neither the strike nor the credit impairment will prevent timely performance. Perhaps it can show that all of the materials have been bought and paid for. If B is satisfied, the matter will end there. If not, further discussions may ensue or B may take the next step.

Fifth, if B has made and S received a "justified demand" and S has failed to provide an adequate assurance "within a reasonable time not exceeding thirty days," the failure is a "repudiation of the contract." 2–609(4). This is the cruncher, for B must determine on imperfect facts whether the demand was justified and whether S's response was adequate under the circumstances of the case. Perhaps these uncertainties dictate continued discussion rather than precipitous action. Nevertheless, if B decides to treat S's response or lack of it as a repudiation and the judgment is sound, a breach has occurred for which B may cancel the contract and pursue damage remedies. See 2–609(4), 2–610(b), & 2–711(1). If B is wrong in his judgment, a cancellation would be a breach by B, for which S might pursue appropriate remedies.

> ***Example VI(1):*** S agreed to deliver goods on October 1 and B agreed to pay for them on December 1. On September 15, S learned from reliable sources that B was having serious financial difficulties. If B is insolvent, i.e., has either "ceased to pay his debts in the ordinary course of business or cannot pay his debts as they become due or is insolvent within the meaning of the federal bankruptcy law," 1–201(23), S's remedy is clear: S may "refuse delivery" on October 1 "except for cash including payment for all goods theretofore delivered. . . ." 2–702(1). This is a risky step, for if B is not insolvent, S's unilateral decision to convert the contract from credit to cash would be a breach. To temper the risk, on October 1 S should demand adequate assurance of payment and, until such assurance is received, suspend delivery of the goods. 2–609(1). In either event, S does not have to deliver the goods until payment or adequate assurance is received.

2. REPUDIATION

Either S or B can repudiate a contract for sale. Except for a failure to give adequate assurance under Section 2–609(4), however, the Code does not define what a repudiation is. But see 2–610, Comment 2. *In general, a repudiation is a manifestation by words or conduct by a promisor to a promisee that he will not or cannot make a future performance under the contract. See Restatement (Second) Contracts § 250.* This standard should govern disputes under Article 2. Thus, if a buyer states that it will "not pay for the goods when tendered" a repudiation has occurred. Similarly, if S sells to a third person goods which are required for performance of the contract with B, a repudiation has occurred. The sale is a voluntary, affirmative act rendering S unable or apparently unable to perform and is a repudiation. Restatement (Second) Contracts § 250(b).

Article 2 does govern the options and remedies available to one party once a repudiation by the other occurs. See 2–610, 2–611, 2–703 and 2–711. Here are the highlights.

First, the remedies are triggered by a repudiation "with respect to a performance not yet due the loss of which will substantially impair the value of the contract to the other." 2–610(a). In short, the repudiation must be material. If not, the aggrieved party's remedy is apparently limited to a demand for adequate assurance. See 2–609(1). Note, however, that the substantial impairment standard is both subjective and objective. One must first know the value of the contract to "the other" (subjective) before it can be decided whether that value is substantially impaired (objective).

Second, if the repudiation is material, the aggrieved party may "suspend his own performance." 2–610(c).

Third, in addition, he may either await performance by the repudiating party for a "commercially reasonable time," 2–610(a), or "resort to any remedy for breach . . . even though he has notified the repudiating party that he would await the latter's performance and has urged retraction." 2–610(b). The first course, awaiting performance, has some risks: the repudiation may be retracted while he waits, 2–611(1), or a wait for an unreasonable time could limit remedial options. The second course puts the aggrieved party into a position both to cancel and to pursue affirmative remedies for breach.

Example VI(2): S promised to deliver 1,000 units of goods to B in 5 equal installments, commencing on March 1. On February 15, S repudiated the entire contract. B elected to wait for performance, and, on March 1, S tendered the first installment and retracted the repudiation. The retraction was effective to reinstate S's rights under the contract because S had neither canceled nor materially changed his position. 2–611(1). But B can still demand adequate assurance from S concerning future performance, 2–611(1), and can claim "due excuse" for any delay in his performance caused by the repudiation.

Example VI(3): Suppose, in *Example VI(2),* that S, on February 15, stated: "I will not deliver the first installment but I will perform the entire contract within the allotted time." B wants to cancel the contract and pursue affirmative remedies. See 2–610(b) & 2–711(1). Cancellation is risky here. The repudiation does not obviously "substantially impair the value of the contract," 2–610(a), and B cannot cancel unless the breach goes to the "whole" contract. 2–711(1). Compare 2–612. B, instead, should use its rights under Section 2–609.

Example VI(4): Suppose, in *Example VI(2),* that S repudiated the entire contract on February 15 and B, in a sharply rising market, waited until the time for contract performance had expired without receiving either a retraction or the goods from S. B then canceled the contract and sought damages measured by the difference between the contract price and the market price at the time when S should have tendered. See 2–713(1).

There is some authority for the conclusion that if B waited more than a commercially reasonable time for S to perform, the damages should be limited by the concept of avoidable consequences to the market price at the time when that reasonable period expired. See VI(D)(2)(d).

3. OTHER TYPES OF BREACH

In addition to repudiation, other and different types of breach flow from the distinct conduct of buyer and seller as performance unfolds. Thus, B may breach by a wrongful rejection or a wrongful revocation of acceptance or a failure to make payment due on or before delivery, 2–703, as well as by repudiation. S may breach by a failure to make any delivery or by such nonconforming performance that supports a rightful rejection or a justifiable revocation by B, 2–711(1), as well as by repudiation. Let us now turn to a more detailed look at the remedies available to the aggrieved party when the other has committed a breach.

C. SELLER'S REMEDIES

The seller's remedies, in general, are catalogued in Section 2–703. Read that Section, please. Note that the Section first lists the types of breach by the buyer, second establishes the nature of the impact the breach must have on the contract, and third provides six possible remedial responses. *Comment 1 states that the "doctrine of election of remedy" is rejected and that the listed remedies are "essentially cumulative in nature" and exclusive.*

1. SELF-HELP

The seller has two remedies that can be pursued without judicial sanction: (a) withholding or stopping delivery of the goods; and (b) cancellation of the contract.

(a) Withholding or Stopping Delivery

The seller has several self-help remedies that involve withholding or stopping delivery of the goods.

Under Section 2–609(1), S may "suspend" performance where the expectation of receiving due performance from B is impaired even though B is not in breach. Similarly, S, in a credit sale, can refuse delivery "except for cash" when B is insolvent. 2–702(1). Where B is in breach, S may "withhold delivery" of any goods directly affected by the breach and "if the breach is of the whole contract," then withhold delivery of the "whole undelivered balance." 2–703(a). These "self-help" remedies enable S to control the movement of the goods in cases where B is in breach or close to it before delivery.

Example VI(5): S agreed to sell B 1,000 units of goods for $5,000, to be delivered and paid for in 5 equal monthly installments. See 2–612(1). S tendered the first installment and B "wrongfully" rejected them, a breach of contract. S need not deliver the first installment and could withhold delivery of the second installment until the first is paid for. 2–703(a). S, however, can not withhold delivery of the balance unless B's breach was of the "whole" contract, i.e., "substantially impairs the value of the whole" contract. 2–612(3). Although this is doubtful on these facts, S can invoke his rights under Section 2–609 and demand adequate assurance of due performance.

Section 2–705 states that S may "stop delivery" of goods in possession "of a carrier or other bailee" when B breaches or becomes insolvent or "for any other reason the seller has a right to withhold or reclaim the goods." 2–705(1). Consider these points.

First, if B is insolvent, S may stop delivery by a bailee or carrier regardless of the quantity of goods involved.

Second, if the goods are in the possession of a carrier and B has breached but is *not* insolvent, S's power to stop delivery is limited to a "carload, truckload, planeload or larger shipments of express or freight." 2–705(1). Convenience to the carrier dictates this limitation.

Third, the power to stop delivery may be exercised until B receives the goods, 2–705(2)(a), or the other events stated in Section 2–705(2) occur, e.g., acknowledgment by the bailee that he holds goods for B or the negotiation to B of any "negotiable document of title covering the goods."

Fourth, the power to stop delivery is exercised by notice so as to "enable the bailee by reasonable diligence to prevent delivery of the goods." 2–705(3)(a). The bailee can demand the surrender of any negotiable document before honoring any notice, 2–705(3)(c), and S must indemnify the carrier for any "charges or damages" incurred in stopping delivery. 2–705(3)(b).

> *Example VI(6):* S stored goods in a warehouse and W issued a negotiable warehouse receipt to "S or order." S sold the goods to B on credit and duly negotiated the warehouse receipt to B. Later, B repudiated the contract and S promptly notified W to stop delivery, the notice arriving before B had arrived to take possession of the goods. The notice came too late: as against B, S may "stop delivery until . . . negotiation to the buyer of any negotiable document of title covering the goods." 2–705(2)(d). The "due negotiation" has occurred.

(b) Cancellation of the Contract
Cancellation, a remedy available to both seller, 2–703(f), and buyer, 2–711(1), occurs when either party "puts an end to the contract for breach by the other." 2–106(4). The legal effect is that the canceling party discharges his duties to the other and "retains any remedy for breach of the whole contract or any unperformed balance." How the contract is canceled is not stated in the

Code: presumably, any manifestation of intention inconsistent with the continued existence of the contract, whether or not communicated to the other, will be sufficient.

Cancellation, however, is not available for every breach by the other. Both S and B may cancel with regard to goods "directly affected" by the other's breach. With regard to any "undelivered balance," however, the breach must be of the "whole" contract, i.e., "substantially impair the value" of the whole contract to the aggrieved party. 2–703(f), 2–711(1) & 2–612(3). Thus, in some cases the breach must be "material" before the other can cancel, and materiality turns upon both the impact of the breach upon the other's reasonable expectations and capacity to perform and the probability that the breacher will cure the deficiency and complete the exchange.

> *Problem VI(7):* S agreed to sell 20,000 tons of lead to B, to be delivered over a three year period. B agreed to pay the price within 15 days of delivery. During the first 18 months of the contract, S was late on several installments and B was late on several payments. These defaults were ignored by the parties. Thereafter, the market price for lead increased. S, reluctantly, delivered the next installment on time but B did not tender payment until 20 days after delivery. S canceled the contract. B's default with regard to one installment justifies cancellation only if it "substantially impairs the value of the whole contract." 2–612(3). See 2–703(f). This would exist if the breach impaired S's capacity to perform (S was depending on B's prompt payment to finance performance) and indicated B's continuing unwillingness to make prompt payment. On the other hand, if B gave adequate assurance of timely future performance, and if S could easily perform regardless of B's non-payment and only one installment was involved, the cancellation would be improper. For an illustrative case decided under the Uniform Sales Act, see *Plotnick v. Pennsylvania Smelting & Refining Co.,* 194 F.2d 859 (3d Cir.1952).

The cancellation problem is further complicated, from B's perspective, by the remedy of rejection. It is clear that B can reject a nonconforming tender by S under Section 2–601 without having the power to cancel the "whole" contract. See 2–711(1). Cancellation, therefore, is a limited remedy available to both parties upon breach by the other. Its occurrence signals an end to the contract and moves the issue of remedies from the level of "self-help" or agreed adjustment to the courts.

2. RECOVERY OF THE PRICE: SECTION 2–709

Section 2–703 provides that where B "fails to make a payment due on or before delivery . . . ." S may have the self-help remedies or damages listed in 2–703 "or in a proper case the price (Section 2–709)." 2–703(e). 2–709(1), in turn, provides that when the "buyer fails to pay the price as it becomes due the seller may recover

. . . the price" in three stated situations. Two of these situations arise after delivery and one arises while S still has possession. We will now examine what is a "proper case" for the price.

Recovery of the price is an efficient remedy with results similar to specific performance: S delivers the goods to B without the loss of volume and recovers, through judgment, levy and execution, the agreed price. In addition, S may recover any incidental damages resulting from the breach. See 2–709(1) and 2–710. Even so, there are some important limitations upon this remedy.

First, B must breach by "failing to pay the price as it becomes due." 2–709(1). A repudiation or wrongful rejection before the price is due will not trigger the price action. Nor will B's failure to make a payment on or before delivery unless the conditions of 2–709(1) are satisfied.

Second, when B has failed to pay the price when due, S can recover the price if at least one of three conditions has been satisfied: (1) B has accepted the goods; (2) The risk of loss of conforming goods has passed to B and they are "lost or damaged within a commercially reasonable time" thereafter; or (3) B breaches before delivery and S is unable after a "reasonable effort" to resell "goods identified to the contract" or "the circumstances reasonably indicate that such effort will be unavailing." 2–709(1)(a) & (b).

Third, when S sues for the price, it must "hold for the buyer any goods which have been identified to the contract and are still in his control." 2–709(2). If the price is recovered, those goods are delivered to B. S "may resell" the goods anytime prior to the collection of the judgment, but B gets credit for the "net proceeds" of any resale and "payment of the judgment entitles him to any goods not resold." 2–709(2).

Fourth, If B has breached the contract but S is not entitled to the price under Section 2–709(1), S "shall nevertheless be awarded damages for non-acceptance" under Section 2–708. Although S can count on this "fall back" remedy, care must be taken in an action for the price to introduce evidence that will sustain damages under the different standards of Section 2–708.

Example VI(8): S agreed to sell B 1,200 units of goods for $60,000, delivery to be in 3 equal monthly installments, shipment FOB point of shipment. B was to pay the price of each installment 15 days after delivery. S shipped and B accepted, see 2–606, but failed to pay for the first installment. S shipped the second installment, but it was destroyed by fire while in the carrier's possession. B repudiated the balance of the contract. S: (1) can recover the price of the first installment because B accepted the goods, 2–709(1)(a); (2) can recover the price of the second installment since the risk of loss had passed to B, 2–709(1)(a); and (3) must wait until the price of the third installment comes due, unless the combination of a partial breach and repudiation of an executory contract persuades the court to accelerate the action. In any event, S must still satisfy at least one of the three conditions in Section 2–709(1).

Example VI(9): S contracted to sell B 10,000 pounds of uranium oxide as fuel for a nuclear reactor. S was to deliver in a single lot and B was to pay the price, $45 per pound, upon tender of delivery. Upon S's tender of conforming goods, B wrongfully refused to accept and pay. At that time, the market price for uranium oxide had dropped to $23 per pound and was still falling. S, concluding that the market was a "shambles" and that a resale could not easily be arranged, stored the identified goods and sued B for the price. B defended on the grounds that the goods were not accepted and that S had made *no effort* to resell them. S can still recover the $45 price if the "circumstances reasonably indicate" that a reasonable effort "to resell them at a reasonable price . . . will be unavailing." 2–709(1)(b). If the circumstances suggest that S could resell them to C for $20 per pound, the court must decide whether $20 is a "reasonable price." Note that S's case is stronger if it made a reasonable effort to resell without success, but if S *in fact* resold the goods at some price (say $15 per pound), an action for the price is not available. The appropriate remedy is under 2–706.

3. RESALE: SECTION 2–706
(a) Availability and Effect

In sum, a successful action for the price under 2–709 satisfies the remedial policy of 1–106(1) with the least possible disruption to the parties. The parties are put in the exact position they would have occupied if B had paid, (the exchange is completed), incidental damages are minimized, see 2–710, and the value fixed by the parties at the time of contracting is preserved. But there is an efficiency norm implicit in 2–709(1)(b) which limits the action for the price to situations where resale is impracticable. If S is in possession of the goods and, as a merchant, can reasonably resell them, it is more cost efficient that S do so rather than to require B to take goods it no longer wants or needs.

This leads directly into 2–706. Suppose that S, after B's breach, has conforming goods on hand and cannot or elects not to recover the price. In this case, S may identify the goods to the breached contract, see 2–704(1)(a), and resell them to a third party. If, as in *Example VI(9)*, the contract price was $45 per pound and the resale price was $20 per pound, S has a potential claim to damages of $25 per pound under Section 2–706(1): *S may "resell" the goods wrongfully rejected or the "undelivered balance thereof" and, where the "resale is made in good faith and in a commercially reasonable manner," may "recover the difference between the resale price and the contract price together with any incidental damages . . . but less expenses saved in consequence of the buyer's breach."* This remedy puts S in the same economic position as if B had paid the price, except that (1) S has incurred costs in arranging the resale, (2) the goods have been delivered to a third party rather than B, and (3) S may have lost volume on the transaction, i.e., S, because of B's breach, has made one less sale than would otherwise have been made. (More on lost volume later.)

The balance of 2–706 contains some rather complex provisions. For example, if S resells by a private rather than a public sale, S "must give the buyer reasonable notification of his intention to resell," 2–706(3), as well as make and conduct the resale in a "commercially reasonable" manner. 2–706(1) & 2–706(2). If S fails to meet these conditions, the resale remedy is not available. As with Section 2–709, however, the general damage remedy under 2–708 is available as a back up. Again, a word of caution for the litigator. To preserve the "back up" remedy, care should be taken to introduce evidence establishing the market value of the goods.

If S attempts a public resale, the conditions are even more complicated. See 2–706(4). Finally, 2–706(5) defines the rights of a purchaser who buys "in good faith at a resale" and 2–706(6) provides that the seller, who is not a secured party, is "not accountable to the buyer for any profit made on any resale."

Here are some illustrations.

> *Example VI(10):* Suppose, in *Example VI(9),* that S agreed to ship the 10,000 pounds FOB point of shipment but that the $45 per pound price by agreement included the cost of shipment, $1 per pound. Upon breach by B, S *properly* resold the goods to C for $20 per pound and incurred $1,000 costs in arranging the resale. C picked up the goods at its own expenses at S's plant.

> On these facts, the $1,000 expended to arrange the resale was incidental damages under Section 2–710 and the $1 per pound not spent in shipping the goods to B (a total of $10,000) was "expenses saved in consequence of the buyer's breach." 2–706(1). Working with the 10,000 pounds promised, S's total damages are the difference between the contract and the resale price, ($25 × 10,000 pounds = $250,000), plus incidental damages, ($1,000), less expenses saved, ($10,000), for a total recovery of $241,000.

> *Example VI(11):* S sold B 10,000 units of goods for $50,000, FOB point of shipment with B to pay the freight upon delivery. B repudiated the contract in a falling market while the goods were in transit. The market price at the point of shipment was $40 per unit and the market price at the point of destination was $20 per unit. S stopped delivery, see 2–705,

and without notifying B, resold them to C for $20,000. S sued B for
$30,000, the difference between the contract and the resale price, plus
$2,000 cost incurred in stopping delivery and making the resale.

Recovery under 2–706(1) should be denied: *First,* S failed to give B any
notice of its intention to resell as required by 2–706(3). This is a
condition precedent to the use of 2–706(1). *Second,* the resale may have
been made in a commercially unreasonable manner or in bad faith. If the
costs involved in reselling at either the point of shipment or the point of
destination are roughly the same and S selects the point that enhances
damages (here the destination point), B should argue that the resale
remedy is not available. Of course, if S was unable to stop delivery and
was required to reship the goods to the point of shipment, the extra cost
and the delay could make a destination resale commercially reasonable.

Nevertheless, S can, in most cases, recover damages for non-acceptance
under Section 2–708(1), measured by the "difference between the market
price at the time and place for tender" (here the point of shipment) and
the "unpaid contract price. . . ." See Comment 8. An exception is
where S attempts to manipulate the remedies by failing to give the
required notice in bad faith. Under these circumstances, some courts
have awarded the damages recoverable under a proper "cover" rather
than higher damages proved under 2–708(1).

Example VI(12): Suppose, in *Example VI(11),* that the market price at
the point of shipment was $20, the market price at the point of
destination was $30, and S, after giving proper notice, resold the goods
for $30 in a commercially reasonable manner at the point of destination.
Later, S sued B for damages under Section 2–708(1), measured by the
difference between the contract price and the market price at the point
of shipment, $30. B claimed that S was limited to resale damages under
Section 2–706(1), $20 per unit: B argued that by complying with the
notice and other conditions, S had elected the resale remedy and that, in
any event, an award of damages under Section 2–708(1) would put S in
better position than full performance would have. See 1–106(1).

Despite disagreement among the commentators, we think that B's
argument should prevail. The argument does collide with the Code policy
favoring the cumulation rather than the election of remedies. See
2–703(1), Comment 1. S's initial choice of remedy, however, was
exercised in a commercially reasonable manner and put S in the same
economic position it would have occupied upon full performance. This
argument is bolstered by implicit policies favoring the resale remedy and
discouraging the use by S of remedial choices to speculate on the market.
Under these circumstances, why should S have two bites of the apple?

Example VI(13): Suppose, in the above examples, that the market price at point of shipment and the point of destination was $40 and the contract price was $50 per unit. Upon B's breach, S stored the goods in a warehouse and sued and recovered $10 per unit damages under Section 2–708(1). Six months later, the market price per unit rose to $60 and S sold the goods to a third party. B complains that because of the resale S either was entitled to no damages under Section 2–708(1) or that it must account to B for the excess of resale over contract price. B is out of luck. S timely pursued the 2–708(1) damage remedy (which yielded no more than a timely resale would have) and assumed the risk that the resale market would go down as well as up. There is no questionable speculation here. Further, the delay would make the subsequent resale commercially unreasonable under 2–706(1). Whether commercially reasonable or not, 2–706(6) responds to B's argument by expressly stating that the "seller is not accountable to the buyer for any profit made on any resale." 2–706(6).

(b) The Lost Volume Problem

The following analysis is oversimplified. S's net profit in a particular sale is measured by the difference between the contract price (KP) and the total cost of performance. (TCP). If the price remedy is available under 2–709(1), S recovers both profit and total cost when B pays. If resale is available under 2–706(1), S may recover all or part of profit and cost from the proceeds of resale and is permitted to make up the difference between the resale and contract price in an action against B. In the case of a resale, however, factual circumstances might exist that would be irrelevant if B accepted the goods and paid the price. Those circumstances are called "lost volume."

Suppose that the contract price is $100 and S resells the goods for $100. S might not be in the same position as full performance if B's breach deprived S of the opportunity to make two profits instead of one. If S had the capacity to and probably would have made the second sale (and more) even if B fully performed, the conditions for "lost volume" are present. The presence of capacity, market demand and second sale probability suggest to most commentators and courts that S should be able to recover the profit earned on the contract with B without any adjustment from the resale. Section 2–706(1) is irrelevant. On the other hand, if S could not have made the second sale "but for" B's breach, there is no lost volume and the resale proceeds under 2–706(1) control the measure of damages.

Some scholars, using economic analysis, have argued against "lost volume" protection on the grounds that the increased marginal costs of the second sale will probably reduce or eliminate its profitability. This argument has persuaded at least one court to place the burden on S to prove that the second sale would have been profitable. See *R.E. Davis Chemical Corp. v. Diasonics, Inc.*, 826 F.2d 678 (7th Cir.1987).

The Code's prescription for "lost volume" is found in 2–708(2). Here is an example before we treat the damage formulas in 2–708.

> ***Example VI(14):*** S was a distributor of a popular power boat manufactured by X. Under the contract, S could purchase up to 10 boats per year from X at a fixed price of $22,500. After S's other fixed and variable costs were added (assume $2,500) and a mark-up for profit was computed, S offered the boat to consumer buyers for $30,000. In early 1992, S had ordered two boats from X and resold them for $30,000 each. In March 1992, B contracted to purchase a boat for $30,000, S ordered it from X and, after preparation, tendered it to B. B wrongfully rejected the boat (a breach), and S promptly resold it to C for $30,000. S sued B for $5,000, the profit he would have made on the sale. B, citing 2–706(1), argued that S had incurred no lost profits because the resale price equaled the contract price.
>
> If S can show that it had the capacity (assume that 7 more boats were allotted by X to S for 1991) and probably would have made the second sale even though B did not breach, it has established the conditions for lost volume and should recover $5,000. The profit prevented by B's breach is measured under Section 2–708(2). If X's boat allotment had expired or S, because of a weak market, probably could not have sold the third boat to C "but for" B's breach, there is no recovery under any section except for whatever incidental damages (costs) were incurred in effectuating the second sale. See 2–706(1) & 2–710.

4. DAMAGES: SECTION 2–708

If S elects not or is unable to pursue an action for the price, 2–709, or resale damages, 2–706, the residual remedy is an action for damages under 2–708. Put more affirmatively, S could sue for damages under 2–708 even though it had completed goods on hand and a resale was feasible or an action for the price was proper.

Section 2–708 has two subsections. Subsection (1) provides a formula that measures damages by the difference between the unpaid contract price and the market price at the "time and place of tender." Subsection (2), which applies "if the measure of damages provided in subsection (1) is inadequate to put the seller in as good a position as performance would have done," provides that the measure is the "profit (including reasonable overhead) which the seller would have made from full performance by the buyer. . . . " The interaction between these two subsections and with 2–706 is important, complicated and the subject of endless debate.

(a) The Damage Formula: Section 2–708(1)

Section 2–708(1) provides, in part, that the "measure of damages for non-acceptance or repudiation by the buyer is the difference between the market price at the time and place for tender and the unpaid contract price together with any incidental damages . . . but less expenses saved in consequence of the buyer's breach." Section 2–708(1) is "subject to" 2–708(2) and 2–723 regarding "proof of market price." See 2–708(1).

It is helpful to view the 2–708(1) formula as a surrogate for the resale remedy. It is a rough approximation of the profit S would have gotten upon the resale of identified goods: the "market price" ("resale price") at the "time and place for tender" (where the resale was made). In terms of actual costs incurred and profit prevented, however, 2–708(1) may totally miss the mark. It may grossly over or under compensate for claimed profits and may ignore any reliance on the contract altogether.

> ***Example VI(15):*** On April 1, S entered two contracts with B for the sale of manufactured goods. The price of each was $10,000 and shipment was to be on May 1, FOB point of origin. In both contracts, S estimated that the total costs of performance (TCP), including overhead, would be $9,000 and that the net profit on each would be $1,000. B repudiated the contracts on April 25 and S had completed goods on hand. At the time and place for "tender," here the point of shipment, the market price was $8,000. The formula in Section 2–708(1) produces damages of $2,000 on both contracts, plus incidental damages, see 2–710, less expenses saved in consequence of the breach (none apparent here). S also has the goods, which are worth about $8,000. On the assumption that S could have resold the goods at the market price, the 2–708(1) formula makes sense. See 1–106(1).

Suppose, however, that in the first contract S had incurred no performance costs at the time of repudiation (the goods were to be purchased from a manufacturer) and in the second contract the goods had been completed at a total cost of $7,000. The formula damages of $2,000 would appear to overcompensate S under the first and undercompensate S on the second contract. In the first contract, if the estimate of $9,000 TCP was reasonable, S would have earned only $1,000 on full performance by the seller. In the second contract, the actual TCP was less than the contract price, and there would have been a $3,000 profit.

These examples illustrate the imprecision of the formula in 2–708(1). In both, 2–708(2) provides a more realistic measure of loss, if it is available to the parties. Under a literal reading of 2–708(2), however, that subsection is not available unless 2–708(1) is "inadequate" to put S in the same position as full performance. Thus, in the first example B could not compel S to use 2–708(2) because S was in a better position than full performance but in the second example S could invoke 2–708(2) because the formula was inadequate. As we shall see, there are some judicially created exceptions to this literal reading.

Example VI(16): Suppose that, in the first contract in Example VI(15), S had incurred no performance costs at the time B repudiated. Thereafter, S contracted to sell the goods to C for $9,500 and *then* completed manufacture at a total cost of $9,500. Under Section 2–708(1), S's damages are computed at $2,000: the remaining $7,500 cost to finish the goods, incurred after breach, does not qualify as incidental damages under 2–710 and, without more, is at S's risk. But if the decision to complete performance was commercially reasonable, S can resell the goods to C under 2–706(1). See 2–704(2) & 2–706(2). If the resale price is $9,500, S can recover $500 from C under 2–706(1) and, of course, can keep the $9,500 paid by C. Thus, S's total costs are fully reimbursed along with $500 in net profit.

In sum, the 2–708(1) formula works best when S has completed goods on hand that could be resold. S can recover the difference between contract and market price (an approximation of profit) and retain the value of the completed goods. But if S (1) has no completed goods on hand or (2) has partially completed goods on hand or (3) is in a "lost volume" situation, 2–708(1) provides an imperfect and incomplete measure of loss. The formula is imperfect in (1) and (3), above, because it cannot consistently measure S's lost profit. The formula is incomplete in (2), above, because it does not compensate for S's reliance in part-performance. All three cases, therefore, are appropriate for the application of 2–708(2).

Other problems in interpreting 2–708(1) have arisen. Suppose that S is a "middleman" or "jobber" working between the manufacturers of aluminum products and prospective buyers. S buys products from M for resale to B. On February 1, 1990, B contracts with S to supply 100,000 tons of described aluminum at $100 per ton, to be delivered in 5 installments starting on July 1 and over the next 15 months. S is expected to secure the needed aluminum from one or more suppliers. By June 1, the market price for the aluminum has dropped to $70 and is expected to go lower. On June 30, before the first delivery was due, B repudiates the contract. The market price was $65 per ton. S cancels the contract for breach and brings suit for damages under 2–708(1). The case will come to trial *after* the date for the last installment has passed. How should S's damages be measured?

First, the repudiation was a breach of the whole contract and S was justified in canceling the contract. See 2–610(b), 2–703(f). Moreover, 2–708(1) damages are available for breach by repudiation.

Second, the measure of damages in 2–708(1) is "subject to" 2–723. Section 2–723(1) provides that if "an action based on anticipatory repudiation comes to trial before the time for performance with respect to some or all of the goods, any damages based on market price . . . shall be determined according to the price of such goods prevailing at the time when the aggrieved party learned of the repudiation." The market price on such date (June 30) was $65 per ton. The rule is designed to reduce the uncertainty in trying to predict what the market prices would be on several dates in the future. But this case will come to trial after the last date for performance, so the damage measure in 2–723(1) does not apply.

Third, without more, S's damages under 2–708(1) will be the difference between the unpaid contract price ($100) and the market price at the time and place for tender of *each* installment. The evidence of these prices will be available at trial. More importantly, B will get the benefit if the market price moves back up before the contract term expires. For a case so holding, see *Trans World Metals, Inc. v. Southwire Co.,* 769 F.2d 902 (2d Cir.1985). Of course, if the case came to trial after the date for three installments had passed but before the last three installments, the rule of 2–723(1) would apply to the last three.

Fourth, the result discussed immediately above is premised on the conclusion that S, a middleman, is entitled to any profit made while taking the risk of securing supplies for future delivery. This time the market went down, not up, and the venture was highly profitable. Suppose, however, that S, by the time of B's repudiation, had entered forward contracts with suppliers to deliver all of the aluminum at $85 per ton. S, in effect, had hedged the risk and established the cost basis for determining profit. Under these facts, S's real profit upon full performance would be $15 per ton, not the "profit" determined under 2–708(1). That "profit" could be as much as $35 per ton. On facts like these, some courts have concluded that since damages under 2–708(1) would put S in a better position than full performance, this result is inconsistent with the policy of 1–106(1). In short, 1–106(1) was invoked to preclude the application of 2–708(1) and to permit the buyer to invoke 2–708(2) to limit S's profit to that actually made on the deal. This result ignores the literal language in 2–708(2) and concludes that 2–708(1) is not applicable when it is "inadequate" to effectuate the remedial policy of 1–106(1). See *Nobs Chemical, U.S.A., Inc. v. Koppers Co., Inc.,* 616 F.2d 212 (5th Cir.1980). Some commentators have applauded this result, see White, *The Decline of the Contract Market Damage Model,* 11 U.Ark.Little Rock L.J. 1 (1988–89), but others have been sharply critical, see Scott, *The Case for Market Damages: Revisiting the Lost Profits Puzzle,* 57 U.Chi.L.Rev. 1155 (1990).

> *Example VI(17):* S agreed to sell B manufactured goods for $10,000, with delivery on May 1. B repudiated the contract on March 1. At that time, the goods were completed, the market price at the time and place of tender was $10,000 and S could have resold them for $10,000. S elected to wait for performance by B. B, however, wrongfully rejected a tender of delivery on May 1, at which time the relevant market price was $9,000. S's damages under the formula in 2–708(1) are $1,000: when

the case comes to trial after the date fixed for performance, market price is determined at the time and place for tender rather than the time of repudiation. See 2–708(1) & 2–723(1). Some experts have argued, however, that since S can only wait for a commercially reasonable time after learning of the repudiation, see 2–610(b), the market price should be determined at the expiration of that time. This is the time when S should have mitigated damages by resale or otherwise. This argument may be sound because it deters speculation on a shifting market, but it finds little support in the language of 2–708(1) or the requirements of 2–706(1) (S is not required to resell the goods). It simply develops by inference the preferred consequences of inaction after a "commercially reasonable time" expires.

In the view of many, 2–708(1) generates more problems of policy and application than it is worth. As a matter of utility, S should prefer either an action for the price, 2–709, or resale, 2–706, over the formula. As a matter of accurate measurement of loss, Section 2–708(2), with its components analysis, seems preferable to the formula. Conceding that there are some strong supporters of formula damages, let us now examine the scope and application of Section 2–708(2).

(b) The "Components" Analysis: Section 2–708(2)
There are two key questions about Section 2–708(2): (1) When does it apply: and (2) How should it be applied?

(1) Applicability
Section 2–708(2) applies when the measure of damages in Section 2–708(1) is "inadequate to put the seller in as good a position as performance would have done." So expressed, it operates as a device to protect the seller from the vagaries of the formula. But as noted in VI(4)(a), despite the express statutory language, 2–708(2) has been successfully invoked by B in some cases where 2–708(1) overcompensated the seller.

There are two and possibly three "cases" where subsection (2) should be applied upon request by S.

Example VI(18): B repudiated a contract for the sale of manufactured goods at a time when S was in the middle of performance. S reasonably elected to stop performance and to salvage the work in progress. See 2–704(2). The contract price was $10,000 and the market price at the time and place for tender was $9,000. After salvage, S had incurred unreimbursed performance costs in the amount of $4,000 and lost profits in the amount of $1,000. Subsection (2) is applicable, because the measure of damages under Section 2–708(1), some $1,000, is inadequate fully to cover S's performance costs, some $4,000. (Note that the phrase "performance costs" is interchangeable with the word "reliance." We will use the former in this discussion.

Example VI(19): In *Example VI(14),* the "lost volume" problem, suppose that the contract price was $30,000 and both the resale price and the market price at the time and place of tender were $30,000. There would be no loss under 2–706(1) if the goods were resold or the formula in 2–708(1) were applied. S, however, is in a "lost volume" situation and would lose a profit of $5,000 on the contract with B. This is true whether the manufacturer attempts to "fix" the price at which S can resell or not. The courts, therefore, have applied 2–708(2) to compensate for the lost volume issue. Otherwise, S could not achieve the position that would have been obtained by B's full performance. See 1–106(1).

Example VI(20): S contracted to sell manufactured goods to B for $10,000. B repudiated before S had incurred any performance costs and S elected not to begin performance. The market price at the time and place for tender was $8,000 and it was estimated that S would have spent $8,000 in variable costs to perform the contract and, thus, earn a $2,000 gross profit. S's recovery under the formula is $2,000 "less expenses saved in consequences of the buyer's breach." 2–708(1). Can S use 2–708(2) in this case?

The answer is *yes* if the language "less expenses saved" in 2–708(1) is interpreted to include the $8,000 not expended in performance. Under this interpretation, the $2,000 difference between contract and market price would be reduced by $8,000, leaving S with a recovery of minus $6,000 in a case where $2,000 in profit would be earned. The solution, of course, is to apply 2–708(2). Nevertheless, we think that this interpretation of "less expenses saved" is wrong.

If the answer is *no* and "expenses saved" is limited to transportation costs and the like, 2–708(1) still does not fit like a glove. It is a rough measure of profit and cannot deal with S's performance expenditures, if any. This has led some commentators and courts to conclude that S can invoke 2–708(2) rather than 2–708(1) in any case where S does not have completed goods on hand ready for resale. In short, 2–708(1) works best when S has completed goods and should be viewed as a surrogate for a resale that could have but did not occur.

(2) Application
The measure of damages under Section 2–708(2) is the "profit (including reasonable overhead) which the seller would have made from full performance by the buyer, together with any incidental damages . . ., due allowance for costs reasonably incurred and due credit for payments

or proceeds of resale." How should this somewhat confusing and incomplete standard be applied? To illustrate, let us reexamine *Examples VI(18–20)* in reverse order.

In *Example VI(20)*, S, at the time of repudiation, canceled the contract and had incurred no performance costs. If 2–708(1) is inadequate, S can claim the "profit (including reasonable overhead)" which the seller would have made from full performance. Normally, this is determined by subtracting the total variable costs (TVC) that would have been incurred in full performance (the "savings realized"), some $8,000, from the contract price. The resulting $2,000 figure is the "profit (including reasonable overhead) which the seller would have made from full performance by the buyer . . ." 2–708(2).

Courts have awarded overhead (or fixed costs) on the assumption that S has allocated part of its overall fixed costs to the particular contract and if they are not recovered, S must allocate those costs to other contracts, thereby reducing their profitability. This assumption has been challenged by economists, (but not accepted by the courts) who argue that increasing marginal costs will, in most cases, undercut the profitability of subsequent contracts regardless of how overhead is treated.

Some courts have permitted S to prove damages under 2–708(2) without proving how much overhead was allocated to the contract and whether it was "reasonable." It is enough simply to prove the difference between the contract price and total variable costs. B then has the burden to prove that any overhead allocated by S to the contract was unreasonable.

In *Example VI(19)*, the "lost volume" problem, S should measure the lost "profit (including reasonable overhead)" in the same way as in *Example VI(20)*: Subtract from the contract price (KP) the total variable costs (TVC) incurred by S at the time of breach. Here, unlike *Example VI(20)*, S has actually incurred those costs (assume $25,000, including the cost of buying and prepping the boat) and they have been reimbursed by the resale of the boat to C for $30,000. But the "lost volume" of $5,000 still remains and is recoverable under 2–708(2).

If S has received $30,000 from the resale, does the language in Section 2–708(2) that B should receive "due credit for . . . proceeds of resale" mean that S's lost profit is neutralized? The answer is no. The courts have held that the "proceeds of resale" language is limited to a case where S, after breach, resells scrap or components on hand, not the case where S resells completed goods. Otherwise, this would undercut the "lost volume" policy and not put S in the position it would have occupied if B had fully performed. To put the matter differently, if S has "lost volume" and has completed goods on hand, Section 2–708(2) is concerned only with the profit prevented not the performance costs incurred. S may or may not resell the completed goods and, if it does, the proceeds will not be used to reduce the recovery. This is the analysis adopted in *R.E. Davis Chemical Corp. v. Diasonics, Inc.*, 826 F.2d 678 (7th Cir.1987), and other courts. See also, Schlosser, *Damages For the Lost Volume Seller: Does An Efficient Formula Already Exist?*, 17 U.C.C.L.J. 238 (1985).

Remember, *R.E. Davis Chemical Corp.*, held that S (not B) must establish the extent to which the second sale would have been profitable. Thus, if S's TVC would have been higher in the second sale than in the first, the profit would be less. It is this lesser profit for which B should be liable.

In *Example VI(18)*, S had started but not completed performance at the time of breach and, exercising commercially reasonable judgment, elected to stop work and salvage the contract. This is a protected option under 2–704(2). Again, S's "profit (including reasonable overhead)" is calculated by subtracting the total variable costs (TVC) from the contract price. But here, S has incurred some but not all of the costs necessary to complete performance. To establish the total variable costs, then, S must prove both the reasonable costs incurred up to the breach and the costs that would have to be incurred to complete performance. Actual costs incurred plus savings realized on breach equal total variable costs for purposes of establishing lost profit and S has the burden of proof on this issue.

What about the performance costs incurred up to the breach, which will not be reimbursed by a payment of profit? Arguably, S can recover them as a "due allowance for costs reasonably incurred." 2–708(2). If, however, S is able, through the mitigation of damages, to sell some of the scrap or components on hand, the "due allowance" should be reduced by the proceeds of that resale. Here is a more concrete example.

Example VI(21): S agreed to manufacture goods for B for $10,000. S estimated the total variable costs would be $8,500 and allocated $500 of its total fixed costs (overhead) incurred in operating the plant to the contract. If all went well, S expected a profit excluding overhead of $1,000. (Profit, $1,000, = KP, $10,000, minus TVC, $8,500, + fixed costs, $500). B repudiated when S was in the middle of performance and S reasonably stopped work. See 2–704. At that time, S had reasonably incurred $4,000 in variable costs, mostly in the purchase of materials, and estimated that it would cost $4,000 more to complete performance. At the same time, S was able to resell some of the materials on hand for performance to C for $2,000.

S's damages under Section 2–708(2) should be calculated as follows:

$10,000 (KP)

less

8,000 (TVC = $4,000 in reasonable variable costs incurred *plus* $4,000 in reasonable variable costs estimated to complete performance)

equals

2,000 (the lump sum amount including profit *plus* reasonable overhead)

plus

2,000 ($4,000 in reasonable variable costs *less* $2,000 proceeds of resale)

equals

$4,000 (total recovery, including net profit, reasonable overhead and reasonable performance costs after mitigation by resale)

Despite complexity and uncertainty, this is the interpretation of Section 2–708(2) that makes the most sense, especially when the general objectives of damages for breach are considered. For an excellent overall analysis, see Sebert, *Remedies Under Article Two of the Uniform Commercial Code: An Agenda for Review*, 130 U.Pa.L.Rev. 360, 383–407 (1983).

5. OTHER PROBLEMS
(a) Mitigation of Damages

As a general rule, damages for breach of contract are "not recoverable for loss that the injured party could have avoided without undue risk, burden or humiliation." Restatement (Second) Contracts 350(1). At the very least, the aggrieved party, after the breach, must make a reasonable effort to avoid or reduce the loss. This principle, although not explicitly stated, pervades seller's remedies under the Code.

First, if B breaches and S has completed goods on hand not accepted by B, S cannot recover the price unless it has made reasonable and unsuccessful efforts to resell or shows that such effort would be impracticable. 2–709(1)(b). And if a resale is effected, it must be made "in good faith and in a commercially reasonable manner" before S can recover damages under 2–706(1).

Second, if S is *not* in a "lost volume" situation and makes a resale that could not have been made "but for" B's breach, Section 2–708(2) is not available. S's damages are determined exclusively by Section 2–706(1) or 2–708(1). Arguably, a proper resale under 2–706(1) trumps damages under the 2–708(1) formula. Suppose S in Ohio agreed to ship FOB point of shipment to B in New York and B wrongfully rejected the goods upon arrival. S made a commercially reasonable resale in New York at or above the contract price. If S subsequently sued under 2–708(1) and proved damages of $5,000 based upon the market price at the time and place (Ohio) of tender, B should get full credit for the resale in New York. This result both implements the mitigation policy and the policy of 1–106(1) against over-compensation. See *Afram Export Corp. v. Metallurgiki Halyps, S.A.,* 772 F.2d 1358 (7th Cir.1985), which supports this result.

Third, the "formula" in Section 2–708(1) has built-in mitigation features. S is limited to the "market price" (a reasonable composite) at the time when S should protect himself (when the breach occurred) and the most convenient place to act (the place of tender).

Fourth, Section 2–704(2) provides that where the "goods are unfinished an aggrieved seller may in the exercise of reasonable commercial judgment for the purpose of avoiding loss and of effective realization either complete the manufacture and wholly identify the goods to the contract or cease manufacture and resell for scrap or salvage value or proceed in any other reasonable manner." If S reasonably stops performance, the problems in *Example VI(17),* including the duty to make reasonable efforts to salvage scrap and materials on hand, are posed. But suppose S elects, after breach, to complete performance and resell. Here is one last example.

> *Example VI(22):* Suppose, in *Example VI(21),* that upon breach by B, S elected to complete performance at a total cost of $8,500. After reasonable efforts, S was unable to resell the goods. S then sued B under Section 2–709(1)(b) for the $10,000 price. B's defense was that S's decision to complete performance rather than to stop work was unreasonable, that it enhanced rather than mitigated damages, and that recovery should be limited to that available under Section 2–708(2), $4,000, rather than the $10,000 contract price. This defense turns on whether S exercised "reasonable commercial judgment" and the burden is on B to show that he did not, "based upon the facts as they appear at the time he learns of the breach." 2–704, Comment 2. Given the Code's pro-resale bias and the usual efficiency if S is able to resell, B's burden is severe indeed. Any honest judgment by S based upon plausible market projections should carry the day.

(b) Incidental Damages

Under Article 2, incidental damages are post-breach expenses incurred by the aggrieved party to salvage part performance, resell, retrieve, "cover" or protect the goods or otherwise mitigate damages. *For the seller, they include "any commercially reasonable charges, expenses or commissions incurred in stopping delivery, in the transportation, care and custody of goods after the buyer's breach, in connection with return or resale of the goods or otherwise resulting from the breach."* 2–710. This flexible standard is limited by the concept of reasonableness and the damages are available as a matter of course with whatever remedy the seller pursues. See, e.g., Sections 2–706(1), 2–708(1) and 2–709(1). For the buyer's incidental damages, see 2–715(1).

(c) Consequential Damages

Consequential damages, in general, are losses resulting from the inability of the aggrieved party to use the promised performance for purposes of which the defendant knew or had reason to know at the time of contracting. In addition to the foreseeability requirement, the losses must be caused by the breach, and proved with reasonable certainty and the aggrieved party must take reasonable steps to avoid or minimize them. See 1–106(1), Comment 1.

There is no provision authorizing the seller to recover consequential damages. Compare 2–715(2), authorizing consequential damages for the buyer. Section 1–106(1) provides that "neither consequential or special nor penal damages may be had except as specifically provided in this Act or by other rule of law." Some courts, relying on 1–106(1), have held that since consequential damages are not "specifically provided" for the seller in Article 2, the seller may not claim them. See, e.g., *Afram Export Corp. v. Metallurgiki Halyps, S.A.,* 772 F.2d 1358 (7th Cir.1985). This reading of 1–106(1) seems to ignore the fact that such damages are permitted under general contract law. In any event, there is no persuasive reason why the buyer but not the seller should be entitled to claim consequentials under Article 2.

> *Example VI(23):* S contracted to sell B an expensive piece of factory equipment, to be delivered in six months, for $250,000. B agreed to pay $50,000 at the time of contracting and the balance at the time of delivery. The contract provided that prompt payment was essential, and S informed B that the money would be needed to pay a loan taken to finance the contract and to purchase additional equipment for the plant. B, without justification, failed to pay on time. In fact, the $200,000 was not paid for another 60 days. As a result, S had to refinance the loan at a higher interest rate and lost business opportunities because the new equipment was not installed.
>
> If the damage claims are consequential, as they appear to be, S should be able to recover them from B. B should pay for S's foreseeable losses resulting from the delay in payment. If the damage claims are classified

as incidental, see 2–710, then they are also recoverable. S could argue, with some plausibility, that the higher interest paid to refinance the loan (that would have been paid off) was a commercially reasonable expense "otherwise resulting from the breach." They were paid to avoid a default on and enforcement of the loan. But stretching such as this could be avoided by treating these and other "opportunity cost" losses resulting from the breach as consequential and permitting their recovery.

D. BUYER'S REMEDIES

1. IN GENERAL

The buyer's remedies upon breach by the seller are catalogued in Section 2–711. Read that Section, please. Note that the 2–711(1) starts with a listing of the types of breach by S and defines the impact the breach must have before B can cancel the contract. Review Ch. VI(C)(1)(b). The available remedies, tailored more or less to the type of breach, then follow. Although the types of breach by S and the uses to which B might put the goods differ, *Section 2–711 and sections following provide B with remedies that parallel those available to S under Section 2–703 and sections following: (1) Specific performance, a judicial order to S to deliver the goods, see 2–711(2)(b), achieves the same function as S's action for the price under Section 2–709; (2) "Cover," i.e., purchasing substitute goods from a third party, see 2–711(1)(a), is a remedy consistent with S's power to resell the goods under Section 2–706(1); and (3) Damages for "non-delivery" serve the same interests as S's damages under Section 2–708.*

But the parallelism is not complete: B appears to have protection different from and additional to that of S. For example, B, in addition to cancellation and more affirmative remedies, may recover "so much of the price as has been paid." 2–711(1). Thus, it is easier for B to have restitution of the price paid to S than it is for S to recover goods delivered to B. See the discussion in Ch. VII(E)(1), *infra*. Further, there is a special remedy when B seeks damages to "accepted goods," i.e., non-conforming goods where there was neither a rightful rejection nor a justifiable revocation of acceptance. See 2–714. This remedy is not listed in the Section 2–711 catalogue. Finally, B, unlike S, receives explicit protection against consequential damages caused by S's breach. 2–715(2). These are losses "resulting from" B's general or particular needs, requirements or uses for the goods "of which the seller at the time of contracting had reason to know. . . ." These remedies, along with incidental damages, 2–715(1), give B's expectations in both obtaining and using the goods comprehensive protection.

> *Example VI(24):* B, a baker, had two delivery trucks. When one was stolen, B contracted with S for a new truck. B paid $5,000 of the $20,000 contract price, with the balance due on delivery. S, knowing of B's special needs, promised to deliver the truck in two weeks. S failed to deliver on time and stated that the truck would not be available for four weeks. B canceled the contract and promptly purchased a similar truck from another dealer for

$25,000, with delivery in two weeks. B may recover from S: (1) the $5,000 down payment, 2–711(1); (2) the difference between the contract price and the "cover" or repurchase price, $5,000, see 2–711(1)(a) & 2–712(1); (3) the reasonable expenses incurred in arranging the cover, 2–715(1); and (4) any foreseeable, consequential lost profits resulting from S's failure to deliver that B could not prevent "by cover or otherwise." 2–715(2)(a).

2.   SELLER REPUDIATES OR FAILS TO DELIVER

Where S repudiates or fails to deliver the promised goods, B has three remedial choices: (1) obtain the goods from S by specific performance, 2–716(1), or reclamation under Section 2–502; (2) obtain substitute goods by purchase or "cover" from a third party, 2–712; or (3) seek damages under Section 2–713. Assuming that B's primary objective is to obtain the promised goods or substitutes, let us examine the content and interaction of these remedies.

(a)   Specific Performance: Section 2–716

Under Section 2–716(1), "specific performance may be decreed where the goods are unique or in other proper circumstances." It is an equitable remedy backed by the contempt power, and the decree orders S to deliver the goods contracted for to B. The specific performance decree is frequently preceded by an injunction against breach by S and may include "such terms and conditions as to payment of the price, damages, or other relief as the court may deem just." 2–716(2). The remedy is part of a larger body of equitable principles which supplement Article 2. See 1–103.

The conditions for specific performance in 2–716(1) are consistent with the general principle that coercive orders are available when legal remedies are inadequate. For example, "unique" goods, such as a Picasso original, are usually required by the contract for performance and, because of special attributes, are not easily replaceable on the market. Neither "cover" nor damages would adequately compensate for their loss. The second condition, "other proper circumstances," refers less to the special attributes of the goods and more to market conditions, the duration of the contract or B's special needs that adversely affect the adequacy of cover or the measurement of damages. The conditions are flexible and are intended to "further a more liberal attitude than some courts have shown in connection with the specific performance of contracts of sale." 2–716, Comment 1.

> *Example VI(25):* B, a coin collector, contracted to buy a 1916 D Mercury dime in uncirculated condition from S, a dealer, for $15,000. The coin was very rare and B needed it to fill his collection of uncirculated Mercury dimes. S repudiated the contract and offered to sell the dime to C for $20,000. The goods are "unique" in quality and the court would probably enjoin S from selling the coin to C and order specific performance. As an alternative, B might seek replevin under Section 2–716(3): the goods are "identified to the contract" and

"circumstances reasonably indicate" that B will be unable to effect cover with reasonable effort. (You may substitute for the 1916–D dime an original Picasso or a limited edition Ferrari and get the same result.)

Example VI(26): B, a canner, contracted to buy all of S's tomato crop, to be grown on 100 acres, for $1.00 per pound. S's field adjoined B's cannery. The growing season was short, and the tomatoes had to be processed immediately after picking to insure peak quality. Between the time of planting and the time of harvesting, the market price increased from $1 to $4 per pound. S harvested the tomatoes, repudiated the contract and offered to sell them on the open market. If similar tomatoes were available without undue delay on the open market, specific performance would probably be denied: a sharp price increase alone does not make the goods "unique" or constitute other proper circumstances. If similar tomatoes were not readily available at any price or if "cover" would unreasonably delay the canning process, specific performance would probably be granted: an inability to meet short term needs through cover or to compensate the loss, here consequential, through damages constitutes "other proper circumstances."

Example VI(27): B, a public utility, contracted to buy 50% of S's output of natural gas at a fixed price with escalation over a 15 year period. The price of natural gas rose beyond the scope of the escalation provision and, after 5 years, S repudiated the contract. B could arrange substitute gas contracts for a 4 year term but not longer. The court would probably order S to deliver 50% of its output over the balance of the contract to B. An adequate "cover" for the long-term was not available and the damages for breach were too uncertain to measure. In addition, the public interest required a reliable and continuous source of energy. In general, courts will routinely grant specific performance of long-term supply contracts without extensive discussion. A leading case is *Laclede Gas Co. v. Amoco Oil Co.,* 522 F.2d 33 (8th Cir.1975).

Again, if specific performance is granted, the court has power to mold the decree to fit the equities of the particular case. For example, if, in *Example VI(27),* the cost of energy exceeded the escalation clause by 300% and S did not clearly assume the risk, see 2–615(a), a modern court might condition the specific performance decree upon B's agreement to a fair price adjustment with S. At least, the power is there even if infrequently exercised. If specific performance is denied, most courts have held that the court may retain jurisdiction to "clean up" the litigation by awarding damages or other appropriate relief.

(b) Recovery From Insolvent Seller: Section 2-502

Section 2-502(1) provides a limited basis for B to recover goods identified to the contract from an insolvent S. B must have paid "a part or all of the price of goods in which he has a special property interest" and keep "good a tender of any unpaid portion of their price." S must become "insolvent within ten days after receipt of the first installment of their price." If these conditions are met, B may "recover them from the seller." If B rather than S identified the goods to the contract, "he acquires the right to recover the goods only if they conform to the contract for sale." 2-502(2).

The parallel with 2-702(2), involving S's right to recover goods delivered on credit to an insolvent B, is obvious. And here, like replevin in 2-716(3), the right to recovery depends upon B having a special property interest through identification of the goods. See 2-501. We will have more to say about the right of seller and buyer to recover goods from an insolvent party and how those rights fare against the claims of other creditors and purchasers to the goods in Chapter VII(3), *infra*. Remember, however, that any right to possession that is triggered by insolvency and is not a perfected security interest under Article 9 is a potential preference under § 547 or other avoidance provisions of the Bankruptcy Code. See Levy, Impact of the New Bankruptcy Code on Article 2, Sales, 14 U.C.C.L.J. 307, 336–338 (1982).

(c) "Cover": Section 2-712

If specific performance or replevin are not available and B still needs the goods, it may attempt to purchase substitutes from a third party. *Under Section 2-712(1), B may "cover by making in good faith and without unreasonable delay any reasonable purchase of or contract to purchase goods in substitution for those due from the seller." Although not clearly stated, the necessary implication is that these conditions must be satisfied before B is entitled to "cover" damages under Section 2-712(2), which are the "difference between the cost of cover and the contract price together with any incidental or consequential damages . . . ., but less expenses saved in consequence of the seller's breach."*

The "cover" remedy is B's analogue to S's power to "resell" under 2-706, except that B is not required to notify S of an intention to "cover." Compare 2-706(3). According to 2-712(3), the "failure of the buyer to effect cover within this section does not bar him from any other remedy." A broad reading of this language would encompass either a complete failure to effect any cover or an actual repurchase in bad faith or with unreasonable delay. The most common residual or "back up" remedy is damages under Section 2-713.

> ***Example VI(28):*** B, a collector, contracted to buy an uncirculated 1916 D Mercury dime from S, a dealer, for $15,000. S changed her mind and failed to deliver. The market price of the described goods at the time B

learned of the breach was $16,000. See 2–713(1). B, after 5 days of effort, uncovered a 1916 D Mercury dime in Extra–Fine rather than uncirculated condition in an estate. She purchased the coin for $18,000, the fair market value. Assuming that B "covered" in good faith and without unreasonable delay, the question is whether there was a "reasonable purchase of . . . goods in substitution for those due from the seller." 2–712(1). If so, B can recover $3,000 plus incidental damages under Section 2–712(2) and 2–715(1). If not, "cover" is not available and B can recover $1,000 plus incidental damages under Section 2–713(1) or, perhaps, seek specific performance.

Arguably, the difference between the two coins, reflected in the prices, suggests that an Extra–Fine is not a "reasonable" substitution for an "uncirculated" coin. In the coin business, the difference in grade is a distinction of substance.

Example VI(29): B, an investor, contracted to purchase 100 Canadian Maple Leaf gold coins from S, a dealer, for $400 each. Due to an international crisis, the price of gold soared and S failed to deliver. At the time B learned of the breach, the market price of Maple Leafs was $500 each. Two weeks later, B, in four separate purchases from four dealers, purchased a total of 100 Maple Leafs at an average price of $550 and, thereafter, sued S under Section 2–712(2), claiming damages of $150 per coin. B claimed that the two week delay was inadvertent: he was busy at the office. Nevertheless, if the delay was "unreasonable" in a rising market or the four contracts were an unreasonable method of "covering," B's damages are limited to the difference between the contract price and the market price at the time B "learned of the breach." 2–713(1).

Example VI(30): Here's one to think about. Suppose, in *Example VI(29),* that B, two weeks after the breach, covered in one contract at $450 per coin. Damages under 2–712(2) are $50 per coin but damages under 2–713(1) are $100 per coin. B sues under 2–713(1) for $100 per coin. S argues that because B "effected" cover, it is barred from recovering damages under 2–713(1). B replies that 2–712 is not applicable because the two week delay was unreasonable and, even so, the remedies are cumulative and no election was made simply because a cover was effected. Who should prevail?

Suppose the buyer, a manufacturer, needs the goods but specific performance is not available (the seller has no completed goods on hand) and no third party can be found who can supply substitutes within a reasonable time. In these circumstances, some courts have recognized that B may "cover" by producing the goods itself and that the cover price is the reasonable cost of producing the goods internally. See *Dura–Wood Treating Co. v. Century*

Forest Industries, Inc., 675 F.2d 745 (5th Cir.1982). Needless to say, this method of cover is not specifically authorized by 2–712 and raises difficult questions about how to measure the cover price and the definition of incidental damages.

(d) Damages: Section 2–713

Section 2–713(1) provides a formula for measuring B's damages for S's "non-delivery or repudiation:" The measure of damages is the "difference between the market price at the time when the buyer learned of the breach and the contract price together with any incidental and consequential damages . . . but less expenses saved in consequence of the seller's breach." The "market price," to be proved under Section 2–723, "is to be determined as of the place for tender or, in cases of rejection after arrival or revocation of acceptance, as of the place of arrival." 2–713(2).

> *Example VI(31):* S, a grain dealer, contracted on March 1 to sell B a carload of wheat for $5,000 and to ship it by November 1, FOB point of shipment. B was to pay the freight, some $500. S failed to ship by November 1, but B did not learn of this until November 5. The market price at the point of shipment was $6000 on November 1 and $6300 on November 5. The market price at the point of arrival, some 1,500 miles away, was $4500 on November 1 and $4600 on November 5.
>
> B's damages under 2–713 are $1300, measured by the difference between the contract price, $5000 and the market price at the point of shipment at the time when B learned of the breach, $6300, less freight costs saved by the breach, $500. The assumption is that the time of breach should correspond to when B had sufficient information to take action and that it is reasonable to determine the market price at the place where shipment was to occur. In this sense, 2–713 is a surrogate for "cover" because a prompt cover at the point of shipment would satisfy the conditions of 2–712(1).

Suppose, in *Example VI(31),* that when B learned of S's breach it promptly covered at the point of arrival for $4600. Later, it sued S for $800 damages under Section 2–713(1). Can S successfully defend on the ground that B has elected the cover remedy and is foreclosed from damages? See *Example VI(30).* The answer is not clear. On the one hand, the Code policy favoring cumulation and disfavoring election of remedies supports B, especially where B's conduct was in good faith. This is consistent with the conclusion that if S resold under Section 2–706(1) it should not be barred from damages under Section 2–708. On the other hand, B's expectations have been fully satisfied by the "cover" and an award of damages under Section 2–713(1) would appear to put him in a better position than full performance. Moreover, the remedial choice, rather than offering better protection, may prompt speculation in an effort to enhance damages. One solution is to revise Article

2 to clarify that a valid cover under 2–712(1) precludes a subsequent action under 2–713. A more complex solution is to assume that B has a choice of remedies unless S can show that B acted in "bad faith" in the enforcement of the contract through a manipulation of remedies in a manner inconsistent with the compensation policy of Section 1–106(1).

A final, vexing problem under 2–713 can arise when S's breach is by repudiation rather than non-delivery. Suppose that S, on May 1, contracts to sell B a carload of wheat for $5000, FOB point of shipment, with shipment by December 1. On June 1, when a carload is worth $6000 at the point of shipment, S repudiates the contract and refuses B's request for a retraction. Assuming that specific performance is not available, what are B's options?

First, B can decide to treat the repudiation as final, cancel the contract and "cover." 2–610(b), 2–711(1)(a) & 2–712. Since proof of market price is not required under 2–712(2), the provisions of 2–723 are not applicable. The time when the case comes to trial is irrelevant.

Second, B could cancel the contract and instead of covering immediately sue for damages under 2–713(1), 2–610(b), 2–711(1)(b). What are B's damages under 2–713? Here 2–723 becomes relevant. If the case came to trial before the "time for performance," here December 1, "any damages based on market price . . . shall be determined according to the price of such goods prevailing at the time when the aggrieved party learned of the repudiation 2–723(1)." That was June 1 and the market price was $6,000.

But if the case came to trial after December 1, damages are to be determined by the market price "when the buyer learned of the breach." 2–713(1). When does B "learn of the breach," (1) when he learns of the repudiation, (2) when he elects to treat the repudiation as a breach and cancels the contract, or (3) when S actually fails to deliver by December 1? Assuming that B has canceled, we think that the answer is option # 2. Since Section 2–610(a) permits B to await S's performance for a "commercially reasonable time" and B has canceled within that time, there is efficiency in measuring damages at the time when B decided to act on rather than when it learned of the repudiation. Unlike a breach by nondelivery, 2–610(b) gives B a reasonable time to reflect. A choice to cancel and sue made within that time negates the risk of any unfair speculation and insures that the market price will approximate that existing when B first learned of the "breach," i.e., repudiation.

Third, suppose B learns of the repudiation and decides to preserve the contract (i.e., does not cancel) until December 1. Consider the following Example.

Example VI(32): On May 1, S contracted to sell B a carload of wheat for $5,000, shipment FOB point of shipment, delivery by December 1. On June 1, S repudiated the contract. The market price at the time and place for tender was $5,500. B insisted on performance and informed S that it would wait until December 1 for delivery. On July 1 the market price was $6,500, on September 1 the market price was $7,500 and on December 1, when S failed to ship, the market price was $8,500. B claims $3,500 in damages under Section 2–713(1), measured by the difference between the contract price ($5,000) and the market price at the time when he "learned of the breach," December 1. B claims that since it elected to ignore the repudiation, it learned of the breach when S failed to deliver. S argues that under the circumstances, the "commercially reasonable" time that B could wait for performance expired no later than July 1 and that B's damages should be limited by the market price at that time, $6,500. S concedes that it would be unreasonable to require B to "cover" at that time, but that fair compensation requires that damages be computed "as if" it had covered. What result?

Assuming that a "commercially reasonable" time expired on July 1, most commentators and some courts favor S, even though B has not elected to treat the repudiation as a breach and the statutory language does not squarely support the result. This outcome is thought to promote realistic loss measurement and to avoid speculation on fluctuating markets. See *Cosden Oil & Chemical Co. v. Karl O. Helm Aktiengesellschaft*, 736 F.2d 1064 (5th Cir.1984). B, on the other hand, argues that assuming a repudiation by S (this may be uncertain in most cases), B, by waiting, assumed the risk that S would retract the repudiation, 2–611, and that the market would go down rather than up. If neither event occurs, B should recover the value of its bargain measured at the time S agreed to deliver. Which side should prevail? Compare *Example VI(17)*.

(e) Incidental and Consequential Damages: 2–715

Both 2–712 and 2–713 provide that B may recover incidental and consequential damages under 2–715. The buyer's entitlement to incidental and consequential damages is treated in Chapter VI, Part 5. Note, however, the B's access to consequential damages may be limited if S has repudiated or failed to deliver and B has decided not to cover under 2–712. For example, suppose that S had failed to deliver factory equipment, B decides not to cover and claims lost profits resulting from the breach. Under 2–715(2)(a), those losses, if otherwise established, can be recovered only if they "could not reasonably be prevented by cover or otherwise." If the goods were readily available and B decided after the breach that they were not needed, it is unlikely that a court would award consequential damages. In short, B has failed to mitigate damages as required by 2–715(2)(a). Even if B has mitigated, it must still establish that (1) the losses resulted from the breach,

(2) S had reason to foresee them at the time of contracting, and (3) the amount is provable with reasonable certainty.

3. NON-CONFORMING TENDER BY SELLER

Overview. As explained in Chapter V(F)(2)(a), when S tenders delivery, B has a right to inspect the goods or documents before payment or acceptance. 2–513(1). If inspection reveals a non-conformity, e.g., a late tender, defects in quality, deficiencies in quantity or improper documents, B may attempt to *reject* the tender under Section 2–601. If the rejection is *rightful*, the goods are, in effect, thrown back on S for disposition, and B may pursue the same remedies as if S had failed to deliver. 2–711(1). If B accepts the goods and later discovers a non-conformity, B may attempt to *revoke* the acceptance under Section 2–608. If the revocation is *justifiable,* then, again, the goods are thrown back on the seller and B may pursue the catalogue of remedies in Section 2–711(1).

After a proper rejection or revocation of acceptance, the goods may be in B's possession until S can dispose of them. In this case, B will have some duties of due care and cooperation, see 2–603, 2–604, 2–605 & 2–608(3), and, if payments have been made or expenses reasonably incurred, B will have a security interest in the goods to secure these obligations of S. 2–711(3).

Of course, a wrongful rejection or revocation by B is a breach of contract, for which S may pursue appropriate remedies. 2–703.

Finally, if nonconforming goods have been accepted, a revocation of acceptance is not justifiable, and proper notice of breach has been given under 2–607(3)(a), B's damages are determined by Section 2–714, plus incidental, 2–715(1), and consequential damages, 2–715(2).

(a) Rejection

Section 2–601 establishes what has been called the "perfect tender" rule. Subject to agreement of the parties and the rules for installment contracts, see 2–612, "if the goods or the tender of delivery fail in any respect to conform to the contract the buyer may (a) reject the whole; or (b) accept the whole; or (c) accept any commercial unit or units and reject the rest." Thus, if S has agreed to deliver 1,000 bushels of # 1 Wheat by October 1 and tenders on October 2 or tenders 999 bushels on October 1, B, arguably, may reject the "whole" tender. To be effective, B must reject within a reasonable time after delivery or tender and must seasonably notify S. 2–602(1). In addition, B should state any defects which are ascertainable by reasonable inspection and upon which the rejection is based. A failure to so state may waive the unstated objection. See 2–605.

> ***Example VI(33):*** S agreed to deliver 1,000 bushels of # 1 Wheat by October 1. S tendered and B properly rejected (2–601) 990 bushels of # 1 Wheat on October 3. B stated that the reason for rejection was "delay in

delivery," but, because of a strike which excused S, the delay was not a proper ground for rejection. B then claimed that the deficiency in quantity justified rejection and S responded that B was now precluded from "relying on the unstated defect to justify rejection or to establish breach." 2–605(1). S is correct only if the defect, "if stated seasonably," could have been "cured" by the seller. 2–605(1)(a). On these facts, S could have cured only if S had "reasonable grounds to believe" that the deficient quantity "would be acceptable with or without money allowance. . . ." 2–508(2). If not, S was prejudiced by the unstated objection and the rejection is rightful.

There are important limitations on the rejection remedy, some stated in Section 2–601 and some not. Here is a brief list of them.

First, the parties may agree that B shall have no right to reject or that it may be exercised only when the breach is substantial. These agreements are normally enforceable. See 2–601 & 2–719(1).

Second, the contract may be an installment contract, i.e., S may be authorized to deliver the goods in "separate lots to be separately accepted." 2–612(1). If so, B may not reject any installment unless the "non-conformity substantially impairs the value of that installment and cannot be cured. . . ." 2–612(2). Thus, if S agreed to deliver 5,000 bushels of # 1 Wheat in 5 installments of 1,000 bushels each and, in the first installment, tendered 990 bushels or tendered 1,000 bushels one day late, B's power to reject would be limited by the substantial impairment test.

Third, in an FOB point of shipment contract, if S fails to notify B of the shipment or fails to make a "proper contract" of shipment, B may reject "only if material delay or loss ensues." 2–504. This limitation and the ones to follow are not stated in Section 2–601.

Fourth, the rejection must be in good faith. B has a duty to enforce the contract in good faith, 1–203, and bad faith for a merchant would include a rejection that was dishonest or inconsistent with "reasonable commercial standards of fair dealing in the trade." 2–103(1)(b). Suppose that S tendered 990 bushels of 1,000 agreed to be delivered in a single lot. If B was honestly dissatisfied with the performance and rejection was a reasonable response in the trade, the rejection would be in good faith. But if, in a falling market, B rejected to avoid a bad bargain rather than from dissatisfaction with S's performance, the enforcement may be in bad faith. Put another way, it is bad faith to seize upon a minor breach as a way to reallocate a market risk which B had fairly assumed at the time of contracting. See *Neumiller Farms, Inc. v. Cornett,* 368 So.2d 272 (Ala.1979). *Caveat*: There is considerable disagreement about the scope and meaning of good faith in this context.

Fifth, B cannot reject if S has power to correct or "cure" the defect under Section 2–508. In some contracts, S has power by agreement to cure defects in material and workmanship after tender and this agreement is a limitation upon rejection. Under Section 2–508, S has a limited, unilateral power to cure *whether B likes it or not* in two circumstances: (1) If the "time for performance has not yet expired" and B has rejected a non-conforming tender or delivery, S may "seasonably notify the buyer of his intention to cure and may then within the contract time make a conforming tender," 2–508(1); and (2) Where the "buyer rejects a non-conforming tender which the seller had reasonable grounds to believe would be acceptable with or without money allowance the seller may if he seasonably notifies the buyer have a further reasonable time to substitute a conforming tender." 2–508(2).

Sixth, as a practical matter, many buyers may accept the goods without discovering a non-conformity that would justify a rejection. As a result, the acceptance cannot be revoked unless the non-conformity "substantially impairs" the value of the goods to the buyer. 2–608(1). In short, there is no "perfect tender" rule after acceptance.

Seventh, even if a rejection is rightful, B does not necessarily have power to cancel the contract. 2–711(1) provides that if the buyer "rightfully rejects . . . then with respect to any goods involved, and with respect to the whole if the breach goes to the whole . . ., the buyer may cancel."

> *Example VI(34):* S agreed to deliver 1,000 bushels of # 1 Wheat by October 1. On September 15, S tendered and B rejected 1,000 bushels of # 2 Wheat. Since the time for performance "has not yet expired," S may cure under Section 2–508(1) by notifying B of his "intention to cure" and then by making a tender of 1,000 bushels of # 1 Wheat by October 1. An offer to accept a reduction in the agreed price for # 1 Wheat would not be a proper cure.

> *Example VI(35):* In previous courses of dealing with B, S had tendered and B had accepted and paid for goods that deviated in quantity from that promised from 10 to 30%. S, in a falling market, tendered 800 bushels in a contract calling for 1,000 bushels and B rejected the tender. Under Section 2–508(2), S has a "further reasonable time to substitute a conforming tender" if he "seasonably notifies the buyer." S had, from the prior course of dealing, "reasonable grounds to believe" that tender "would be acceptable with or without money allowance."

> *Example VI(36):* S, a retailer, tendered and a consumer rejected a T.V. set with a defective picture tube. S, with a right to cure under Section 2–508(2), offered either to replace the picture tube or to reduce the contract price. B insisted upon a new T.V. set. The question is whether S has made a "conforming tender." Unless the circumstances indicated

that B would accept the defective T.V. with a price adjustment, the offer of a price adjustment is not a cure. In some cases, an offer to replace the defective part has been held to be sufficient especially if the replacement can be made quickly and without affecting overall quality. For more complex goods, such as a new car, some courts have required S to tender a new car to cure a material defect in the first tender. B, arguably, would not have purchased a new car knowing that it needed repairs and requiring B to accept and pay for a repaired car would, in the absence of agreement, be unfair.

Enough has been said to suggest that the "perfect" tender rule of 2–601 is something less than perfect and that the exceptions, explicit or hidden, may eat up the rule. This reality, the risk of its abuse and the fact that CISG employs a concept of "fundamental breach," see Articles 46(2) & 49, have lead some commentators to urge rejection of the perfect tender rule. See Sebert, *Rejection, Revocation and Cure under Article 2 of the UCC: Some Modest Proposals,* 84 Nw.U.L.Rev. 375 (1990). Others, urging that the rule gives needed remedial leverage to consumer buyers, have argued for the status quo. What do you think?

One final set of rejection problems involves B's rights and duties regarding goods in his possession after a rightful rejection under 2–601. Here are some illustrations.

> *Example VI(37):* In a contract for the sale of machinery, B paid S 50% of the price before delivery. Upon tender by S, B took possession of the goods to inspect them and, after the expenditure of $1,000 found a serious defect. B rightfully rejected the goods and canceled the contract. S directed B to ship the goods to him but refused to return the down payment or to reimburse B for inspection costs. Under 2–711(3), B has a security interest in the rejected machinery to secure repayment of the price and inspection expenses "reasonably incurred." This is a possessory security interest arising under Article 2 rather than a security interest created by agreement. See 9–113. If S refuses to pay, B may resell the goods "in like manner as an agreed seller" under 2–706(1) and satisfy S's debt from the proceeds. Unlike the normal procedure under 2–706(6), however, B must remit surplus proceeds to S. 2–711(3), Comment 2. See 9–504(2).

> *Example VI(38):* B, a merchant, rightfully rejected grain in his possession for defects in quality. The market price was dropping rapidly and S, by telephone, requested B to resell the grain promptly for S's account. Does B have a duty to resell here?

If B has no security interest in the goods, its general duty is to hold the goods "with reasonable care at seller's disposition for a time sufficient to permit the seller to remove them." 2–602(2)(b). If S gives no instructions within a reasonable time, B may store, resell or reship them for S's account and such action is not "acceptance or conversion." 2–604.

A merchant B, however, has somewhat greater obligations under Section 2–603. At a minimum, it must "follow any reasonable instructions received from the seller with respect to the goods." Even if no instructions are received, if the goods are perishable or "threaten to decline in value speedily," B must take "reasonable efforts to sell them for seller's account." 2–603(1). In a falling market, therefore, the merchant B must comply with S's reasonable request to resell and may have such a duty in any event. In complying with these requirements, B is "held only to good faith and good faith conduct," 2–603(3), and is to be reimbursed for reasonable expenses incurred. 2–603(2).

Example VI(39): S tendered and B took possession of a suite of furniture for purposes of inspection. Later, B rightfully rejected the "commercial unit" for defects in the wood and stored the goods in his basement. Even later, B brought the bed upstairs and used it. B is in trouble. B, by an exercise of "ownership" over one piece of a commercial unit which is "wrongful as against the seller," has accepted the commercial unit. See 2–606(2), 2–601(c) & 2–602(2)(a). S may either sue for the price, adjusted for any breach of warranty, or sue in tort for conversion. 2–606(1)(c). Either way, S gets paid.

Suppose B is in possession of goods wrongfully rejected. Section 2–602(3) states that the "seller's rights with respect to goods wrongfully rejected are governed by the provisions of this Article on Seller's remedies in general (Section 2–703). In the usual case, B's wrongful rejection would be an acceptance of the goods, see 2–606, and S could recover the price. See 2–607(1), 2–709(1)(a). In the unusual case, where S wants the goods back and is satisfied with damages, B would presumably have duties with respect to the goods which are analogous to those upon a buyer who has rightfully rejected.

(b) Revocation of Acceptance
We examined the nature and effect of an acceptance in Chapter V(F)(2). The question now is what, if anything, can B do if she discovers a non-conformity after the goods have been accepted? *One answer is that B may "revoke" the acceptance under 2–608 and, thereafter, have the "same rights and duties with regard to the goods involved as if he had rejected them." 2–608(3). There are two preliminary hurdles, however, to a buyer who has accepted goods: (1) The burden is on B to "establish any breach with respect to the goods accepted, 2–607(4); and (2) B must "within a reasonable time after he discovers or should have discovered any breach notify the seller of breach or be barred from any*

remedy," 2–607(3)(a). If these hurdles are cleared, B must next deal with the complex conditions to revocation of acceptance imposed by 2–608.

First, the non-conformity must "substantially" impair the "value to him" of the accepted "lot or commercial unit." 2–608(1). Note that the test has both objective and subjective elements: it is subjective in that B's particular requirements, whether foreseeable to S or not, must be taken into account and objective in that the particular requirements must be "substantially" impaired.

Second, if B accepts with knowledge of the non-conformity, revocation is difficult if not impossible. The knowing acceptance, to be revoked, must be on the "reasonable assumption" that the non-conformity would be cured and it has not been "seasonably cured." 2–608(1)(a). See 2–607(2). The assumption may be based upon what S said, a prior course of dealing, or the like.

Third, if acceptance occurred "without discovery of such non-conformity," B may revoke only if the acceptance was "reasonably induced either by the difficulty of discovery before acceptance or the seller's assurances." 2–608(1)(b).

Fourth, revocation must occur "before any substantial change in condition of the goods which is not caused by their own defects." 2–608(2). Thus, the acceptance of unmerchantable melons, which deteriorate because of mold, may be revoked, but if the melons are first destroyed by fire, a subsequent revocation will be too late.

Fifth, the revocation "must occur within a reasonable time after the buyer discovers or should have discovered the ground for it . . ." and is not effective until B notifies S of it. 2–608(2). Thus, B may accept goods with defects not discoverable upon reasonable inspection and, then, lose the right to revoke because he failed to discover the defect within a reasonable time after acceptance.

> *Example VI(40):* B purchased a race horse warranted to be "sound" at an auction for $30,000. B inspected the horse after the hammer fell, found nothing wrong and loaded her on his van for the 200 mile ride to his stable. The next morning, B's trainer inspected the horse and found a fractured shin bone in the right foreleg. B promptly telephoned S, informed him of the defect, and stated that he would not take the horse. S insisted that the horse was B's and that he must pay the full price. Assuming that B can prove that the bone was broken (the horse was not sound) when the horse was tendered after the auction, consider the following questions: (1) Did B accept the horse? 2–606(1). If not, has there been an effective rejection? 2–601 & 2–602(1). (2) If the horse was accepted, can B revoke acceptance under Section 2–608? (3) If so, has

there been an effective revocation? 2–608(2). (4) If there has been no effective rejection, has B given timely notice of breach under Section 2–607(3)(a), so as to preserve his claim to damages? On the facts of this case, the failure to discover and give notice of the non-conformity until the day after the sale may bar *any remedy.*

Three final points that have created some uncertainty:

First, does S have the right to "cure" after a justifiable revocation of acceptance? Suppose, for example, that the time for performance has not yet expired. A literal reading of 2–508 suggests that the cure right is limited to cases of rejection. Section 2–608(3) states, however, that a buyer who rightfully revokes has the same "rights and duties" with regard to the goods as if he had rejected them." As a matter of policy, then, shouldn't S have the same right to cure as if B had rejected the goods? The answer, for us at least, is yes.

Second, what are B's duties with regard to rightfully (or wrongfully) revoked goods? Again, 2–608(3) states that a "buyer who revokes has the same rights and duties with regard to the goods involved as if he had rejected them." Sections 2–602 through 2–605, therefore, would seem to apply and B's duties would be defined therein. Similarly, the wrongful revocation would not alter B's acceptance and liability to S for the price.

Third, suppose B, because of S's delay in giving directions or B's necessities, uses the goods (i.e., a mobile home) after a justifiable revocation. At what point does the use negate the justifiable revocation? When the goods are returned, should B compensate S for the use? The UCC does not answer these questions and there is disagreement among the courts and the commentators. Some plausible answers are that a reasonable use under the circumstances does not negate the revocation and that B, in any event, should pay S the reasonable value of the use.

4. **DAMAGES IN REGARD TO ACCEPTED GOODS: SECTION 2–714**
If, in Example VI(40), B had accepted the race horse, was unable to revoke acceptance but had given reasonable notice of breach, the remedial posture would be as follows: (1) B would owe S the price, 2–709(1)(a) & 2–607(1); (2) B could claim damages to accepted goods under Section 2–714 and, upon notifying S, could "deduct all or any part of the damages resulting from any breach of the contract from any part of the price still due under the same contract," 2–717 and (3) B could also claim incidental and consequential damages in a proper case. See 2–714(3), 2–715(1) & 2–715(2).

Section 2–714(1) provides that a buyer who has accepted goods and given S notice of breach under Section 2–607(3)(a) "may recover as damages for any non-conformity of tender the loss resulting in the ordinary course of events from the seller's breach as determined in any manner which is reasonable." This very general standard is, presumably, subject to the remedy policy expressed in 1–106(1) and the limitations on consequential damages stated in 2–715(2)(a).

Section 2–714(2) provides a special rule for breach of warranty cases:

> *The measure of damages for breach of warranty is the difference at the time and place of acceptance between the value of the goods accepted and the value they would have had if they had been as warranted, unless special circumstances show proximate damages of a different amount.*

These two subsections provide overlapping and sometimes confusing measures of direct damages for breach by S with regard to accepted goods. Here are some examples.

Example VI(41): S contracted with B to manufacture 4 pieces of factory equipment, which was regarded in the trade as a commercial unit. S tendered and B accepted under protest 3 pieces. B put the 3 pieces into operation and gave S notice of breach. Under 2–714(1), the non-conformity of tender went to the quantity of goods sold. The direct "loss resulting in the ordinary course of events" is the value of the 4th piece in the commercial unit. This might be determined from either the market value of the 4th piece or from the difference in value between the commercial unit with and without the 4th piece. The loss, as "determined in any manner which is reasonable," should be deducted from the contract price. A similar analysis should be employed if S was late in delivering the commercial unit. What was the loss to B "resulting" from the delay?

Example VI(42): B contracted to purchase a piece of machinery from S for $5,000. At the time of acceptance, the market value of the machine was $4,500. After acceptance, B discovered that the machine was unmerchantable and worth only $300. Under Section 2–714(2), the damages for this breach of warranty are $4,200: The measure is the "difference at the time and place of acceptance between the value of the goods accepted" ($300) and the "value they would have if they had been as warranted." ($4,500) The contract price, $5,000, is regarded as presumptive value, subject to proof that actual value was more or less. On the other hand, if the market value had been $5,500 rather than $4,500, B would have made a better bargain and the damages under Section 2–714(2) would be $5,200. Note how 2–714(2) allocates shifts in the market value of the goods as warranted between the time of contracting and acceptance. This could not occur if the value of such goods was the contract price.

Example VI(43): Suppose, in *Example VI(42)*, that the market value and contract price at the time of acceptance were $5,000 and the machine as accepted was worth $300. B spent $4,000 to repair the machine. S argues that the difference in value should be measured by subtracting the value of the goods received ($300) from the total of $300 plus the reasonable cost to repair ($4,000) for damages of $4,000. Put another way, $4,300 not $5,000 is the value of the goods as warranted, a functioning machine. This argument, however, deprives B of the value of its bargain for a *new* machine measured at the "time and place of acceptance" and should be rejected. B's damages are $4,700.

Example VI(44): Suppose, in *Example VI(43),* that the value of the goods as warranted was not clear. B spent $5,000 to repair the machine. These costs were reasonable and necessary to achieve the warranted result. S argues that B's damages should be limited to $4,700, because the total of the value of the goods received ($300) and the reasonable cost to repair them ($5,000) cannot exceed the contract price ($5,000). Otherwise, B would be overcompensated.

Although all courts concede that the reasonable cost to repair is relevant to proof of the value of the goods as warranted at the time of acceptance, a few have imposed the contract price as a limitation. Others disagree, concluding that unless B gets the full $5,000 in repairs, it will be deprived of the value of the bargain, a merchantable machine. This latter line of cases is sound. If the reasonable cost of repair plus the value of the goods warranted exceeds the contract price, it simply proves that the value of the goods as warranted exceeded the contract price. Thus, B's bargain should be protected.

Example VI(45): B, a tomato farmer, purchased 5 bags of tomato seeds from S, a dealer, for $100. S knew that B's soil was highly acid and stated that the seeds, described as Pips # 1, would "do well in acid soil." The seeds were in fact Flips # 2 and would not flower in highly acid soil. The market value of 5 bags of Flips # 2 was $100. B prepared and fertilized the field, planted the crop and tended to the plants. Despite reasonable effort the entire crop failed. B claims that a successful crop would have been worth $10,000 on the market and that after B's expenses were deducted would have netted $7,000. What are B's damages? One conclusion is that since the difference in market value between the two seeds was 0, there were "special circumstances" and that the proximate damages of a "different amount" were the net value of the lost crop, $7,000. This, however, confuses direct with consequential damages. A better analysis is as follows: (1) B's damages under Section 2–714(2) should be the difference in value between the seeds as warranted, ($100) and their value for B's particular purpose, of which S was aware, (0). Thus, B has direct damages of $100. (2) The net crop loss, $7,000, is consequential damages under Section 2–715(2)(a), for it reflects B's loss from the inability to use the seeds as warranted. Thus, B's total damages is $7,100 and represents a mix of direct and consequential losses caused by S's breach.

Example VI(46): Here is a problem to solve. S, the manufacturer of computer systems, visits B's business to assess current needs. After two days of discussions, the parties agree that B needed a computer and software that will do X, Y and Z. S then agrees to sell B an existing system (named EZ 440) for $50,000 and states "this will do the trick." EZ 440 is installed and B accepts the system. Unfortunately, EZ 440 will only do X (not X, Y and Z) and there is nothing that S can do about it. S now says there is an existing system that will do X, Y and Z. That system is called EZ 1000 and it sells for $150,000. The parties agree that the value of the EZ 440 at the time of acceptance was $20,000. To what damages, if any, is B entitled?

5. INCIDENTAL AND CONSEQUENTIAL DAMAGES

(a) Incidental Damages

The buyer, like the seller, see Ch. VI(C)(5)(b), may claim incidental damages upon breach by the other. See 2–712(1), 2–713(1) & 2–714(3). See also, 2–716(2). *Under Section 2–715(1), B's incidental damages include post-breach expenditures of the following types: (1) expenses "reasonably incurred in inspection, receipt, transportation and care and custody of goods rightfully rejected;" (2) "commercially reasonable charges, expenses or commissions in connection with effecting cover;" and (3) "any other reasonable expense incident to the delay or other breach."* Put another way, incidental damages are reasonable post-breach expenses incurred in perfecting remedies, performing duties with regard to the goods and otherwise attempting to mitigate damages. It is, therefore, a distinct category of damages which is free from the conditions and limitations imposed by the Code on direct and consequential damages.

> *Example VI(47):* B purchased and accepted two pieces of machinery from S for $5,000 each. The goods were defective.
>
> B spent $1,000 in an unsuccessful attempt to repair the first. He then revoked acceptance under Section 2–608, canceled the contract and sued S for damages under 2–713(1). Here, the $1,000 qualifies as incidental damages under 2–715(1). They are "reasonable" expenses "incident to the . . . breach."
>
> B spent $1,000 in a successful attempt to repair the second machine and did not revoke acceptance. Here the $1,000 spent to repair is relevant to the difference in value test under Section 2–714(2). It helps to establish the value of the goods as warranted. Thus, the damages are direct rather than incidental and would be compensated under 2–714(2). See *Example VI(44).*

(b) Consequential Damages

The buyer, unlike the seller, see Ch. VI(C)(5)(c), has a special provision for consequential damages, Section 2–715(2). To illustrate, suppose that B, a baker, has decided to expand its business. It explains this to S, a manufacturer of ovens, and S agrees on May 1 to deliver an oven of a specified capacity by November 1 for $25,000. After the contract was signed, B spent $50,000 in expanding the bakery and preparing to receive the new oven. B also entered into 6 new contracts with retailers for the delivery of bread from the expanded bakery. S failed to deliver the oven on November 1 and, in fact, had resold it to another baker for $30,000. B promptly "covered" by purchasing a substitute oven from C for $27,500 (the cover cost was $1,000) and the oven was installed on February 1. B wants to sue S for breach.

Here is an analysis that affords maximum recovery to B.

First, B's *direct* damages (loss of bargain in obtaining the goods) are measured by the difference between the "cost of cover and the contract price," some $2,500. 2–712(2).

Second, B's *incidental* damages are measured by the "commercially reasonable charges, expense or commissions in connection with effecting cover and any other reasonable expense incident to the delay or other breach," some $1,000. 2–715(1).

Third, B's consequential damages (losses resulting from being deprived of the use of the goods) include "any loss resulting from general or particular requirements and needs of which the seller at the time of contracting had reason to know and which could not reasonably be prevented by cover or otherwise." 2–715(2)(a). Here, the damages result from the delay in obtaining a new oven and, at the very least, could include any profits provable with reasonable certainty that B would have made during the three month period of delay. Nevertheless, there are 3 important conditions that must be satisfied: (1) The loss must result from B's "general or particular requirements and needs;" (2) The seller must have "reason to know" of those requirements and needs "at the time of contracting" (the limitation of *Hadley v. Baxendale*); and (3) B must make reasonable efforts to prevent the losses "by cover or otherwise."

On this analysis, B has a good claim for consequential profits lost from the delay. S knew of B's particular needs and requirements (a business expansion) and had reason to know that lost profits might result from a breach. Under Section 2–715(2)(a), there is no requirement that S have reason to know that lost profits would probably result or that S "tacitly" agreed to assume the consequential losses. See Comment 2. Further, B in fact covered to minimize the delay and, apparently, took all reasonable steps to avoid the loss. Finally, the claimed lost profits can be proved with reasonable certainty from figures on profit levels before and after the expansion or from figures on the contracts B was unable to perform because of the breach.

Example VI(48): Suppose, in our oven problem, that B, after S's failure to deliver, decided for sound business reasons to discontinue the expansion. He settled claims under the 6 bread contracts for $10,000 and salvaged the investment in the expansion with a net loss of $15,000. Finally, he estimated that he lost net profits of $20,000 over the next 12 months because of the breach. What consequential damages can B recover?

(1) Lost profits are doubtful. On the facts, B could have avoided 9 months of losses through "cover or otherwise." On the 3 months delay, the alleged lost profits were probably not caused by the breach (B intervened by a decision not to expand) or not provable with reasonable certainty (there are no provable levels of post-expansion profits for comparison.)

(2) The salvaged reliance expenses, totalling $25,000, are recoverable if the losses result from "general or particular requirements and needs of which the seller at the time of contracting had reason to know." 2-715(2)(a). B's reliance investment was clearly foreseeable at the time of contracting and B made reasonable post-breach efforts to minimize the losses. These consequential losses should be recovered.

Example VI(49): Suppose that S delivered and installed an oven with dangerous defects in B's plant. The oven exploded in use, causing damage to the oven, to surrounding personal property and to B and B's employees. In addition to the commercial losses recoverable under Section 2-715(2)(a), consequential damages also include "injury to person or property proximately resulting from any breach of warranty." 2-715(2)(b). This case, however, is on the wavering line between tort and contract and, in some states, may be governed by principles of strict tort liability rather than the Code. Even so, plaintiffs within the scope of extended warranty liability can still sue under Article 2 for damages to person and property. See 2-318 and review Ch. V(E)(6)(b).

E. AGREED REMEDIES

The general Code policy that the "effect of provisions of this Act may be varied by agreement . . .," 1-102(3), finds concrete expression in Sections 2-718 and 2-719. Section 2-718 regulates the power of the parties to a contract for sale to liquidate or limit damages for breach of contract. Section 2-719, which is subject to Section 2-718, regulates agreements which modify or limit other Article 2 remedies, such as B's power to reject, 2-601, or the right to consequential damages.

1. **LIQUIDATED DAMAGES**
    (a) Basic Policy
    A liquidated damages clause attempts, by agreement of the parties at the time of contracting, to fix the damages resulting from a breach by one or both parties. Under 2–718(1), the clause must meet two conditions to be enforceable: (1) From the perspective at the time of contracting the amount fixed must be "reasonable in the light of the anticipated or actual harm caused by the breach, the difficulties of proof of loss, and the inconvenience or nonfeasibility of otherwise obtaining an adequate remedy," and (2) From the perspective of the time of breach, a "term fixing unreasonably large liquidated damages is void as a penalty." Thus, even though the amount may be a reasonable estimate of loss at the time of contracting, a court can review the clause in light of actual events to determine if it is "unreasonably large."

    Example VI(50): S agreed to manufacture goods for B for $20,000. At the time of contracting, the general market for goods of that kind was uncertain, the cost of finding a resale buyer should B breach was viewed as high and the complexities involved if S were caught with uncompleted goods on hand by B's repudiation were viewed as extreme. S and B, therefore, agreed that if B repudiated the contract at any time before the goods were completed, S could recover the "contract price as liquidated damages and not as a penalty." B repudiated before the goods were completed and S, using reasonable commercial judgment, stopped work and salvaged. Under Section 2–708(2), S's damages would be $7,000, including $2,000 in lost profit. S cannot enforce the liquidated damage clause: (1) The amount was not reasonable "in the light of the anticipated or actual harm caused by the breach." To be reasonable, the amount should take into account the nature of the breach, the condition of the goods at the time of breach and the remedial options available to S; (2) In retrospect, a $20,000 payment for a $7,000 loss is "unreasonably large" and the clause is void as a penalty; and (3) The effect of Section 2–709(1), which establishes 3 conditions for recovery of the price, arguably cannot be varied by agreement. On these facts, a liquidated damage clause might be enforceable if stating, in effect: "If B repudiates before the goods are completed and if S elects reasonably to stop work and salvage, then considering the estimates of loss and difficulties of proof, B shall pay S $10,000 as liquidated damages."

    Example VI(51): At the time of contracting, S and B agreed that if S failed to deliver an oven on time and B made reasonable efforts to find a substitute, B would have foreseeable consequential damages for an uncertain period in an indefinite amount. Given B's prior profit levels and future projections the parties estimated the loss at $20,000 and S agreed to pay that amount as "liquidated damages." S failed to deliver and B, after efforts to mitigate suffered actual damages of $10,000. The liquidated damages were probably a reasonable forecast of "anticipated or actual harm" at the time of contract but, in retrospect, arguably "unreasonably large" and void as a penalty. Efforts to liquidate consequential damages, however, have met with judicial favor and, thus, the scope of reasonableness may be greater here than in *Example VI(50)*. See *California & Hawaiian Sugar Co. v. Sun Ship, Inc.*, 794 F.2d 1433 (9th Cir.1986), which enforced a clause liquidated delay damages at $4,000,000 despite actual damages of only $360,000. Many commentators have urged that the "unreasonably large" limitation should be deleted from 2–718(1) because it improperly interferes with rational efforts to allocate risk and agree on the consequences of breach.

Example VI(52): Suppose, in *Example VI(51)*, that the damages were fixed at $20,000 and the actual loss was $100,000. Can a term fixing an unreasonably *low* damage figure be invalidated? If the parties intended to liquidate rather than to limit damages, i.e., were trying to fix an amount that would fully compensate B rather than to impose an artificial limit on S's exposure, the answer would depend upon the first sentence of Section 2–718(1): was $20,000 "reasonable" in light of the anticipated or actual harm caused by the breach, etc. If not, the clause fails. If so, the text of 2–718 (but see the title) does not explicitly deal with a clause which, in retrospect, is unreasonably low. Comment 1 states that an "unreasonably small amount . . . might be stricken under the section on unconscionable contracts or clauses," presumably in that a clause which deprives B of a minimum adequate remedy, although conscionable at the time of contracting, see 2–302(1), operates in an unreasonable manner.

Although the line is difficult to draw, a distinction should be observed between an effort to liquidate and an effort to limit damages. In the former, the parties attempt to assess and agree upon the predictable losses resulting from breach. In the latter, S tells B, in effect, no matter how great your actual loss, my risk or exposure will *never* exceed X. This clause limits rather than liquidates damages. It may be unenforceable because it either is unconscionable at the time of contracting or leaves B without a minimum adequate remedy, but not because the attempt to forecast loss was unreasonable.

(b) Restitution for Buyer in Default
Section 2–718(2) & (3) deals with a breaching buyer's ability to obtain restitution of any price paid from a seller who is protected by a liquidated damage clause. Thus, if B has paid $5,000 of the $10,000 price in advance and agreed that if he does not accept a timely tender S may recover $2,500 in liquidated damages, B, after breach, may recover in restitution the amount by which the advance payment exceeds the valid liquidation, $2,500. 2–718(2).

If there is no liquidated damage clause, B may recover any amount in **excess** of 20% of the value of the total performance, $2,000 on these facts, or **$500,** whichever is smaller. 2–718(2)(b). That would be $4,500 on these facts. But this amount may be reduced by any damages to which S is otherwise **entitled** or any benefits received by B "directly or indirectly" by reason of the contract. 2–718(3).

2. MODIFICATION OR LIMITATION OF REMEDY
(a) Scope and Effect of Section 2–719

In summary, Section 2–718 deals with the enforceability of agreements liquidating or limiting damages for breach of contract. An effort by the parties to forecast damages is regulated by the policy against punitive damages for breach. 1–106(1). An effort by the parties to limit **damages** regardless of foreseeable or actual loss is regulated by the policy that the parties should have, at least, a "fair quantum of remedy." See Comment 1, 2–719. This latter policy raises somewhat different problems than an avowed effort to forecast damages. The focus is on whether the clause was unconscionable at the time of contracting (because of unfair surprise or oppression), see 2–302(1), and, if not, whether the limitation takes too much from the minimum remedies that commercial law ought to provide. See 2–719(3). All of this is, of course, very imprecise.

Section 2–719, which is subject to Section 2–718, provides in subsection (1)(a), that the "agreement may provide for remedies in addition to or in substitution for those provided in this Article and may limit or alter the measure of damages recoverable under this Article, as by limiting the buyer's remedies to return of the goods and repayment of the price or to repair and replacement of non-conforming goods or parts." Section 2–719(1)(b) provides that resort to the agreed remedy is "optional unless the remedy is expressly agreed to be exclusive, in which case it is the sole remedy." There are two limitations upon these general principles: first, where "circumstances cause an exclusive or limited remedy to fail of its essential purpose, remedy may be had as provided in this act," 2–719(2); and second, a limitation or exclusion of consequential damages must be conscionable, 2–719(3). Here are a few examples.

> ***Example VI(53):*** In a contract for sale, S and B agreed that if B accepted and failed to pay for conforming goods, S's remedy was limited to recovery of any profit prevented by the breach and that this was the exclusive remedy. Since the agreement directly limits the amount of damages recoverable, its enforceability is governed by Section 2–718(1) rather than Section 2–719(1). Since a fair quantum of remedy here is the full contract price, 2–709(1), the limitation on damages to profit is, arguably, unreasonable.

> ***Example VI(54):*** S and B agreed that B was to accept and pay for any goods tendered without inspection, that B had no power to reject the

tender and that if B justifiably revoked any acceptance, the exclusive remedy was restitution—B would return the goods and S would refund any price paid. The agreement is enforceable. 2–719(1)

Example VI(55): In a contract for sale, S expressly warranted that the goods were "free from defects in material and workmanship" and the agreement provided that the "exclusive remedy" for breach of warranty was that the goods would be repaired or defective parts replaced. Consequential damages were expressly excluded. On these limited facts, if the goods are defective B cannot revoke acceptance and pursue normal remedies under Section 2–711. S must be give a reasonable opportunity to "cure" under the agreement and if that effort is successful B has its "exclusive" remedy. Put differently, B has given up its claim to damages in exchange for S's commitment to "cure" any defects in material and workmanship.

If no "cure" is effected within the time stated, the exclusive remedy has, arguably, failed its "essential purpose" and B may have "remedy . . . as provided in this Act." 2–719(2). Except for consequential damages, see *Example VI(56), infra,* B could try to revoke acceptance under 2–608 or claim damages under 2–714.

Example VI(56): Suppose, in *Example VI(55),* that the agreement explicitly provided: "In no event shall B recover any consequential damages caused by any breach by S." This clause is enforceable unless unconscionable, and in commercial cases, i.e., where the "loss is commercial", the clause is not prima facie unconscionable. 2–719(3). Thus, if S successfully repairs or replaces defective parts, B assumes the risk of any consequential damages, unless it can establish unconscionability. The test is one of unfair surprise or oppression at the time of contracting, and most courts have refused to apply Section 2–302 to invalidate the clause in commercial cases.

If S fails to repair or replace, however, B could argue that the limited remedy of "cure" has failed its essential purpose and that the clause excluding consequential damages drops out with it. B would rely on 2–719(2) which provides that where "circumstances cause an exclusive or limited remedy to fail of its essential purpose, remedy may be had as provided in this act." This argument has been successful where the clause excluding consequential damages is found to be dependent upon the clause creating the limited remedy. If the latter fails, so does the former. See *Waters v. Massey–Ferguson, Inc.,* 775 F.2d 587 (4th Cir.1985). If the exclusion clause is independent, however, it will be enforced unless unconscionable at the time of contracting or enforcement leaves B without a minimum adequate remedy. In these cases, minimum adequate remedy means that at the very least B should be able to recover the price paid. For a helpful discussion, see Foss, *Failure of Essential Purpose: An Objective Approach,* 25 Duq.L.Rev. 551 (1987).

(b) Agreed Remedies and Consumer Buyers

Suppose the buyer is a consumer, i.e., a person who buys goods "primarily for personal, family or household purposes?" See 9–109(1), 2–103(3). Article 2 contains no special provisions for consumer protection in this situation. But see 2–719(3), where personal injuries are involved. In theory, consumer buyers are treated the same as a commercial or merchant buyer under 2–719.

Some help comes from Congress in the form of the Magnuson–Moss Warranty Act. 15 U.S.C.A. §§ 2301–2312. If a seller makes a written warranty, the buyer's protection includes mandatory disclosure of essential information by the seller, § 2302, invalidation of efforts to disclaim (but not limit their duration) implied warranties, § 2308(a), no requirement of contractual privity, and judicial remedies in the federal courts that include class actions and the recovery of attorney fees. § 2310(d). This protection follows if the seller makes a "limited" rather than a "full" express warranty. See § 2303.

If the seller makes a "full" warranty (and it is not required to do so), then the buyer is given important additional protection. § 2304. For example: (1) The warrantor may not limit the duration of any implied warranty; (2) Any attempt to limit or exclude consequential damages must "conspicuously" appear on the face of the warranty; (3) As a "minimum remedy," the warrantor must "remedy such consumer product within a reasonable time and without charge, in the case of a defect, malfunction, or failure to conform with such written warranty;" and (4) If the warrantor is unable "after a reasonable number of attempts" to cure the defect, the consumer may elect "either a refund for, or replacement without charge of, such product or part . . . ."

Since most warrantors do not make "full" warranties and since Article 2 does not provide comparable protection, many states have enacted so-called "lemon" laws governing the sale of new cars. While the terms vary, an essential feature is that a consumer buyer is entitled to a car that conforms to the warranty given by the dealer or manufacturer, that the seller is obligated to "cure" nonconformities and that if the seller fails to "cure" after a reasonable number of tries, the buyer may elect to have a full refund or a new car. Thus, consumer buyers of new cars have "lemon law" protection that is comparable to that given under a "full" Magnuson–Moss warranty. Consumer buyers of other products, however, must rely upon Article 2 or other state law.

(c) Warranty Litigation: A Reprise

In contracts for the sale of machinery, automobiles and other complex manufactured goods, S will frequently induce B to agree to a warranty "package" with four components: (1) An express warranty for a limited period of time that the goods are free from defects in material and workmanship; (2) The combination of a disclaimer of all other warranties, express or implied, which satisfies Section 2–316, and a "merger" clause stating that the writing is the "final and exclusive statement of the terms and conditions" of the contract; (3) A limited and exclusive remedy that upon breach of the express warranty, S shall repair the goods and replace defective parts; and (4) A clause excluding any and all liability for breach of warranty, negligence or any other liability for consequential damages. In short, S limits both the scope or warranty liability and remedies for breach for which B gets a commitment from S to repair the goods and replace defective parts, presumably within a reasonable time. Thus, B pays for the prospect of repaired goods and assumes the risk of consequential damages while breach of the express warranty is being remedied.

Suppose, however, that S, after reasonable efforts, is unable to repair or replace at all or in time for B to get the benefit of his bargain. Must B pay the full price for goods that S won't or can't fix and be foreclosed from any direct or consequential damages? There are some cases where the answer is yes. Yet B should achieve some success if the court accepts any or all of the following arguments.

First, if the "repair or replacement" remedy is interpreted as a promise, the failure to repair or replace amounts to a second breach of contract, for which B is entitled to some damages. At a minimum, B might justifiably revoke acceptance, 2–608, or seek damages to accepted goods.

Second, the inability to repair might justify the conclusion that "circumstances" have caused the "exclusive or limited remedy to fail of its essential purpose" and that "remedy may be had as provided in this Act." 2–719(2). At a minimum, B would have the usual Code remedies for breach of the express warranty but not consequential damages.

Third, the court might be persuaded that the entire warranty "package," including the consequential damage exclusion, fell with the limited remedy under Section 2–719(2). If so, the "disclaimer" and the "repair and replacement" remedy and the exclusion of consequential damages would fall, leaving B with a full plate of Code remedies. This argument is most persuasive where the parts of the warranty "package" are interpreted as dependent upon each other, or S has acted in bad faith or, possibly, the breach was so fundamental that otherwise B would be deprived of a fair quantum of remedy. Where S has acted reasonably and in good faith and the consequential damage exclusion is clearly independent of the "package,"

(M.& S.) Sales & Leases of Goods BLS—8

however, most courts have limited B's remedies to "direct" damages and enforced the exclusion of consequential damages, if it was not unconscionable at the time of contracting.

Example VI(57): S, a manufacturer, sold B, a farmer, a machine designed to pick and sort tomatoes and to keep them cool after sorting. B assented to the warranty "package" just discussed, which was contained in a standard form contract drafted by S and offered on a take-it-or-leave-it basis. The clause excluding consequential damages was clearly independent of the "package" which gave a limited express warranty, disclaimed all other warranties, and limited the remedy to "repair or replacement of defective parts." B started to pick the tomatoes, but the machine did not work properly—the fruit jammed up in the sorting mechanism and much of it was either missorted or damaged. Further, the cooling system failed. S made reasonable efforts to repair the machine and, although some success was had, the defects and resulting delays cost B 40% of his crop. On these facts, B, at a minimum, should be able to recover direct damages under Section 2–714(2), incidental damages under Section 2–715(1), and consequential damages if the exclusion clause was unconscionable. 2–719(3). Even though the loss was commercial, if B was relatively inexperienced and was not fully aware of the exclusion clause at the time of contracting, the court might conclude that the exclusion was unconscionable. For such a case, see *A & M Produce Co. v. FMC Corporation,* 135 Cal.App.3d 473, 186 Cal.Rptr. 114 (1982).

F. STATUTE OF LIMITATIONS

The statute of limitations for Article 2 is found in 2–725. The following points should be kept in mind.

First, other notice provisions can bar claims even before the statute of limitations has run. For example, the remedies of both rejection and revocation are conditioned upon prompt notice by the buyer, 2–602(1) & 2–608(2), and the buyer's claim for damages may be barred if the buyer does not notify the seller of breach "within a reasonable time after he discovers or should have discovered any breach." 2–607(3)(a).

Second, 2–725 is a tolling rather than a notice statute of limitations. A cause of action accrues and the statute starts to run "when the breach occurs, regardless of the aggrieved party's lack of knowledge of the breach." 2–725(2). A "notice" statute of limitations begins to run when the plaintiff knew or should have known about the cause of action.

Third, an "action for breach of any contract for sale must be commenced within four years after the cause of action has accured." 2–725(1). On the other hand, the parties by their "original agreement . . . may reduce the period of limitation to not less than one year but may not extend it." 2–725(1).

Fourth, special rules are provided for breach of warranty claims. Thus, a "breach of warranty occurs when tender of delivery is made, except that where a warranty explicitly extends to future performance of the goods and discovery of the breach must await the time of such performance the cause of action accrues when the breach is or should have been discovered." 2–725(2). Thus, although the usual warranty claim is controlled by the "tolling" statute of limitations, an explicit extension to future performance converts the limitation to a "notice" statute.

Fifth, a special rule is provided for terminated actions commenced before the statute has run, 2–725(3), and the "law on tolling of the statute of limitations" is not altered by 2–725. See 2–725(4).

> *Example VI(58):* In a written contract for the sale of office furniture, S agreed to ship 50% of the goods FOB point of origin on July 1, 1988 and the balance on August 1, 1988. B agreed to pay the full contract price on August 15, 1988. Consider the following:
>
> (1) S delivered all of the furniture but B failed to pay on August 15, 1988. S did not learn of this failure until August 20, 1988. Nevertheless, the breach occurred on August 15, 1988, 2–725(2) and S must commence its action for the price "within four years after the cause of action has accrued." 2–725(1). Similarly, if S failed to ship goods on July 1, 1988 and B did not learn of this until July 20, 1988, the cause of action still accrued on July 15, 1988. Review 2–713(1), which permits B to use the market price "at the time when the buyer learned *of the breach*" even though the breach occurred at an earlier time.
>
> (2) Suppose that S delivered 50% of the furniture on July 1, 1988 but sent a letter repudiating the balance of the contract on July 5, 1988. B received the repudiation on July 9 and, after waiting a commercially reasonable time, see 2–610(b), decided to cancel the contract and cover on July 25. When does the cause of action accrue? The answer is on July 9, 1988, when the repudiation was received. That is the date of breach, even though B can wait before acting and S could retract it. There would be no breach by repudiation, however, until the words or conduct were communicated to B.
>
> *Example VI(59):* Under a contract for sale, S delivered and installed factory equipment purchased by B from S. The installation was completed on July 1, 1988. Under the contract, S expressly warranted that the goods would be free from defects in materials and workmanship for one year and agreed to "cure" any such defects until July 1, 1989. B agreed to bring any suit for

breach of express warranty within 1 year after the cause of action accrues. Implied warranties were not disclaimed. On June 1, 1989, B discovered a defect in workmanship which S, after six months of effort, was unable to cure. B had the equipment repaired by C at considerable cost and now contemplates litigation against S. By what dates must the action be commenced?

(1) If the defect breached an implied warranty of merchantability, the action must be commenced before July 1, 1992. The cause of action accrued when the equipment was installed on July 1, 1988 (i.e., when the tender of delivery was made) and the warranty did not explicitly extend to future performance. See 2–503 on when a tender of delivery is made.

(2) If the defect breached the express warranty and was discovered within the one year period, the cause of action accrued when the breach was "discovered," here on June 1, 1989. This is a case where the express warranty was explicitly extended to future performance (one year), but limited to a one year period. But the parties have limited the time for initiating the action to one year after the cause of action accrues. Thus, B must sue before June 1, 1990. This time might be extended for an additional six months if, as some courts have held, S's unsuccessful efforts to cure the defect tolled the statute of limitations. See 2–725(4).

(3) S breached the agreement to repair or replace defects in material and workmanship when it failed to effect a cure. Since the repair clause was part of the contract for sale, B has four years from the date of breach to sue for breach of contract.

For additional discussion and criticism, see Comment, *UCC § 2–725—A Statute Uncertain in Application and Effect,* 46 Ohio St.L.J. 755 (1985).

G. REVIEW QUESTIONS

VI–A. S contracted to sell goods to B on credit. Before delivery, S received reliable information that B was insolvent. S claims that if B is insolvent, S can cancel the contract and sue B for damages.

1. Is S correct?

2. If not correct, what is S's remedy on these facts?

3. Under what circumstances would S be able to cancel and sue for damages?

VI–B. S and B entered a contract where S was to deliver goods in six equal installments and B was to pay for each installment within 15 days of delivery.

S delivered three installments. B paid for the first two on time but had not paid for the third installment before the fourth delivery was due. In the meantime, the market price for the goods had risen sharply and S has several buyers for the balance of the goods.

1. Can S cancel the contract for B's breach and sell the remaining goods without liability?

2. If not, what should S do on these facts?

VI–C. When S delivers conforming goods to a carrier in an FOB shipment contract, both title and risk of loss pass to B. If B breaches or becomes insolvent before the goods arrive, under what circumstances can S recover the goods from the carrier? What is S's position *vis a vis* the reclaimed goods?

VI–D. *True or False:*

1. From S's standpoint, an action for the price is the best remedy.

2. If, at the time of B's breach, S has not procured or started work on the goods, the resale remedy, 2–706, is not available.

3. The proper remedy where lost volume is involved is found in Section 2–708(1).

4. If S tries to resell under Section 2–706(1) but does so in bad faith, he is barred from any remedy.

5. If S gives notice and properly resells under Section 2–706, he is limited to the difference between the contract and the resale price.

VI–E. S contracted to manufacture goods for B for $20,000. Before S commenced performance, B repudiated the contract. S immediately canceled the contract but still decided to manufacture the goods. They were completed at a cost of $19,000, but S, after a reasonable effort, was unable to find anyone to purchase them. S would like to sue B for the $20,000 contract price. B will argue that S failed to "mitigate" damages and, on these facts, is limited in damages to the difference between the contract and market price at the time and place of breach.

1. Under what circumstances could S recover the price?

2. If the price is not recoverable, is S limited in damages to the Section 2–708(1) formula?

VI-F.   S contracted to manufacture goods for B for $20,000. B paid $10,000 in advance and agreed to pay the balance upon delivery. S completed and identified the goods to the contract and failed without justification to deliver. The market price of similar goods at the time and place that B learned of the breach was $25,000. It would take six months for delivery of the goods if B purchased them from another source. Which of the following remedies are available to B on these facts:

1. Recover the goods from S under Section 2–502.

2. Cancel the contract, obtain restitution of $10,000 paid and recover $5,000 in damages under Section 2–713(1).

3. Replevin the goods from S under Section 2–716(3).

4. Cancel the contract and seek damages under Section 2–714.

5. Recover incidental and consequential damages under Section 2–715.

6. Obtain specific performance under Section 2–716.

7. Other?

VI-G.   *True or False:* If B effects a proper "cover" under Section 2–712 he is barred from recovering damages under Section 2–713.

VI-H.   S contracted to sell B 100,000 gallons of fuel oil with a sulphur content not to exceed 1%, delivery by May 1. S, relying on a representation from the refinery that the sulphur content did not exceed .8%, tendered delivery on April 30. B inspected the oil, discovered a 1.1% sulphur content and, on May 3 rejected the tender. The market price for fuel oil at this time was dropping sharply. When B elected to cancel the contract, S argued either that B's rejection was in bad faith or that S had a right to "cure" the nonconformity under Section 2–508. As a cure, S tendered a negotiable bill of lading for 100,000 gallons of fuel oil described as "sulphur content less than 1%" and stated that delivery was available within 24 hours. B still wants to cancel. What result?

VI-I.   On August 1, S, a dealer, sold and delivered a new T.V. to B, a consumer. Two weeks later, B discovered a latent defect in the picture tube and justifiably revoked acceptance. B demanded a new T.V. or her money back. S argued that it was customary to "cure" defects of this type by supplying a new picture tube and that he had reason to believe that this would be acceptable. S attempted to "cure" under Section 2–508 and B resisted. May S cure?

VI–J.   Answer the questions raised in *Example VI(40)*. When you have completed that, please answer the question posed in *Example VI(46)*.

VI–K.   S sold B a new pick-up truck for farm use on July 1. On August 1, B complained about excessive wear on the front tires and S realigned and balanced the vehicle. B was still not satisfied: the tires continued to wear and strange noises came from the front end. On November 25, the truck was damaged in an accident without B's fault or negligence. B's insurance covered 50% of the loss. On December 1, without any further discussion with S, B notified S that acceptance was revoked, canceled the contract and filed suit for recovery of the price paid plus damages under Section 2–713. Which of the following arguments by B should the court accept:

1. B is barred from any remedy by failing to give reasonable notice of breach under Section 2–607(3)(a).

2. If B is not barred, revocation of acceptance is not proper under Section 2–608.

3. If revocation is not proper, B's damages are measured by Section 2–714, thereby foreclosing any recovery of the price paid.

VI–L.   B, operator of a trucking company, purchased a new truck from S to replace an older model. S had done business with B before and was familiar with his business. The new truck had a serious defect in the engine and S refused to repair it. The contract price for the truck was $25,000. It is estimated that the value of the truck as warranted was $24,000 and the value of the truck with the defective engine was $10,000. B spent $6,000 to replace the engine. In addition, he spent $1,000 to rent a replacement truck which was available for one-half of the time that the new truck was out of commission. B estimates that he lost profits in the amount of $5,000 during the three months wait to replace the engine. B sues S for damages for breach of warranty. How much should B recover?

VI–M.   S contracted to sell B, a retailer, a smoke detection and alarm system for his warehouse. During negotiations, B stated that the average value of inventory in the warehouse was $100,000 and that if the alarm system did not work he would like some protection against inventory losses. S replied: "The answer is insurance. Our contract provides that if the alarm system fails for reasons within the warranty, we will refund the price and pay as consequential damages not more than $500 for each breach. Take it or leave it." B took it and, later, took it on the chin. The system failed miserably and despite heroic efforts by firefighters the entire inventory was destroyed. B's insurance covered 50% of the loss, the total of which was $5,000. B sued for $5,000 in consequential damages and S defended on the contract clause—no more than $500. Is the clause enforceable?

VI-N. One last problem for Chapter VI. Suppose, in Question VI-L, above, that S had effectively disclaimed all warranties, express or implied, except an express warranty that the goods were free from defects in material and workmanship. Also, the contract stated that as an exclusive remedy for breach of the express warranty, S, for a 12 month period, would repair or replace all defective parts or workmanship. Finally, the contract excluded all liability for consequential damages. Three months after delivery, the truck developed a violent shimmy which made it unsafe to drive. S tried for three months to remedy the problem without success. S stated that there were no defects in parts and workmanship that it could find and although it regretted the shimmy, "we've done all that we can do, the rest is up to you." B would like to revoke the acceptance, cancel the contract, recover the price paid, recover damages under Section 2–714 and recover incidental and consequential damages under Section 2–715. Which, if any, of these forms of relief are available?

VII

THIRD PARTY CLAIMS
TO THE GOODS

Analysis

A. IN GENERAL

The parties to a contract for sale have broad power to allocate risks between themselves by agreement. See 1–102(3). But their agreement alone cannot resolve the claims of third parties to the goods. These claims typically take three forms. *First,* Owner (O), claiming title, seeks to replevy goods purchased by B from S or, in the alternative, claims damages from B for conversion. *Second,* a Secured Party (SP) under Article 9, seeks to reposses goods from B to enforce a security interest created by B's seller, S, or some other debtor. *Third,* an unsecured creditor of either S or B obtains a judicial lien (and becomes a Lien Creditor) on either, (a) S's goods delivered to B to be purchased or resold, or (b) goods purchased by B from S but left in S's possession. In each case, Article 2 has something to say about these claims. In addition, Section 2–312 establishes the scope of S's warranty liability to B if, after a sale, O is able to replevy or SP is able to repossess the goods from B.

B. OWNERSHIP CLAIMS

1. THE BASIC RULE

Suppose that a thief (T) steals goods from O and sells them to S, who pays value in good faith and without knowledge of O's title. S resells the goods to B, a good faith purchaser. Later, O learns that B has "his" goods and attempts to replevy them. *On these facts, O will prevail under the first sentence in 2–403(1): a "purchaser of goods," even though a good faith purchaser, (GFP) acquires "all title which his transferor had or had power to transfer. . . . "* Here, S, "his transferor," had neither title nor power to transfer title because he purchased from a thief. As between O and B, both innocents, the risk is placed upon B. B's remedy is against S for breach of warranty of title, see 2–312(1)(a), and S's recourse is against T, if T can be found. This is the basic common law rule, which was thought to preserve the security of property.

2. THE CODE EXCEPTIONS

Section 2–403 gives B better title than S had power to convey in two situations: (1) Where O delivers the goods to S in a "transaction of purchase," which is voidable for fraud or some other defect, and S sells the goods to B, a GFP; and (2) Where O entrusts the goods to S, a merchant who deals in goods of that kind, and S sells them to a "buyer in the ordinary course of business." (BIOCB) See 1–201(9). In both cases, O has intentionally done something—delivered the goods to S—and created a risk that B will be mislead by S's possession. But the purpose of the delivery is different: in the first case, O intends to sell the goods to S and in the second he does not. In both, however, B has an excellent chance to obtain good title.

(a) Transaction of Purchase

Section 2–403(1) provides that a person with "voidable title has power to transfer a good title to a good faith purchaser for value." The terms, "good faith," "purchaser" and "value" are defined in 1–201. A classic example of voidable title is where O has been induced to sell goods by S's fraudulent misrepresentation. As between O and S, O can avoid the contract for sale and recover the goods. Between O and a GFP who has taken delivery, however, O loses.

2–403(1) provides further that when "goods have been delivered under a transaction of purchase the purchaser has such power [to pass good title] even though (a) the transferor was deceived as to the identity of the purchaser, or (b) the delivery was in exchange for a check which is later dishonored, or (c) it was agreed that the transaction was to be a 'cash' sale, or (d) the delivery was procured through fraud punishable as larcenous under the criminal law." These four situations were included to clarify and expand the GFP's protection in a transaction of purchase and to avoid the conclusion sometimes reached at common law that S's title was "void" rather than "voidable." An example of "void" title would be where O was induced by fraud to sign a writing thinking it was a bailment agreement when in fact it was a contract for sale. If O delivered goods to S and S resold them to a GFP, O could replevy them from the GFP because S got "void" rather than "voidable" title. See *Inmi–Etti v. Aluisi*, 63 Md.App. 293, 492 A.2d 917 (1985). Making substantive outcomes turn on such fine distinctions did not appeal to the drafters of the Code.

Note that S need not be a merchant and B need not be a BIOCB for good title to pass. The key is whether delivery is under a "transaction of purchase" and whether B is a good faith purchaser for value.

(b) Entrusting

Even though a delivery is not under a "transaction of purchase" it may be an entrusting as defined in 2–403(3): *"Entrusting includes any delivery and any acquiescence in retention of possession regardless of any condition expressed between the parties to the delivery or acquiescence and regardless of whether the procurement of the entrusting or the possessor's disposition of the goods have been such as to be larcenous under the criminal law."*

The importance of an entrusting lies in what it gives B power to do. According to 2–403(2): "Any entrusting of possession of goods to a *merchant* who deals in goods of that kind gives him power to transfer all rights of the entruster to a *buyer in the ordinary course of business.*" Thus, if S was a merchant, 2–104(1), and resold the goods to a BIOCB, see 1–201(9), O's title would pass to the BIOCB even though S had "void" title and the goods were not delivered in a transaction of purchase.

This result is justified in terms of fairness to the BIOCB, who relied upon the merchant's possession, and the need to protect sales in the ordinary course of business. In addition, O, the entruster, has created the risk by delivery to a merchant and is in a better position than the BIOCB to insure that the merchant does not violate the terms of the entrustment. *Note that BIOCB has a special definition. It "means a person who in good faith and without knowledge that the sale to him is in violation of the ownership rights or security interest of a third party in the goods buys in ordinary course from a person in the business of selling goods of that kind. . . ." 1–201(9).* The BIOCB, therefore, must meet a higher standard than the good faith purchaser.

> *Example VII(1):* O, the owner of a valuable painting, was approached by S, an art dealer, who said: "I would like to borrow the painting for a month to display in my gallery. If you agree, please sign this bailment agreement so that I can have the painting insured." O, without reading it, signed the alleged "bailment" writing which, in fact, was a contract for sale. S displayed the painting for a while and then sold it to B, a private collector, for $25,000. Can O replevy the painting from B?

> The answer is uncertain if B defends upon the "transaction of purchase" exception to Section 2–403(1). S's conduct constituted fraud in the execution (he misrepresented the character of the writing) and, as such, got "void" rather than "voidable" title. O was not deceived as to the identity of someone to whom he intended to sell the painting, see 2–403(1)(a), he was deceived as to the character of the transaction. Even so, the delivery is treated like a transaction of purchase if "procured through fraud punishable as larcenous under the criminal law." 2–403(1)(d). Whether S's conduct was a crime must still be determined from other state law. If so, B gets good title. If not, O can replevy.

> The answer is probably no if B relies upon the entrusting exception. O's delivery to S was an entrusting, 2–403(2), S was a "merchant who deals in goods of that kind," 2–403(2), and if B was a BIOCB, he acquires "all rights of the entruster." 2–403(2). Whether B was a BIOCB will depend upon the facts of the case.

> *Example VII(2):* O sold a painting to S, a private collector, for $5,000 and delivered the painting in exchange for a check in the amount of the price. S promptly resold the painting to B # 1, an art dealer, for $10,000 cash and then stopped payment on the check issued to O and left town for an extended vacation. B promptly resold the painting to B # 2, a BIOCB, for $15,000. May O, upon learning of S's conduct, replevy the painting from B # 2?

The answer is *no* if C relies upon the "transaction of purchase" exception. Even though S's payment was conditional upon the check being paid, O delivered the goods in a transaction of purchase and S's power to transfer good title to B # 1 (and B # 1's power subsequently to transfer good title to B # 2) was not impaired by the subsequent dishonor. 2–403(1)(b).

The answer is *yes* if C defends on the entrusting exception. Although O entrusted the goods to S, S was a private collector rather than a "merchant dealing in goods of that kind." 2–403(2). Thus, S had no power to transfer O's title and neither B # 1 nor B # 2 (a BIOCB) could take a greater interest than S.

Note, however, that if B # 1 took good title from S on any theory, the claim of B # 2 to good title would be sheltered by B # 1's status. This is true even though B # 2 knew of O's claim at the time of purchase.

In sum, if there was neither a "transaction of purchase" nor an "entrusting," B loses to O regardless of B's bona fides. If there was a "transaction of purchase," B must be a good faith purchaser for value. Unless B is a merchant, the test for good faith is subjective. See 2–103(1)(b). See also *Johnson & Johnson Products, Inc. v. Dal Intern. Trading Co.*, 798 F.2d 100 (3d Cir.1986), applying the subjective test. If there is an "entrusting" to a merchant, B must be a BIOCB. Here the good faith test is subjective (B will probably not be a merchant) but there are objective elements to consider since B must "buy in the ordinary course from a person in the business of selling goods of that kind." 1–201(9).

C. SECURITY INTEREST CLAIMS

Suppose that Secured Party (SP) created (by a written security agreement) and perfected (by filing a financing statement) under Article 9 a security interest in Dealer's (D's) inventory, i.e., goods held for resale. The security interest secured a loan from SP to D which D promised to repay in installments with interest. Later, D sold a unit of that inventory to B, a consumer, for cash. Shortly thereafter D defaulted on his loan to SP and SP, among other things, tried to repossess the goods from B, claiming that they were still subject to the security interest created by D. Is SP correct?

The answer, which is found in Article 9, is no if either of two conditions are met: (1) SP authorized the sale of inventory by D "in the security agreement or otherwise," 9–306(2); or (2) B is a BIOCB who "takes free of a security interest created by his seller even though the security interest is perfected and even though the buyer knows of its existence." 9–307(1). There is a parallel with 2–403 here, since in both cases SP entrusted the goods to a merchant who deals in goods of that kind. Where SP consented to the sale, it is difficult later to claim that B is still subject to the original security interest: SP knows that it will be sold and must look to the proceeds of that sale as security for the loan. See 9–306(1). Where there is no consent, however, fairness to the BIOCB and a broader policy facilitating a free and reliable market for the sale of goods justify the protection of 9–307(1). Unlike 2–403(2), where the BIOCB claims a greater title than his seller had, the BIOCB under Section 9–307(1) seeks to free his admittedly good title from the security interest.

The purchaser has even greater protection when the security interest is *unperfected*, see 9–301(1)(c).

Here are some simple examples.

> ***Example VII(3):*** D sold goods subject to SP's perfected security interest to C, a BIOCB, and C resold the goods to G, a GFP, but not in the ordinary course of business. D defaulted and SP sought to repossess the goods in G's possession. Assuming that SP did not consent to D's sale, G cannot claim the direct protection of Section 9–307(1): G was not a BIOCB and the security interest involved was not "created by his seller." But C was protected by Section 9–307(1), and G, a purchaser from C, should receive the same protection through the "shelter" principle. See 3–203. Put another way, if C "takes free" of the security interest under 9–307(1), so should its purchaser, whether a GFP or not.

> ***Example VII(4):*** D, a dealer, sold goods to C, a consumer, who purchased for "use primarily for personal, family or household purposes." See 9–109(1). The sale was on credit, and D created a security interest in the goods. Under Section 9–302(1)(d), a security interest in consumer goods is perfected without filing a financing statement. C then resold the goods to C # 2 for value, the goods also to be used for personal, family or household purposes. C then defaulted on his obligation to D and D claimed that the security interest continued in the goods in C # 2's possession.

> D is wrong. Section 9–307(1) does not apply, since C # 2 was not a BIOCB. But C # 2, a consumer, took free of D's perfected security interest if he bought "without knowledge of the security interest, for value and for his own personal, family or household purposes. . . ." 9–307(2). But the goods must be consumer goods in the hands of both C and C # 2, and if D files a financing statement before the purchase, C # 2 does not take free of the security interest. 9–307(2).

There are a few remaining problems.

First, at what point does a buyer become a BIOCB? The Code does not say. Assuming that the essential conditions of 1–201(9) are satisfied, most courts have concluded that the status arises when the goods are identified to the contract for sale, see 2–501(1), not when they are delivered or when title passes. Thus, protection arises earlier rather than later in the deal. See *Daniel v. Bank,* 144 Wis.2d 931, 425 N.W.2d 416 (1988).

Second, does the "objective" or "subjective" definition of good faith apply when a buyer seeks to take free from a security interest under 9–307(1)? Again, the Code is not clear. Most courts have concluded that the "subjective" definition, found in 1–201, applies even though the purported BIOCB is a merchant buying goods from a seller who is also a secured party. They reason that the "objective" definition is limited to merchants in transactions governed by Article 2. See 2–103(1)(b). Whether a buyer takes free of a security interest is governed exclusively by Article 9. See 9–307(1).

Third, is there any way other than Article 9 that a BIOCB can take free of a perfected security interest in the goods? Some courts have used 2–403(2) in cases where the security interest was not created by BIOCB's seller but where, nevertheless, the secured party has entrusted the goods to that seller. See, for example, *Executive Financial Services, Inc. v. Pagel,* 238 Kan. 809, 715 P.2d 381 (1986). The basis for this result is anything but clear. Although the language of 2–403(2) is broad enough to include security interests, 2–403(4) explicitly states that the "rights of other purchasers of goods . . . are governed by the Articles on Secured Transactions (Article 9) . . ." See also 2–402(3)(a).

These uncertainties will undoubtedly be resolved in the next revision of Articles 2 and 9.

D. SELLER'S WARRANTY OF TITLE

1. SCOPE OF WARRANTY
Section 2–312(1) provides that unless excluded or modified "there is in a contract for sale a warranty by the seller that (a) title conveyed shall be good, and its transfer rightful; and (b) the goods shall be delivered free from any security interest or other lien or encumbrance of which the buyer at the time of contracting has no knowledge."

In disputes over ownership, the warranty of title is breached if it is determined that in a dispute between O and B, B did not receive "good" title or that S's transfer to B was not "rightful" against O. In short, S warrants that B received "a good clean title transferred to him also in a rightful manner so that he will not be exposed to a lawsuit in order to protect it." Comment 1. But if title was good or the transfer was rightful, S does not warrant that B's possession will be undisturbed by a law suit. In short, there is no warranty of quiet possession under 2–312(1), although "disturbance of quiet possession . . . is one way, among many, in which the warranty of title may be established." Comment 1.

In disputes over security interests the warranty is breached when the goods are delivered subject to the security interest, unless B has actual knowledge of it at the time of contracting. See the definition of "knowledge" in 1–201(25). There is no breach if the goods were delivered free of a security interest, even though it takes litigation with SP to establish that result.

Example VII(5): O entrusted goods to D, a merchant who dealt in goods of that kind, for the limited purpose of repair. As security for a loan to D, SP then created and perfected a security interest in the goods and other inventory of D. D then sold the entrusted goods to B, a GFP but not a BIOCB. Upon D's default, O sought to replevy and SP sought to repossess the goods.

O's replevin action should prevail: There was no "transaction of purchase, 2–403(1)," and B was not a BIOCB. See 2–402(2). B did not get good title. B, however, has an action against D for breach of the implied warranty of title. 2–312(1).

SP's attempt to repossess the goods should not prevail. D was simply a bailee of goods owned by O. D either had no rights in the goods to which SP's security interest could attach or SP took subject to O's rights. See 9–203(1) (debtor must have "rights" in collateral). Either way, the claimed security interest is not enforceable (B took "free" of it) and B's rights do not depend upon 9–307(1). As such, B has no breach of warranty claim against D under 2–312(1)(b).

See also Section 2–312(3), dealing with the warranty of a merchant that the "goods shall be delivered free of the rightful claim of any third person by way of infringement." 2–312(3).

Example VII(6): O, who lived in Italy, owned a painting valued at $1,000,000. Because of its historical significance, the painting could not be exported from Italy without a special license. Nevertheless, O sold the painting without a license to D, a dealer in New York, for $1,200,000 and D resold the painting to B, a private collector, for $1,500,000. Neither D nor B had knowledge of the Italian export restriction. Later, the Italian government publicized the illegal export but did not attempt to recover the painting. Neither did O, who was quite happy with the $1,000,000. Without the export license, however, the painting was worth only $250,000 on the open market. B sues D for breach of warranty of title.

In a case on similar facts, a court suggested that there was no breach of warranty. No one had sued to recover the painting. B got good title and the transfer was "rightful" against O. The illegal export was not "rightful" against the Italian government, but its claim was neither a security interest nor a lien or encumbrance under 2–312(1)(b). Neither 2–312 nor the comments supported the conclusion that the improper export breached the warranty of title. See *Jeanneret v. Vichey,* 693 F.2d 259 (2d Cir.1982), reversing, 541 F.Supp. 80 (S.D.N.Y.1982). Nevertheless, there was a cloud on the title that affected the value of the painting.

2. EXCLUSION OR MODIFICATION

The warranty provided in 2–312(1) can be excluded or modified by "specific language" in the contract for sale. 2–312(2). Presumably, this requirement is satisfied by language that there are "no warranties of title or rightful transfer" or that the goods are "delivered free from any security interest." There is no explicit requirement that this language be CONSPICUOUS, compare 2–316(2), but the Code's general policy against unfair surprise suggests that the language be so. See 2–302(1). The "only" other basis for exclusion or modification is "circumstances which give the buyer reason to know that the person selling does not claim title in himself or that he is purporting to sell only such right or title as he or a third person may have." These circumstances arise most frequently in sales by auction. 2–312, comment 5. See 2–328.

> ***Example VII(7):*** A, professional auctioneer, sold goods purporting to belong to S to B. Later, O established good title and replevied the goods from B. Without more, the "circumstances" give B "reason to know" that A "does not claim title in himself." Thus, A made no warranty of title. S, however, did make such a warranty unless there were other "circumstances" that modified or excluded it.

> Note that art dealers who acquire art and finance its sale *and* who sell at auction should be distinguished from auctions where the auctioneer provides only professional services. In the former case, the "circumstances" may not give the buyer reason to know that the auctioneer "does not claim title in himself or that he is purporting to sell only such right or title as he or a third person may have." In these cases, the warranty should be disclaimed by "specific language." 2–312(2).

3. DAMAGES FOR BREACH

In most warranty of title litigation, B has accepted the goods sold by S before O or SP asserted a claim to them. Thus, 2–714 and 2–715 will control the damage questions. Moreover, B must give the notice to S required by 2–607(3)(a) and beware of the statute of limitations. 2–725.

Suppose that B paid S $5,000 for a painting and that, later, O successfully replevied it. (O might, instead, sue B for conversion). B's damages would be the difference in value between the goods with "good" title, say $5,000, and goods with a defective title, say $0, measured at the "time and place of acceptance." 2–714(2). In addition, B can recover "incidental" damages, which include the cost of defending the lawsuit, see 2–714(3) & 2–715(1), and consequential damages. Arguably, incidental damages in these cases include attorney fees, since S warranted that the transfer was "rightful." The difference in value test measures direct damages "unless special circumstance show proximate damages of a different amount." 2–714(2).

Example VII(8): On July 1, 1980, S sold B a painting which had been stolen from O for $50,000. On June 1, 1992, O successfully replevied the painting, then worth $1,000,000 from B. Most courts have given B the appreciated value of the painting rather than the value at the time of contracting. The result is justified on the grounds that there were "special circumstances" justifying a different amount, or that the appreciated value, when taken from B, was a foreseeable form of consequential damages. See 2–715(2)(a).

Unfortunately, the statute of limitations has run on B's claims against S. The cause of action for breach of warranty accrued on July 1, 1980 when the "tender of delivery" was made, 2–725(2), and was barred "four years after the cause of action" accrued. 2–725(1). None of the exceptions in 2–725 apply here.

Example VII(9): S sold B, who resided in Illinois, a used truck for $10,000. Unknown to B, the truck was subject to an Illinois state lien for unpaid taxes in the amount of $2,000 and could not be driven in the state until the lien was paid. B conducted a multi-state business, however, and the truck could be driven in other states. S has made and breached a warranty that the truck was free of any "lien or encumbrance." 2–312(1)(a). The direct damages for breach are $2,000, the cost to B in removing the lien and obtaining the full value of the bargain.

E. CLAIMS OF OTHER CREDITORS AND PURCHASERS

1. AGAINST THE RECLAIMING SELLER

After S sells and delivers goods to B, its power to retrieve them from B and also free from the claims of B's creditors or purchasers from B is sharply limited. In a credit transaction, S can create and perfect a security interest under Article 9 and, if B defaults, can repossess the goods from B with priority over the claims of most creditors and some purchasers. *In the absence of a perfected security interest, S's right to retrieve is limited to two situations: (a) reclamation from an insolvent buyer, 2–702; and (b) cash sales, where the check bounces, see 2–507(2). In both, S must act fast before the claims of third parties have intervened.*

(a) Reclamation From Insolvent Buyer

If, in a credit transaction, B becomes insolvent, see 1–201(23), and S learns of this before delivery, S may refuse to deliver "except for cash, 2–702(1). Similarly, if B becomes insolvent and the goods are still in the possession of a carrier or bailee, S may be able to stop delivery under 2–705(1). The power of S to stop delivery under 2–705, at least, illustrates a possessory security interest arising under Article 2. See 9–113.

But suppose that S discovers B's insolvency *after* delivery and has not created and perfected a non-possessory security interest under Article 9? *Under*

2–702(2), S may *"reclaim the goods upon demand made within ten days after the receipt"* unless B has misrepresented his solvency in writing to S *"within three months before delivery,"* in which case the ten day limitation *"does not apply"* and a reasonable time limitation is available. See *1–204.* As between S and B, then, reclamation turns on a delivery by S to an insolvent buyer in a credit transaction and a timely demand. B's failure to disclose the insolvency is treated as fraud, and 2–702(2) provides the exclusive right of S to "reclaim goods on the buyer's fraudulent or innocent misrepresentation of solvency or of intent to pay." See also 2–702(3), which provides that a successful reclamation of goods excludes all other remedies with respect to them.

S's reclamation right under 2–702(2), however, is made "subject to the rights of a buyer in ordinary course or other good faith purchaser under this Article (Section 2–403,)" 2–702(3). Thus, if the rights of a BIOCB or a GFP have intervened *before* a timely reclamation demand, S is out of luck. Note that under a 1966 Amendment to Section 2–702(2), a "lien creditor" was removed from the category of third parties against whom S might lose. The purpose of this change was to preserve the pre-code priority of the defrauded seller over the lien creditor and, thus, the trustee in bankruptcy under the "strong arm" clause of the Bankruptcy Code. See 9–301(3). This priority has been honored by most courts and was adopted in Section 546(c) of the Bankruptcy Code. *Thus, in most cases a seller who can reclaim goods from the buyer under 2–702(2) can also reclaim them from B's lien creditor or its trustee in bankruptcy, even though the judicial lien attached before the reclamation demand was made.* Here is an Example in review and with a new twist or two.

> *Example VII(10):* On October 1, S delivered goods on credit to B, who was insolvent. At that time, B was financed by SP, who had created and perfected a security interest in all B's "inventory, existing and after acquired." Under this so-called "floating lien," SP's security interest attached to the goods sold by S to B on October 1 when B obtained rights in them. Three events then occurred: (1) On October 4, B filed a petition in bankruptcy. (2) On October 5, S demanded reclamation from B under Section 2–702(2). (3) On October 6, B contracted to sell the goods to a BIOCB, who paid cash but did not take immediate possession. How should this mess be resolved?
>
> *First,* since the reclamation demand was timely, S may recover the goods from B, 2–702(2), and probably from its trustee in bankruptcy. Section 546(c)(1) of the Bankruptcy Code, however, requires that S's demand be in writing. In addition, the sale from S to B must be in the "ordinary course" of S's business and the written demand must be made "before" (not "within", see 2–702(2)) ten days after receipt of such goods by the debtor. These minor variations from 2–702(2) should be kept in mind.

Second, because S's demand was made before B sold the goods to BIOCB, reclamation should be successful. S's claim is based upon B's fraud rather than title or a security interest, and the BIOCB takes subject to it. It is not clear in 2-702(3) when BIOCB has "rights" that might prevail over S. Presumably, they arise, at the earliest, when the goods are identified and BIOCB has a special property interest in them. See 2-501(1). Thus, if the transaction between B and BIOCB occurred on October 3 rather than October 6, S should lose unless BIOCB, who left the goods in S's possession after paying the price, is found to be in bad faith.

Third, the status of SP, who had a security interest in the goods before the demand was made, is a matter of some disagreement. Is he an "other good faith purchaser under this Article (Section 2-403)?" 2-702(3). The definition of "purchaser" is broad enough to include a secured party, see 1-201(33), but 2-403 deals with purchasers who take title to goods, not those who take free of security interests. Under this narrow reading of "purchaser," a secured party, like a lien creditor, would be excluded from that class of persons to whom the defrauded seller could lose. Most courts, however, have held that SP is a purchaser and prevails over S where the security interest attaches to the goods sold *before* the reclamation demand is made, even though the security interest arises under an after acquired property clause. In short, S's reclamation claim, even though a remedy for B's fraud, is treated like a security interest, see 1-201(37), in the competition with SP. As such, it will not prevail over SP's security interest, which attached and was perfected before the reclamation demand was made.

If S makes a timely demand after the goods have been sold to a BFP or BIOCB, who has priority to any identified proceeds of the sale? More to the point, should S, reclaiming under 2-702(2), or SP, asserting a perfected security interest under Article 9, have priority? Most courts have held that S's reclamation right does not extend to proceeds. Under this approach, SP wins. Other courts have concluded that the reclamation right extends to proceeds and that S should have priority over general creditors of B but not over SP. This conclusion makes practical sense, (it preserves the integrity of Article 9), even though there is no explicit support for it in the statute. See *United States v. Westside Bank,* 732 F.2d 1258 (5th Cir.1984).

(b) Cash Sales

S's reclamation right against B is even more tenuous when the sale is for cash rather than on credit. In the usual cash sale, S will deliver the goods to B in exchange for a check, which is normally a conditional payment. See 2-511(3). If the check is dishonored by the drawee bank, the conditional payment is defeated "as between the parties." 2-511(3). S, then, can recover the goods from B: *Under 2-507(2), B's "right as against the seller to retain or*

*dispose" of the goods "is conditioned upon his making the payment due."
Comment 3 boldly states that the "ten day limit within which the seller may
reclaim goods delivered on credit to an insolvent buyer is applicable here," see
2–702(2), and many courts have agreed.* See *Holiday Rambler Corp. v. First
National Bank & Trust Co.,* 723 F.2d 1449 (10th Cir.1983).

Unlike 2–702(3), 2–507(2) does not mention or define the rights of third
parties. But 2–403(1)(b) and (2) make it clear that S's reclamation claim is
subject to the rights of a GFP or a BIOCB. In short, these purchasers win
again.

The matter is not so clear where the claims of creditors are involved. A
plausible solution is to apply the results reached under Section 2–702(3) to
the cash sale, namely that S always wins over lien creditors of B but not over
secured parties whose security interests attach before the reclamation
demand. The matter is controversial and has not been clearly resolved by the
courts. See Mann & Phillips, *The Reclaiming Cash Seller and the Bankruptcy
Code,* 39 S.W.L.J. 603 (1985) for a complete discussion.

(c) Consignments; Sale on Approval and Return

There are at least two contracts for sale where it is understood that goods
delivered to B may be returned to S even though they conform to the
contract. The first is a "sale on approval" and the second is a "sale or
return." See 2–326(1). In a "sale on approval" the goods are delivered to B
"primarily for use" and are returned if they are not approved by B. The
agreement, of course, will provide the standards for B's disapproval. See
2–326(1)(a). In a "sale or return," the goods are delivered "primarily for
resale" and are returned if B is unable to sell them. 2–326(1)(b). Both
transactions are treated as sales, but with special incidents. Thus, in a "sale
on approval" the risk of loss remains on S until B accepts the goods,
2–327(1)(a), and in a "sale or return" the risk of loss is on B until return.
2–327(2)(b).

What are the rights of creditors of B to goods in B's possession under these
two transactions? *Section 2–326(2) provides: "Except as provided in subsection
(3), goods held on approval are not subject to the claims of the buyer's
creditors until acceptance; goods held on sale or return are subject to such
claims while the buyer's possession."* The assumption is that the two
transactions are "strongly delineated in practice" and that the presumption
favors a "sale or return" when the goods are delivered to a merchant for
resale. Comment 1.

In a consignment, O delivers goods to an agent or factor (C) with power to
sell. O retains title to the goods. If C is able to sell to B, title passes directly
from O to B and C remits the purchase price, less a commission. If C is
unable to sell, the goods are returned to O. Under no circumstance does O

sell the goods to C. In most consignments, O has power under the agreement to reclaim the goods from C upon stated events of default before any sale or return by C.

As with a "sale or return," the problem is the rights of creditors of C rather than purchasers from C. Purchasers are fully protected, because O has given C power to sell. See 2–403(1). Suppose, then, that C, in possession of O's goods on a consignment, grants a security interest in them to SP or that LC obtains a judicial lien on the goods. How does this affect O's right to reclaim the goods on default by C?

First, the goods are "deemed to be held on sale or return" with respect to claims of creditors of C when they are delivered "to a person for sale and such person maintains a place of business at which he deals in goods of the kind involved, under a name other than the name of the person making delivery . . . ." 2–326(3).

Second, like goods held on "sale or return," consigned goods are subject to the claims of C's creditors while in C's possession 2–326(1)(b) & (2), subject to the notice exception in 2–326(3).

Third, the exception turns upon whether sufficient notice has been given to third parties that C is dealing in the goods of others. If so, O's claim to the goods will prevail over C's creditors. Sufficient notice is given when C is "generally known by his creditors to be substantially engaged in selling the goods of others" or because O "complies with the filing provisions of the Article on Secured Transactions. . . ." 2–326(3)(b) & (c). *A consignor, therefore, should always consider the wisdom of filing an Article 9 financing statement, see 9–402(1), in the proper place, see 9–401(1). This will give sufficient notice to creditors of C under Section 2–326(3) and, to the extent provided by 9–114, insure priority over secured parties who have a perfected security interest in the goods.*

> *Example VII(11):* SP created and perfected a security interest under Article 9 in C's "inventory, existing and after-acquired," to secure a loan. O consigned goods to C for sale. The goods qualify as inventory, and SP would have a "perfected security interest in the goods if they were the property" of C. 9–114(1). If it was established that C was "generally known by his creditors to be substantially engaged in selling the goods of others," 2–326(3)(b), SP is deemed to have notice and should be subject to O's claim. If this notice cannot be established and O is "required" to file a financing statement to protect its interest under 2–326(3)(c), O must comply with the special requirements of Section 9–114(1) to have priority over SP. Read that section, please, and remember that if O's consignment is not a security interest and the exacting notice requirements of Section 9–114(1) are not met, O is

subordinate to a person who would have a perfected security interest in the goods if they were the property of the consignee. 9–114(2).

Here is a final reminder. The reclaiming seller under either 2–702 or 2–511 and the consignor under 2–326(3) are not secured parties seeking to enforce an Article 9 security interest. Their interest is based respectively upon claims of fraud, conditional payment and title. But the effect—reclamation from B—is the same and, in most cases, the creditors of either B or C, the consignee, will have no knowledge of the claim. Thus, the tension is predictable—S asserts what amounts to a "secret" claim to goods in the possession of B, frequently a merchant, and third parties have, arguably, relied upon that possession in making purchase and credit decisions. The policy question, therefore, is whether these claims should be treated like security interest subject to Article 9 or whether the common law distinctions should still be recognized. With consignments, at least, a hybrid approach has been developed—the consignor's interest is not a security interest, but notice can be given and priority assured by complying with Article 9. Whether this will stand the test of time remains to be seen.

2. CLAIMS TO GOODS IN SELLER'S POSSESSION

Assume that after conforming goods are identified to the contract, S repudiates the contract or fails to deliver to B. Suppose, also, that B has paid all or part of the price in advance. When can B recover the identified goods from the seller under Article 2?

Three possible routes are specific performance, 2–716(1), replevin, 2–716(3), and the limited claim to identified goods held by an insolvent seller under 2–502. See Chapter VI(D)(2). Another possibility, which we will not discuss here, is under Article 9. B could create and perfect a security interest in goods sold to him to secure advances made on the price. In each case, B could obtain possession of the identified goods on S's default.

If B has no claim to the goods against S, then there will be no competition for the goods between B and creditors of or purchasers from S. But if B could recover the goods from S, we must determine the extent to which that claim is subject to the claims of S's purchasers and creditors. The remedies of specific performance and replevin have already been explored in Chapter VI. With one example of Section 2–502, we will assume thereafter that B has a claim against S to the goods and focus upon the competing claims of B and S's purchasers and creditors.

Example VII(12): S agreed to manufacture goods for B. B paid one-half of the price at the time of contracting and promised to pay the balance when the goods were delivered. Unknown to B, S was insolvent at the time of contracting. Thirty days later, after the goods were identified but did not yet conform to the contract, S repudiated the deal. On these facts, B may recover the identified goods from S, even though they do not conform to the contract.

B has paid "a part or all of the price of goods in which he has a special property" under 2–501(1) and S became "insolvent within ten days after receipt of the first installment on their price." 2–502(1). B, however, must make and keep "a tender of any unpaid portion of their price." Note, however, that if the goods were not identified or if S became insolvent more than ten days after receipt of the part-payment, the Section 2–502(1) claim would fail. Note also that unlike S's reclamation right under 2–702(2), there is no section in the Bankruptcy Code blessing B's rights under 2–502. Most commentators believe that the 2–502 rights, if exercised, would be a preference under Section 547 of the Bankruptcy Code.

(a) Purchasers From Seller

Suppose, in *Example VII(12)*, that S, after identifying conforming goods to the contract, sold them for cash to C. On the facts, B has a "special property interest" in the goods, 2–501(1), but not title. In most cases, the goods must be delivered to B before title passes. 2–401(2). S, on the other hand, still had title to the goods but no actual authority to sell them to C. And, certainly, the goods were not delivered by B to S in a transaction of purchase. See 2–403(1). Without more, then, C could acquire only the title which S "had or had power to transfer," 2–403(1), and would take subject to B's rights, if any, against S to possession under Article 2.

But B, by acquiescing in the retention of possession by S, has entrusted the goods to S. 2–403(3). *Thus, if S is a "merchant who deals in goods of that kind" and C qualifies as a BIOCB, S has power to "transfer all rights of the entruster" to C. The bundle of rights acquired by the BIOCB, then, would include title from S and freedom from the special property interest held by B. Short of the entrusting exception, however, the Code appears to say that if C were just a GFP, he would take title from S subject to B's special property interest and the remedies it supports under 2–502(1) or 2–716.*

(b) Creditors of Seller

Creditor is defined to include a general or unsecured creditor, a lien creditor, a secured creditor and a trustee in bankruptcy. 1–201(12). To what extent is the buyer's right to recover goods from the seller subject to the claims of creditors of the seller? Section 2–402 provides some of the answers. Here are a few examples.

> *Example VII(13):* B purchased a mink coat from S, paid $500 down and left the coat with S for 90 days, at which time the $2,500 balance of the price was due. In the interim, S became insolvent but did not file bankruptcy. C, an unsecured creditor of S, demanded that the coat be made available to pay C's claim.

2–402(1) provides that the "rights of unsecured creditors of the seller with respect to goods which have been identified to a contract for sale are subject to the buyer's rights to recover the goods." Thus, if B has "rights" under 2–502 or 2–716, they prevail over C. C, or any creditor, however, might attack S's retention of goods sold or identified to B as fraudulent "under any rule of law of the state where the goods are situated." See 2–402(1) & (2). If fraudulent, the contract for sale is "void" against S. But 2–402(2) provides a preemptive rule that protects B in this standard "layaway" plan: "Retention of possession in good faith and current course of trade by a merchant-seller for a commercially reasonable time after a sale or identification is not fraudulent." This rule preempts other state law on the matter. So holding is *In re Black & White Cattle Co.*, 783 F.2d 1454 (9th Cir.1986) (California law).

Example VII(14): S owed B $10,000 on a note. On July 1, S sold B a mink coat for $5,000. On July 10, S became insolvent and, shortly thereafter, identified a mink coat to B's contract in order to secure the $10,000 debt. On July 12, LC obtained a judicial lien on S's property, including the mink coat. Who is entitled to the coat, LC or B?

First, Article 2 does not provide a rule of priority in contests between a judicial lien and a special property interest. One must look to other state law where, without more, priority might be given to the party whose interest arose first.

Second, LC is a creditor, as defined, and under Section 2–402(2) could argue that S's identification of the goods was fraudulent or could assert with even more authority that the identification was made not in the current course of trade "but . . . as security for a preexisting claim for money" and, as such, constituted a fraudulent transfer or a voidable preference. 2–402(3)(b). Either argument, if established under relevant state law, makes the identification void against LC. Further, the identification on these facts is clearly a preferential transfer under Section 547(b) of the Bankruptcy Code. In this case, therefore, S's conduct is not entitled to protection under 2–402.

Example VII(15): S sold inventory to B in the ordinary course of business. B paid cash and left the goods in S's possession until it could clear a place for them in its building. S then borrowed money from SP, who created and perfected a security interest in S's "inventory, existing and after-acquired." Thereafter, S defaulted on the loan and SP repossessed the inventory, including that sold to B, before B obtained possession. B claims from SP the goods identified to its contract for sale.

If S's identification or retention of possession was *not* fraudulent under 2–402, the rights of SP with a security interest and B with a special property interest should be determined under Article 9. At the very least, nothing in Article 2 is intended to impair the rights of SP under the provisions of Article 9. 2–402(3)(a). Since a BIOCB takes free of a security interest *after* it is created, 9–307(1), logic would dictate no less protection when the sale to a BIOCB occurs *before* the security interest. But when does he become a BIOCB? Does it depend upon the taking of possession of the goods? Some courts have held no, concluding that where B has paid for the goods and S's retention was neither fraudulent nor misleading to other creditors, B's special property interest should have priority. In short, the special property interest arising under Article 2 has priority over the later Article 9 security interest. Since this conclusion is not clearly supported by either Article 2 or Article 9, caution dictates that B take prompt possession to solidify its Article 2 rights to the goods. Cf. 9–113.

In summary, B's Article 2 rights to the goods, like those of S, are not based upon a security interest and are not communicated to those who deal with S. When the interests of buyers from and creditors of S are considered, B's case is weakest when S's identification is preferential, the retention of possession is irregular or tends to mislead creditors and B, because it has paid all or part of the price in advance, looks and acts more like a creditor than a buyer of goods. In this uncertain borderland between Article 2 and Article 9, caution dictates that B perfect a security interest under Article 9 if it is financing S's acquisition and production of the goods or obtain prompt possession of identified goods which have been paid for in whole or in part.

F. SECURITY INTERESTS ARISING UNDER ARTICLE 2

In a credit sale, i.e., where the seller has agreed to deliver goods sold in exchange for the buyer's promise to pay the price, the overlap and tension between Articles 2 and 9 can be illustrated as follows.

First, S and B can, before delivery, enter a security *agreement* creating a security interest in the goods and S can perfect the security interest by filing a financing statement in a designated public office. This is a security interest arising under Article 9 and its enforceability, perfection, priority and enforcement are governed by that Article. See 2–102. If B defaults under the security agreement, S can enforce the security interest by repossessing and disposing of the goods under Article 9, Part 5. Compare 2–706, permitting S to resell goods in its possession upon breach by B.

Second, if S delivers the goods and retains "title" until B pays the price, the effect is to create a security interest even though there was no express security agreement. 1–201(37), 2–401(1). This is, nevertheless, a security interest arising under Article 9. S, upon B's default, could enforce it by repossessing the goods. But unless the security interest is perfected by filing or otherwise, it is subordinate to the claim of an intervening lien creditor and the trustee in bankruptcy. 9–301(1)(b) & Section 544(a) of the Bankruptcy Code.

Third, if B becomes insolvent or fails to pay all or part of the price due on or before delivery, S can withhold delivery and retain possession of the goods. 2–703(a). See 2–702(1). S may still have possession of the goods, or it may stop delivery while they are in the possession of a carrier or bailee. 2–705. At common law, S was thought to have a possessory lien on the goods to secure the price. The lien arose by operation of law in the course of the sales transaction rather than by agreement. Under 9–113, this lien is now called a "security interest arising solely under the Article on Sales . . ." The security interest is "subject to" the provisions of Article 9 "except that and so long as the debtor does not have or does not lawfully obtain possession of the goods (a) no security agreement is necessary to make the security interest enforceable; and (b) no filing is required to perfect the security interest; and (c) the rights of the secured party on default by the debtor are governed by the Article on Sales. . . ." By virtue of 9–113, therefore, S has a perfected possessory security interest arising under Article 2 whose priority is determined by Article 9 but whose enforcement is governed by Article 2. Here is a simple example of how this works and what difference it makes.

> *Example VII(16):* S contracted to sell B a carload of goods for $50,000, shipment FOB point of shipment. B agreed to pay S's agent, located at the destination point, $25,000 when the goods were shipped and the balance 4 weeks later. S shipped the goods without reserving a security interest. S then learned that B had failed to pay part of the price and was able to stop the goods in transit. See 2–705. In the meantime, LC had obtained a judicial lien on B's interest in the goods in transit.

> As between S in possession and LC, S has priority. Under 9–113, S has a perfected possessory security interest arising under Article 2 which has priority over LC under Article 9. See 9–301(1)(b). S can enforce its security interest by resale of the goods under Section 2–706, provided that the conditions established there are met. See Chapter VI(C)(3). If the resale nets a profit, S has no duty to account for it to B. If the security interest were enforced under Article 9, however, S would have a duty to account for any surplus realized over the secured obligation. See 9–504(2).

> Suppose, however, that S had delivered possession and then properly regained it from an insolvent B, see 2–702(2), or from B who issued a check in payment which bounced, see 2–507(2). Does S still have a security interest arising under Article 2? The answer is probably no in the fraud claim: "Successful reclamation of goods excludes all other remedies with respect to them." 2–702(3). The answer is probably yes in the conditional delivery if the claims of creditors or purchasers have not intervened before possession was regained. S has lawfully regained possession upon B's default in a "cash" sale

SALE OF GOODS: ARTICLE 2

and, unless the failure of condition is treated like a retention of title, the principle and policy of Section 9–113 should apply.

Problem: S shipped more than a carload of goods to B "fob" point of shipment. B then sold the goods to C while they were in transit. The contract was made through an exchange of telexed messages and C paid the price by wire transfer. B agreed to deliver the goods to C after they arrived. S learned that B, despite the sale, was insolvent and properly stopped delivery before B received the goods. 2–705. C, who has title to the goods, 2–401(1), claims that it took free from S's security interest arising under 9–113. Is C correct? Consider 9–113, 2–705, 9–307(1) and 2–403. Would C prevail if C were a BIOCB?

G. REVIEW QUESTIONS

VII–A. T stole a valuable painting from O. After fabricating evidence of title, T delivered the painting to S, an art dealer, with authority to sell for not less than $200,000. Five months later, S sold the painting to B, a BIOCB, for $240,000. S did well for T, for the fair market value at time of delivery to B was $190,000. Five years later, O traced the painting to B and demanded its return. At that time, the fair market value was $250,000.

1. Can O replevy the painting from B?

2. If so, what, if anything, can B recover from S?

VII–B. What is the difference between a security interest, see 1–201(37), and a special property interest, see 2–501(1)? Consider both differences in definition and legal effect.

VII–C. SP created and perfected a security interest in D's car. D defaulted, SP repossessed the car and delivered it to S, a dealer in new and used cars, for work on the engine. S had no actual authority to sell. Nevertheless, S sold the car to B in the ordinary course of business, B paid cash, signed an application for a certificate of title, and was told that the car and a certificate of title would be ready in three days. SP learned of the sale and took possession of the car from S before delivery to B.

1. Did B take free of SP's security interest?

2. If not, what, if anything, can B recover from S?

VII–D. On July 1, S, a manufacturer, sold and delivered a new backhoe to B, a dealer, in exchange for a $20,000 check for the purchase price. B, who had not dealt with S before, was insolvent and in need of cash. On July 2, B stopped payment on the check and on July 3, B sold and delivered the backhoe to C, a farmer, for $10,000 cash. C, a regular customer, knew that B was in financial trouble and was told by B that he would "get the papers to him" after the holiday. On July 6, S learned that the check had been dishonored and promptly demanded return of the backhoe from B. B reported that it had been sold but would not say to whom. On July 12, S discovered that C was the purchaser and sought to replevy the backhoe from him.

1. As between S and C, what result?

2. What, if anything, can C recover from B?

VII–E. M is a merchant who both repairs and sells a wide variety of jewelry. On July 1, M's inventory contained jewelry (1) delivered by A for repairs; (2) delivered by B under a contract for "sale on approval," (3) delivered by C under a contract for "sale or return," and (4) delivered by D for sale under a consignment contract. On July 1, T, an unsecured creditor of M's, obtained a judicial lien on all of the inventory. As between T and M's customers, A, B, C and D, who is entitled to possession of the jewelry?

*

PART THREE

LEASING OF GOODS

Analysis

*

VIII

GENERAL SCOPE
AND POLICIES

A. THE NEED FOR 2A

Article 2A, Leases, regulates an important transaction, the lease of goods. Leasing of personal property has long existed but in recent years has experienced exponential growth. In 1987 alone, the Department of Commerce estimated the value of lease receivables outstanding in the United States at more than $310 billion.

The governing law has been a hodgepodge of principles drawn from the common law of real and personal property. The resulting uncertainty provided a field day for manipulating case law precedent and analogical application of Articles 2 and 9 to achieve opportunistic results. For example, the common law lease—"a bailment for hire"—was neither a sale nor a secured transaction. *If the transaction could be characterized as a sale, however, the lessee might obtain the benefit of Article 2's warranty provisions. Similarly, if the contract was classified as a secured transaction rather than a lease, the lessor might have an unperfected security interest, vulnerable in bankruptcy, because no financing statement was filed.* Either classification was possible with courts in wide disagreement over appropriate classification and governance. A lease is a transfer of an interest in personal property and therefore could arguably come within the Article 2 scope section of "transactions in goods." But many sections of Article 2 apply expressly only to "sellers" and "buyers." Article 9 comes into play only if a transaction is properly characterized as creating a "security interest," a classification inappropriate for a lease.

As courts struggled with the uncomfortable fit between the Code articles and lease transactions, committees composed of practitioners and law professors began the laborious process of drafting what would become the first new article to be added to the UCC since its promulgation. The initial product, the Uniform Personal Property Leasing Act, was approved by the National Conference of Commissioners on Uniform State Laws in 1985. A decision was then made to make the UPPLA a part of the UCC. Accordingly, a revised draft, now called Article 2A, Leases, and an amended definition of "security interest" in Article 1–201(37) designed to exclude the lease were promulgated by the Commissioners in 1986; the UCC's Permanent Editorial Board and the American Law Institute approved the changes in 1987. Twenty-four amendments, primarily concerned with transfers of the lessor's interest and rights of the lessor's secured creditors against the lessee, were officially approved and adopted in 1990. The discussion in this BLACK LETTER is based on the amended version. As of January 1, 1992, some version of Article 2A has been enacted in 20 states and introduced in 16 more.

Fortunately for the authors of this BLACK LETTER, it is unnecessary to devote extensive discussion to the factors which prompt a user to lease rather than purchase goods. These factors have to do with the arcane worlds of accounting and tax. The payment obligations of a lessee need not appear on its financial statement as a debt incurred by a credit buyer, a potential downside to loan acquisition. And an equipment lessee may receive more favorable tax treatment than a credit buyer. The lease is a deductible business expenditure, while the interest on a credit purchase may not be.

These considerations are properly left to other courses and sources. But they illustrate the importance for the Code to contain provisions to distinguish the "true" lease from a credit sale disguised as a lease. *Issues of filing and available remedies are at stake.*

1. FILING

Leases do not require filing for the lessor to achieve protection against creditors of the lessee. 2A–307. But if the transaction that purports to be a lease is characterized as a credit sale disguised as a lease, it would be subject to the perfection and filing requirements of Article 9. An unfiled interest loses to perfected and lien creditors including the ubiquitous Trustee in Bankruptcy. 9–301. The problem may be avoided, however, by the simple expedient of filing a financing statement under 9–408. Under this section, a financing statement may be filed using the term "lease" and although such a denomination will not be a factor in determining the true characterization of the transaction, it will provide the creditor with perfected status if a court construes the transaction to be a credit sale in disguise (a secured transaction).

2. AVAILABLE REMEDIES

Significant differences in the remedies provided for default exist depending on whether the transaction is an actual lease or a security interest. See the discussions on lease remedies in Chapter XII and sales remedies in Chapter VI.

(a) Lease or Sale: *The Code Solution:*

The Code now seeks to distinguish the "true" lease from the credit sale by a combination of 1) a specific exclusion of "security interest" in 2A–103 and 2) an elaborate redefinition of "security interest" in an amended 1–201(37). 2A is therefore limited to provisions governing the "true" lease defined as ". . . a transfer of the right to possession and use of goods for a term in return for consideration." 2A–103(1)(j). The amended definition of "security interest" is discussed in VIII(C), *infra.*

B. THE SCOPE OF ARTICLE 2A

The scope of 2A includes ". . . any transaction, regardless of form, that creates a lease." 2A–102. *"Lease," in turn, is defined as a "transfer of the right to possession and use of goods for a term in return for consideration, but a sale, including a sale on approval or a sale or return, or retention or creation of a security interest is not a lease."* 2A–103(1)(j). "Lease" also includes a "sublease," unless the "context clearly indicates otherwise." Thus, the transactions to which 2A applies are sharply delineated.

Three scope determinants worth noting include:

1. CONTRACTING OUT
Except where provided otherwise, the effect of the provisions of 2A may be varied by agreement of the parties. See discussion in IX(C), *supra.*

2. CHARACTERIZATION BY ANALOGY
A court may "apply this Article by analogy to any transaction, regardless of form, that creates a lease of personal property other than goods, taking into account the expressed intentions of the parties to the transaction and any difference between a lease of goods and a lease of other property." Comment, 2A–102.

3. PREEMPTION BY OTHER LAW
A lease governed by 2A may also be subject to other law, including statutes of the United States, state certificate of title statutes, and consumer protection statutes. 2A–104.

One final note: As a transfer of possession of goods for a consideration, the lease bears a close similarity to a sale. One should not be surprised to expect to find the governing standards of 2A to parallel closely those of Article 2. To facilitate this conscious parallelism, the Cross References of each section of 2A cite the Article 2 analogues, and in addition, the Official Comment to each 2A section cites a "Uniform Statutory Source." In this BLACK LETTER, where the provisions of 2A do not depart significantly from those of Article 2, reference will be made to Part II, SALE OF GOODS where the issues have been discussed. In this Part III, LEASING OF GOODS, the treatment will concentrate on those portions of Article 2A which are unique to leasing. Despite the similarity between a lease and a sale, the following example illustrates the risk of relying on analogy to apply Article 2 to a lease transaction.

> *Example VIII(1):* In a recent case from a jurisdiction which had not yet adopted 2A, the lessee entered into a "Retail Lease Agreement" for the use of a new Jeep. Several days after the lessee took possession, the motor exploded causing extensive damage to the engine. Repairs were made but numerous other problems caused the lessee to return the vehicle and revoke acceptance under 2–608. The trial court granted summary judgment for the defendant holding that the parties had unambiguously intended to create a lease. In affirming the judgment, the appellate court rejected arguments based on analogy stating that any extension of the UCC's sales provisions to lease agreements must necessarily be the result of legislative action. (Note: On similar reasoning, the court refused to apply the consumer protection provisions of the federal Magnuson–Moss Warranty Act because there was no initial sale directly related to the lease.)

C. THE "TRUE" LEASE

No single issue under the Code has caused more difficulty or spawned more litigation than whether a given transaction should be characterized as a lease or as a disguised security interest (a conditional sale). The difference makes a difference in a variety of contexts. Three of the most litigated are 1) the filing requirement for perfection under Article 9 (only the incautious should be embroiled in such litigation since in case of doubt, 9–408 expressly recognizes the use of a precautionary filing in lease transactions), 2) the status of the creditor in bankruptcy proceedings, and 3) whether the creditor must adhere to the procedural requirements of Article 9 in pursuing a remedy for default. The volume of litigation can best be illustrated by the 1986–1991 Cumulative Supplement of the Uniform Commercial Code Case Digest in which 160 cases are digested in the fine print of 34 pages. While the newly amended definition of "security interest" may resolve some of the issues, its complexity guarantees that much litigation will continue. *Please read 1–201(37).*

The revised 1–201(37) helps to distinguish between a lease of goods and a security interest in goods rather than between a sale and a lease of goods. The latter distinction is less important now that Article 2A has been promulgated. Recall that Article 9 applies to "any transaction (regardless of its form) which is intended to create a security interest in personal property or fixtures including goods. . . ." 9–102(1)(a). Under 1–201(37), first paragraph, "security interest" means "an interest in personal property or fixtures which secures payment or performance of an obligation." If, in a contract for sale, the seller delivers goods to the buyer on credit and reserves "title" until the price is paid, the "retention or reservation of title . . . is limited in effect to a reservation of a 'security interest'." 1–201(37), first paragraph. Thus, the seller must comply with Article 9 or suffer the consequences.

> *Example VIII(2):* After negotiations, Buyer agrees to purchase new farm equipment from Seller for $25,000, with $10,000 down on delivery and $15,000 due in six months. Under the written contract for sale, Seller retains "title" to the goods until the price is fully paid but does not file a financing statement. After the goods are delivered, Buyer borrows $15,000 from Bank, which creates an enforceable Article 9 security interest in the farm equipment and perfects by filing a financing statement. The consequences are that if Buyer defaults in both transactions, Seller has an enforceable but unperfected security interest in the goods and Bank, which has perfected its security interest, has priority. 9–301(1)(a).

Suppose in the example above, the parties had called themselves "lessor" and "lessee" and labeled the transaction a "lease of goods." For reasons to be elaborated, the transaction creates a security interest rather than a lease and Article 9 controls. The newly amended definition of "security interest" in 1–201(37) focuses on economic factors to distinguish the true lease from the disguised conditional sale contract which would be governed by Article 9. The former definition's use of intent ("Unless a lease . . . is intended as security . . . .") has been abandoned in favor of objective criteria based on ". . . the facts of each case. . . ." *Basic to the characterization of a true lease is the lessor's retention of a meaningful residual interest in the goods. By contrast, where the effect of the transaction is to transfer the full economic value of the goods to the transferee, it is a sale.* Beginning with a recognition that "the facts of each case" are to be determinative, 1–201(37) contains three paragraphs of guidelines and examples (two pages worth!) to achieve its objective.

To be a security interest, the transaction must not be terminable by the lessee (a requirement designed to overturn the holding of a prior case to the contrary) and, in addition, must satisfy one of four additional requirements. 1–201(37) (first a-d). Their content may be summarized under the headings of "economic life" and "nominal consideration."

1. ECONOMIC LIFE

If the transaction is for the full "economic life" of the goods (or if the lessee is bound to renew for such a period), it is a security interest (the lessor would have no residual interest). The economic life is to be determined on a prospective, not retroactive, basis. 1–201(37)(y). That the economic life becomes greater or lesser because of events unanticipated at the time of the original lease is irrelevant to the characterization.

> *Example VIII(3):* Lessor and Lessee enter into a 3 year lease of equipment reasonably expected to have an economic life of 6 years. New technology makes the equipment obsolete in the third year. Although the economic life of the lease coincides with the term of the agreement, it remains a true lease since the transaction must be viewed prospectively. It is, in other words, the life which the parties would reasonably have expected it to be at the inception of the transaction.

2. NOMINAL CONSIDERATION

Where the lease contains an option either to purchase or renew for the full economic life of the goods for a "nominal consideration," the transaction is a security interest since the lessor would have no meaningful residual interest. 1–201(37) (first c and d). But what is "nominal"? 1–201(37)(x) provides examples of what would *not* be nominal: leases in which the consideration for the exercise of the option is to be the fair rental (the option to renew) or the fair price (the option to purchase) determined at the time the option is to be performed. The economic reality is that the exercise of the option will require the lessee to pay the lessor a fair value for the lessor's residual interest, a result consistent with the nature of a true lease. It is a lease, in short, if the lessor has something of significant value at the conclusion of the term; if not, the transaction is a security interest.

> *Example VIII(4):* Lessor and lessee enter into a 3 year lease in which the total of the monthly payments approximate what the purchase price plus interest would be. The goods were specially manufactured for the lessee's use

and customized with the lessee's logo. The lease contained a clause granting an option to renew at a fair market rental to be determined at the time of the exercise of the option. Despite the presence of the option clause which would satisfy the "non-nominal" provision of 1–201(37)(x), the transaction should be considered a security interest. The other clauses make it clear that there will be *no* significant "market" rental. Since the goods have been customized, no one other than the original lessee will want the goods.

The above examples should not be confused with those discussed in another section of the definition (1–201(37) (second a-e) which begins with the phrase "A transaction does not create a security interest merely because it provides that . . ." Subsections (d) and (e) of this paragraph describe options in which the price for exercising the option is fixed in the original transaction and is equal to or greater than the "reasonably predictable" fair rental (the option to renew) or the fair value (the option to purchase) of the goods at the time the option is to be performed. Thus these "fixed price" or "full payout" options will *not necessarily* be security interests.

> ***Example VIII(5):*** Lessor and Lessee enter into a 5 year lease providing for monthly payments of $5,000. A clause grants an option to renew at a fair market rental to be agreed upon by the parties at the time of the renewal. The rental agreed upon is $1000 per month. The transaction is a true lease because the additional consideration is not nominal under the terms of 1–201(37)(x). If the option price had been agreed upon at the time of the original transaction (a fixed price option), 1–201(37)(d) would govern and one could only conclude that the transaction does not create a security interest *merely* because it contains such a provision.

Other examples in the category of provisions which will not make a transaction a security interest *merely* because of their presence are 1) where the present value of the consideration paid by the lessee is substantially equal to or is greater than the fair market value of the goods at the time the lease is entered into (the "full pay out" lease) (1–201(37) (second a)), 2) the lessee assumes the risk of loss, or agrees to pay taxes, insurance, filing, recording, or registration fees, or service or maintenance costs with respect to the goods (1–202(37) (second b)), and 3) the lessee has an option to renew the lease or to become the owner of the goods (1–201(37) (second c)). Common to each of these categories is the notion that their presence alone is not sufficient to determine the true nature of the transaction.

It should be emphasized that the above guidelines do not furnish a bright line test for characterizing transactions in which the agreed upon consideration for the exercise of the option is less than the fair market value. The Official Comment states: "There is a set of purchase options whose fixed price is less than fair market value but greater than nominal that must be determined on the facts of each case to ascertain whether the transaction in which the option is included creates a lease or security interest." One can only conclude that the section leaves a wide area of discretion in the courts to determine when the difference between the value of the goods and the price of the option is sufficiently disparate that the transaction should be treated as a security interest.

> ***Example VIII(6):*** A 3–year equipment lease contains a provision granting the lessee an option to purchase the equipment at the end of the three years for $1000. The reasonably predictable value is $5,000. These economic facts make it clear that portions of the monthly payments were being made to compensate the lessor for the residual interest, an economic reality inconsistent with a true lease. Although the Code definition does not dictate a result, the five to one disparity between option price and predictable value suggests that the transaction should be characterized as a security interest.

Problem: Your client sells or rents new pickup trucks. It is common practice to rent under the following terms: (1) Lessee agrees to pay a fixed rent over a stated term (say 4 years); (2) At the time of leasing, the parties estimate the residual value of the truck at the end of the lease (say $2,500); (3) At the end of the lease, an appraiser determines the actual value of the residual interest (say $3,000); (4) Once the actual value is determined, payments are made under a "terminal rental adjustment clause" (TRAC) depending upon the actual value of the residual. If actual value is higher than estimated value, Lessor pays the Lessee (here $500). If actual value is lower than estimated value, Lessee pays the Lessor. Client wants to know whether this transaction is a "true" lease.

IX

GENERAL PROVISIONS

Analysis

A. DEFINITIONS UNIQUE TO 2A

Many of the definitions in 2A, see 2A–103, have such close analogues to the General Definitions in Article 1, see 1–201, and those in Article 2, see 2–103—107, that they do not require separate discussion. *This section, therefore, will highlight those definitions that are unique to 2A.*

1. GENERAL DEFINITIONS

2A contains several definitions that relate to leases of goods in general. Among other things, these definitions help to determine the scope of Article 2A. See in particular the definitions of "lease," 2A–103(1)(j), "leasehold interest," 2A–102(1)(m), and "lessor's residual interest," 2A–103(1)(q). See also the definitions of "lease agreement," "lease contract," "lessee," "lessee in the ordinary course of business," "lessor," "merchant lessee," and "sublease" in 2A–103(1). These definitions should be distinguished from the Article 2 definitions of "sale," "contract for sale," 2–106(1), "title," 2–401, and "special property interest," 2–501(1).

2. GOODS AND FIXTURES

2A's definition of "goods," 2A–103(1)(h), is both more inclusive and more limited than that in Article 2, 2–105(1), 2–107(1). A lease of goods includes "fixtures" but excludes "minerals or the like, including oil and gas, before extraction." Thus, a lease of fixtures is covered by 2A but a lease of natural gas to be extracted by the lessor or lessee is not.

The inclusion of "fixtures" as goods is important. If the leased goods are fixtures, a determination to be made under real estate law, see 2A–309(1)(a), then the lessor should make a fixture filing in the "office where a mortgage on the real estate would be filed or recorded." 2A–309(1)(b). The filing requirement is imposed in 2A–309 rather than by Article 9. Thus, if the lessor's interest is perfected by filing, it will have priority in most cases over a subsequent conflicting interest of a mortgage or owner of the land. 2A–309(4). If the lessor's interest is perfected by filing, it will not have priority over an earlier recorded mortgage interest in the land and fixtures unless there is a "purchase money lease." 2A–309(4)(a). If the lessor's interest is not perfected, it will have priority only if the fixtures are classified as "readily removable" equipment. 2A–309(5)(a).

> *Example IX(1):* Lessee owns land which is used in natural gas production. The land contains gas rigs, pipes and storage tanks, all of which are fixtures. Lessor agreed to lease new replacement pipes and storage tanks to Lessee. At the time of the lease, a mortgagee of the lessee-owner had a recorded mortgage interest in the land and fixtures. Since the mortgage was first in time to file, it would, in most cases, have priority over Lessor, even though Lessor made a later fixture filing. An exception is made for a "purchase money lease," 2A–309(4)(a). On the facts here, the lease is "purchase money" because the lessee did not have possession of the goods or a right to use

them before the lease, 2A–309(1)(c). Thus, Lessor would have priority over the mortgagee if it made a fixture filing thereafter. Note, however, that the fixtures are not "readily removable equipment" since the rig, pipes and storage tank are "primarily used or leased for use in the operation of the real estate." Thus, this possible exception to the mortgagee's priority could not be invoked in this case. See 2A–309(5)(a).

3. CONSUMER LEASE

Although the Code is not a "consumer protection" statute, 2A does contain a number of sections which make special provisions for the "consumer lease." As defined in 2A–103(1)(e), " *'Consumer lease' means a lease that a lessor regularly engaged in the business of leasing or selling makes to a lessee who is an individual and who takes under the lease primarily for a personal, family, or household purpose[, if the total payments to be made under the lease contract, excluding payments for options to renew or buy, do not exceed $_____].*" Whether and to what extent there should be a dollar limitation is left up to the individual states. Special provisions for consumer leases are found in 2A–106 (choice of law and choice of forum clauses), 2A–108(2) and (4) (unconscionability), 2A–109(2) (acceleration of rental clauses), 2A–208(2) (no-modification-except-by-writing clauses require separate signature), 2A–503(3) (limitation of consequential damages), 2A–504(3)(b) (formula for limiting consumer lessee's liability), and 2A–516(3) (lessee's failure to give notice of infringement not a bar to remedy against lessor). See also, 2A–407(1).

4. FINANCE LEASE

The finance lease is normally a three party transaction in which the lessor (typically a leasing company) is a financier whose primary function is to extend credit to the lessee. The *lessee* selects the goods from a *supplier;* the *lessor* purchases the goods from the supplier; and the lessor in turn leases the goods to the *lessee.* Two transactions are involved and interrelated: A sale from the supplier to the lessor and a lease from the lessor to the lessee. To be a finance lease, it must qualify as a "true" lease. There must be a residual interest in the lessor so that it does not run afoul of the disguised security interest classification discussed in VIII C.

As defined in 2A–103(1)(g), " 'Finance lease' means a lease with respect to which (i) the lessor does not select, manufacture, or supply the goods [provides the justification for exempting the lessor from what would otherwise be implied warranty liability]; (ii) the lessor acquires the goods or the right to possession and use of the goods in connection with the lease [insures the interconnectedness between the sale and the lease]; and (iii) one of the following occurs: . . . ." The "following" consists of 4 different procedures each of which is designed to insure that the lessee will be informed of the representations, warranties, promises, and disclaimers contained in the contract between the supplier and the lessor. These procedures provide the lessee with the basis for its reliance on the obligations of the supplier with reference to the quality and performance of the goods.

> ***Example IX(2):*** A code comment (2A–407, c. 3) provides the following hypothetical: A, the financier and the potential lessor, has been contacted by B, the potential lessee, to discuss financing the lease of an expensive line of equipment that B has ordered from C, the manufacturer of the goods. The negotiation is completed and A, as lessor, and B, as lessee, sign a lease of the equipment for a 60 month term. B, as buyer, assigns the purchase order with C to A who makes payment to C. The equipment is delivered by C to B. B signs and delivers copies of the certificate of acceptance to A and C. The lease qualifies as a finance lease since A did not select, manufacture, or supply the goods, the goods were acquired in connection with the lease, and the documents insure that B, the lessee, has knowledge of the warranties, covenants, and promises contained therein. The consequences of determining a lease to be a finance lease are treated in X(C) and XII(B) of this BLACK LETTER.

B. CHOICE OF LAW AND FORUM

Section 1–105(1) provides two general choice of law principles. First, the parties may agree that the law of "this state," i.e. the forum, or another state governs "when a transaction bears a reasonable relation to this state and also another state." Second, if there is no agreement, "this Act applies to transactions bearing an appropriate relation to this state." *Article 2A narrows these general principles in two ways:*

1. CONSUMER LEASES

Recognizing the danger that lessors may induce consumer lessees to agree to clauses providing that the applicable law will be that of a jurisdiction with the least favorable consumer protection or to a forum inconvenient to the lessee, 2A–106 provides more restrictive rules for the *consumer* context than the Article 1, choice of law section, 1–105. *The jurisdiction must be one in which the lessee either resides or will reside within a 30 day period and the forum chosen cannot be one which would not otherwise have jurisdiction over the lessee.*

2. CERTIFICATES OF TITLE

Leases of motor vehicles, trailers or boats may be subject to the certificate of title legislation of "this state" or "another jurisdiction" as well as Article 2A. 2A–104(1)(a) & (b). If so, the lessor's interest in the vehicle must be noted on the certificate. Under 2A–105, "compliance and the effect of compliance or noncompliance with a certificate of title statute are governed by the law (including the conflict of law rules) of the jurisdiction issuing the certificate until the earlier of (a) surrender of the certificate, or (b) four months after the goods are removed from that jurisdiction and thereafter until a new certificate of title is issued by another jurisdiction." *Since the interests of third parties who rely upon the certificate are involved, this choice of law rule cannot be varied by agreement.*

> *Example IX(3):* Lessee, a consumer residing in State A, leases a used car from Lessor, a dealer doing business in State B. The car will be used in State A. The certificate of title laws of State B do not require that a lease interest be noted on the certificate. A clause in the lease provides that the law of State B shall govern all aspects of the transaction. Apart from the certificate of title law, the agreement choosing the law of State B is not enforceable under 2A–105. However, State B's certificate of title law governs in State A until Lessee surrenders the certificate in State A or until the "four month" condition is satisfied, whichever is earlier.

C. PRIVATE AUTONOMY

Article 2A explicitly incorporates the general principle of 1–102(3) that ". . . the effect of the provisions of this Act may be varied by agreement except as otherwise provided in this act and except that the obligations of good faith, diligence, reasonableness and care prescribed by this Act may not be disclaimed by agreement. . . ." 2A–103(4). The exceptions in 2A include those which protect the rights of third parties (2A–303(4) and (6)) and provisions curbing abusive clauses in consumer leases. See 2A–106 & 2A–109.

D. UNCONSCIONABILITY

2A–108 includes an almost verbatim replica of its 2–302 counterpart in Article 2. In addition, the comments to 2–302 are incorporated by reference into 2A and relevant case law is said to be "persuasive but not binding" in interpreting 2A–108. See Comment, 2A–101. 2A–108 does, however, include provisions taken from the Uniform Consumer Credit Code making "conduct" in inducing a lease contract or clause or collecting a claim a source of unconscionability. It also permits the court to award attorney's fees either to the successful claimant or to the party against whom the claim was made if an action has been brought which the claimant "knew to be groundless."

*

X

FORMATION AND CONSTRUCTION

Analysis

A. General
B. Statute of Frauds
C. Finance Lessee a 3rd Party Beneficiary
D. Warranties

A. GENERAL

2A's provisions with reference to parol evidence, formation, firm offers, offer and acceptance, course of performance or practical construction, modification, rescission, waiver, casualty to goods, identification of goods and warranty disclaimers track those of Article 2. Two exceptions: The first deals with the Sales Article on modification which requires that the statute of frauds must be satisfied ". . . if the contract as modified is within its provisions." 2-209(3). This provision was not incorporated into 2A-209 since it was considered unfair to allow an oral modification to make the entire lease contract unenforceable if the modification takes it a few dollars over the dollar limit (the $1000 total payments requirement of 2A-201(1)(a)). On the other hand, it was not considered appropriate to provide that the lease in its pre-modified state would be enforceable since in some cases enforceability might be worse than no enforcement at all. Resolution of this issue is therefore left to the courts based on the facts of each case. 2A-209 (Purposes). The second exception is the omission of a "battle of the forms" provision (2-207). For reasons that are not self-evident, the drafters did not consider the issues significant to leasing transactions.

> *Example X(1):* The parties entered into an oral lease in which the total payments were $950. Subsequently, the parties made a single modification increasing the total payments to $1050. The oral modification may not be enforceable, but it would probably be considered unfair to make the entire lease unenforceable because of the slight increase in the total payments.

B. STATUTE OF FRAUDS

2A-201 is the lease analogue to the Sales provision (2-201). It differs in two significant respects. First, it does not include the 2-201(2) provision which states a special rule for the merchant who does not respond to a written memorandum. The comment explains that the number of such transactions involving leases, as opposed to sales, would be few. 2A-201 (Purposes). Secondly, there is no exception for cases in which payment has been made since, unlike a sale, a lessee does not tender payment in full for goods delivered. Rather, the lessee makes periodic payments and the making of such rental payments was not considered an adequate substitute for a writing.

C. FINANCE LESSEE A 3RD PARTY BENEFICIARY

As previously discussed, the finance lease is normally a three party transaction in which two related contracts are formed: a contract of sale between a supplier and the lessor and a contract of lease between the lessor and lessee. 2A-209 provides expressly that the seller's promises to the lessor in the first contract extend to the lessee under the lease contract, a codification of contract (third party beneficiary) law. Restatement, Second, Contracts 302.

D. WARRANTIES

Article 2 recognizes two implied warranties, the warranty of merchantability and the warranty of fitness for a particular purpose. Prior to 2A, the courts applied the merchantability warranty to the merchant-lessor by analogy. But what about the finance lessor who finances the transaction but who has no special knowledge with reference to the goods? 2A provides a statutory exemption for the finance lessor. Each of the two warranty sections (2A–212 and 2A–213) begins with the words: "Except in a finance lease. . . ." The exemption's effect is to take the finance lessor out of the loop; the seller is treated as making all such warranties and promises directly to the lessee. The lessor consequently has no liability for defects or other problems. It is important to note, however, that the lessor remains liable for any express warranties made to the lessee.

Other provisions in 2A with reference to express warranties and disclaimer of warranties are unremarkable except for a minor deviation from the Article 2 provision on disclaimer of merchantability. The 2A version requires the disclaimer to be in writing.

*

XI

EFFECT OF LEASE CONTRACT

Analysis

A. GENERAL

Part 3 of 2A begins with a deceptively simple provision modeled after that which introduces the "validity" and "enforceability" section of security agreements in Article 9 (9–201). 2A–301 states: "Except as otherwise provided in this Article, a lease contract is effective and enforceable according to its terms between the parties, against purchasers of the goods and against creditors of the parties." The "except" clause introduces the sections which follow and which contain a series of complex rules and exceptions with reference to third party issues. 2A–302 negates any significance of the separation of title and possession; 2A–303 governs the transfer of rights and delegation of duties under the lease contract; 2A–304 and 2A–305 are twin provisions relating to good faith transferees of the goods from the lessor and lessee; 2A–306 and 2A–307 deal with liens and attachments; 2A–308 governs fraudulent transfers and preferences; 2A–309 and 2A–310 relate to fixtures and accessions; and 2A–311 provides that the parties may alter the statutory priorities by agreement.

B. TRANSFER AND ALIENABILITY

Although free transferability is the general rule, 2A–303 provides a number of complex qualifications. Provisions in lease agreements which prohibit transfer and which are made expressly unenforceable are detailed in 2A–303(3) and (4), the former dealing with security agreements and the latter with the transferor's right to transfer rights to payment where the transferor has performed the entire obligation. Other prohibitory provisions are dealt with in 2A–303(2), a sub-section which makes the transfer effective but subjects the transferor to the liabilities specified in 2A–303(5). Under this subsection, if the transfer was made an event of default, the aggrieved party will have the remedies provided in Part 5 of Article 2A. If the transfer was not made an event of default in the lease agreement, the aggrieved party will have an action for damages if the transfer ". . . materially impairs the prospect of obtaining return performance by, materially changes the duty of, or materially increases the burden or risk imposed on, the other party to the lease contract. . . ." 2A–303(5)(b). Compare 2–210(2).

> *Example XI(1):* On February 1, A, a manufacturer, leases 6 combines to B, a farming corporation, for a 12 month term. A agreed to defer payment of the first two months rent until April 1. On March 1, B found it did not need all 6 combines and B thereupon subleased two combines to C. The transfer is effective despite the presence of a clause prohibiting the transfer and making it an event of default. A has no remedy against C. A's remedy is against B pursuant to the default provisions of 2A–303(5)(a) and 2A–501(2). If the transfer was not made an event of default, A would have an action for damages against B only if he can establish that the transfer materially increases A's risk. 2A–303(5)(b). Had this been a consumer lease, the prohibitory clause would have to be specific, written and conspicuous. 2A–303(8).

C. PRIORITY DISPUTES

1. NON-CREDITOR TRANSFEREES

2A–304 and 2A–305 are twin sections dealing with priority disputes as to leased goods as the result of transfers by the lessor and the lessee, respectively. Where a lessor has transferred the goods to a subsequent lessee, the dispute will be between the two lessees. Where the lessee has transferred the goods, the dispute will be between the lessor and the transferee. The two sections are derived from Section 2–403, which states the general policies on the good faith purchase of goods. In general, the transferees take subject to the existing leases. The exceptions involve situations where the transaction involves a transferee "in the ordinary course of business" from a transferor "who is a merchant dealing in goods of that kind." 2A–304(2) and 2A–305(2).

> *Example XI(2):* Merchant leases goods to A. A returns goods to Merchant for repair. Merchant leases goods to B, a lessee in the ordinary course of business. B, the subsequent lessee, takes the goods free from the existing lease. 2A–304(2).

> *Example XI(3):* Lessor leases goods to A, a merchant dealing in goods of that kind. A leases the goods to B, a lessee in the ordinary course of business. B takes the goods free from the existing lease. 2A–305(2).

2. CREDITORS

Third party creditors' rights need to be considered in the light of the previous discussion of the "true" lease/security interest issues. Since 2A deals only with "true" leases, filing under Article 9 is not required for priority determinations although the uncertainty involved in the characterization issue should prompt the cautious lessor to make a permissive filing under 9–408.

Creditors of the lessee are subject to the rights of the lessor under the lease and therefore have rights to the leasehold interest of the lessee but not to the residual interest of the lessor. 2A–307. Creditors of the lessor also take subject to the lease contract with an exception which would give a secured creditor priority if that secured creditor would have had priority under Article 9 by having filed its interest at the time the lease contract became enforceable. The lessee, in other words, takes his interest subject to the perfected security interests of creditors of the lessor. The lessee is treated as a hypothetical secured party in determining priority issues. For protection against secured creditors of the lessor, the lessee should therefore do a UCC search. If the lessee is a "lessee in ordinary course," however, the lessee will take free of the security interest. 2A–307(3).

> *Example XI(4):* Merchant grants security interest to Creditor who files on January 1. Merchant leases goods to Lessee on February 1. Unless the lessee qualifies as a lessee "in the ordinary course of business" (2A–103(1)(*o*)), lessee's interest in the goods will be subordinate to that of Creditor.

D. COMPETING CLAIMS IN FIXTURES

Although 2A–309 is modeled after the fixture section of Article 9 (9–313), a number of changes were made to reflect leasing terminology and to add new material. Of particular significance to lessors of goods which are or may become fixtures is the effect of 2A–309(9). This subsection subjects the lessor's interest to the filing requirements of Article 9 even though the lease agreement does not create a security interest. Thus a fixture filing becomes essential to protect the lessor in priority contests with the real estate claimant. First to file constitutes the general rule. Similar to the "purchase money security interest" exception in 9–313(4)(a), 2A–309(4)(a) grants priority to a "purchase money lease" over a prior real estate interest provided that the lease is perfected by a fixture filing within 10 days after the goods become fixtures.

E. SALE AND LEASEBACK

A special section, 2A–308(3), countenances the "sale-leaseback" transaction where the seller sells goods to a buyer but possession of the goods is retained by the seller pursuant to a lease contract between the buyer as lessor and the seller as lessee. Such a transaction is one entered into for financing purposes where the buyer is a leasing company and is willing to extend credit to the seller. The buyer becomes the financier-lessor and the seller becomes the lessee in a transaction in which the goods have never left the possession of the seller. The statutory and common law of a number of states had treated transactions where possession is retained by the seller as fraudulent per se or prima facie fraudulent. 2A–308(3) immunizes the sale-leaseback from this attack as long as the buyer ". . . bought for value and in good faith."

XII

PERFORMANCE

Analysis

A. General
B. Promises in Finance Leases

A. GENERAL

Part 4 of 2A is the shortest of its 5 divisions, containing seven sections, only one of which requires discussion other than that already given to the Article 2 analogues. The sections dealing with insecurity, adequate assurance of performance, anticipatory repudiation, retraction of anticipatory repudiation, substituted and excused performance, and the procedure on excused performance (2A–401 through 2A–406) make no significant changes from the parallel provisions in Part 4 of Article 2 (page references).

B. PROMISES IN FINANCE LEASES

The lessee's third party beneficiary rights to hold the supplier to its obligations under the sales contract do not come without a price. Once the goods have been accepted, 2A–407 validates the "hell or high water" clause in a finance (not a consumer) lease. Without any need for special provisions in the lease contract, this section makes the lessee's promises irrevocable and independent. The rationale is that in a finance lease the lessee is relying on the supplier to perform the essential commitments. Upon acceptance of the goods, the lessee must make payments to the lessor "come hell or high water." This does not, however, preclude the lessee from having an action against the lessor for breach of an express warranty or from having rights as a third party beneficiary against the supplier in the sale contract.

> *Example XII(1):* In *Example IX(2),* assume that after acceptance of the goods, the equipment malfunctions. Since it is a finance lease, no implied warranties are made by the lessor and the lessee's obligation to make payments to the lessor continues as it became irrevocable and independent when lessee accepted the goods. The lessee does, however, have a remedy against the supplier as the beneficiary of the warranties in the sale contract between the lessor and the supplier.

DEFAULT

A. GENERAL

As originally promulgated, the Part 5 remedies division of Article 2A became the most controversial and stirred immediate debate with California adopting a much altered version. The drafting committee went back to the drawing boards and 24 amendments were promulgated in 1990. 14 of the Amendments are in Part 5. Its opening section, 2A-501, departs from other Code remedial treatments by making it clear that whether a party is in default is determined by provisions of 2A as well as the agreement, thus creating what some commentators are characterizing as "statutory" and "contractual" defaults. Basically, all of the rules are subject to the rights of the parties to add, modify or substitute, limited only by concepts similar to those in Article 2 (the parenthetical citations are to the Article 2 counterparts): the consequence of an exclusive remedy failing of its essential purpose, 2A-503(2), (2-719(2)), the unconscionability of limiting consequential damages for injury to the person, 2A-503(3), (2-719(3)), and the liquidation of damages at an amount reasonable in the light of the anticipated harm, 2A-504(1), (2-718(1)). The liquidated damages section differs from its Article 2 analogue only by adding a provision permitting liquidation by use of a "formula," a practice common in leasing transactions. 2A-504(1).

Remedies are stated to be cumulative, 2A-501(4), with the Official Comment explaining that this is in furtherance of the Code policy of 1-106 which seeks to put the aggrieved party in as good a position as if the other party had fully performed. The comment warns that such cumulation or selection is not permissible if it would put the party in a *better* position.

The remedies of cancellation and termination and their effects are provided in 2A-505 and do not differ from their Article 2 counterparts. The Statute of Limitations section, 2-506, differs in two respects: 1) it does not prohibit the parties from extending the statutory period (4 years) on the ground that it makes little sense to encourage litigation in a lease transaction in which claims of breach of warranty diminish with the passage of time, and 2) a more liberal rule permits the start of the period of limitation to be the later of the date when the default occurs or when the act on which it is based is or should have been discovered.

B. DEFAULT BY LESSOR

2A-508 is an index to the lessee's remedies which are individually treated in the subsequent sections. Many of them are similar to buyers' remedies in Article 2. Only the most significant departures are discussed herein.

1. COVER

In most instances the aggrieved lessee will seek a replacement lease for the one which is in default. Two factors which require a different treatment from that afforded in the 2-712 cover section are present:

(a) The differences between two sales contracts are likely to be less than the difference between two leases. Cost differences may not accurately measure the difference in the comparable worth of two leases with substantially different terms and periods. 2A–518 addresses this problem by requiring that the covering lease agreement be "substantially similar." The standard is admittedly and perhaps necessarily flexible. The section does recognize that adjustments need to be made for what will usually be the different periods of time of the two leases.

(b) Article 2's cover remedy is premised on a replacement cash purchase. By contrast, the covering lease will involve periodic future payments which the section recognizes must be reduced to present value to make the proper comparison. A 1990 amendment changes the date from which to measure the damages. The original version specified the date of default. The amendment, recognizing that the lessee's cover injury begins when cover takes place, designates the date of ". . . the commencement of the term of the new lease. . . ." 2A–518(3).

> *Example XIII(1):* On January 1, Lessor leases equipment to Lessee for a 12 month term at $500 per month. Lessee properly terminates on June 30 and enters into a "substantially similar" replacement lease on August 1. The new lease is for a 12 month term at a monthly rental of $700. Lessee's cover damages (in addition to whatever incidental and consequential damages were suffered) should be measured by the present value (measured as of August 1) of $1,000 ($200 times the number of months remaining under the original lease).

2. CONTRACT/MARKET DIFFERENTIAL

As is true with the Article 2 remedial structure, cover is not mandatory and the aggrieved lessee may choose not to replace the lease but rather to sue for damages based on the difference between the contract price of the lease and its market value. The 2A section differs from its Article 2 analogue only in its recognition that the amounts compared must be reduced to their present value. 2A–518.

> *Example XIII(2):* Lessor leases equipment to Lessee for 12 months at a monthly rental of $5,000, the goods to be tendered at Gotham on January 1, 1990. Lessor repudiates. Lessee purchases (does not lease) replacement goods. The market rental at Gotham is $6,000. Lessee may recover $12,000 (the monthly difference of $1,000 times 12, the number of months remaining on the lease).

C. DEFAULT BY LESSEE

The Lessor's remedies are indexed in 2A–523. Only those which differ significantly from their Article 2, Seller counterparts will be discussed.

1. REPOSSESSION AND DISPOSITION

Repossession and disposition is the analogue to the Article 2 remedy of resale by a seller and the corollary to the lessee's cover remedy. Repossession and disposition by the lessor under 2A–525 and 2A–527 involves some of the same problems previously discussed under the cover remedy (XIII(B)(1), *supra*). Disposition must be by a lease "substantially similar" and the amounts must be adjusted to reflect present values. The lessor is not accountable to the lessee for any profit made on the disposition. Under the formula of 2A–527, the lessor should receive 1) rent due under the original lease, 2) the present value of the difference between the rent under the original lease and the rent under the replacement lease for the term of the original lease, and 3) incidental damages, if any. Costs saved must be deducted.

> *Example XIII(3):* On January 1, 1988, Lessor leased equipment to Lessee for 5 years at a monthly rental of $3,000. On January 1, 1989, Lessee defaulted and Lessor repossessed. Lessor re-leased the equipment on March 1 to another lessee for 5 years at a monthly rental of $2,500. Lessor should recover $6,000 (two months unpaid rent) plus the present value (measured as of March 1) of $23,000 (the $200 monthly difference in rental times 46, the number of months remaining under the original lease).

2. CONTRACT/MARKET DIFFERENTIAL

If the lessor chooses not to use or is unable to use the repossession remedy, 2A–528 permits calculation of damages utilizing the market rent standard. This is similar to that provided for sellers in 2–708(1). Once again, the difference in the structure of payments under a lease from the lump sum of the price in a contract of sale requires adjustments. The formula must take into account 1) the present value of the difference between remaining rent of the defaulted lease and the market rent which would be payable on the hypothetical lease, 2) comparable durations, 3) place of tender, 4) incidental damages, and 5) expenses saved by the lessee's default.

> *Example XIII(4):* On January 1, 1990 Lessor leases equipment to Lessee at a monthly rental of $5,000 for a term of 2 years. Lessee defaults on June 1 and returns the goods on August 2. Lessor does not re-lease the goods but sells them to a third party in September. Lessor could have re-leased the goods on August 1 at a monthly rental of $4,000. Lessor is entitled to $10,000 (the unpaid two months rental between the default and the time when the goods could have been released) plus the present value (measured at August 1) of 17,000 (the monthly difference between the lease and market rentals times 17, the number of months remaining on the lease).

3. PROFITS

The second subsection of 2A–528 provides: "If the measure of damage provided in sub (1) is inadequate to put the lessor in as good a position as performance would have, the measure of damages is the profit . . ." The language parallels that of its Article 2 counterpart, 2–708(2), the section which deals with the problem of the "lost volume seller." The lessor may be a "lost volume lessor" if the conditions of capacity, market demand and second lease probability are satisfied. (See discussion of these conditions in Chapter VI.)

4. ACTION FOR THE RENT

The action for the rent under 2A–529 is limited to those occasions when it is impossible or impracticable to utilize other remedies. Its Article 2 analogue is 2–709, the seller's action for the price. Under the 1990 amended version, the lessor may sue for the actual rent owed plus the present value of rent payable under the defaulted lease for the remaining term of the lease agreement provided one of four conditions are satisfied: 1) the lessee has retained possession of the goods, 2) the goods have been lost or damaged within a commercially reasonable time after the risk of loss passes to the lessee, 3) the lessor is unable after reasonable effort to dispose of the goods at a reasonable price or 4) the circumstances indicate that effort will be unavailing. 2–529(1)(a) and (b).

5. RESIDUAL ACTION FOR DAMAGES

The 1990 amendments added a sub-section to 2A–523 (the index section) to recognize that a lessor who is entitled to exercise any of the above discussed remedies may choose not to do so. In such cases, the lessor may recover ". . . the loss resulting in the ordinary course of events from the lessee's default as determined in any reasonable manner, together with incidental damages, less expenses saved in consequence of the lessee's default." 2A–523(2). For example, where lessee has defaulted in the payment of rent, the lessor may merely sue for the unpaid rent as it comes due plus lost interest or other damages "determined in any reasonable manner." A new sub-section, 2A–523(1)(f), expressly negates any doctrine of election of remedies.

D. REVIEW QUESTIONS

A. True or False

1. It is possible under Article 2A and Article 9 to draft an effective agreement that creates both a lease and a security agreement.

2. It is unnecessary to file a lease to achieve protection against creditors of the lessee.

3. The "economic life" of leased goods is to be determined as of the time when the lease term ends.

4. Where the present value of the total rental payments under a lease is substantially the same as the market value of the goods at the time the lease is executed (the "full payout" lease), the transaction is a security interest.

B. Answer the problem set forth on page 244.

C. X, a construction company, required the use of certain equipment manufactured by Y. X notified Z, a leasing company, of its needs whereupon Z contracted to purchase the equipment from Y. At the same time, Z contracted to lease the equipment to X for a 5–year term, supplying X with a copy of its purchase contract with Y.

1. How does Article 9 characterize this transaction?

2. Assume that the equipment malfunctions in the 5th month of the lease. What are the rights and remedies of a) X against Z and b) X against Y?

D. Lessor leased an aircraft to Lessee. Lessor obtained a loan from Bank assigning the rental payments to Bank as security. Upon notification that it was to make payments to the Bank, Lessee sought to cancel the lease. Lessee relies upon a clause in the lease forbidding assignment of Lessor's rights under the lease. What result and why?

E. SP held a perfected security interest in equipment sold to Contractor–Debtor. Debtor leased the equipment to Lessee. Upon default by Debtor, SP seeks to repossess from Lessee. What result? What if Debtor was a merchant in the business of selling such equipment?

F. Lessor leased equipment to Lessee for a three-year term at a monthly rental of $500. Lessee defaults by repudiating in the third month, having made 3 monthly payments.

1. What remedies are available to Lessor?

2. How should the recoveries be measured?

APPENDIX A

ANSWERS TO QUESTIONS

PART I

CHAPTER I

I–A.   See IB(2). These persons will, typically, assert claims to the goods or for damages against the parties.

I–B.   See IB(1). A consumer is determined by the use to which he or she puts the goods or the loan. A merchant is determined by its experience with the goods in the trade. The consumer is normally given greater protection than the ordinary party and the merchant is frequently held to higher standards than the ordinary seller or buyer.

I–C.   It's just the other way around. See ID(1).

I–D.   *False.* The agreement of the parties may control or other state or federal law may preempt the UCC.

CHAPTER II

II-A. The "best" argument is that a knowing misrepresentation is fraud **rather** than an express warranty and fraud is not "displaced" by Section 2–313(1). See 1–103. In fraud cases, the normal remedy is rescission with restitution and the parol evidence rule does not apply. As for punitive damages, Section 1–106(1) states that punitive damages may not be awarded "except" as specifically provided in "this Act or by *other rule of law.*" If punitive damages were awarded for certain types of fraud under non-Code law, they should be awarded in this case. Compare Section 2–721, which invites the aggrieved party to use Article 2 remedies for fraud.

II-B. See II(C)(1). Some techniques include the purposes and policies stated in Section 1–102(1), the "principle" of construction stated in Comment 1 to Section 1–102, the broad scope and content of agreement, see 1–201(3), **and** the UCC's preference for standards, e.g., good faith, rather than rules.

II-C. *No.* On the facts, the limitation is manifestly unreasonable. See II(C)(2). Compare *Example III(12).*

II-D. *False.* The statute of frauds states a fundamental policy on liability and, by implication, cannot be varied by agreement. The parties, however, can create a statute of frauds for modifications of the contract. See Section 2–209(2).

II-E. At least four defined words are listed in the definitional cross references, two defined in Article I and two defined in Article 2. What is a "reasonable time" is defined in Section 1–204(2). The words "offer" and "consideration" are not separately defined, although they may be indirectly covered by the definition of "agreement," 1–201(3).

II-F. The purpose of this exercise is to show that the parties to commercial transactions have different purposes, that each Article of the UCC responds to and facilitates or regulates those purposes and that the interests of parties and non-parties define the scope and content of legal protection. Thus, a sale and a lease have different functions, title differs from a security interest, **and** the lessor is not a secured creditor. Have you made a little list?

II-G. 1. *True and false.* Neither Article 9 nor Article 2 apply.

2. *Mostly true.* An exception might arise if non-Code law was inconsistent with contract formation policies in Article 2. Judicial creativity would then be required.

3. *Not necessarily.* If the seller has made a written warranty, the Magnuson–Moss Warranty Act will apply. See *Example II(13).*

4. ***False.*** Section 9–103 governs in perfection disputes under Article 9. Sections 1–105(2), 2A–105 and 2A–106 govern Article 2A.

5. ***True.*** Beyond question. But we still recommend that you read Professor Gedid's article, cited in the Text.

II–H. At common law, there is an accord and satisfaction and the claims are discharged. S can't accept B's offer of $3,000 and reserve rights. It is either accept or reject. The question is whether Section 1–207 alters the common law result. Prior to the 1990 Official Text, the courts disagreed. Most courts, however, held that 1–207 did not displace the common law, especially where payment was tendered by check. Despite the language of 1–207, the majority concluded that it was limited to disputes over the performance of continuing contracts for sale, not attempts to discharge the contract. The matter has been resolved in favor of the common law in the 1990 Official Text. New Section 1–207(2) provides that 1–207 does not apply to an accord and satisfaction and new Section 3–311 regulates the use of a check to achieve an accord and satisfaction. So, we have a bit of history and another limited exercise in methodology.

PART II

CHAPTER III

III–A. A good list might include:

1. Was the subject matter goods, see III(A)(2)? If not, Article 2 does not apply.

2. If so, was the transaction a contract for their sale? If so, Article 2 applies.

3. If goods were involved but a sale was not, does any section of Article 2 apply directly to the dispute?

4. If both goods and services were involved, which predominates, goods or services? If the former, Article 2 applies to the entire transaction. If the latter, Article 2 does not apply unless the court applies the gravamen test, i.e., Article 2 will apply to disputes over the goods involved.

5. If all else fails, the court might extend Article 2 by analogy.

III–B. In a sale of goods, title passes from S to B for a price. 2–106(1). Title cannot pass until the goods are existing and identified, 2–105(2), and then title passes by agreement or under the rules of Section 2–401. See III(B)(2).

III–C. *True.* See 2–106(1).

III–D. The statement is *false*. The special property interest passes upon identification of the goods, 2–501(1), title normally passes upon delivery. 2–501. The special property interest is important in risk of loss disputes and is necessary for some "goods oriented" remedies of the buyer. Title has been rejected as a problem solving device in most cases. See III(A)(3) and (B)(2). Note, however, that title and special property could pass at the same time, compare 2–501(1) and 2–401, and the whereabouts of title is important in disputes over ownership.

III–E. The emphasis upon standards, the deemphasis of title and the broad scope of transaction planning facilitate private agreement. The merchant concept, by imposing higher standards upon that class, and unconscionability and good faith, which police conduct at the time for contracting and during performance, regulate the contract. All of this is done, however, by courts. Bad faith is not a crime under Article 2—it simply limits the scope and effectiveness of the agreement or efforts to enforce it in court.

III–F. In all probability, the court will dismiss the complaint. Section 2–314(1) applies specifically to a "contract for the sale of goods." Although goods are involved in this transaction, they do not dominate. Construction services do. Thus, Article 2 does not apply directly and the courts are reluctant to extend it by analogy to construction contracts. Under the gravamen test, however, if the defective connector caused the loss, O might persuade some courts to apply Article 2 to the relevant issues of liability and remedy relating to the goods.

CHAPTER IV

IV–A. *False.* The consideration requirement is implicit in the definition of agreement, which requires a "bargain in fact."

IV–B. 1. *No.* The quick answer is that the "crossed offers" for different quantity do not show agreement and, therefore, cancel each other out. 2–204(1). S's subsequent shipment of 1,000 units, therefore, was a new offer which B could accept or reject. If, however, B's offer was received and S first shipped 1,000 units and then mailed the letter, a contract for 1,000 units would be created. 2–206(1)(b).

2. *Yes.* There is a conduct by both parties which recognized the existence of a contract and there is no apparent disagreement over price or quantity. See 2–204(1). The fact that the letters disagree is irrelevant.

VI–C.   Unless the parties have agreed on quantity, the contract fails for indefiniteness: there is no reasonable quantity term which the court can supply. 2–204(3). In addition, the agreement runs afoul of the statute of frauds, which states that it is not enforceable beyond the quantity of goods shown in the writing signed by the party to be charged. 2–201(1).

IV–D.   *No.* B's telegraph was not an offer, because S was not reasonable in believing that B had made a firm proposal to buy 5,000 units from S at S's best price. B was still negotiating. Thus, S made the offer and B could reject it without liability. Remember that Article 2 does not define offer. Without conduct by both parties showing intention to contract, resort must be had to common law principles.

IV–E.   There is some controversy, but here is our analysis. (1) At common law, S's response plus shipment was a counteroffer to sell at $25 per unit. B's acceptance of the goods without objection created a contract on S's terms. (2) Section 2–207 arguably changes that result: (a) there was no contract under 2–207(1)—S expressly conditioned assent on B's agreement to $25; (b) 2–207(3) seems to apply—there is conduct by both parties recognizing the existence of a contract and the writings of the parties do not agree on price. Thus, both price terms "drop out" and the court is invited to supplement the failed agreement with a reasonable price. See 2–305(1). The analysis of most courts and commentators supports this result. (3) But if S clearly expressed his reservation in something other than a standard form (a letter typed for the particular deal) and if B received that writing before accepting the goods, will B be "unfairly surprised" if held to a contract on S's terms? Some commentators argue that when the material terms are "dickered" rather than those in standard forms, Section 2–207(3) ought not to control. B knew or had reason to know of S's price and should object before acceptance. Result: contract on S's terms.

IV–F.   The defense should not prevail. The oral agreement was within the scope of the statute, 2–201(1), and both parties have signed writings indicating that a contract for sale has been made. The problem is that neither signed writing specifies a quantity: the only written specification is in an unsigned internal memo from S. Yet all three writings can be related to the same transaction by their contents. Without parol evidence, it is clear that S's internal memo, even though unsigned, relates to another writing that is signed. This should be sufficient to neutralize the perjury risk, except for one issue of statutory interpretation: does the phrase "such writing" in the last sentence of Section 2–201(1) refer to the signed writing required in the first sentence or does it refer to "a writing" which states quantity whether it is signed or not? As a matter of policy, the latter interpretation should prevail on these facts.

CHAPTER V

V-A. The parties must intend to adopt a writing as a partial or a total integration. Intention to integrate is either expressed in a "merger" clause or inferred from the probability that if the parties had agreed to the term during negotiations it certainly would have been included in the writing.

V-B. It excludes from the written agreement both prior or contemporaneous agreements which either contradict the terms of the writing or supply consistent additional terms. It does not exclude evidence from any source that explains or aids in the interpretation of terms in the writing.

V-C. *False.* The "plain meaning" rule has been rejected.

V-D. The conditions for the proof of trade usage are set out in Section 1–205. It is admissible to "give particular meaning to and supplement or qualify terms of an agreement." Review V(B)(2)(b)(3).

V-E. *True,* unless the parties intended to contract despite their failure to agree. In that case, the court should attempt to supply a reasonable term. See 2–204(3).

V-F. S must prove that B, at the time of contracting, knew or had reason to know that S intended to deliver stewing hens. The sources of this possible proof include the agreement of the parties as a whole, including prior course of dealing and trade usage, and other "circumstances" in the commercial setting, i.e., the agreed price was more consistent with the sale of stewers than fryers or that trade definitions of "chicken" excluded fryers. If B knew that S intended stewers and failed to speak, B has committed a form of commercial fraud. If B had reason to know from all of the facts and circumstances, the conclusion is that S's meaning is more reasonable than B's and should prevail.

V-G. 1. *True.* Credit is a creature of agreement.

2. *False.* Either party can tender first but neither is required to distinguish the case where a date for performance is fixed but S's preparation for performance will extend over a long period of time. S must tender first on these facts.

3. *False.* The duty of good faith applies to the performance and enforcement of the contract.

4. *True.* The duty of good faith both provides consideration and regulates the exercise of reserved discretion.

V–H. Review V(C)(4)(b). The statement is a minority position. The policy question is whether the parties can, at the time of contracting, "contract out" of judicial review of S's reasons for termination. The less that those reasons have to do with B's performance and the more they concern S's potential financial loss, the more likely the court is to apply the duty of good faith and give B a reasonable chance to recoup its investment.

V–I. 1. All of the goods unless "circumstances" give S authority to deliver in lots. 2–307. Review V(D)(1)(a).

       2. The seller's place of business. 2–508.

       3. S must comply with the requirements of Section 2–503(1).

V–J. If the goods are to be delivered without being moved, S must procure an acknowledgment from the bailee of B's right to possession. Although 2–503(4)(a) does not expressly say so, the bailee should acknowledge to B, not S.

V–K. In the destination contract, S must at his own risk and expense transport them to the destination and tender delivery there. 2–319(1)(b). In the shipment contract, S tenders by a proper delivery to the carrier. 2–504. In the destination contract, B bears the risk and expense of shipment until tender at the destination. 2–509(1). Review V(D)(1)(c)(3).

V–L. S can obtain payment of the price upon presentation of the draft and documents before B has an opportunity to inspect the goods. Since this device requires B to extend credit to S, it must be agreed to in the contract. Unilateral action by S is a breach.

V–M. The question is whether the "unreasonably disproportionate" language in Section 2–306(1) is a limitation upon B's discretion to cease having any requirements in good faith. Although there is some disagreement, the answer is no. In the absence of a commitment to order a minimum amount each year, the limitation, derived from a course of performance, controls wild swings in the exercise of discretion to order *something* rather than a good faith decision to have no requirements whatever. If S wants to control the risk of no requirements, the appropriate agreement is B's promise to order a minimum amount each year.

V–N. They are similar in that they all seek to supplement or fill gaps in the agreement about what quality S agreed to supply. They tend to complement each other and all three warranties could exist in the same transaction. The differences involve difficulties in proof, who can make the warranty, ease of disclaimability, etc. For example, the implied warranty of merchantability may be the easiest to prove but it takes a merchant to make one and it is the hardest to disclaim.

V–O.   If S makes an affirmation or promise or provides a sample or a description, they presumptively become part of the basis of the bargain, whether made before or after the time of contracting. S must rebut with evidence that B did not rely on the representations or could not reasonably have believed them. Some representations are not presumptively included if they affirm "merely" the value or are merely the seller's opinion or commendation. The line is sometimes difficult to draw.

V–P.   *True.* Check it out. See 2–315 and 2–316(2).

V–Q.   The question is whether B's claim that he purchased goods where the breakage rate would not exceed 5% in any soil can be supported. S agreed to meet B's generally stated needs but did not affirm or promise the 5% level of performance. The express warranty claim, therefore, is weak. Similarly, if B had a particular purpose or need for 95% durability, it was not fully communicated to S. Even though S knew B was relying on his skill and judgment, can it reasonably be implied that he warranted a particular durability on the information provided by B? Probably not. See 2–315. B's best bet may be to prove that the tool was normally used in all types of soil with a breakage rate of not more than 5%. He must prove that it was not fit for "ordinary" purposes, i.e., was not merchantable. If so, B's particular purpose becomes an ordinary purpose for which the tool was not fit. On the facts, Farm # 3 provides the biggest challenge.

V–R.   The statement is essentially true. A few states protect economic loss caused by unmerchantable goods in strict tort and others have enacted Alternative C to Section 2–318. Other states, by judicial decision, have protected consumers against direct rather than consequential economic loss, especially where the retailer is insolvent or out of business. In commercial cases, however, the "gap," with its jurisprudential collision between contract and tort, flourishes.

V–S.   S is wrong. His express warranty "explicitly extends to future performance of the goods." Thus, B's cause of action accrues when he discovered or should have discovered the breach rather than upon tender of delivery by the seller. See 2–725(2). In warranty litigation under the Code, unless there is language of explicit extension, the cause of action arises upon tender of the defective goods whether or not B knows of the breach. In strict tort litigation where a defective product has caused damage to person or property, the cause of action arises when B discovered or should have discovered the injury.

V–T. Under an open price, neither party bears the risk of market price fluctuations. Under a fixed price, the risk of market fluctuations is allocated—if the market price goes up, S is disadvantaged, if the price goes down, B squirms.

V–U. When it has agreed to pay before inspection "against" documents, COD or the like. Both parties must agree to these terms.

V–V. Review V(F)(2)(c). See 2–607. This is important stuff.

V–W. Normally, B has no duty to pay until the goods have arrived and it has inspected them. On the facts, S had no basis to demand cash before shipment or to withhold delivery: B was not insolvent and had given adequate assurance of due performance. Thus, S's shipment "under reservation," by requiring B to pay before inspection, was not justified by B's conduct and was not agreed to. In short, B wins: it was a breach of contract.

V–X. If B did not rightfully revoke acceptance under Section 2–608, the risk of loss passes and he owes B the full contract price. See 2–510(1). If the revocation was rightful, B avoids liability for the price and must return the goods or their market value to S. Under 2–510(2), the deficiency in B's insurance coverage is $5,000 and, to that extent, the risk of loss remains on S. Thus, S can recover $5,000 from B but not the full value of the goods, $10,000. If B were fully insured, S could recover the full value of the goods. If B had no insurance, the full risk would be on S. In any event, B's insurance company has no subrogation rights against S.

V–Y. 1. The government embargo and its impact were risk events which were foreshadowed in the negotiations. Arguably, S, by failing to insist upon a risk allocation clause, tacitly assumed the risk by agreement. In any event, the embargo was not a contingency the nonoccurrence of which was a basic assumption of the parties, even though S can claim that performance as agreed was made commercially impracticable. Thus, S assumed the risk and should have provided for it in the contract or otherwise. Even if excuse were found, S's relief is seemingly limited to excuse from delay or non-performance. Neither Section 2–615 nor any other section authorizes performance under an adjusted price unless B agrees. S's last argument is that compliance with a government regulation made performance impracticable, but this is weak where the government regulation was a risk event that both parties anticipated as likely to occur.

2. The modification is probably enforceable under Section 2–209(1). Review the discussion in C(V)(I)(1) at p. 147.

V–Z. Number 4 is correct. The risk had not passed to B—S had agreed to deliver the goods to B in New York. See 2–509(1)(b). S was not excused under Section 2–613 because the goods were not identified at the time the contract was made. S was not excused under Section 2–615 because this type of risk, destruction of the goods before risk of loss passes, is allocated to S by Section 2–509 unless otherwise agreed. In short, S is in the best position to anticipate and to insure against damages to goods in his possession and control.

CHAPTER VI

VI–A. 1. *No.* Insolvency alone is not a breach.

2. S may refuse to deliver except for cash, 2–702(1), or suspend performance and demand adequate assurance. 2–609.

3. Without an actual breach or explicit repudiation by B, Section 2–609(4) is the only way.

VI–B. 1. *No.* This is an installment contract and B's default with regard to one payment installment must substantially impair the value of the whole contract before S can cancel. We need more information on B's capacity and willingness to pay and on the impact of B's non-payment on B's capacity to perform. S's desire for a quick cancellation in a rising market without this information is the stuff of which bad faith is made. See 2–612(3).

2. S could suspend performance, demand adequate assurance, 2–609, and sue for the price of the particular installment that had been accepted.

VI–C. The circumstances are set forth in Section 2–705. Review VI(C)(1). The effect is that S has a possessory security interest in the goods arising under Article 2. See 9–113. This interest secures B's obligation to pay the price and is enforced by resale under Section 2–706. We will discuss this in more detail in Chapter VII(F).

VI–D. 1. *True.* The goods are moved to B and lost volume is avoided.

2. *False.* See Section 2–706(2). S could obtain, identify and resell after breach.

3. *False.* The correct section is 2–708(2).

4. *False.* Section 2–708(1) is available upon proper proof.

5. *A close case.* Code remedies are cumulative. If S acts in good faith under Section 2–706, he should be able to select the 2–708(1) formula if the yield is higher. But S's choices are limited by the remedial policy in Section 1–106(1), and some courts might refuse to apply 2–708(1) if it put S in a better position than full performance would have.

VI–E.   1. If S exercised reasonable commercial judgment in the decision to complete the goods, 2–704(2), and was unable after reasonable efforts to resell them, an action for the price should lie. 2–709(1)(b). One could question the judgment of any seller who elected to complete performance without an existing resale contract, especially if the goods were unique or the market was unstable.

2. *Yes.* It is a surrogate for the resale remedy.

VI–F.   1. *No.* S is not insolvent. Even so, there is not enough information to assess whether other conditions have been met.

2. *Yes.* See 2–711(1).

3. *No.* B could reasonably effect cover.

4. *No.* B has not accepted the goods. Even so, cancellation is no help, since B owes the price and S has fully performed and refuses to cure.

5. *Yes.* Both are possibilities, depending upon the facts.

6. *Perhaps.* The goods are not "unique" but a six month delay in cover plus resulting damages of a speculative nature may qualify as "special circumstances."

7. *Yes.* B could cancel the contract, recover the price and cover. See 2–711(1). "Cover" is necessary if the project is to continue and if B is to mitigate consequential losses.

VI–G.   The answer should be the same as in V(I–D)(5): B is not barred simply because he has, in good faith, effected cover. But there is dissent from this position, particularly where B's use of 2–713 after cover appears to put him in a better position than S's full performance would have. Stay tuned, this issue is still open.

VI–H.   The good faith argument might work if the deviation is truly insubstantial and B's primary motive is to avoid a disadvantageous bargain. There is, however, some debate over whether good faith is a limitation on the rejection power and, so far, there is no authoritative judicial interpretation. A similar result has been reached, however, by stretching the "cure" provision to protect S: where S is reasonable in thinking that the tender will conform to the contract (here S relied on a representation) or that B will accept it anyway (prior course of dealing might help) and can promptly and completely cure and the defect is relatively insignificant, S should be able to cure even if the time for performance has expired and the conditions of Section 2–508(2) are not squarely met. This creative manipulation avoids some hardships of the perfect tender rule.

VI–I.   *No.* The right to cure in Section 2–508 is expressly limited to rejection, not revocation of acceptance. S can propose the "cure" but B need not accept it. Even so, there is some question whether S has cured when a repaired rather than a new T.V. is tendered. This is especially true in consumer transactions.

VI–J.   A.   *Example VI(40):* The answers turn on questions of fact. B did accept the horse if the time for reasonable inspection expired before the horse was shipped from the auction. This will turn on whether B should have been accompanied by his trainer and whether inspection by the trainer would have discovered the defect. If not, the next day is soon enough and the attempted rejection is effective. If B accepted by not rejecting before the horse was shipped, the shoe is on the other foot. B must prove that the bone was broken upon tender of delivery and, if so, that the acceptance was induced by the "difficulty of discovery before acceptance." 2–608(1)(b). If B did not in fact inspect, evidence of what a reasonable inspection would have revealed is necessary. In addition, B must revoke within a reasonable time after he discovered or should have discovered the defect. So if B could have discovered the defect with a reasonable inspection, the revocation route is down the tube. Finally, B may lose any claim if his notice of breach comes too late. If B can prove that there was a defect at tender and that he gave notice as soon as he could, it is unlikely that a court will conclude that an unreasonable amount of time has expired. It is one thing to bar rejection and revocation and quite another to bar any claim.

     B.   *Example VI(46):* S has made an express warranty that EZ 440 is fit for B's particular computer needs. This warranty was breached after acceptance by B and there was no cure. The normal damage formula in 2–714(2) will not put B in the same position as full performance. The difference in value between EZ 440 as warranted and EZ 440 as delivered is $30,000. It will cost B an additional $100,000 above the contract price to obtain an EZ 1000. Thus, the warranty of fitness for particular purposes and the inadequate damages under 2–714(2) are "special circumstances" that justify application of another measure of damages. B should recover as damages the difference between the value of EZ 440 as delivered and the value of a system (EZ 1000) that would meet B's computing needs, some $120,000. Incidental and consequential damages may also be recoverable.

VI-K.   1. *This is doubtful.* B did inform S of a breach and invoked his assistance in cure. But B did not inform S that the cure didn't work until 4 months had elapsed. Some courts have held that notice of the first breach won't carry over to a complaint that the cure failed: S is entitled to know that as well. If 4 months is an unreasonable delay, then B may be barred. But it is doubtful, isn't it?

2. *Correct.* There has been a substantial change in the condition of the goods not due to their own defects. 2-608(2).

3. *True.* Upon acceptance, B is liable for the price, subject to adjustment for damages under Section 2-714.

VI-L.   At best, B can recover $14,000 under 2-714 plus $1,000 under 2-715(1) plus $5,000 under 2-715(2), or $20,000. Should B be limited to the $6,000 cost of repairs under Section 2-714(2)? No, because this is an alternative method of measurement when there is no persuasive evidence of value. The consequential damages might be reduced to the extent they were not reasonably foreseeable or proved with reasonable certainty or not reasonably avoided by cover or otherwise. See 2-715(2)(a).

VI-M.   The clause underliquidates damages by limiting the extent of liability for consequential damages. There was no attempt to make a reasonable forecast of actual loss at the time of contractings. The clause is enforceable if it was conscionable at the time of contracting, see 2-302, and did not operate to deprive B of a minimum adequate remedy. Since B could recover the price paid and S could have excluded all liability for consequential damages, see 2-719(3), the clause should be enforced, especially where B knew of the risk and could have insured fully against it.

VI-N.   If the truck is one big defective part, B should get all of the relief he requests, subject to the scheme of agreed remedies. Some courts have held that B, under such a scheme, gives up the right to revoke acceptance and is left to damages for accepted goods. All courts would conclude on these facts that the limited, exclusive remedy failed its essential purpose, i.e., to give B a complete repair within a reasonable time with minor losses. Thus, B should get his remedies under Section 2-714. Most courts have held that a well drafted exclusion of consequential damages does not fall with the rest of the remedy package . . . it stands alone for separate evaluation. With one or two exceptions, the exclusion has been upheld in commercial cases over claims that it was unconscionable at the time of contracting. Thus, the probabilities are that B can't revoke, can recover damages under 2-714(2), can recover incidental damages under 2-715(1) but cannot recover consequential damages.

CHAPTER VII

VII–A.   1.   Yes. The painting was stolen by T. There was neither a transaction of purchase between O and T nor an entrusting by O to S.

2.   S has clearly breached the warranty of title. 2–312(1). Most courts will award B damages based upon the difference between the value of the painting as warranted at the time of replevin, $250,000, and the value of the painting as received, here nothing, to B. 2–714(2). But note that the statute of limitations has run on these facts and B has no enforceable claim. See 2–725(1) & (2).

VII–B.   A security interest in goods secures D's obligation to pay the price or the loan. It is enforceable under Article 9 if D defaults. A special property interest is given to a buyer of goods upon identification. 2–501. It gives B an insurable interest in the goods and limited rights under Article 2 to the goods upon breach by S. But it does not secure S's obligations under the contract.

VII–C.   1.   B does not take free of the security interest under Section 9–307(1), even if a BIOCB, because the security interest was not created by his seller, S, but by D. But SP entrusted the goods to S and B might prevail as a BIOCB under Section 2–403(2). But does that Section cut off SP's security interest? And is B a BIOCB before he takes possession with a certificate of title? Although there is some debate on both questions, some courts have protected B by cutting off SP's security interest and by holding that B becomes a BIOCB when the goods are identified to the contract.

2.   If SP can repossess, S has breached his warranty that the goods are free from "any security interest." 2–312(1)(b). B had no knowledge of SP's interest and, at a minimum, should recover any amount expended to pay off the security interest plus expenses. Of course, D still had title to the car—SP's entrustment of the car to S would not give S power to transfer D's title. Thus, S has breached both a warranty of title and "no security interest" and B's remedy should be so structured.

VII–D.   1.   Although B was insolvent, the transaction was a "cash" sale and S's reclamation rights are governed by Section 2–507(2). But C's rights as a purchaser, which arose before the reclamation demand, are, in the view of most courts, determined under Section 2–702(2). C arguably is not a "good faith purchaser" under Section 2–403: he paid too little and he knew too much. Thus, if S could reclaim the goods from B under 2–702(2) he should also be able to replevy them from C.

2. C's action against B, if any, depends upon whether C took in bad faith. If so, that fact may exclude any warranty of title and place the risk on C. If not, does B warrant to C that the goods are free of a third party's reclamation rights? Yes, since B warrants that the goods are "delivered free from any security interest or other lien or encumbrance of which the buyer at the time of contracting has no knowledge." S's reclamation claim to the goods surely qualifies. As between S and B, a successful reclamation from B (or C) is S's exclusive remedy. 2–702(3).

VII–E. 1. The lien does not attach to the property delivered by A for repairs. Although there is an entrusting, 2–403(3), there was no transfer in the ordinary course of business. 2–403(2). Thus, the common law rule protecting the bailor applies.

2. The lien does not attach to B's goods, delivered to M on approval. 2–326(2). Note, however, the definition of creditor includes a "lien creditor." 1–201(12).

3. The lien does attach to C's goods delivered to M for "sale or return." 2–326(2). The same is true of goods delivered on consignment or the like to a person within the scope of 2–326(3). If M qualifies under 2–326(3) and satisfies the public notice requirements in that subsection, however, the goods are deemed not to be on sale or return and the lien does not attach. Presumably, a true "sale or return" would be protected from M's creditors if the public notice requirements of 2–326(3) were satisfied.

PART III

A. 1. *False:* The newly amended definition of "security interest" in 1–201(37) is designed to distinguish a security interest from a lease with each being subject to different articles of the Code, the former by Article 9 and the latter by 2A.

2. *True:* Leases do not require filing for protection against creditors. But the cautious draftsman will make a precautionary filing under 9–408 in the event that a court later determines the lease to be a security interest in disguise.

3. *False:* The "economic life" is to be determined with reference to the facts and circumstances as of the time the transaction is entered into. 1–201(37)(y).

4. *False:* This transaction may still be a lease since these economic facts are not determinative. "A transaction does not create a security interest *merely* because it provides. . . ." (emphasis added) 1–201(37) (second a). The intent of this language is to cover instances where the lessor has an

expectation that the goods will appreciate in value and thereby provide the lessor with a meaningful residual interest.

B. 1–201(37) does not furnish a bright line test for characterizing the "open end" or "TRAC" lease. Case law has been divided on the issue. Where the lease allocates the risk of market appreciation or depreciation to the lessee, it may be argued that the lessee is in the same position as a debtor with an "ownership" interest in the goods, an interest which is inconsistent with that of a "true" lease. We think this argument ignores what should be considered the more determinative factor, namely that, despite the adjustment clause, the lessor has retained a significant residual interest in the goods thus warranting its classification as a true lease.

C. 1. The transaction constitutes a "finance lease." The three conditions of the definition in 2A–103(1)(g) are satisfied: The lessor (Z) had nothing to do with the selection, manufacture, or supply of the goods; the lessor acquired the right to the goods "in connection with the lease"; and the lessor (X) received a copy of the purchase contract.

2. a. X (lessee) against Z (lessor): No remedy. 2A insulates the finance Lessor from implied warranty liability for defective goods (2A–212) and makes the lessee's promises (to make payments) irrevocable and independent upon the lessee's acceptance of the goods (2A–407). The provisions constitute a statutory "hell or high water" clause recognizing the reality that the lessor's responsibility should not extend beyond its function as a financer of the transaction.

b. X (lessee) against Y (supplier): Applying a statutory third party beneficiary theory, 2A–209 extends to the lessee the full benefit of a supplier's promises to the lessor under the supply contract including all express or implied warranties. 2A–519 provides the remedy for breach of warranty: the present value of the difference between the value of the use of the goods accepted and the value if they had been as warranted for the lease term.

D. 2A–303(4) precludes the enforceability of a clause which prohibits a transfer of a right to payment under a lease contract. It states expressly that such a transfer is not a transfer that materially impairs the prospect of obtaining return performance by, materially changes the duty of, or materially increases the burden or risk imposed on, the other party to the lease contract.

E. SP is entitled to repossess. 2A–307(2)(c) provides that a secured creditor does not take subject to the lease if its interest was perfected before the lease contract became enforceable. If, however, the lessee qualifies as a "lessee in the ordinary course of business," it will take free from the security interest even though the interest was perfected and the lessee knew of its existence (2A–307(3)). Having leased from a dealer in good faith, lessee qualifies for this special protection (2A–103(o)).

F. 1.   Remedies of the Lessor: The failure to pay an installment coupled with a repudiation of the balance substantially impairs the value of the whole lease and therefore triggers the laundry list of remedies in 2A–523(1). They include cancellation (2A–505), repossession and redisposition of the goods by sale, lease or otherwise (2A–525 and 2A–528), retention of the goods (2A–528), and an action for the rent (2A–529).

    2.   Measurement of Recovery

        a.   Repossession and Redisposition Damages: Where lessor redisposes of the goods by re-leasing them, the measure of damages includes the accrued and unpaid rent plus the present value of the total rent under the original agreement minus the present value of the rent under the new lease agreement applicable to that period of the new lease term which is comparable to the then remaining term of the original lease agreement.

        b.   Retention and Damages: Where lessor retains the goods, the measure of damages is the accrued and unpaid rent plus the present value of the total rent for the then remaining lease term of the original lease agreement minus the present value of the market rent. If this measure is inadequate (the "lost volume lessor"), damages may be measured by the present value of the profit (2A–528).

        c.   Action for the Rent: Where lessor is unable after reasonable effort to dispose of goods at a reasonable rental or price or the circumstances reasonably indicate that such effort will be unavailing, lessor may recover the present value of the rent for the then remaining lease term (2A–529(b)).

                            *

APPENDIX B

PRACTICE EXAMINATION

QUESTION I
(90 Minutes)

You have just been appointed to the Great UCC Court in the Sky, with a specialty in Article 2. You have been handed two documents by the Clerk, the Buyer's version of a current dispute and the reaction of the Seller's attorney. Your job, if you choose to accept it, is to critically analyze the conclusions reached by the Seller and to identify and analyze any other issues raised by the facts but not addressed by the Seller. The objective is to reach conclusions that are sound under the applicable sections of Article 2. Go for it!

Buyer's Version

Around April 1, we were preparing to bid on a sewer project for the City of Chicago—the contractor was to dig an open trench about six feet deep for three blocks through clay, shale and loose gravel. Another company was to lay the pipe. Bids were due on April 25. Then we saw this ad in a trade magazine by Sluice, Inc. for a 12' Tunnel Boring Machine (TBM). The ad stated that the TBM was designed for open trench projects up to seven feet deep and had a "solid record of success." We called Sluice in Pittsburgh and they sent their sales manager out to look at the job specifications, some test borings and the job site. He stated several times that the 12' TBM would "cut through that stuff like paper." When pressed a bit, he stated that "this thing eats shale for dinner." We were interested, so I went out to Pittsburgh for a demonstration and to discuss a possible purchase. They had a demonstrator in place over a four foot trench and the TBM worked well in soil that was 90% clay. They then showed me a TBM that was for sale. The basic machine, weighing 40 tons, was new, but the accessories—cutting blades and retractable legs for different depths—were used. Their asking price for the complete unit was $90,000 with new accessories. I could not wait for new accessories so, after some bargaining, we agreed upon a $75,000 price for the unit before us. We agreed that the seller was to ship the unit promptly FOB Pittsburgh. None of this was in writing. In the bargaining, Sluice knocked $5,000 off the price because the accessories were used and $10,000 off if we would agree to delete their usual warranty package in sale of this kind—you know, the express warranty against defects in material and workmanship coupled with a promise to repair and replace for one year after acceptance. We did agree. About that time the sales manager stated rather firmly that this sale is "as is where is" but I objected with equal force—used accessories or not, we wanted some protection. I then gave Sluice a $5,000 down payment (a check I believe) and agreed to pay the balance sixty days after delivery.

I quickly returned to Chicago and, counting upon the cost savings that the TBM would generate, bid on the sewer project. We had the low bid of $500,000, the contract was awarded on May 1 and the work was to be completed by August 1. For each day of unexcused delay we were to pay liquidated damages of $1,000. On May 3, we received a letter from Sluice "confirming" the purchase at $75,000 and stating that the TBM would be shipped FOB Pittsburgh by the end of May. I was so furious that I didn't pay much attention to the last paragraph of the letter which, as you can see, reads, in part, that the 12' TBM is sold "AS IS WHERE IS" and that "Sluice shall not be liable for any loss or damage resulting directly or indirectly from the use or loss of use of the machine" and, finally, that "this letter constitutes the complete and exclusive statement of the terms of the agreement." I telephoned the sales manager and blew my cool—we need that TBM "yesterday" and said that unless that "damn thing is delivered in seven days we will hold you accountable." I was assured that the TBM would be shipped tomorrow but, in fact, it was not shipped until May 17 and because of problems in assembly it was not on the job site until June 1. We were already three weeks behind and in the hassle of getting going I did not call Sluice about the delay. From then on, things went from bad to worse. For the next 45 days we had constant problems—the used cutter blades quickly dulled and broke, the retractable legs kept collapsing and the machine failed to generate enough power to dig through the soil, which at places was solid shale. During this period I kept telephoning Sluice in Pittsburgh complaining about our problems and asking for advice. They sent several letters with helpful hints but never offered to send anyone out. Around July 1, they sent a letter reminding us that the price was due. After that I stopped calling and we just plugged along on the project. I replaced the cutter blades several times, repaired the legs at least twice and, finally, had the power system in the TBM overhauled, all at a cost of $50,000. We finally finished the job on November 1, 120 days late, and the City refused our claim that the delay was excused. More importantly, our total costs on the project, excluding liquidated damages, exceeded the contract price by $250,000. With liquidated damages, I figure we took a $370,000 bath on this contract. Around November 1, when I could see the extent of the disaster, I sent Sluice a letter claiming that they had breached the contract of sale and that we were holding them accountable for damages. We still have not paid the balance of the contract price, some $70,000.

End of sad story.

Sluice's Legal Reaction (prepared by esteemed Summer Associate)

Ho Hum, how easy! Assuming that everything the buyer said is true, the buyer owes us $70,000 on the contract and we have no liability whatever. This conclusion is plain and clear under Article 2 of the UCC.

> 1. No express warranties were made under UCC 2–313 and, even if they were, they were excluded from the final agreement by the parol evidence rule, UCC 2–202.
>
> 2. Any implied warranties were excluded by the "AS IS" clause in the letter, UCC 2–316(3)(a).
>
> 3. Consequential damages were properly excluded by the agreement, UCC 2–719.
>
> 4. Even so, the buyer failed to give adequate notice of breach under UCC 2–607(3)(a).

There, that should do it. When do I get my Summer bonus and my offer to be a permanent associate at $80,000 per year?

QUESTION II
(One Hour)

In 1986, Blinko, a public utility, commenced construction of a nuclear power plant, to be completed in 1991, and was interested in obtaining a long-term source of fuel. Strump operated a plant which produced uranium oxide, an important nuclear fuel ingredient. At that time, the worldwide demand for UO was high. The market price for UO had risen from $22 per pound in 1980 to $40 per pound in 1986. In addition, inflation and other factors had increased the average cost of producing one pound from $18 in 1980 to $36 in 1986. After negotiations with several producers and some hard bargaining, Blinko determined that the best deal it could get was that proposed by Strump. The final package, offered on a "take or leave it" basis, included the following:

> 1. The contract was to last 12 years, but after 2 years Strump (but not Blinko) could terminate upon giving 90 days notice in writing.
>
> 2. Blinko was obligated to take annually 50% of Strump's output from Plant # 2. The plant had a capacity to produce 600,000 pounds of UO per year and had been

operating at 70% of capacity. It was understood that Blinko would take monthly deliveries of what was estimated to be 17,500 pounds. The goods were to be shipped by rail "FOB origin" and Blinko was to pay the price of each shipment within 15 days of delivery.

3.   Blinko was to pay the higher of either the market price, to be determined by a formula expressed in the agreement, or an adjusted base price (ABP), to be determined by adjusting upward or downward a base price of $36 under labor cost and production cost indices which were included in the contract.

4.   Strump was to be excused from certain delays and nondeliveries under a broad-gauged *force majeur* clause, but the contract was silent with regard to excuse for Blinko or any other adjustment.

A written agreement containing these and other terms was signed by both parties on June 1, 1986. At that time, the market price for UO was $41 per pound and the adjusted base price, under the contract formula, was $38 per pound.

For the first five years of the contract, the following performance figures emerged:

Year	S Output	Amt. Taken by B	Average Market Price	Av. ABD
86–87	420,000	210,000	$41	$38
87–88	410,000	205,000	$42	$40
88–89	400,000	200,000	$43	$42
89–90	410,000	205,000	$43	$44
90–91	430,000	215,000	$41	$45

During this period, Blinko stored the UO in anticipation of the completion of construction of the nuclear power plant in early 1991 and Strump operated at close to 70% of capacity. In the middle of 1991, however, the following events occurred:

1.   Due to a public protest of nuclear power safety in general and concern about subsurface conditions around Blinko's construction site in particular, the Nuclear Regulatory Commission, in cooperation with state officials, suspended construction on Blinko's plant "indefinitely." At best, the estimated delay was five years. At worst, the project would have to be canceled.

2.   Due to a worldwide collapse in the demand for UO, the market price dropped from $41 per pound in March, 1991 to $32 on June 1, 1991. Although inflation had eased, the average base price per pound remained at $43 on June 1, 1991. By June 1, 1992, the market price had declined to $20 per pound and the average base price had declined to $40 per pound.

3.   From March, 1991 until June, 1992, Strump lost 75% of the business of Plant # 2 that was not obligated under the contract with Blinko. Since the demand for

UO was now low and Strump's cost of production remained high, this business could not be replaced. In the meantime, Blinko was paying $40 per pound for UO it could not use, which was worth between $20 and $25 on the open market.

Questions

The time is June 1, 1992 and Blinko has had enough. Blinko informs you that for the past six months Strump has continued to produce at 70% of capacity and has insisted that Blinko take and pay for 17,500 pounds of UO per month at the adjusted base price. During this time, Strump has refused to discuss a modification of the contract and has insisted that the risk was on Blinko. Blinko would like "out" of the contract and has requested a memo from you identifying and evaluating the grounds upon which it might terminate the relationship without liability. Please comply.

QUESTION III
(45 Minutes)

S, a manufacturer of kitchen hardware in Seattle, received a written order from a distributor in Cincinnati for 200 units, (a truckload) at a total price of $100,000. On the same day, May 1, S telephoned D and stated that they would not ship the goods unless a check for the full contract price had been issued and delivered to S's agent in Cincinnati. D agreed and, later that day, the agent called to confirm that the check had been received and deposited. On May 2, S shipped the goods by truck to D "FOB origin" and took a non-negotiable bill of lading naming S consignor and D consignee. It was estimated that the truck would arrive in Cincinnati late in the afternoon of May 5. On May 5 at 9:00 AM Seattle time, the agent in Cincinnati telephoned S to report that the $100,000 check had "bounced" and that there were rumors that D was in financial trouble. In addition, the agent reported (reliably, it turned out) that E, a distributor in Columbus, had purchased the truckload from D and had issued to D a check, later certified by the Payor Bank, for $80,000. Finally he reported that D and E were headed to the depot to take delivery of the goods when they arrived. At the time of the call, the truck was reported to be somewhere between Indianapolis and Cincinnati on I 74.

Questions

(A) It is now 10 AM in Seattle and you have just gotten a telephone call from your client, S. His questions are: "What should we do?" and "Where do we stand?" Advise him.

(B) Assume that S is able to stop delivery free of E's claims. S directed the agent in Cincinnati promptly to resell the goods and, within 24 hours, the hardware was sold to a dealer in Indianapolis for $70,000. The agent, however, neglected to give D any notice of the resale. It is stipulated that the market price at all relevant times for the goods in Cincinnati was $75,000 and in Seattle was $55,000. It is also clear that S incurred expenses of $200 for stopping delivery, $300 for arranging the resale and

$500 in transporting the goods to Indianapolis. What damages can S recover from D? Please explain your answer.

QUESTION IV
(90 Minutes)

Your client, Ace Leasing, is in the business of leasing office equipment and computers to business and consumer lessees. Ace has continuing relationships with five manufacturers. In some situations, (75% of all deals) Ace first buys the equipment from the manufacturer and leases it to customers. In other cases, (25% of all deals) Ace helps a customer finance a lease. In these cases, the customer first selects the equipment needed from the manufacturer and then approaches Ace for financial assistance. Ace then buys the equipment from the manufacturer and leases it to the customer. The consideration for the lease includes appropriate finance charges. [The finance lease arrangement is an alternative to conventional financing, where the customer buys the equipment directly from the manufacturer with the purchase financed either by the manufacturer or a bank. In these cases, the manufacturer or bank would extend credit and perfect a security interest in the equipment under Article 9.] In all cases, Ace is thoroughly familiar with the nature and quality of the goods leased.

Prior to the enactment of Article 2A, there were no statutes in the state dealing with leases. The case law, however, extended Article 2 by analogy to all leases made by Ace, regardless of type or whether the lessee was a business or a consumer. In essence, Ace, as a merchant lessor, made the same warranties to the lessee as were made by a seller to a buyer. In addition, Ace had the same power to disclaim warranties and to limit remedies as did a seller under the UCC. Finally, the lease warranties extended only to the immediate lessee and the lessee's remedies for breach of warranty were the same as those under Article 2.

Article 2A has now been enacted in Ace's state and will be effective on July 1, 1992. You have represented Ace before, and are now asked for the following advice. Assume that the advice is tentative and that there will be time for refinements.

Dear Lawyer:

We have heard something about Article 2A and want to know how it will affect our business. Things have been running smoothly under the old system, so we are a bit concerned.

1. We have heard that 2A deals with something called a "finance lease." We need to know exactly what this is and whether it covers any of our existing business. If so, please tell us how this affects our risks if the goods leased are of poor quality and what, if anything, we can do to take advantage of any benefits from the finance lease.

2. If we lease goods and the transaction is not a finance lease, does 2A alter our liability regarding the quality of the goods? You told us before 2A that our liability was the same as that under UCC Article 2. Can you give us the same advice under 2A?

3. Finally, we lease 30% of our total volume to consumers. You told us that Article 2 had few, if any, special rules for consumer protection in the area of warranties, disclaimers, agreed remedies and privity. How about 2A? Are there any special consumer protection rules in warranty cases that we should be aware of?

We don't need a lengthy memo now. That can come later. For now, however, we'd like you to support your answer with appropriate but brief analysis and citation to the relevant 2A provisions. This memo will be helpful to us management types and to our in-house attorney. Also, don't hesitate to give any relevant advice beyond that requested in this letter.

Yours sincerely,

Ace

ANSWERS TO EXAMINATION QUESTIONS

QUESTION I. B has accepted the TBM and did not revoke acceptance. Thus, his damages, if any, would be determined under §§ 2–714 & 2–715. The key issues are whether B can ever reach the damage questions and the answers turn on the scope and interpretation of the parties' agreement. If S's contentions are sound, B's damage claims are sharply limited. If B's responses are accepted, the "grab bag" of direct, incidental and consequential damages will be opened. Here are some issues that you should have considered and resolved.

1. *Was "any" remedy barred by lack of notice under § 2–607(3)(a)?* No. Despite a lack of communication from 7/1 until 11/1, B repeatedly advised S that the TBM was not working after delivery. This was a notice "of breach" and informed S that the transaction was "troublesome" and should be watched. Similarly, B complained of an announced delivery date that would have been a delay if followed. Since S knew that B regarded any delay as a breach, the failure of B to complain further once the delay actually materialized could not prejudice S.

2. *Was the statute of frauds satisfied?* Yes. B received and accepted the goods. § 2–202(3)(c). In addition, S's confirmatory memo of 5/3, signed by S, satisfies the statute against S if not B. 2–201(1).

3. *What was the agreement between the parties?* As of 4/25, the parties had the following oral agreement, upon which B had relied in submitting a bid:

(a) $75,000 price for new TBM with used accessories;

(b) Prompt shipment FOB point of shipment;

(c) Warranty package excluded in exchange for price reduction;

(d) From advertisements, statements at site visit and demonstration of a TBM model, a plausible claim that S made an express warranty that the TBM was fit for B's particular construction purpose, see § 2–313(1).

(e) Implied warranties of merchantability, § 2–314(1).

(f) Disagreement over "AS IS" disclaimer—clearly excluded.

On 5/3, S mailed a confirmation of the oral agreement, which operated as an acceptance under § 2–207(1) and proposed additional and different terms. B objected to the delivery date, which was a different term, but failed to object to the "As Is" disclaimer, the exclusion of consequential damages and the Merger clause. B, in fact, accepted and used the TBM without objection. Did S's terms become part of the agreement or did they "drop out" under § 2–207(2)?

B's Arguments. Whether the "As Is" and Excluder clauses are additional or different terms is unimportant because B, in the earlier negotiations, objected to both of them. In fact, B's price reflected S's agreement that consequential damages would not be excluded. The Merger clause is an additional term, but B did not expressly assent to it. In fact, all of the terms materially alter the bargain and in no case did B expressly assent to the term. See Comment 3. In short, there was no need to object and express assent cannot be inferred from the conduct of accepting the goods.

S's Arguments. The confirmation proposed a modification in a letter, not in a standard form. The terms were clear and conspicuous. B was not unfairly surprised and by objecting to one term without objecting to others, B has expressly assented. S has relied upon B's objective conduct of assent without objection and the terms, therefore, are part of the agreement. S's arguments are persuasive, are they not?

4. *Legal effect if S's arguments prevail.* There are three related questions here.

(a) Were any implied warranties excluded under Section 2–316(3)(a) by the "As Is" language? S clearly made an implied warranty of merchantability, § 2–314, and arguably an implied warranty of fitness, § 2–315. Is an "As Is" disclaimer which does not satisfy the conditions of § 2–316(2) sufficient to exclude? The answer is probably yes with regard to the *used* accessories but without well understood trade usage it is unlikely that a court would conclude yes with regard to the TBM or the total system. Otherwise, important quality undertakings would be undercut with inadequate communication.

(b) If S made an express warranty that the system was fit for B's particular excavation purposes (and this seems likely under § 2–313(1)), did that warranty drop out of the final agreement because of the Merger clause? Remember, S may be unable to disclaim an express warranty but both parties can agree to drop it in a final writing adopted as a total integration. See §§ 2–316(1) and 2–202. B, a commercial buyer, is in trouble here if the Merger clause becomes part of the agreement under § 2–207: if he has manifested assent to the clause without unfair surprise, most courts will give it legal effect.

(c) Was the clause excluding consequential damages unconscionable, see § 2–719(3)? Again, if B had information and an opportunity to object to the clause and accepted the goods without objection, how can he argue that the clause was unconscionable at the time of contracting? B might argue, under § 2–209(1), that the modification was in bad faith because of S's extortion, but the facts as developed don't really support this.

If S's arguments prevail, then, B has no claim for consequential damages caused by S's delay (excluded) and only a limited claim that the new TBM was unmerchantable.

5. *Legal effect if B's arguments prevail.* If S's terms are not part of the agreement, B can begin to develop the factual basis for damages. He has suffered direct damages measured by the difference in value between the TBM system delivered and the system as warranted, i.e., a system that would meet B's particular purposes. Some of the repair costs incurred are relevant to that value. Other post-breach expenses will be incidental damages, although the line is not clear on these facts. The liquidated damages paid to O and other costs incurred because the machine was not available on time are consequential damages, § 2–715(2)(a). Again, we need more facts to determine what S could reasonably foresee, whether B reasonably mitigated damages, what losses were caused by the breaches, etc.

On balance, S's arguments are likely to be accepted by the courts.

QUESTION II. What arguments can B make to avoid the now oppressive contract and what are the chances of success?

1. *The contract was unconscionable at the time of contracting.* No way. Admittedly, S had some discretion that B did not (termination power and contractual excuse). But the pricing mechanism seemed realistic based upon existing trends and there is no evidence of unfair surprise or oppression. See

§ 2–302. The hardship to B arises from changed circumstances and § 2–302 does not help very much.

2. *There was no consideration given by S.* Nonsense. There was a power imbalance, but S did not reserve a free way out of the deal: time must pass, notices must be given, good faith must be exercised, etc. Put another way, the bargain does not lack mutuality.

3. *S failed to negotiate over or agree to a modification reasonable in light of the changed circumstances.* So far, this argument is a wash in the courts. S has no duty to negotiate in good faith unless imposed by agreement.

4. *B is excused from performance under § 2–615.* Most courts assume that § 2–615 should be applied to B even though only sellers are mentioned. The question is whether the suspension of construction and the market collapse are contingencies the nonoccurrence of which were a basic assumption of the contract and which make performance as agreed commercially impracticable. The answer is probably no. There is no persuasive evidence to support this risk allocation conclusion. The suspension frustrated B's purpose, but so long as there is some use or market for the goods, most courts will not excuse. Even though the market collapse may make performance impracticable, most courts have held that the parties assume the risk up or down under their pricing arrangement. B should argue that the combination of events, suspension and collapse, were, at the time of contracting, not foreseeable as likely to occur and seriously disrupt the agreed contract. This is appealing but, so far, no court has accepted the line.

5. *S is in bad faith in maintaining a constant output in light of the economic disaster around him.* There is no argument that S's output is disproportionate to prior output—clearly it is not. But it is disproportionate to the realistic demand for the product. In short, S has artificially maintained the same output to exploit the pricing mechanism in the contract with B. Arguably, this is bad faith under § 2–306(1) (or B should argue). In principle, there is no difference between S maintaining output to exploit a favorable contract than B varying requirements to exploit increased demand and a favorable price. This argument, when combined with S's reserved discretion, B's frustration of purpose and the market collapse, make a persuasive case for some relief from the contract. But what? If S's bad faith is a breach, why can't B cancel the contract? There is no clear precedent for this result, so we are on the edges here.

QUESTION III. (A) A bounced check is grounds for stoppage in transit. See §§ 2–705(1) & 2–511(3). The conditions for stoppage appear to have been met: a truckload is involved, § 2–705(1), and B has not received the goods, § 2–705(2)(b). (FOB delivery is not "receipt") see § 2–103(1)(c). Thus, S should promptly notify the carrier to stop delivery. § 2–705(3)(b). At this point, S is seeking to assert a security interest arising under Article 2. See § 9–113. But what about E's rights as a BFP. E will argue that S delivered the goods to B (to the carrier in an FOB origin) shipment in a transaction of purchase, title passed to B and before stoppage B resold the goods to E, who fully qualifies as a BFP. In addition, since the goods were identified at the time of contracting, E can argue that B's title, which he acquired upon S's delivery to the carrier, passed to E. See § 2–401(1). See § 2–403(1)(b). E's argument should prevail unless a court would conclude that there is no delivery to B in a transaction of purchase until B has physical possession of the goods or that E must take physical possession before he can finally qualify as a BFP. This is also dubious: there is no such possession requirement if all other conditions for BFP status are met. The question, however, is whether E took free of S's possessory security interest under § 9–113. So long as S retains control, the answer is no. Neither § 9–307(1) nor § 9–403(2) help here. Do you see why?

(B) S's failure to give notice deprives him of his resale under § 2–706(1) and, according to the prevailing wisdom, relegates him to damages under § 2–708(1). But note what S gets there: the difference between contract and market price at the time and place of tender (Seattle in an FOB origin contract), $45,000, minus expenses saved, 0, plus incidental damages, $1,000, for $46,000. Is something fishy here? S actually got $70,000 for the goods in Cincy and will get $46,000 more in damages under § 2–708(1), or a total of $116,000 on a deal with a $100,000 contract price. Is S in a better position than full performance under this approach? See § 1–106(1). Yes, but what can we do about it? If B waives objections to lack of notice and S is fully protected under the resale, why not limit S to § 2–706(1)? This result would be easier if S had intentionally failed to give notice so as to take advantage of the lower market in Seattle—bad faith in enforcement.

QUESTION IV

Dear Ace:

Article 2A *will* have an impact on the way you have been doing business, both in regard to the transactions where you buy from suppliers and then lease to customers and those transactions (25% of total) where the customer first selects the equipment and you in turn purchase it from the manufacturer and lease to your customer. To respond specifically to the three questions asked in your recent letter:

1. The finance lease, defined in 2A–103(1)(g), is an innovative concept under 2A. Under it, the lessor has no implied warranty liability to the lessee for the goods leased. To qualify as a finance lease, the transactions must be structured as follows: *First,* you must not select, manufacture, or supply the goods desired by the lessee. Your passive role justifies exempting you from implied warranty liability. You remain liable, however, for any express warranties made. *Second,* after your customer has selected the goods and the manufacturer (2A calls the manufacturer a "supplier") from whom they are to be obtained, you will purchase them from the supplier with the understanding that you are a buyer who intends to lease the goods to a lessee. This satisfies the definitional requirement that you have acquired the goods "in connection with the lease." *Third,* you must satisfy one of the four requirements of

2A–103(g)(iii). In general, these requirements are designed to inform the prospective lessee about the terms of the supply contract between you and the supplier *before* the finance lease is signed. For example, you have satisfied the requirement if the lessee receives a copy of the contract with the supplier "before signing the lease contract." If you don't want to reveal all of the terms of that contract, the requirements are satisfied if the lessee is informed in writing of terms that relate to warranties or the supplier and the lessee's rights are clearly identified in writing before the lease is signed. But these requirements are tricky and will require some further discussion on how best to implement them. The purpose, however, is clear: Since the lessee under a finance lease is a beneficiary of the supply contract and enforces it against the supplier rather than the lessor, it must be informed of its rights, duties and risks under that contract before signing the lease. See 4A–209.

In addition to immunity from implied warranties under the finance lease, there is another advantage to the lessor. Once the lessee accepts goods furnished under a finance lease, its promises and commitments to the lessor become irrevocable and independent of any claims for breach of warranty that the lessee may have against the supplier. In commercial leases at least, lessee must pay lessor "come hell or high water." See 2A–407.

By the way, the lease must be a "true" one, in that it is not a security interest in disguise. See 1–201(37). A precautionary filing under Article 9 should be made to protect against this eventuality, see 9–408, and to insure priority against subsequent creditors of the lessee. See 2A–307.

2. If there is no finance lease, your potential warranty liability and power to disclaim warranties and agree to limited remedies as a lessor is essentially the same as it was before. Except for some minor variations, which we can discuss later, the exposure of a "regular" lessor of goods under 2A is the same as that of a seller of goods under Article 2. This means that through disclaimers and agreed remedies you have power to contract into the same immunity position that would be achieved by structuring a finance lease.

3. There are several special rules for consumers in 2A, but only one provision, 2A–407(1), is relevant here. Under that provision, a *consumer* who accepts goods under a finance lease does not remain liable to the lessor "come hell or high water" unless the lease provides that the lessee's promises are "irrevocable and independent" upon acceptance and that clause is otherwise enforceable. 2A–407(3). Thus, we must review the lease provisions in consumer finance leases to determine what revisions, if any, are required.

In sum, you may wish to increase the volume of business under finance leases. If so, we need to review your business practices and establish a system to insure that 2A's requirements are met. In addition, we should discuss exactly how to deal with consumer lessees under finance leases and devise clear and conspicuous terms that contract into the "hell or high water" protection.

APPENDIX C

TEXT CORRELATION CHART

Sales Black Letter	Countryman (2d ed)	Schwartz (2d ed)	King	Benfield (2d ed)	Whaley (2d ed)	Epstein (3d ed)	Jordan (2d ed)	Eddy (2d ed)	Honnold (5th)	Speidel (4th)	Farnsworth (4th)
Part One: General Considerations											
Chapter I. Commercial Law in General									1–9	1–4	
Chapter II. Uniform Commercial Code	895–99	1–28	1–15; 77–80.	2–18		1–8		1–7		4–14	1–16
History			1241–53								
Basic Policies								29–32			
Substantive Content								—			
Methodology								399–430	10–29		
Part Two: Sale of Goods	901–913; 954–55; 1005–06; 1039–44; 1057–76.	29–31									
Chapter III. General Scope and Policies			63–77; 105–09.	18–37; 199–202.	1–17						
Scope & Definitions		9–13	15–33	95–125	17–23.	227–229	1016–35	465–70	137–50	411–423	622–634
Policies		33–44	40–62	481–85	153–55		905–06; 940–48.	413–31		423–441.	
Chapter IV. Contract Formation Agreement											
Offer and Acceptance	926–40	66–85	81–102	38–49; 68–78; 90–94.	46–63	230–39	785–92	465–471; 498–503.		445–481	
Statute of Frauds	913–26	31–48	84–97	49–68	27–40	240–41	792–819	471–83	10–29	481–96	
Chapter V. Performance of the Contract for Sale											
Scope and meaning of agreement	940–49; 1047–50.	48–66	101	125–51	40–46	242–47	792–819	483–492		498–523	379–98
General obligations	1109–1143	230–232		151–70; 532–69.	147–53; 289–311.	247–50	1046–56	492–98	275–89		
Seller's obligations—in general	1120–39; 1095–1118.	61–62; 68; 97–98; 70–85.	15–13; 101–02; 219–26; 450–49.	171–81	163–75			505–535	295–203	405–06; 424–26; 655–59; 684–92.	

Sales Black Letter	Countryman (2d ed)	Schwartz (2d ed)	King	Benfield (2d ed)	Whaley (2d ed)	Epstein (3d ed)	Jordan (2d ed)	Eddy (2d ed)	Honnold (5th)	Speidel (4th)	Farnsworth (4th)
Seller's obligations—Warranty	895–1015; 1023–39.	104–144; 172–75; 225–29.	133–196	213–268; 294–338.	67–90; 112–45.	256–86	882–907; 954–84; 1001–15.	653–674; 711–28.	33–54; 70–87; 87–137; 150–66.	755–822; 828–41; 852–55; 866–71.	517–54; 571–621; 634–50.
Buyer's obligations		230–32; 239–40.	226–31	169–70	147–53		828–53		290–95	409–410; 526–50.	363
Risk of loss	1091–1109	83–103	114–127	181–198	156–63; 220–225.	250–55	1117–1137	535–543	467–205	646–571; 709–15.	477–516
Excusable nonperformance	969–83	436–487		463–480	224–42	309–16		543–552		551–80	
Modification	949–55			78–89			819–27				
Chapter VI. Remedies for Breach of Contract for Sale — Breach of contract		312–51	213–19	437–462	178–82; 243–45; 281–82.	328–334	858–881	578–83		582–93	
Seller's remedies Self-help / Price / Resale / Damages / Other problems	1207–1222	353–91; 517–26.	285–333; 379–85.	419–36; 516–31	245–64	317–328; 341–44.	1178–1243	585–611	251–53; 380–409.	581–614	696–619; 742–50.
Buyer's remedies	1185–1207	157–171	333–349; 357–366. 370–85	388–410	264–81	317–334; 342–43.	1138–1178	617–52	253–73	615–45	680–96
Seller repudiates or fails to deliver 2–716 2–502 2–712 2–713		391–430	226–65						234–50		
Non-conforming tender	957–68	232–311		340–388	182–220	287–309	828–58	553–78	206–34; 303–310.	709–56	651–79
Rejection, Revoke Accepted goods	927–40			395–99; 419–423.				644–52	234–50		
Incidental and consequential D.						334–341					554–71

Sales Black Letter	Countryman (2d ed)	Schwartz (2d ed)	King	Benfield (2d ed)	Whaley (2d ed)	Epstein (3d ed)	Jordan (2d ed)	Eddy (2d ed)	Honnold (5th)	Speidel (4th)	Farnsworth (4th)
Agreed remedies	1039–66	176–203	158–68	268–94	91–111		907–40	611–616 674–711			
Liquidated D		204–225; 430–35.									
Limitation of remedy			385–97	410–18			948–54		70–87	866–83	
Statute of limitations	1068–84		398–407		282–88		984–1001	517; 566; 721.		822–27	
Chapter VII. Third Party Claims to Goods											
Ownership claims	1174–80	488–502	409–26	481–508			134–35	518–26 294–99	410–435	897–908 909–913	17–44
Security interest claims		512–17									
Seller's warranty of title		144–57		338–39	65–67		1035–45		59–70	919–32	
Claims of other creditors and purchasers	218–32	527–41		202–212					380–402; 445–51.	933–39	720–42
Security interests arising under A.2											

APPENDIX D

TABLE OF U.C.C. CITATIONS

(M.& S.) Sales & Leases of Goods BLS—11

Sec.	This Work Page	Sec.	This Work Page	Sec.	This Work Page
2–716(3)	60	2–721	41	Art. 2A (Cont'd)	247
	62	2–723	170		248
	181		171		249
	183		185		252
	210		186		253
	227	2–723(1)	171		257
2–716, Comment 1	181		172		263
2–717	34		173		265
	113	2–725	122	2A–101	249
	139		125	2A–102	40
	194		152		239
2–718	8		206	2A–102(1)(m)	246
	62		207	2A–102, Comment	40
	199		221		240
	201		222	2A–103	239
	202	2–725(1)	113		246
2–718(1)	63		124	2A–103(1)	246
	122		207	2A–103(1)(e)	22
	200		222		247
	201	2–725(2)	113	2A–103(1)(g)	22
	202		124		35
	262		131		247
2–718(1)(a)	202		206	2A–103(1)(h)	40
2–718(2)	201		207		246
2–718(2)(b)	202		222	2A–103(1)(j)	40
2–718(3)	201	2–725(3)	207		239
	202	2–725(4)	207		246
2–718, Comment 1	201		208	2A–103(1)(n)	22
2–719	8	Art. 2A	1	2A–103(1)(o)	257
	62		2	2A–103(1)(p)	22
	199		3	2A–103(1)(q)	246
	202		11	2A–103(1)(x)	22
	204		12	2A–103(3)	33
2–719(1)	189		13	2A–103(4)	249
	202		14	2A–103, Comment (t)	22
	203		17	2A–104	240
2–719(1)(b)	202		22	2A–104(1)(a)	248
2–719(2)	63		23	2A–104(1)(b)	41
	202		30		248
	203		33	2A–104(1)(c)	23
	205		34	2A–104(1)(d)	41
	262		39	2A–104(3)	41
2–719(3)	47		40	2A–105	43
	61		41		248
	63		42		249
	122		43	2A–106	23
	126		54		247
	202		57		248
	203		81		249
	204		238	2A–106(1)	32
	206		240		43
	262		241	2A–108	249
2–719, Comment 1	202		246	2A–108(2)	247

APPENDIX E

INDEX

Note: Each chapter begins with a detailed, analytical table of contents and concludes with a set of review questions, answers to which are provided in Appendix A, 267–283. Appendix B, 285–296, contains four practice examination questions and answers. Finally, Appendix C, 297–300, is a correlation chart citing the sections of this BLACK LETTER to the relevant sections of leading casebooks.

313

†